# THAT TYRANT, PERSUASION

# That Tyrant, Persuasion

## HOW RHETORIC SHAPED THE ROMAN WORLD

J. E. LENDON

PRINCETON UNIVERSITY PRESS

PRINCETON & OXFORD

Published by Princeton University Press
41 William Street, Princeton, New Jersey 08540
6 Oxford Street, Woodstock, Oxfordshire OX20 1TR

press.princeton.edu

All Rights Reserved
ISBN 978-0-691-22100-7
ISBN (e-book) 978-0-691-22102-1
Library of Congress Control Number: 2021948742

British Library Cataloging-in-Publication Data is available

Editorial: Rob Tempio and Matt Rohal
Production Editorial: Karen Carter
Jacket/Cover Design: Pamela L. Schnitter
Production: Erin Suydam
Publicity: Charlotte Coyne and Alyssa Sanford

Jacket art: Giovanni Battista Piranesi, *Gruppo di Scale*. From the compilation "Prima Parte di Architetture e Prospettive," Italy, 1749. The New York Public Library / Gado Images / Alamy Stock Photo

This book has been composed in Arno

Printed on acid-free paper. ∞

Printed in the United States of America

10 9 8 7 6 5 4 3 2 1

For Elizabeth, again and always

πειθὼ δὲ τὴν τύραννον ἀνθρώποις μόνην

—EURIPIDES, HECUBA


omnium regina rerum oratio

—PACUVIUS, HERMIONE

# CONTENTS

"LIFE IMITATES ART" quipped Oscar Wilde, in a passage now not wholly forgotten but perhaps not well enough remembered.[1] Anyone can think of examples. One of my personal favorites is from Mark Twain, who, in his recollections of *Life on the Mississippi* (1883), complained that

> a curious exemplification of the power of a single book for good or harm is shown in the effects wrought by *Don Quixote* and those wrought by *Ivanhoe*. The first swept the world's admiration for the medieval chivalry-silliness out of existence; and the other restored it. As far as our South is concerned, the good work done by Cervantes is pretty nearly a dead letter, so effectually has Scott's pernicious work undermined it.[2]

The South, under Sir Walter Scott's sway, which the North quickly shook off, became different and strange: Scott "sets the world in love with dreams and phantoms . . . with the sillinesses and emptinesses, sham grandeurs, sham gauds, and sham chivalries." Under the influence of Scott the South became obsessed with "windy humbuggeries," with rank and title, with pride and honor, preserving dueling after it vanished in the North. In sum, Twain concluded with a wink, "Sir Walter had so large a hand in making Southern character, as it existed before the [US Civil] war, that he is in great measure responsible for the war."[3]

Or consider sunny California. This was the name of the realm of Amazons, warrior-women who lived without men, in an early printed chivalric romance (1510) entitled *Las Sergas de Esplandián*, where the imaginary dominion of California was named for the Amazon queen, the formidable Calafia. *Las Sergas* was the fourth sequel to the ground-breaking *Amadis de Gaulia* (1508), one of a line of books that emerged at the very beginning of secular printing: a new medium desperate for content, as we might now say. As such these works were widely read among the lay literate, translated as necessary into all the languages of Europe, and came to constitute, for a time, a shared literary culture. That a conquistador should name California after a kingdom in one of these books was only natural. But of far more than onomastic importance was the search those books inspired for real Amazons in the New World. The classically educated, of course, could have known of Amazons from their Greek and Latin reading; but Amazons were brought far more forcefully to contemporary attention in the vernacular *Sergas de Esplandián*. And so it was that real Spanish officialdom would quiz explorers and governors in the New World about whether they had found Amazons and urge them to seek them out; and those in the New World would (naturally) sometimes report that they had indeed found them, not least along the river Amazon, which takes its name from this quest; and the search for such exotic creatures became a minor but real engine for continued Spanish exploration and conquest in the Americas.[4]

Examples of the influence of art—books—on life can be extended almost indefinitely.[5] "There are two novels that can change a bookish fourteen-year old's life: *The Lord of the Rings* and *Atlas Shrugged*. One is a childish fantasy that often engenders a lifelong obsession with its unbelievable heroes, leading to an emotionally stunted, socially crippled adulthood, unable to deal with the real world. The other, of course, involves orcs."[6] Nor are examples lacking from the ancient world: Alexander the Great notoriously emulated Achilles, of whom he had learned from his reading of the *Iliad*. Later figures—Pompey, Julian—imitated Alexander the Great in their turn. And an intriguing proposal has recently been made that the emperor Tiberius had a similar relationship with the Homeric hero Odysseus.[7]

The potential power of shared reading to create action was pondered in the 1970s by the anthropologist Victor Turner, upon whose concept of the Root Paradigm—"the presence and activity of certain consciously recognized (though not consciously grasped) cultural models in the heads of the main actors"—it is appealing to draw to understand such phenomena. Valuable as well is his forthright argument that such models can be so mighty in the human mind that they may make those who embrace them act, obviously as it would seem to us, against their own practical interests, even to the point of going open-eyed to their deaths.[8]

The most powerful form of shared reading is of course common education, and that is the subject of this book, which speculates about the influence of the education of the Greco-Roman ruling class—education in rhetoric and its preliminaries—on the deeds, the public actions, done by those who received that education. As such, it plows a somewhat lonely furrow. Investigation of the influence of rhetorical education on fine writing among the Greeks and Romans, by contrast, is well over a century old, the fact of such influence is universally accepted, and the writing on the subject now perfectly enormous.[9] But while the positive case for rhetorical influence on ancient literature is easy to make, on an anecdotal basis, simply by collecting passages in ancient authors that appear to show such influence, no agreed-upon principles exist for calculating the relative strength or weakness of such influence.[10] Did taught rhetoric extend its roots to the same depth in every ancient literary genre and every ancient author and every work? Or did loyalty to the traditions of different genres in some cases confine the influence of formal rhetoric to a glittering surface of winter ice, while mightier currents drove the dark river beneath?[11]

This is an intractable puzzle, and this book does not address it directly. Instead this book argues for the influence of rhetorical education not upon texts, but upon deeds: after a survey of how young men were taught rhetoric, and the social and historical significance scholars have attributed to such teaching (section i), it suggests that the murder of Julius Caesar followed a script taken from rhetorical education (section ii); postulates that rhetorical education may have had an influence on the building of civic structures under the Roman Empire, especially in the cities of the Roman East (section iii); and investigates changes in the Roman law that may have occurred under the influence of rhetoric (section iv).

These several subjects have been chosen because they represent different degrees of rhetorical influence upon action. The case of Caesar's murder seems to offer a clear case for such influence; it was also chosen for its fame. In the case of buildings the results are mixed: the argument is that rhetorical education drove the construction of two types of structures—monumental nymphaea and colonnaded streets—while offering ambiguous advice on a third, city walls built during the Roman peace. Finally, although the present author argues, with all the ingenuity he can muster (and the assistance of many other scholars), for the influence of rhetoric on the substantive Roman law, the only fair conclusion he can arrive at is that such influence was, ultimately, rather limited. The law of the Romans was hardly impervious to change inspired by rhetorical training—and many examples are suggested—but rhetoric nibbled around the edge and effected little fundamental change in the logic and grounding principles of that law. The murder of Caesar, public building, and the Roman law are also disparate, and so can represent (however inadequately) the entire Roman world of public action. Finally, the book's conclusion attempts to make sense of this varied picture of the influence of rhetorical education upon public action in the Roman world, about the Roman Empire its rhetorically educated leaders imagined they lived in, and about the consequences of that imaginary empire for the real empire of the Romans.

It should be made quite clear at the outset that the argument of this book is speculative. Education plays a large role in creating the world we consider normal and expected, and it is rarely given to mankind to peer behind that education to realize that much of what it teaches is arbitrary as well as untraceable. Rhetorical education, that is, worked upon the Roman mind at a level beneath the conscious grasp of the ancients, and so the influence of that education on how people behaved in the real world was as unlikely to be overtly commented upon as is the influence of our own education on how we go about our lives. No Greek or Roman *says* "I did this thus and so because of what I learned in school." We must find cases where education seems to drive action, and I hope to persuade, by looking at three very different fields of action, that—with interesting exceptions—this was often the case.

Finally, this investigation proposes a new approach to the challenge of the influence of taught rhetoric on literary texts, because it tests ways in which the influence of taught rhetoric, in any realm, might be blocked and channeled. In the real world, more clearly than in literature, when a man tries to act according to what he was taught in school, reality often fights back. (Think: economics!) Some things rhetoric suggests prove impractical in fact, while others can be discouraged as impractical before the fact by the logic of brass tacks. In other cases too the influence of rhetoric is countered by well-established traditions that fight against, and may well defeat, the plans suggested by rhetoric. This book, then, is a study of the influence of rhetoric on real life, but also a study of the fences around the influence of rhetoric, fences that, *mutatis mutandis*, might apply both to the real world and to the world of the pen.

# ACKNOWLEDGMENTS

GENEROUS SUPPORT for the writing of this book was provided by the Gerda Henkel Stiftung, the Institute for Advanced Study, the Alexander von Humbolt Stiftung, the Loeb Classical Library Foundation, my employer, the University of Virginia, and my department, the Corcoran Department of History. Among individuals, thanks are due first to those who have read the entire manuscript: Michael Peachin and Henriette van der Blom, the readers for the Press, whose comments have immeasurably improved the final version. A. J. Woodman did the same mighty deed from friendship, and Elizabeth Meyer (several times) from love. Individual chapters were read and invaluably commented upon by Barbara Burrell, Ari Bryen, Tony Corbeill, Gary Gallagher, and Martin Jehne. Ulrike Babusiaux, Nicolas Lamare, and Michael Peachin were kind enough to provide copies of their writings before publication; the journal *Chiron* granted permission for me to reprint my article "Rhetoric and Nymphaea in the Roman Empire," *Chiron* 45 (2015) 123–149, which is adapted into chapter 6; and the University of Vienna supplied a copy of W. M. N. Reiter's unpublished *Magisterarbeit*. Georgia Aristodemou, John Bedell, Glen Bowersock, Angelos Chaniotis, David Cohen, Anna Dolganov, Stephen Harrison, Margaret Imber, Christopher Jones, Georgy Kantor, Nicholas Lindberg, Rubina Raja, Dylan Rogers, Christian Witschel, and Cecily Zander benevolently answered specific queries. The book could not have written without the gentle efficiency of the University of Virginia Library's Interlibrary Loan and Library Express On-Grounds offices; the Heidelberg and MIT libraries were also indispensable. Timothy Brannelly undertook the immense task of checking the references; Claire Weiss arranged the illustrations and defeated many intractable computer problems; Pam Marquez copyedited the manuscript; and Michael Powers prepared the index. Rob McQuilkin (an old and trusty friend) and Max Moorhead prepared the book for the market, and Rob Tempio and Matt Rohal welcomed it into the snug environs of the Princeton University Press.

Translations are my own unless otherwise indicated. Errors too are my own, as is the general perversity of the book.

# The Strange World of Education in the Roman Empire

WHO LANGUISHES in perplexity about the force of education in the affairs of men may find it pleasant to ponder the empire of the Romans. The formal education of young men of the ruling strata was long, narrow, and strange to us, and so its sway over the ancient mind should be easy to discern: the contrast to our own education provides perspective.[1] From the first century BC at the latest this education was also so similar from place to place—within the Latin-speaking West and the Greek-speaking East and also shared between them—and so similar too over many centuries, that investigating its force is little hindered by regional eccentricity or by the need to trace changes over time in the mechanism of that influence, education in rhetoric and its prerequisites.[2]

# 1

# Education in the Roman Empire

EDUCATION IN THE ERA of Rome's rule consisted of three main stages: first, for young children, the learning of letters and basic arithmetic in a primary school, the *ludus* in Latin.[1] Then, childish things—such as mathematics—having been laid aside, from the age of seven or thereabouts came language under the "grammarian," language taught primarily through analysis of poetry, chiefly the *Iliad* in the East and (when it became available) the *Aeneid* in the West.[2] After the grammarian (at age fourteen or fifteen, perhaps) came several years of instruction under the *rhetor*, the rhetorician, who taught rhetoric and its theory.[3] This was accomplished primarily by "declamation," giving and listening to speeches on imagined topics—topics that were similar or identical East and West and over many centuries.[4] In the West at least, deliberative topics—*suasoriae* or speeches of advice, often given to or in the character of a famous historical or mythic personage—tended to be taught first, and then *controversiae*, imaginary court-cases.[5] By the late second century BC, but likely even earlier, an intermediate curriculum, a sequence of *progymnasmata* or *praeexercitamina*, "preliminary exercises" (preliminary to declamation, that is) had evolved between grammar and rhetoric.[6]

Although the curriculum was static, where it was taught and the people who taught it varied considerably.[7] The children of the rich might take the first, and some the second, stages at home with private tutors; if only the first stage was provided at home they might start at the school of the grammarian at a younger age.[8] In grand families in the

Latin West much of early education might be given in Greek and through Greek texts, to promote the bilingualism hoped for in young men of rank; the Greek East did not return the compliment by learning Latin, except under the late empire and at a later stage of education.[9] Whether the *rhetor* or grammarian taught the *progymnasmata*, or how they were divided between those worthies, varied, as did the number and order of those exercises.[10] Slaves and the children of the poor stayed on at the (very cheap) *ludus* until they had the words and numbers necessary for the futures their parents or masters envisioned for them, or until the money ran out (free education being unknown), never advancing to the far more expensive grammarian and *rhetor*— the privilege of the rich and socially ambitious—who taught nothing useful for business, unless it was the business of language itself.[11] If their trade needed computational skills beyond those of the *ludus*, poor children and slaves might attend the no less modest school of the *calculator*, the teacher of arithmetic; after that, if there was money left, came apprenticeship.[12]

Rich young men who pursued the course of education under grammarian and *rhetor* to its end would learn much poetry, read much oratory (especially Demosthenes if Greek-speaking or Cicero if Latin-), and incidentally consume some unsystematic history and philosophy if the authors were regarded as good models of style (as Plato and Xenophon were).[13] Education at the level of grammarian and *rhetor* might be expected to be available in any major town.[14] But systematic instruction in, say, philosophy, was yet a further stage of education beyond the instruction of the *rhetor*, and in most periods was undertaken only by a tiny number of enthusiasts and often required a long and expensive stay in a city far away, ideally violet-crowned Athens. How education in what we anachronistically call the "professions," architecture and especially medicine, fit in, we must honestly confess that we do not see clearly (for law see section iv).[15] In the case of medicine we know both of schools that taught theory—that at Alexandria being the most famous—and of learning by apprenticeship. A guess is that lower-status aspirants became apprentices, and the sons of the wealthy (medicine being a profession that took in both) had at least some rhetoric before they moved to

medical school and subsequently (we devoutly hope) attached themselves for a period to a practicing doctor.[16] In the education of the doctor we know best, Galen, we see ghostly traces of a parallel course of
education, where philosophy replaced rhetoric after grammar.[17] How
common this was, other than that it appears to have been far less common than education in rhetoric, we cannot say.

Education through the level of declamation under the *rhetor* was general among the sons of the ruling class of the empire: those of Roman
senators, equestrians, and the far more numerous sons of the prosperous
class who made up the city councils, the *curiae* or *boulai,* that governed
the cities of the empire—and thus, in practice, governed the empire,
whose administration was for the most part divided among its cities.[18]
These were the boys who would grow up to make the great decisions of
town and empire; and, if inclined, they might also read and write literary
works, the ruling and writing classes of the empire being for the most
part indistinguishable.

## The Evolution of Rhetorical Education

The tale of the ascendency of rhetoric begins in epic Greece, with the
predilection even of heroes for taking great decisions after public debate
and deliberation.[19] In Homer, among whose bloody-handed barons
little trace of democracy can be found, public assemblies are held and
the heroes compete in, and admire, eloquence in council.[20] In one of
Homer's most striking similes we meet Odysseus, standing with his eyes
cast down and his staff still, uttering "words like unto the snowflakes of
winter, and then no mortal man could vie with him."[21]

About the ultimate origins of formal rhetorical instruction in Greece
there is inscrutable controversy; good fortune that it matters little to
us.[22] But whether they presided over classrooms or not, by the late fifth
century BC there were men in Greece—"sophists"—who would teach
you public speaking, if you could afford it, of whom the best-known is
Gorgias of Leontini, who arrived in Athens—subsequently the center
of such instruction—in 427 BC, when the Peloponnesian War was
raging.[23] It is natural to associate the demand for training in speaking

with the mass assemblies and lawyerless law courts of the Athenian democracy, and this temptation should not be too much resisted. But every Greek state of which we have knowledge, even where local ways limited the franchise, knew both public deliberation by debate and cases at law decided by weighing the competing speeches of litigants: Gorgias was a success even in rude Thessaly, and such habits existed at Sparta as well, even if Spartan men practiced their famous "laconic" speech, in which they competed in brevity and pith.[24] We may perhaps trace this Spartan idiosyncrasy to the same passage of the *Iliad* in which Odysseus's eloquence was praised: Menelaus, Homer's king of Sparta, "spoke fluently, in few words but clear, for he was not verbose nor did he speak at random," and so, in the same way, did his countrymen the Spartans speak for centuries after him.[25]

Suffice to say that by the second half of the fourth century BC—by the period of the anonymous *Rhetoric to Alexander* and Aristotle's *Rhetoric*—rhetoric was a mature intellectual discipline divided into three sorts—forensic, for the courts; deliberative, for the assemblies and councils and to give advice to potentates; and finally, demonstrative or display, mostly panegyric, the oratory of praise. There was a teaching curriculum, and one of the two main later theoretical arms of rhetoric, *idea* theory (which taxonomized style and delivery) was already quite developed.[26] The period after the death of Alexander is a dark place in our evidence. Very little educational material survives. But it is generally agreed—at least for cities with significant Greek populations—that in this period classroom instruction in rhetoric became generally available, was mostly standardized, and that by the second century BC at the latest, the name we associate with this is Hermagoras, the second great arm of rhetorical theory, *stasis* theory (*status* in Latin, which investigated the fundamental issue at stake in a speech) had also become mature.[27] Declamation, the method by which advanced rhetoric was taught, also developed in this period, although it had earlier roots.[28] And it is likely that, lost to us in the Captain-Nemo murk of the era, there was fought the titanic battle that by the first century BC left the science of the grammarian—the rule-bound manner of writing and speech at some distance from everyday usage that was taught by microscopic analysis of poetry, in no way an inevitable preliminary to the study in rhetoric—triumphantly in charge of education at the intermediate stage.[29]

What we really want to know, of course, is how much time in any era the average Greek or Roman boy from a wealthy family spent learning rhetoric. The traditional education of upper-class Athenians was split between letters, music, and athletics.[30] Education in "music" (which included poetry, and its composition, not merely recitation), continued strong in the Greek-speaking Hellenistic world.[31] So too did athletics thrive: the gymnasium was one of the characteristic institutions of the Hellenistic city, as was the *ephebeia*, a one-to-three year course of military training found in many cities.[32] It may, however, be significant that while grave reliefs from Classical Athens had shown departed youths naked, as athletes, by the late second century BC the grave reliefs of young men from Smyrna represent the departed clothed and grasping book-rolls—emphasizing, in other words, their literary education.[33] What of intellectual subjects other than grammar and rhetoric? Plato advocated that boys be taught mathematics beyond the calculations necessary in the vegetable market, to include number theory, geometry, astronomy, and the theory of music.[34] After the death of Alexander we come to hear of the *enkyklios paideia*, the "encyclic" or "complete" or "general" education. This included grammar and rhetoric, and also dialectic, arithmetic, music theory, geometry, and astronomy.[35] But Ilsetraut Hadot showed as early as 1984 that if this broader education existed at all, it was limited to Athens and to those preparing for further study in philosophy, which most young men had no ambitions to pursue, while the term *enkyklios paideia* (*artes liberales* in Latin) itself was so vague that it could apply to nearly any formal education undertaken by persons of superior social standing, and was frequently applied to the overwhelmingly common narrow education in language and public speaking.[36] Reality was apparently more like the *Clouds*, where Aristophanes presents as available a paid education in Socrates's *phrontisterion*, or "thinking shop," concerning the nature of the universe, astronomy, geometry, theoretical geography, the theory of grammar, meteorology, biology, and musical theory, but his prospective student wishes to learn nothing but rhetoric, to help him in court and to allow him to evade his creditors.

When Greek education spread to Rome, there was nothing left but grammar and rhetoric. Two routes to that end were possible. The disinclination of Romans to exercise naked and the social stigma attaching to theatrical or musical performance at Rome may account for the loss of Greek athletics and music, and the fact that there was no regular training for Roman soldiers until the reign of Augustus, and then only for the lower ranks—the Romans preferring their warriors to learn by experience—may have rendered superfluous organized military training such as the Greek *ephebeia*.[37] Alternatively, there may have been little to change. For reasons unclear, inscriptions attesting Greek educational institutions—fees for teachers, honors for visiting lecturers, contests in athletics and poetry—become rarer in the course of the first century BC.[38] This might be no more than a matter of epigraphical fashion, and the Hellenistic education system might still have been lively, although less visible to us. Or it could be that Greek education was itself narrowing, and that the Roman curriculum mostly limited to grammar and rhetoric was not the result of Roman philistinism and prudishness, but was the curriculum that contemporary Greek boys were already, for the most part, following.[39]

When we consider Rome, the question is not when rhetorical training became available—we can see it from 161 BC, when Greek teachers of rhetoric were ordered expelled, and it was probably a good deal older—but, again, how intensively it was pursued in earlier times.[40] Among the lofty class of which we can see something, military service, potentially starting at seventeen, was obligatory until the late second century BC (and it was best undertaken as early as possible by those intending a political career, ten campaigns being required before election to *quaestor*), while many young men continued to go to war long after such service had ceased to be compulsory.[41] The teaching of rhetoric in the classroom had also to fight for time with what scholars traditionally call the *tirocinium fori*, an apprenticeship in public life of a year or more that involved following a great man around, a practice that was still very much alive in the late 60s BC, probably into the 40s, and perhaps later as well.[42] The facts that teachers of Latin rhetoric endured the formal disapproval of the censors in 92 BC and that the 80s saw the first rhetorical treatises in Latin that survive to us (with the same declamatory themes—situations or scenarios—that would be used centuries later) illustrates, again, that such training was available, but not how prevalent it was; nor is there any other direct evidence.[43] But perhaps there is a hint. Members of the generation of Roman politicians born around 85 BC (the generation of Brutus and Cassius, about which we know a great deal) and those older than they, were very apt to go to Greece as adults to polish up their rhetorical educations.[44] But of those born in the 60s, it was mostly teenagers who were sent. Cicero's own experience, going to Greece as an adult, and that of his son and nephew, going as teenagers, stand for many.[45] The implication of the belated second educations of the older generation is that the rhetorical instruction they had received in Rome before or in the 60s was somehow unsatisfactory, that they felt that they were falling behind younger men, that they felt that their eloquence needed its tires rotated.[46] Perhaps the most economical interpretation is that in the 50s BC for Romans of the highest classes an education involving much rhetoric but many other calls upon a young man's time as well passed to an education consisting mostly of language and rhetoric, including an early sojourn in Athens.

It might be thought that when in the 40s and 30s BC the Roman Republic was ruled by embattled magnates, rent by civil war, and when peace finally achieved took the form—however well concealed—of the autocratic regime of Augustus, oratory, as far less useful amidst the thud of swords on shields and decisions made privily in the overlord's court than it had been in the free Republic, would have been less valued, and that its decline would be reflected in change and decline in rhetorical education. Not so. Contemporaries certainly complained about the decline of oratory (and would long continue to do so), but they still sent their sons to learn it, and if anything the 40s and 30s, we guess, was a period when rhetorical education strengthened and was further formalized.[47] For once we arrive in the Roman Empire, a standard set and sequence of primary, grammatical, and rhetorical education is clearly occupying all or almost all of the educational time of most upper-class boys, and change in education practice—never fast—thereafter becomes even slower. And between the 40s and the reign of Augustus a battle over style in Latin oratory—a group of purists who called themselves "Atticists" accused the more ornamented speeches of some of their contemporaries of "Asianism"—was fought to exhaustion.[48] Students in the rhetorical schools of that period would presumably have had to tread as carefully through that battlefield as they did through the contemporary battlefields of war and politics. And regardless of how picayune the controversy appears to us, it assures us of the intellectual liveliness of the field of rhetoric in that epoch.

On the Greek side, the late second or early third century AD saw the development of the Hermogenic corpus of three—eventually five—guidebooks for teachers (modern scholars think only two of them are really by Hermogenes; no matter), and the use of these became standard in late antiquity once the rival system of Minucianus had been put to flight.[49] The role of epideictic (demonstrative) oratory—the display oratory of praise (mostly) and blame—in the curriculum remains a puzzle.[50] Encomium was certainly taught among the *progymnasmata*, before declamation, but while one author of a work on *progymnasmata* strongly implies that the topic would be returned to later, presumably at a more advanced level, a second insists that it was taught only there.[51] Evidence for epideictic school declamations (at the highest level of teaching, in contrast to the more basic *progymnasmata*), is, moreover, lacking, in both Greek and Latin, although declamations in the other two genres might naturally contain encomiastic passages.[52] The best solution may be that, under the Empire, over time the progymnasmatic exercise of encomium was simply given a larger and larger proportion of the time at that stage of teaching.[53] Perhaps the culmination of this trend is the fourth-century AD sophist Athanasius of Alexandria, who thought encomium should be taught first and that most of the other progymnasmatic exercises should be taught as parts of it.[54]

Still, at its highest levels, and in both Greek and Latin, the curriculum remained dominated by deliberative declamation (*suasoriae*) and especially forensic declamation (*controversiae*).[55] In the former, the teacher proposed a theme such as "Agamememnon considers whether or not to sacrifice Iphigenia," or "Advise Sulla, in a public meeting, whether to resign his dictatorship."[56] Here the speaker had both to adjust his tone to the figure he was addressing and the figure he, as speaker, was impersonating (it being difficult for a boy to represent an elder of great deeds and dignity). And he must also master *stasis*, especially whether this was a matter of honor, expediency, or necessity, and know the subcategories of each. Finally, he must also be prepared to arouse the full range of emotions in his listeners.[57]

In a forensic declamation the teacher chose one or several from a set of laws traditional to the practice.[58] Perhaps, "An action at law shall lie against him who violates a tomb." The teacher then created a scenario that set this law against another, or against apparent justice: "A hero lost his weapons in combat, so he borrowed a set from the tomb of a dead hero. After fighting valiantly for his city, he returned the weapons. He is charged with violating the tomb."[59] The declaimer must then either prosecute or defend the hero. In variations the rules might be implicit (stating the illegality of crimes such as murder being superfluous) and the scenarios posited wonderfully intricate:

> A man had a blind son whom he had made his heir. He then married a stepmother [the Roman reader would know that stepmothers are almost invariably wicked] and removed the boy to the secluded part of the house. In the night, when he lay in his bedroom with the stepmother, he was murdered, and the next day his son's sword was found affixed in the wound, and the wall between his room and that of his son bloodied with palm prints. The blind son and the stepmother accuse each other.[60]

There were rules. The cases were supposed to be balanced enough to allow compelling speeches on both sides. The facts laid down as the basis of the declamation could not be altered: the declaimer could not produce a homicide victim alive. Laws from the real world could not be introduced (although other rhetorical laws could, and many real laws had rhetorical analogues); legal technicalities were usually avoided. "Inartificial" proofs—calling (imaginary) witnesses or proclaiming the existence of a document that settled the case—were not approved. The contest was in developing a persuasive backstory that set the stated facts in a favorable context (*color* in Latin), in maintaining a verbal style consistent with the nature of the litigant the declaimer was pretending to be (*idea* theory), in grasping the issue or issues at stake (*stasis* theory), in the persuasive argument of plausibilities, in evoking emotion in the hearer, in inventing *sententiae*, or catchy, pithy, memorable phrases. Revolting tortures could be described, but sex, never. Regional accents were scorned, voice and diction were closely watched, and only a confined lexicon of words was allowed: nothing that clanged vulgarly of the new. In the Greek world this patrol of the lexicon would eventually take the form of Atticism—not to be confused with "Atticism" in Latin, mentioned above—trying to use no word that could not be found in Athenian writers before the death of Alexander, or the early poets who were considered Attic by courtesy. Gestures too must be just so.[61]

There is a much-loved body of ancient complaint about declamation as a mode of teaching—a body to which Quintilian himself, by far our best known teacher of Latin rhetoric, was happy to contribute—complaining of the fancifulness of the themes, their impracticality as training for actual pleading in the courts, and the overwrought style sometimes encouraged in the schools.[62] But these are all internal critiques: suggestions about how the teaching of rhetoric could achieve its agreed-upon aims better, rather than proposals for significantly different educational aims—math perhaps? home economics?—or different institutional arrangements. The triviality of traceable changes over time in this education—astonishing to us, given the complete lack of central or official regulation, legal requirements to send children to school, or a system of public examinations that would tend to hold teachers to the same material and methods—also suggests that parents were quite content with it, it being in their power to move or remove their sons at an instant.[63] The third and fourth centuries AD did bring in new institutions and courses of study: now it was possible to take formal instruction in Roman law (at Beirut, Rome, and eventually elsewhere), to learn Latin (if one was a speaker of Greek), or to take instruction in shorthand writing, which last seemed for a short period to promise high preferment in imperial service. Libanius of Antioch, the fourth-century teacher of Greek rhetoric, naturally inveighed against such newfangled teaching, which is why we know about it. But careful examination of his writings reveals that he does not fear primarily that students might abandon the *rhetor* for such education, merely that they might curtail their time in his school or, more likely, undertake these studies—as they would philosophy—after their rhetorical training was done, and his writings suggest that only a small minority even did that.[64] In other words, despite the contemporary carping, and despite our own wonderment, education in grammar and rhetoric appears to have been, judging by its longevity, the most successful form of education in the history of the West.

# 2

# The Social and Historical Significance of Rhetorical Education

IN THE YEAR 1847, on the verge of a general European revolution, Dr. Wilhelm Adolf Schmidt, professor of history at the University of Berlin, hurried into print his *Geschichte der Denk- und Glaubensfreiheit im ersten Jahrhundert der Kaiserherrschaft und des Christenthums*. In the next year he was a member of the short-lived Frankfurt Parliament that strove unsuccessfully to bring liberal representative government to Germany. In 1851 he wisely accepted a position in safe, republican Zurich. His *History of Freedom of Thought and Belief* represented a perfervid trawl through all the writings of the first century AD (and much before, and much after) for every antimonarchical sentiment he could find, and his eye naturally fell upon the surviving declamations about the slaying of tyrants (on which see section ii below).[1]

Schmidt took it for granted that such declamations were expressions of protest and rebellion against the Roman imperial regime: he noticed that Caligula once banished a rhetorician who delivered a declamation on tyranny, and that Domitian had one executed.[2] Such a political interpretation of declamation as an attack on the imperial system has attracted approval from time to time,[3] but could ultimately make little headway against the abundant indications of the fact that the imperial regime made no systematic efforts—no efforts at all, the isolated cruelties of Caligula and Domitian aside—to suppress declamations about tyranny in the schools, which remained so popular that Juvenal could describe them as a teacher's staple food: "What iron innards you must have, Vettius . . . when your thronging class slays savage tyrants! . . . That same cabbage day after day kills wretched teachers!"[4] Not only were tyrant themes not stifled, but their familiarity made them a convenient tool with which the imperial regime and its creatures beat usurpers. Formerly abused as "bandits" and "pirate chieftains," usurpers were transformed, in the reign of Constantine and after, into "tyrants."[5] And comparison to the same familiar figure was also used by orators to bludgeon wicked officials (usually when they were safely departed from their provinces), a habit also regarded as supportive of imperial rule, because the emperors of Late Antiquity were happy to be thought of as the allies of their people against the abuses of their own subordinates.[6]

Declamation was hardly a form of sedition against the imperial regime, but Schmidt's argument has recently risen revenant, as arguments parallel to his have been offered: that declamation was subversive of the Roman social order or Roman paternal authority. These arguments reproach a slightly prior sociological interpretation, that declamation *reinforced* social hierarchy. And alongside the sociological understandings, there are also historical ones. Agreement on the deeper significance of rhetorical education has not been reached.

I anticipate myself. For centuries modern students accepted declamation at face value, as a mere form of education (even if they often thought it perverse in objective and method) without a subterranean social significance, and were happy to allow it the purposes ancient teachers claimed for it, the production of eloquence and (secondarily) moral improvement.[7] And they had the powerful backing of the Renaissance, which tried its best to revive Roman rhetorical education exactly in order to revive Roman eloquence and to effect the moral elevation of students.[8]

But the middle of the twentieth century brought doubts about the value of fluency of speech (having had much experience of it used for ill) and eventually also about the practicality (or wisdom) of teaching morality in school. And these doubts were projected upon Roman education, to undermine ancient statements about its value. So scholars were ready to discard the utterances of the ancients about the functions of rhetorical education, long before modern students found anything to put in their place. This was finally supplied in the late 1990s, when the interpretative schools of the 1960s, 70s, and 80s, mostly borrowed from literature and finally leaching into classics, brought with them sociological analyses and suggestions of the covert consequences of rhetorical education.[9] "What"—as a scholar in 2007 summarized the question— "did rhetoric teach all those who studied it without becoming political leaders, famous speech writers, or performing sophists? Was it genuinely useful for emperors, administrators, soldiers or women, or just a conventional, decorative accomplishment? In what ways does rhetoric train one to think, to analyse, to criticize? How did it affect the cognitive development of those who learned it or their sense of identity?"[10]

At a minimum, rhetorical education taught its students to speak like gentlemen, and at a minimum fathers paid to equip their sons with a marked, and marked as socially superior, way of talking. Rhetorical education, moreover, taught not only artificial habits of speech, but also comportment: posture, gait, and physical mannerisms, which gestures to employ and which to avoid as vulgar. These too set their students socially apart and above.[11]

The question is the ultimate importance of such a superior manner in a world (unlike ours) where status was already so clearly and visibly marked. Social standing in the Roman world was normally immediately evident from clothing: type, decoration, condition, and cleanliness. Libanius, as a teacher of rhetoric, naturally insists upon the additional importance of rhetorical training: "If anyone came upon you with your slaves, all naked and chatting, and knew nothing else about you, he wouldn't think it just for you to have power over them."[12] And so, Libanius goes on, his addressees should rededicate themselves to rhetoric, to underline the vital social distinction between free man and slave. But Libanius's scenario is desperately contrived. How many of the notables of an ancient city—the class of persons Libanius is addressing—would be unknown to their townsmen? How frequently would the master and his slaves all be undressed? And even if they were unknown, and all naked as jaybirds, how often would master and slaves be joshing each other on terms of equality, rather than the slaves serving and assisting the master, another everyday mark of relative status?[13] We may be forgiven for taking away from Libanius the realization that making distinctions between high and low was likely a secondary contribution of rhetorical training.[14]

Still, Roman parents of the ruling class were indeed concerned that their children should talk properly. They were concerned that the slaves attending even upon tiny babies speak well; to offer good examples of speech some parents—even rich parents, who could easily afford slaves to do the dirty work—cared for their young children themselves.[15] Moreover, plentiful *exempla*, so powerful among the Romans whether true or not, provided models of the noble teaching their own children: we think of the mother of Julius Caesar and Cornelia, mother of the Gracchi.[16] Extra training of the childish voice happened in the *ludus*, the primary school, with the grammarian, and indeed all through the education of wealthy boys.[17] Might this be because excellence in rhetoric, both in speech and deportment, in addition to its practical value in a world of councils and courts of law, served also as a form of competition between relative equals high in society? Was this a competition parallel to that of seeking public office, or making public benefactions, a competition in a society that seems to have had an infinite appetite for such contests?[18] Roman-period education was itself highly competitive.[19] A chance reference reveals that a primary-school teacher might be known colloquially as a *harenarius*, an "arena attendant," and we are suddenly faced with the unsettling possibility that the proper sense of *ludus*, the Latin primary school, was less "playground" than "gladiator school."[20] At a higher level, competition was baked into the very structure of declamation, as one boy advised "yes" and his opponent "no" in *suasoriae*, speeches of advice, and as one boy argued for guilt and his opponent for innocence (or another's guilt) in *controversiae*, imaginary court cases. It is easy to suspect that like parents today who become over-involved in their children's sports, Roman fathers, who themselves had gone through the same education, were their sons' most passionate fans and critics, and that such fathers had a very good sense of which boys in the schools were good and bad speakers, as we are told happened when Cicero was a boy (the truth of the tale is beside the point) when the fathers of other boys would visit his school to hear him, and grumpily reproach their own sons for admiring rather than bettering him.[21]

Among adults we can tell from inscriptions that rhetorical excellence was admired—and competed in, as if school competition never ended—among perfectly average members of the civic ruling classes of the empire. In surviving literature and inscriptions, nearly all the praising references to superiority in education or literary culture (and their number is vast) imply superiority over relative social equals, not the ignorant masses (over whom such superiority was assumed).[22] In the fourth century AD a student returning home from rhetorical studies in a distant city was expected to give a public oration to show off his skill in the face of a whole chamber of rivalrous critics, a much-feared experience.[23] Perhaps rhetorical training, then, served more to distinguish among the high—in the competitive culture of the Greek and Roman upper classes—than to distinguish the high from the low.

In the Greek East, this competition in public speaking as an end in itself manifested itself eccentrically in a small body of itinerant star performers in rhetoric—the so-called "sophists"—just as the Roman world knew star athletes and gladiators, star mimes and pantomimes (actors), star charioteers, and star lions in the arena. These sophists competed for supremacy among themselves and could gather masses of eager listeners to their public performances.[24] For their displays, they specialized in speeches on mythical themes (the Trojans consider an offer of alliance from Achilles) and historical ones (defend Miltiades for his failure, in the aftermath of Marathon, to capture Paros): all themes from before the death of Alexander the Great. To a greater or lesser degree (but mostly greater, over time) they competed also in rigorous Atticism, confining themselves to the Greek of Athenian writers from before that same date.[25] Extravagantly revered (not least by themselves) as heroes of high culture—the tired but inevitable comparison is to operatic tenors—sophists could command the deference of Roman officials and even emperors, and so exerted a degree of power in the world outside rhetoric, often representing their cities on embassies to Rome.[26] But it is unlikely that power in the great world was ever the main point of rhetorical education, or even of pursuing a career as a sophist; had it been so there would have been sophists in the West, and more than a handful in the East. It was rather an incidental side effect of the fact that, since education in rhetoric was nearly universal above a certain social level, and rhetorical expression was therefore the *lingua franca* of the ruling class, governors and emperors expected to be addressed rhetorically, eloquence was admired, and therefore that its most skilled practitioners were accordingly esteemed and respected by all persons who shared that education.

Competition aside, if we look into actual surviving speeches given by declaimers, we notice that they not only often spoke as the advocates of people unlike themselves—the poor, women, slaves, whores—but sometimes even spoke in the voices of those persons (their utterances being imagined by the advocate, or the usual ancient exclusion of women and slaves from pleading in court being suspended so they could impersonate such figures). This role-playing aspect of declamation, it has been suggested, was intended (in the Latin case at least) to educate rich young men for their eventual roles as head of a Roman family, which required an understanding (conveyed by representing, or even impersonating in declamation, women, slaves, and freedmen) of the viewpoints of those under their protection, legal and otherwise, and of the potential conflicts inherent in their role, between the terrible, potentially lethal power of *patria potestas* and the expected *pietas* and affection towards family and servants that restrained such power.[27]

"A humanistic interpretation of this social practice would posit that such role playing through participation as performer and audience member might broaden the child's perspectives," suggests a scholar.[28] And why not? But such a humanistic interpretation was rejected (even by the writer of those words) under the prompting of the theoretical methods of the time of writing. To make the function of declamatory role-playing congruent with the theory that rhetoric was a marker of social superiority, it was required that the result of such role-playing (and declamation in general) was the ultimate *reaffirmation* of social

roles.[29] Thus, it was argued, the themes of declamation, and their conventions (who might speak for themselves, who was obliged to be spoken for) reinforced in the young declaimer's mind social hierarchies
between men and women (and effeminate men), rich and poor, free
men and slaves, Romans and easterners, and Greeks and non-Greeks,
not least by presenting the second type in each pairing as wicked and
socially disruptive.[30]

Whence these ideas, bubbling up in the 1990s? It is significant to the
argument of this present book, which often dwells on the consequences
of academic accident, that these arguments—rhetorical education as a
marker of status and as an education in hierarchy—are themselves the
result of such an academic accident. This was the chance adoption or
assimilation (by osmosis in the universities) by the small number of
classicists initially interested in social theory of the views of Michel Foucault, Judith Butler, and Pierre Bourdieu, and the subsequent person-
to-person, article-to-article and book-to-book spread of those views
among a wider set of students of the ancient world. But Clifford Geertz
was writing at the same time as Foucault and Bourdieu. And had those
classicists read Geertz instead, it is possible that the interpretation of
declamation from a "humanistic perspective" that allowed it to broaden,
rather than constrict, the mind of the student of rhetoric would not have
been scorned. In such a case, we might read rather of declamation working as a commentary on the social order, as offering an understanding
of the deep structures of and contradictions in society, and as a way to
grasp how society's various groups and those groups' ideals fall into
conflict or work together, such knowledge being understood as an end
in itself, and not as a means to power.[31] By now, perhaps, both interpretations would be equally dated. But I emphasize: the Foucault-, Butler-,
and Bourdieu-inspired teaching-of-hierarchy school of the interpretation of rhetorical training that long prevailed was in no way inevitable.
It was an accident of life in the modern university.

And no less accidental was the rejoinder. For there chanced to be
present in the universities at much the same time a rival body of theory,
mixing Antonio Gramsci and Foucault (and his followers) with James C.
Scott's *Weapons of the Weak* (1985), which produced a habit of thinking

that identified phenomena under study not as invariably supporting the existing structures of power, but rather as invariably subverting them.[32] At its extremes, when "resistance" was identified in activities (such as rug-making and hair-dressing) where neither the notional resisters nor the notional oppressors recognized it as such, this approach was justly suspected. But declamation under the Roman Empire is not such an extreme and unlikely case.[33] Even the most cursory reading of the surviving declamations reveals that the weaker partner of the pair of stock characters who find themselves in conflict—the Poor Man against the Rich Man, the Son against the Father, the female (provided she is not a stepmother) against the male—is both more frequently represented and more sympathetically presented. Declaimers, moreover, thunder astonishingly frank reproaches against abusive wealth and paternal and husbandly cruelty: astonishingly frank, or so it seems to us, for a world content with hierarchy and *patria potestas*, where wealthy fathers were paying the teachers, and an odd form of training for courts in which the judges and their advisors would be exactly such wealthy fathers and husbands.[34] Did, then, declamation poke, or could it poke, or did it at least equip its students with sharp sticks for poking, the social order in which student and teacher lived?[35] That declamation could indeed be subversive the ancient textbooks themselves confess. Where a genuinely dangerous subject was contemplated—a reflection on the emperor or his family, perhaps—the textbooks describe at length something called "figured speech," a speech that sounded innocent, but was intended to be understood by the cognoscenti in a sense other than, or opposite to, that of the words spoken.[36] And one might note that there is no parallel self-conscious ancient discussion—similar to that of subversive figured speech—within the rhetorical textbooks of the role of declamation in *reinforcing* social hierarchies.

Still, about subversion, one wonders. The ancient complaints against declamation that survive to us bemoan the fantastical quality of declamatory themes and the distance of school declamation from actual pleading in the courts, but never complain that declamation places the power of fathers in peril or undermines the wider social order. Nor, as far as we can tell, did rich fathers furiously remove their sons from school because their teachers assigned them declamations in which they denounced the cruelty of rich fathers. Whatever the purposes of pronouncing subversive sentiments in declamation, then, the practice of declamation as a whole was not received as subversion by authorities, fathers, or society at large. This is perhaps exactly because of the frame of unreality in which declamation operated, the unreality that attracted such complaint. Being defined categorically as "fiction" (if we may apply that dangerous word to any ancient literature), that categorization protected declamation, declamation's teachers, and declamation's students.

So we bid farewell to the sociological interpretations of school declamation, leaving them in an intractable state of conflict, dominated by sharply opposing points of view: declamation undergirding hierarchy versus declamation subverting hierarchy, a standoff like that of Dr. Seuss's North- and South-Going Zax. And we realize sadly that the existence of such a contention among scholars does not encourage wholesale acceptance of the views of either side. But there is still much that is useful to take away: the competitive quality and the role-playing of declamation signal the simple force and intensity of this form of education. It involved much reading, even at higher levels (and the more the better, Quintilian and Libanius would have agreed), but that reading was not proved by written essay or exam or monotone *Referat*. The end product was frequent (perhaps daily) public performance by the student. If modern analogies be sought, education in declamation was less like attending a modern school or university and more like instruction in a musical conservatory or drama school, or perhaps athletic coaching.[37] Quintilian inadvertently reveals the pressure exerted by such education on its pupils when he complains that students were too eager to praise the declamations of other students, to the point of leaping ritually to their feet and cheering repeatedly in the middle of their speeches.[38] Of course they did: each boy knew that he would be speaking next, or very soon. And it is, I think, fair to suppose that such education would have the deeper impact on the student that we have come to expect from today's up-close coaching, rather than the weaker impact of today's more distant lecturing-and-testing style of teaching. Perhaps what the students learned was odd to us, but it should be emphasized that what they did learn they learned very deeply indeed. This may help to explain the continued practice of declamation in adulthood, visible in Seneca the Elder for the West and in the great competing sophists in the Greek world. Declamation was taught at so profound a level that it was often impossible to leave declamation behind. It haunted the minds of its students all through their lives, as the relentless appearance of rhetorical habits in the Latin literature of the Empire abundantly proves.[39]

How rhetorical education molded its students has primarily been the study of classical philologists. What rhetorical studies did *not* teach——what we might consider the gaps it left in the Roman intellect—have mostly been the study of historians of antiquity. The great scholar of ancient education Henri-Irénée Marrou pointed out how narrow this education was, excluding all significant mathematical and scientific learning, and that such humanistic knowledge as was conveyed—philosophy, history, geography—was chopped up into fragments for the use of rhetoric and taught without any organization or system. Marrou thought that this educational *sclérose sénile* contributed to the *décadence* of the late Roman empire, and, by implication, to the coming of the Middle Ages.[40] In 1945, Andreas Alföldi, contemplating Stalin's tanks advancing on his native Budapest and about to be expelled from his house by German staff officers, conceived the notion that rhetorical education of the third and fourth centuries AD created a conflict between the educated Roman senatorial aristocracy and the warrior emperors of the time, especially the warlike and practical Valentinian (AD 364–375). This theoretical conflict not only explains the abuse to which those emperors were subjected by the literary tradition, but the disaster that ensued when the senators won the contest upon the succession of Valentinian's son Gratian, the senators' effete creature, wholly ill-equipped by his education to deal with the crisis on the borders inspired by the western march of the Huns that culminated in the disastrous battle of Adrianople (AD 378). Thus rhetorical education is to blame, at least in part, for the fall of the empire in the West.[41] To Ramsay MacMullen it was the third-century crisis in particular in which rhetorical education played a role, by compelling Roman leaders (no longer sometimes happily immune to such education, as in Alföldi), to see the crisis in moral—rather than, for example, economic—terms, and thereby making them incapable of formulating a useful response.[42] To his student Susan Mattern such an education—both the ethnic stereotypes it purveyed and the accurate geographical knowledge it did not— had a large and obnoxious impact on how the Romans conducted their foreign affairs.[43] Another of his students, this author, has argued that the way in which rhetorical education taught reverence for the past, yet without placing the events of the past in clear logical and chronological sequence, could inspire a reactionary military overhaul that in the second through fourth centuries AD turned Roman tactics back towards those of the classical Greeks, once again with grim consequences for the empire.[44] We might add that, with an education that was apt to scorn words and ignore events after the death of Alexander, the whole of history after that event was a dark age to a Greek with a conventional rhetorical education: if he wanted to know what came later, between Alexander and his own day, he had positively to seek out historical works to read.[45] The Romans were less given to historical themes in declamation, but from what we can tell theirs ended with the death of Cicero.[46] About the period after that, unless they sought out histories and antiquarian treatises for themselves, they knew nothing from their education in rhetoric.

Theories that depend upon assertions about what ancient people allegedly did not know and could not think have been known to suffer empirical come-uppances. A learned man once argued with passion and cogency on the basis of ancient texts that the Romans did not possess the intellectual apparatus to formulate large-scale military strategy, but another, even more cogent and more passionate, showed from different ancient texts that they did.[47] We cannot find examples of sophisticated Roman thinking on the imperial economy—they sound like angry toddlers on the subject—but by the fourth century AD, if not before, they seem to behave as if they knew and understood far more than they wrote on the subject. There is also a cheerful anachronism about taxing the ancients with ignorance of our own academic subjects and for not thinking like we do, an anachronism no less dangerous for being freely admitted.

Combining the contributions of the philologists and the historians—while shying away from the more extreme conclusions of both—we may conjecture that students of rhetoric under the Empire knew what they knew with great force and intensity (more than we are used to, from our systems of education), but what they knew with such vigor is not what we know. Even if we put aside the historians' suggestions of a ruling class afflicted by their education with drastic ignorance of much of the knowledge we would consider necessary for that ruling, still, what the members of that class were positively taught by rhetorical education will have stood first in their minds, and been likely in principle to have the greatest historical impact. Testing that hypothesis is the purpose of the rest of this book.

# SECTION II

# Killing Julius Caesar as the Tyrant of Rhetoric

# 3

# The Carrion Men

THE DISPUTE was sordid and the dictator was late.[1] But, then, why should Caesar hurry to the Senate to hear a debate—an embarrassing contention between two of his own minions—that turned on exactly how illegal one of his own appointments was? Caesar's wife, besides, had suffered nightmares, his doctors told him to stay home, and his diviners agreed: the omens were, in a word, poor. The conspirator Decimus Brutus had gathered a body of gladiators in the Portico of Pompey, under the excuse of games in the theater connected to it. The Senate was meeting in the Senate House—the Curia—of Pompey, also attached to that Portico.[2] Rightly fearing delay, Decimus Brutus had to go to Caesar's house and wheedle him out.[3]

So it was that, eventually, Caesar allowed himself to be enticed from his house, through the streets, through the Campus Martius, into the Portico of Pompey, and past Decimus Brutus's gladiators. Then he allowed himself to be talked past another set of poor auguries, performed at the very door of the Curia, and finally into the chamber (where none could go but senators, thus stripping Caesar of his retinue); and there, finally, he took his seat.[4]

By plan of the conspirators Caesar's fellow consul and friend Mark Antony was held in conversation outside,[5] while Tillius Cimber, under pretence of piteous petition, got a good grasp on Caesar's toga—which was intended both as the signal for the attack, and to hold the dictator in his seat for the butchery to follow.[6] But then things grew odd. There was no crash of Decimus Brutus's gladiators into the Curia of Pompey to execute the deed of blood. Nor did a few carefully chosen members of the widespread conspiracy—doughty officers of the legions well used to the sword—step forward to cut Caesar down. Rather, Caesar's attackers flocked around their victim so thickly that none of them could get a good swing with the daggers they produced from beneath their clothes. Servilius Casca did no more than nick Caesar in the shoulder, while Cassius got in an awkward blow at the dictator's face, and Decimus Brutus merely gouged him in the thigh. By then Caesar had freed himself from Cimber and was up and fighting.

He whirled and flung Casca—bleating "in Greek in his excitement" to his brother for help—violently away. As Caesar twisted to rid himself of Casca, that more stalwart brother found an opening, and got in the first good blow, a jab deep into Caesar's side. But in the face of the fifty-five-year-old's vigorous resistance, the assassination was now verging into farce. Cassius tried to stab Caesar once more but succeeded only in hitting Marcus Brutus in the hand, and the obscure conspirator Minucius Basilus stabbed the even more obscure Rubrius Ruga.[7] Caesar, meanwhile, had got hold of the first Casca brother's dagger, and now there was a running fight, the throng of conspirators trying to get a clear blow, as Caesar defended himself, spinning and darting, and running and shouting, in an attempt to break free of the swarm of his attackers.[8]

Eventually Caesar was borne down by sheer numbers. Or, in the more romantic telling, when he saw even his protégé Marcus Brutus advancing with dagger in hand—presumably in the hand Cassius had *not* ineptly stabbed—he simply yielded to his fate, saying in Greek "You *too*, my son?" before sinking down beneath the statue of Pompey and drawing his toga over his head. Now the murderers worried him like curs, and Brutus himself delivered a deep wound to Caesar's groin.[9] All the senators present and in the conspiracy stabbed Caesar, most of them after he was dead. Thirty-five wounds were later counted on his body.[10]

Those senators in Pompey's Senate House who were *not* part of the conspiracy took to their heels, expecting perhaps to suffer the same fate Caesar just had, and in their panic created a crush at the door. Many members of the Senate were Caesar's supporters, after all, and known to be so, for Caesar had packed that venerable body with his allies, increasing its numbers from six hundred to nine hundred. These additions were held in due contempt, naturally, by the senators of ancient lineage, and the names of some of them, such as Fuficius Fango, were no doubt as comic to the Romans as they are to us.[11] Surely, with Caesar dead, the assassins would turn on them.[12]

To anyone with even a rudimentary sense of how Roman politics worked—of how power at Rome was assembled through networks of affinity and gratitude—the slaughter of at least Caesar's more powerful supporters will have seemed inevitable. Such a slaughter, indeed, had many of the conspirators urged. But the stern Marcus Brutus (the efficient Decimus Brutus was only a distant cousin) had insisted that none should die but Caesar alone, and many of those same conspirators had been recruited largely for their admiration of the character of Marcus Brutus and his family tradition of ridding Rome of unwanted monarchs, so he got his way.[13] This perplexing mercy was extended even to Mark Antony, Caesar's co-consul and closest political ally. Although Antony, whose fists alone might have turned the tide of the nearly botched assassination, was understood to be so dangerous that he needed to be held outside the Senate House during the murder, he was suffered nonetheless to flee with the rest after Caesar was killed.[14] Brutus, who seems to have expected the Roman Senate somehow to intuit that the assassins meant none of them harm, advanced into the chamber to deliver a reassuring speech, only to be embarrassed by the discovery that it was empty of senators other than his fellow conspirators.[15]

The flight of nearly all the senators had, in fact, spawned a rolling panic, first in the near-by theater of Pompey, and then more widely in the city, and soon people were running every which way, in flight from wild rumors: Gladiators were slaughtering the Senate! The city was being sacked! Caesar had been murdered! The poor plundered the markets as the rich fortified themselves in their houses.[16] Antony lay low, while Caesar's other mighty supporter in the city, Marcus Lepidus (holding the post of master of horse, he ranked second to the dictator himself), heard the news of the attack while about his business in the Forum, and ran to Tiber Island where a small unit of soldiers—the only soldiers immediately available—was camped. He marched them to the Campus Martius where he awaited Antony's instructions. Lepidus was a third obvious and necessary target for the conspirators, but they had made no plans to slay or seize him either.[17]

Having mysteriously failed to predict the panic of the Senate, the conspirators had puzzlingly also failed to predict the panic of the people at large. So when the assassins emerged from Pompey's Portico and proceeded to the Forum, waving their bloody daggers and with a cap of liberty perched on a spear as their standard, and crying out all the while that they had slain a tyrant, rather than being received as heroes, they found themselves reduced to the function of blood-stained policemen trying to still the confusion. Decimus Brutus's gladiators had joined them as soon as they emerged from the Curia of Pompey, and also in the Forum slaves from the conspirators' houses. So too did a gaggle of senators who had not been in at the kill but, eager to share the credit for it, were waving daggers around as well, and also presumably the majority of the conspirators who, not being senators, had not been able to participate in the murder.

In this company the conspirators ascended the neighboring Capitoline Hill, placing guards at vulnerable points.[18] The seat of Rome's holiest shrines, where, according to one late account, the conspirators gave thanks to the gods, the Capitoline Hill was also a natural fortress.[19] Other senators joined them on the Capitoline now, including Cicero, not a member of the conspiracy, but enthusiastic in the aftermath. He urged Brutus and Cassius to summon the Senate to the Capitoline, but nothing was done.[20] The conspirators spent the night on the Capitoline Hill, presumably in some discomfort; Antony, having recovered his nerve, spent it instead by beginning the process of moving Caesar's treasure (by one estimate over 375 US tons in weight) to his own house.[21]

The next morning, commoners having been gathered in the Forum (partly by payments) and bade to bellow for peace in the city, those commoners were treated to a series of speeches by the conspirators and their friends, speeches that were variously received. First the praetor and relative of Caesar, Cornelius Cinna, harangued the crowd, naming Caesar a tyrant, and calling those who had killed him virtuous tyrannicides who should be called down from the Capitol and given a reward. But the crowd (too much of it, alas, unbought) did not echo his appeals (in one version they shouted violently against him) and the paid part of the crowd did exactly as they had been paid to do: they bellowed for peace, and nothing else.[22]

Cinna was followed by the glittering young Cornelius Dolabella, garbed as consul: Caesar had designated him to succeed to the consulship when he himself planned to lay it down in a few days. It was indeed the propriety of this succession that the Senate had met to debate on March 15, for Dolabella was only twenty-five (under law the minimum age for the consulship was forty-two); Antony loathed him, opposed his appointment, and swore to use his power as an augur to block it. Now that Caesar was dead, Dolabella simply elevated himself to the tremendous office that had been promised him, descended the Capitoline, and addressed the crowd, seconding Cinna's pleas, but with greater success: finally voices were heard calling for the leaders of the plot themselves to descend and address the people.[23]

So Marcus Brutus and Cassius Longinus finally did come down—the former still visibly bleeding from being stabbed by the latter—with a heavy escort of gladiators, and addressed the crowd with much praise of each other and the other conspirators, urging the Roman people to recapture their ancient liberty. But their speeches were greeted by a sinister silence, and they retired back up the Capitoline. The crowd in the Forum dispersed and worked to perfect the security of their own houses.[24]

We wonder not so much why this cycle of speeches failed, but rather what good end the conspirators expected had it succeeded. For one thing was sure: this was all taking time, and time, as they well knew, was against the conspirators. At the moment of the assassination, the balance of armed forces in the city was perhaps equal. Favoring the conspirators were Decimus Brutus's gladiators and sheer surprise; against them was the small force on Tiber Island of which Lepidus had hastened to take command. But Rome itself and all the towns around were filled with Caesar's veterans, veterans who had been or were expecting to be rewarded for their services with allotments of land in colonies throughout the empire. Those in the city were camped in groups on the grounds of the temples and sanctuaries, organized in bodies under banners and officers and about to set out.[25] And, given that the supreme commander under whom a veteran had served was traditionally responsible for arranging boons such as land in colonies, Caesar's death placed their anticipated grants in considerable doubt.

Caesar's veterans—dangerous because they were owners of their own war-gear in the Roman manner—were furious at their leader's death, and loyal to his lieutenants. Summoned and not, the veterans soon began to rally to Antony and Lepidus, and by the afternoon or evening of March 16 those two Caesarian loyalists felt sufficiently strong to march their forces from the Campus Martius into the Roman Forum—an act atrocious to Roman tradition, which barred soldiers in arms from the city proper—placing the conspirators on the neighboring Capitoline under siege.[26] Those who had watched and waited to see which side was likely to prevail took omen and heart from this display of force and now flocked to the Caesarians. Influential men who had benefitted from Caesar's generosity also presented themselves before Lepidus and Antony, summoned by a blizzard of letters from Caesar's loyalists noting that the felicity they enjoyed depended on Caesar's generous acts not being overturned. There was now open talk in the streets that the killing of Caesar must be avenged in blood.[27] All of these developments were ill news for the conspirators. But what else, we must ask, can the conspirators have expected?

Now there was nothing for the conspirators to do but begin or return to negotiations with Antony and Lepidus, a task that Brutus and Cassius undertook through intermediaries: weighty men, former consuls.[28] Antony and Lepidus might have stormed the Capitoline by this time, we guess, but not without much effusion of blood and upset to the gods whose temples crowded the hill. Antony would also have remembered with a wince that only three years before he had led troops from the Capitoline into the Forum—one account speaks of eight hundred killed—to expel the followers of the versatile Dolabella (then a turbulent tribune urging the abolition of debts, and likely also the lover of Antony's wife), and earned the commons' hatred as a result; now with the commons still in play, it was best not to remind them.[29] Moreover, if Decimus Brutus escaped the Capitoline, as governor-designate of Cisalpine Gaul (Northern Italy) he would be the first to arrive at Rome with a sizeable army.[30] Antony and Lepidus naturally declined the assassins' invitation to come and confer on the Capitoline, with its grim guard of gladiators.

So it was that both sides eventually agreed to place the matter in the hands of the Senate, called by Antony as consul to meet early the next morning in the temple of Tellus, a safe distance from the Capitoline, and close to Antony's own house. Had Antony and Lepidus been in an ironical frame of mind, they might have recalled that this temple was located on the very site of the razed house of Spurius Cassius, who had attempted to make himself king of Rome, and was an ancestral relation of the conspirator Cassius brothers. There Antony went without soldiers, but with a breastplate under his toga. Lepidus was not so trusting: his soldiers surrounded the temple with the paradoxical result that supporters of the assassins—including Cinna, ill-fated orator of the day before—rejoiced in the incongruity of being rescued from Caesarian mobs by Lepidus's Caesarian troops.[31]

Unlike in the streets, opinion was decidedly in favor of the conspirators in the Senate, which voted them safe-conduct and invited them to join the Senate's deliberations; although the leaders of the conspiracy did not dare to descend the Capitoline to do so. It was proposed that they should formally be named tyrannicides and given rewards by the Republic. Others urged that they merely be thanked, not having undertaken the deed in search of rewards, while yet others urged that they be granted no more than impunity for the deed. This discussion of generous options was brought to a halt by Antony's feline observation that if Caesar were deemed to have been killed rightly, as a tyrant, then his rule, and all his many enactments, must be considered lawless and invalid. This reduced the Senate to confusion, because those enactments included—quite illegally, of course—designation of Rome's magistrates five years in advance: Caesar had been planning to campaign in the East and had wanted things at Rome settled before he left. Naturally those selected did not want to lose the lofty posts promised them. Particularly exercised and prolix in defense of Caesar's acts was the nimble Dola-bella, ally to the assassins in the Forum the day before, who had already taken up the consulship Caesar had pledged to him. During this debate both Antony and Lepidus left the building to admonish the ever-growing crowds outside the temple who were crying that Caesar's mur-der must be avenged, the pair struggling to prevent actual violence while at the same time maintaining the mob's fury at a potentially useful boil.[32]

The eventual compromise struck in the Senate was that Caesar's acts should be confirmed but that his assassins should enjoy impunity for their deeds. The sequel is known to every lover of Shakespeare, who compresses, but does not much falsify, the events that followed. Three days later Caesar's will was read, in which the Roman citizenry discov-ered that he had granted them three hundred sesterces apiece and many of his properties along the Tiber to enjoy as public parks. Two days after that Caesar's funeral was held, at which the dictator's body (or an ac-curate model of it) was displayed with all its wounds and Antony, deliv-ering the eulogy, whipped up the commons to riot against the conspira-tors.[33] Now the assassins were besieged in their houses, and the poet Helvius Cinna was torn to pieces in the street by mistake, being con-fused with the conspirator Cornelius Cinna. Alarmed by this incident in particular, the conspirators began to make their way secretly out of the city. By mid-April Antony was in control of Rome, Lepidus had set out for the provinces Caesar had granted him and the Senate had con-firmed, and a thin eighteen-year-old, wrapped against the chills and influenzas to which he was chronically subject, had arrived back from school in Greece, having been named in Caesar's will, to the general surprise, the dictator's heir. His name was Gaius Octavius, and no one took him very seriously at all.[34]

# 4

# Puzzles about the Conspiracy

IN RETROSPECT, contemporary observers knew that the conspiracy had been a shambles. It was carried out, Cicero wrote, with "a manly spirit but childish planning."[1] But why? The chief historical puzzles that the details of the conspiracy present might be catalogued as follows:

- Decimus Brutus had armed gladiators near the Senate House of Pompey. Why did they not kill Caesar?
- Why did all the conspirators in the Senate House want to stab Caesar themselves, producing a confused melee?[2]
- Why did the conspirators do nothing about Mark Antony and Marcus Lepidus, or any other followers of Caesar, not even arrest them for kid-glove treatment if the fastidious Brutus insisted? It was especially leaving Antony alive that Cicero later regarded as "childish."[3]
- Why did Brutus think that after the assassination he would be able to address the Senate? Why did he not expect the senators, most of them loyalists of Caesar, to be terrified at the deed?[4]
- Why were the conspirators apparently surprised by the panic their deed caused in the city?
- Why did the conspirators go up the Capitoline Hill?
- Why did the conspirators spend March 16 giving speeches in the Forum?[5]

- Why, other than descending to give speeches, did the conspirators apparently have no plans for what to do after they ascended the Capitoline Hill, given that the reactions of Lepidus, Antony, their troops, and Caesar's veterans could have been predicted?[6]

Once upon a time some of the oddities of the conspiracy against Caesar were explained by the suggestion that Marcus Brutus was a legal and constitutional rigorist.[7] And the Romans too were a legally minded folk, and sticklers for legal technicalities—so especially scholars in the old days thought—and many in the conspiracy will have agreed with Brutus in wishing to remove Caesar with the absolute minimum insult and injury to the laws.

Thus Julius Caesar, who had become dictator for life, had placed himself outside the Roman constitution, and so could properly be killed.[8] But no such clear charges could be laid against Antony and Lepidus, so they could not.[9] Besides, a more general slaughter would obscure the lawful purpose of the deed: rather than a morally pure vindication of the laws, the affair would look like another sleazy stage in the battle between Caesar and the followers of Pompey (who probably constituted much of the conspiracy).[10] The strange inactivity of the conspirators after Caesar's murder was thought consequent upon the fact that although the conspiracy was thick with praetors (Marcus Brutus, Cassius, Cinna, possibly Cimber and P. Naso) and tribunes (Cassius's brother Lucius, and Casca),[11] Antony was consul; that legally a praetor could only summon the Senate if no consul was available (so Cicero's suggestion that the Senate be called to the Capitoline could not be acted upon); and that, as the highest executive officer of the state, it was for the consul Antony to lead the way.[12] Since constitutionally little could be done without Antony's sanction, the conspirators were reduced to sending messengers to him, even as he and Lepidus, less pettifogging about the law, organized their forces and marched soldiers into the city. Having undertaken to kill Caesar in vindication of the law, Brutus and his likeminded conspirators were by that same law, either from conviction or consistency, trapped.

But was Marcus Brutus really afflicted by a "mania for legalism?"[13] The slightly mad letter of Brutus to Cicero usually cited of old in support of this contention—"May the gods and goddesses take everything from me before my conviction that none, with my consent, be more powerful than the Senate and the laws! I did not allow it in the case of the man I killed [Caesar], I will not allow it in the case of his heir [Octavian], and I would not allow it in the case of my own father, were he to come back to life!"—is now generally denounced as spurious, and if by some wonder it is not, it was written more than a year after the Ides of March.[14] And if Brutus and his fellow conspirators were prisoners of legalism, it was extremely selective. "Why, this is *vis*, you!" Suetonius reports that Caesar cried when Tillius Cimber first grabbed him in the Curia of Pompey, a fatuity if *vis* be taken in its wider sense, as violence of any sort, but exactly right if Caesar was accusing Cimber of violating the Roman law that punished using force against public officials.[15] Murdering Caesar without legal process was hardly the act of fanatics for legalism.[16] And other parts of this theory fall apart upon closer examination. It made sense to scholars with orderly minds that a praetor could not summon the Senate if there was a consul available, but this was known to be false as far back as Mommsen.[17] Antony also, no less than Dolabella, was legally too young to be consul, so in principle he could be ignored by legal rigorists, or, if they admitted that he was a legitimate consul, they could by the same logic claim the same for Dolabella, who had taken up the consulship and, as friendly to the conspirators (so they thought then), could summon the Senate for them. A general sense of vindicating the laws and liberating the state so that the laws and constitution could operate freely, of returning the Republic to a state of *libertas* as the coins of Brutus and Cassius were to cry out after the fact—the *libertas* that was Brutus's watchword at the battle of Philippi where he took his life and *libertas* was finally lost—may certainly have motivated Brutus and other conspirators.[18] But legalism does not explain the perplexities—the ultimately fatal perplexities—of the plot to murder Caesar.

Was Marcus Brutus's impractical enthusiasm perhaps philosophical rather than legal? Brutus was only one of some many dozens of conspirators, but we are told that he was the leader and moral center of the undertaking, and many had joined the conspiracy because of his leadership.[19] And it was he, our authors tell us, who insisted upon grounds of justice, but perhaps also because of misplaced optimism about the character of Mark Antony, that no action be taken against Antony, Lepidus, and the rest of Caesar's supporters, although why anyone could have objected to their being placed under gentle restraint until the city was safely in the hands of the conspirators is hard now to fathom.[20] Leaving them free was, of course, the decision that ultimately doomed the hopes of the conspirators.

Brutus's philosophy may indeed help to explain his own adherence to the conspiracy, despite his personal closeness to Caesar. For the historical Marcus Brutus was a follower of the so-called Old Academy, that is to say, a fundamentalist Platonist.[21] And old-fashioned Platonism was a more activist creed than the prevalent Stoicism of the time (or, for that matter, the Epicureanism that Cassius affected).[22] In the face of tyranny, Platonism offered fewer easy escapes into quietism than other contemporary philosophies.[23] Indeed, there already existed a strong tradition of Platonist tyrant-killing and tyrant-expelling, including, most famously, the glorious deeds of Plato's students Chion and Leonides, who slew Clearchus the tyrant of Heraclea (himself a student of Plato, the distinction between Platonic "philosopher-king" and tyrant being a bit hard to make in practice). And also, of course, Dion of Syracuse, who heroically drove out of that place the tyrant Dionysius the Younger. That Dion then became tyrant himself, and was himself murdered by Callipus of Athens, yet another student of Plato, who then, inevitably, became briefly tyrant in his stead until his own assassination, was easily overlooked. [24]

As odd as it may seem to us that so large a body of men were willing not only to follow Brutus and his philosophy, both in his hope to kill Caesar (for which, of course, most had other motives as well) but also in his perverse refusal to kill anyone else, we should remember that, of all the generations from Socrates and until today, Rome in the time of Cicero and Caesar knew perhaps the greatest enthusiasm for philosophy ever seen among a historical ruling class; that within that very tiny group philosophy was something in the way of a mass phenomenon.[25] And so we must imagine Brutus backed by other Platonist conspirators just as eager to slay a tyrant as he was.[26]

The problem is that, although his Platonism may help to explain Brutus's personal motivation and that of some of his followers, it does not explain the plans (such as they were) for the assassination. To the contrary: the more we look into Platonism, and more broadly into Greek philosophical views of tyranny, the more baffling the acts of the conspirators become. Plato insisted that men became tyrants because they had tyrannical souls. If denied the opportunity to rule as tyrants— as they naturally would be in a well-regulated state—men with tyranni-cal souls became common criminals. But if the opportunity presented itself, such men would gang together and raise the one among them possessed of the *most* tyrannical soul to be actual tyrant over the state, while the others with slightly less tyrannical souls would become his evil henchmen. Such henchmen, then, could never become or be rendered less wicked: they were wicked by nature, by virtue of the quality of their souls, and they fell into a small category of persons—the "incurables"— who could never (despite Plato's general optimism about the teaching of virtue) become better.[27] So, according to the Platonic philosophy Brutus espoused, it would be unimaginable to concert with (necessarily wicked) former supporters of Caesar such as Decimus Brutus, and, if Caesar were to be killed as a tyrant, his present supporters—Antony, Lepidus, and much of the Senate—were also irredeemably evil, and, rather than spare them (as we are told Brutus insisted upon), Brutus should have been the first to demand their destruction.

Had Brutus—and there was "not a single Greek philosopher, to put it simply, of whom he was ignorant or to whom he was indifferent"— also recalled his Aristotle, he would have discovered there too the need to make careful plans for what happened after the slaying of a tyrant.[28] The kind of government that arose after a tyrant fell, Aristotle wrote in his *Politics*, was unpredictable: it might be no better, another tyranny.[29] Tyrants intentionally and unintentionally divided their subjects and set them against each other, destroying all bonds of friendship and affinity, natural or man-made, and such divisions in the state characteristically led to *stasis,* that state of civil unrest or civil war that Greeks dreaded as the ultimate failure of politics.[30] Simply to kill the tyrant, to spare his henchmen, and to let the political chips fall where they may, all of that lay quite athwart the teachings of the Greek philosophers.[31]

Philosophy, then, like legalism, may have motivated some of the assassins, but it hardly provided them with their plan. What, then, of Brutus's family tradition? Marcus Junius Brutus and his contemporaries accepted that he and his distant cousin Decimus were descended from the Lucius Junius Brutus who had in early times led the revolt at Rome against Rome's king Tarquin the Proud, and so established the Roman Republic (creative dodges were employed to explain how the con-temporary Bruti could be plebeians while Lucius Junius Brutus was a patrician, and how the elder Brutus could have any descendants at all, having, notoriously, executed his sons as traitors).[32] As a *triumvir mon-etalis* in the 50s BC Marcus Brutus had depicted the ancient Brutus on his coins.[33] As a people, moreover, the Romans prided themselves on their hatred and intolerance of kings—a healthy disposition of which they were reminded every February 24 by the repetition of the rite of the *Regifugium,* or King-Runs-Away, which celebrated the expulsion of Rome's last monarch.[34] We read that attempts were made to urge Brutus against Caesar by the scrawling or posting of anonymous messages read-ing things such as, "Would that you were with us now, Brutus!" and "You are no true Brutus!"[35] This implies, perhaps, that those at the top of society could feel real popular pressure from those lower down to do something about Caesar.[36] Before the murder there was, moreover, great suspicion that Caesar had actual monarchical ambitions—there was play with crowns and royal acclamations, which were thought by some to be Caesar testing the waters among the commons to see how being proclaimed king would be received.[37] And, indeed, in one tradi-tion the conspirators cried out that they had killed a king.[38] Did his family tradition help to urge Brutus against Caesar?[39] Did the anti-monarchical tradition of the Romans—and the leadership of Brutus, whose family represented that tradition—drive some of the other con-spirators?[40] Quite possibly. But it still does not explain how they acted. For Tarquinius Superbus and his family were driven out of Rome, not

killed, and so details of the liberation of Rome from the Tarquins offered
no guidance to assassins. Legend reported, moreover, that the Tarquins
made at least three attempts to re-establish their rule at Rome with the
help of allies (Lars Porsenna of Clusium being only the most famous).
No Roman pondering upon the Tarquins would be likely to be as insouci-
ant as the conspirators were about what was to happen after their deed.[41]

Nor was useful guidance offered by three other early stories of seekers
after despotic power at Rome who came to bad ends.[42] Spurius Maelius,
who was thought to be aspiring to kingship (439 BC), was, according
to legend, killed by Servilius Ahala with a dagger hidden in his armpit
(thus the *cognomen* Ahala, "armpit"). Three of the conspirators against
Caesar could claim to be related to Ahala, Brutus through his mother
Servilia, and both brothers Casca (whose *gens* name was Servilius), and
we know that Brutus had Ahala on his mind when he was younger
because when he was a moneyer in the 50s he also minted coins depicting that ancient worthy.[43] But the version of the killing of Spurius Maelius circulating at the time of the conspiracy against Caesar made Servilius Ahala a magistrate—master of horse to the great Cincinnatus,
who was hurriedly appointed dictator to deal with the crisis—ordered
by that dictator (who had the legal right to issue such an order) to kill
Maelius, and, if we may expand the story somewhat from later accounts,
Ahala had not even intended to kill Maelius with a dagger, but resorted
to it when the commons defended Maelius from his summons to appear
before Cincinnatus.[44] Not much guidance there for the assassins of
Caesar, nor in the pursuit of royal power by Spurius Cassius (486 BC),
executed either according to the sentence of the quaestors or killed by
his own father (from whom Caesar's killer Cassius descended) wielding
the terrible might of his *patria potestas*; nor in that of M. Manlius Capitolinus (384 BC), who was also executed in accordance with a vote of
the Roman people in the centuriate assembly.[45] Inspirations to the conspirators such killings may have been, but legend had come to cast them
all as formally legal executions and did not give the assassins of Caesar
a road map telling them how to proceed.[46]

The same is true of Rome's more recent nonlegendary political
murders or (depending on one's political opinion) just and necessary

removals of demagogues aiming at kingship or tyranny: Tiberius Grac-
chus beaten to death with the legs of benches; his brother Gaius killed
under some cover of legality at the urging of Rome's first *senatus consultum ultimum* (statement of the will of the Senate); Saturninus pelted to
death with roof tiles; Livius Drusus done to death by night (and his
assassin never found); Catiline killed in battle, and his supporters executed in a dungeon at the order of the consul, Cicero, under cover of
another *senatus consultum ultimum*.[47] Nor, finally, did the historical
Greek tradition of tyrant slaying offer much direction to the conspirators, the deeds better known (to us and them) having little in common
with the actions of those who killed Caesar, although they may account
for one of the roads not taken: one of the plans the conspirators rejected
was to murder Caesar on the *Via Sacra*, the analogue at Rome to the
Panathenaic Way at Athens where Harmodius and Aristogeiton, the most
famous would-be tyrant slayers of all—they managed to kill the tyrant's
brother Hipparchus, but not the tyrant Hippias himself—attempted
their immortal deed.[48]

## Killing the Tyrant of Declamation

While not discounting as motives legalism, love of liberty, philosophy,
Brutus's family tradition, the Roman tradition of hostility to monarchy,
or Greek history, we still need to look elsewhere for the outlines of the
plan to kill Caesar.[49] Although contemporaries knew the conspirator
Marcus Brutus as a philosopher, they knew him perhaps better as an
orator, a talent for which Cicero praises him in his dialogue of 46 BC re-
counting the history of oratory, in which Brutus serves as one of Cicero's
interlocutors, and which was called the *Brutus* after him.[50] Orators had
much to say about tyrant slaying. Indeed, in rhetorical training, they
relentlessly used a script for tyrant slaying that comes very close to what
the conspirators against Caesar actually did.

If we wish to blame the failure of the conspiracy to bring liberty to
Rome on an intellectual contagion among the conspirators, we should
look to a contagion likely to have been general among the conspirators.
Marcus and Decimus Brutus were both born (probably) in 85 BC and

the year before that (probably) saw the birth of Cassius. Where we can estimate from the dates of their office holding, the other conspirators were much the same age or at most slightly younger.[51] It thus appears that the conspirators all grew to manhood in a generation when formal training in rhetoric had become a considerable part of Roman education, if not (as it would become under the Empire) almost the whole of it. It is very likely that Marcus Brutus and every single one of the other conspirators had, during their schooling, frequently rehearsed the ubiquitous rhetorical theme of tyrant slaying.[52]

*Controversiae*, forensic declamation (most rhetorical training was forensic), depended upon a set of stock characters—the Hero, the Cruel Father, the Rich Man, the Poor Man, the Pirate—and a body of laws that gave legal form to the differences between them, and thus the necessity for speeches such as those given in court. Our interest here is in an overwhelmingly popular pair of those stock characters, the Tyrant and the Tyrannicide, and the law declamation used to pit them against one another, that "The man who kills a tyrant shall receive a reward from the city."[53] An example: "A painter sets up in the street, where the tyrant was wont to pass by, a painting of the punishments in Hades. The tyrant comes upon it, and kills himself. The painter asks for the reward due to a tyrant slayer. The city refuses."[54] The declaimer argues the case of either the painter or the city.

That the figure of the Tyrant of declamation hovered over Julius Caesar at least since he captured Rome in early 49 BC is clear from Cicero, who wrote to his friend Atticus in March of that year that he had developed a set of *theses* (simulated arguments)—practicing *theses* was another rhetorical exercise—about the proper conduct of the statesman under tyranny, *theses* that he was arguing on both sides, both in Greek and in Latin, to take his mind off his troubles and to contemplate "something serviceable."[55]

That the rhetorical tyrant-killing theme was on the minds of the conspirators as well appears clear in our historical accounts of the conspiracy. It is not only that the assassins themselves cried out that they had killed a tyrant.[56] When Cornelius Cinna addressed the Roman people in the Forum "he called Caesar a 'tyrant' and his destroyers 'tyrannicides'" and urged that the assassins be summoned down from the Capitoline and rewarded. And the next day in the Senate it was proposed that the assassins should formally be named "tyrannicides" and, again, given a reward.[57] Whatever the possible muddle produced about what exactly was shouted and said in the Senate by Greek authors using the terminology of tyranny familiar to them, that well-attested reward, twice proposed, comes right from the declamatory law about tyrant killing.[58] And the existence of that law in the minds of the conspirators explains another oddity of the recorded events. All the conspirators present in the Senate stabbed Caesar; in fact, the crowding and the resulting tangle—the conspirators' stabbing each other by mistake—almost let Caesar escape. Why did they *all* have to participate with their own hands?

It turns out that the declamatory themes hanging on the law "that the man who kills a tyrant shall receive a reward" sometimes involved disputes between *several* claimants to the reward as to who had really killed the tyrant. "A man ascended the acropolis in order to kill a tyrant. The tyrant fled, and another man, coming upon him, killed him. The men dispute over who should receive the prize."[59] To anyone who had declaimed in school on the topic of tyrant slaying, establishing who got credit for the deed was a perfectly predictable consideration. And so it was also quite natural that the plan did not have Decimus Brutus's gladiators force their way into the Senate House and kill Caesar—or kill him on the way in or out—but for all the assassins present in the Senate to stab Caesar in order that, whether or not there was to be a material reward for killing Caesar, they could all claim the glory of being proper tyrannicides, and deny it to lesser men such as gladiators.[60]

The tyrant and his death formed a well-worn plot. For the tyrant was perhaps the most fully worked-out character in the small zoo of the *personae* of declamation: the stock tyrant had the fullest taken-for-granted backstory. This was in part because he was only partially distinct from the tyrants told of in history and tragedy and the stock tyrant of philosophy, and the orator could call also upon commonplaces about those well-known figures.[61] But if the tyrant of declamation was morally and psychologically similar to the tyrant of philosophy, he was set apart by his story arc, the standard sequence of events (rarely all present, however, in a single declamation) that took him from seizing the tyranny to his death at the point of the sword of a tyrant slayer.

The tyrant of declamation is among the rich and well-born of the city: the stock declamatory character of the Rich Man is often under suspicion of aiming at tyranny, and aspiring to tyranny is a recognized crime in rhetoric.[62] (But was the Rich Man really so aspiring? He has weapons and other "tyrannical apparatus" hidden in his house. Please declaim on the subject.)[63] He becomes tyrant by seizing the city's high, fortified citadel, its acropolis or *arx*.[64] There he lives in luxury.[65] He is joyfully cruel and revels in torturing those whom he suspects of plotting against him, or anyone else he can get his hands on.[66] (With his menacing headquarters and his gloating sadism, the tyrant of declamation has a good deal in common with extroverted villains in whom we delight, when we watch, say, James Bond films.)[67] Of course the tyrant has good reason to be suspicious, because a stream of people—usually young men, hardly distinguishable from the declamatory stock character of the Hero—attempt to kill him, in order to enjoy the reward for tyrannicide stipulated by the law of city, which is (like many declamatory laws) in force even if it is not mentioned as the law upon which a particular declamation is grounded.[68] Such is the tyrant's fear that he sometimes abdicates his tyranny on carefully negotiated terms in return for immunity for his crimes (his adherence to these terms, or not, offering other opportunities for declamation).[69] But if the tyrant is indeed killed, the tyrannicide is escorted down from the citadel in his glory to receive his reward. . . . But someone sues to prevent it, and the claimant and his opponent must try to make good their cases before the court. Whoever wins the case at law, however, once the tyrant is dead the state returns to its pretyrannical constitution and its prior felicity as if nothing had ever happened. So certain is it, according to the conventions of declamation, that everything will return to normal that those suffering under a tyranny can be imagined consoling each other with the thought that "it will stop soon. When he dies we'll soon be free."[70]

The stock elements of the story of tyrant and tyrannicide fit the historical details of the murder of Caesar well enough that it is appealing to deduce that the killing of the tyrant of declamation dominated the minds of the slayers of Julius Caesar, and provided, as it were, a script for their deeds.[71] The stock tyrant lives on the *arx*. This is why the conspirators felt they had to liberate the citadel of Rome, the Capitoline Hill, which even contained an area called the *arx* (although the fact that it could be relatively easily defended was not lost upon them, and they did post sentries).[72] They also needed to ascend the *arx* to be escorted down from it in triumph, even if, given the chaos in the city, that happy event did not in fact, apparently, transpire.[73] The slaying of the stock tyrant is greeted with celebration.[74] This is why Brutus was surprised when those senators not part of the conspiracy bolted from the Senate house. That is why the conspirators themselves ran out waving their daggers and shouting that they had killed a tyrant. And that is why they were equally surprised at the chaos and rioting in the city when they emerged. According to the script, Rome should revert immediately to a peaceful, biddable, constitutional state, reveling in its new, tyrant-free happiness.

Antony and Lepidus appeared nowhere in that script, so they were ignored.[75] Brutus explained that the conspirators "would win the glory of tyrannicides if they killed Caesar *alone* as a king; but if they killed his friends they would appear to be members of Pompey's faction acting out of hate."[76] It was also safe to ignore Caesar's lieutenants because, according to the script of declamation, after the tyrant slaying Rome would automatically revert to a prelapsarian state where such creatures posed no threat. For unlike the tyrant of philosophy, whose evil retainers are a major theme of philosophical treatment, henchmen of the declamatory tyrant powerful in their own right (their existence, the danger they presented, and any soldiers they might have lurking on Tiber Island) simply did not feature much in the plot of declamatory tyrant slaying.[77] In rhetoric the death of the tyrant by implication automatically eliminates or renders powerless his entire (dimly seen) regime. And if the state is imagined to revert to perfect constitutional government after the death of the tyrant, the extraconstitutional power of the tyrant's henchmen surely poses no danger. As a declamatory tyrant slayer boasts, "Even now you are enjoying the fruits of my deeds! The citadel, as you can see, is empty of evil men. No one issues commands. . . . Everything is peaceful. All the laws are in force, freedom is patent, democracy is firm, marriages are not outraged, children are free from fear, maidens are safe, and the city is rejoicing in its common felicity."[78]

Now we understand why the conspirators against Caesar made no useful plans for the aftermath: in declamation, after the death of the tyrant, the city returns *automatically* to its free constitution without any further effort.[79] Why did declamation take this reversion for granted? Because in the real world of declaimers and their teachers, the whole point is to deliver contending speeches about the prize for killing the tyrant. So a sharp snap-back to civic normality by the imagined city of the declamation is necessary in order that the city be in a condition to hear those speeches and grant, or refuse, the prize. Any obstruction within the story to the delivery of these speeches—such as surviving evil tyrannical henchmen—must yield to the real-world demands of educational declamation, and so vanish.

And the speeches: Brutus had a speech prepared for the Senate because giving a speech (the declamation) is what a tyrannicide was expected to do after his deed. This expectation of a speech was deep-set in the minds of those who thought about killing tyrants. Reporting on the killing of Nabis the tyrant of Sparta in 192 BC, after which the Spartans gathered, disorderly but armed, and drove the assassins out of the city, Livy comments, "Nor would this uproar have occurred, if the people had immediately been summoned to an assembly—their weapons left aside—and if an oration suitable to the occasion had been delivered" by Alexamenus, the leader of the plot against Nabis. The chaos in Sparta was only settled when Philopoemen, hero of the Achaean league, arrived and, "having summoned the leading men, gave a speech such as Alexamenus should have given."[80] And Cicero, who had much fault to find in retrospect with the actions of the conspirators once Caesar was dead, emphasizes particularly the missed opportunities for speeches: an address should have been made to the people, he thought, and he claims that at the time he urged the praetors (including both Brutus and Cassius) to summon the Senate to the Capitoline Hill.[81]

That Cicero imagined that either the senators, who had fled while Brutus tried to address them, or the tumultuous people would have gathered promptly to be thus addressed (even by the eloquent Cicero) shows how immovable the assumption was that a tyrant slaying had to be followed by a speech (or shows Cicero's no less immovable self-opinion).[82]

In fact, details aside, the conspirators were at one with Cicero on the need to give speeches, and speeches they gave, or at least tried to. First Marcus Brutus, unsuccessfully to the Senate, and then the sequence of orations given by Cinna, Dolabella, and Brutus and Cassius to the people the next day. In declamation the giving of speeches ended the script, bringing the story to an end. Loyally following that script, the conspirators gave their speeches, but when no end came, they could find nothing to do but to read over the last page of the declamatory script again, and give yet more speeches, in the hope that the magic would eventually work.

# 5

# Who Was Thinking Rhetorically?

THE READER will have been concerned for some pages now that this present author seems oblivious to the obvious interpretation of the similarities between the events of 44 BC and the script for tyrant slaying that was lodged deep in declamation: that the apparent parallels are the result of our six main sources—Nicolaus of Damascus, Plutarch's *Brutus* and his rather different *Caesar*, Suetonius, Appian, and Cassius Dio, or their sources in turn, all other than Nicolaus writing at least a century and a half after the events they describe—consciously or unconsciously assimilating the events of history to the model of rhetorical tyranny these authors learned in school. In other words, to what degree do our accounts of the murder of Caesar sound like tyrant slaying in declamation because of the influence of their educations on our authors' writing, rather than the influence of their educations on the deeds of the historical actors? To this we might respond first, somewhat impertinently, Why assume that men's education has a greater impact on what they write than on the deeds they do? Is such thinking not anachronistic, a product of our own assumption that literature is an independent realm that primarily influences other literature? But second, the historical tradition does present details where this kind of literary influence is strongly to be suspected, and so obvious are these embellishments that they help to strengthen the argument that the rest of the tradition is sound, as does the absence of declamatory simplification or augmentation where these could have been useful, or could have made delightful, indeed virtuoso, additions.

In his *Brutus* (and no other source—not even the same author's *Caesar*—agrees) Plutarch has Brutus address the Roman people on the Capitoline on the day of the assassination and then has all the conspirators descend the hill in a procession, with Brutus "surrounded by many of the most distinguished men, escorted with great glory from the citadel and set upon the rostra," and then has Brutus address them again, amidst "good order and silence." But it appears from Cicero that no such orations to the people were actually given on the Capitoline that day, and the glorious procession down from the *arx* sounds very much like something taken from declamation, where such a procession down from the *arx* was a feature.[1] Appearing for the first time in our latest main authority, Cassius Dio, is the suggestion that the weapons used to kill Caesar were not carried into the Senate on the persons of the conspirators, but instead in document boxes. It is attractive to suppose that this contamination of the tradition may be the result of the recurrent anxiety in declamation about smuggling weapons past the tyrant's guards.[2]

Even more striking is the tale of Brutus's wife, Porcia, and the test to which she subjected herself, a story current in outline by the time of the emperor Tiberius in the early first century AD, but which had changed significantly by the time of Cassius Dio in the early third.[3] Porcia was the daughter of that stern traditionalist Cato the Younger, who had committed suicide at Utica in 46 BC during the civil wars that brought Caesar to supremacy in Rome. In 44 BC Porcia, as Cassius Dio tells the story, suspected that something was up by observing her husband Brutus deeply pondering, and suspected too what the secret might be. But Brutus would not tell her when she asked. And Porcia concluded that this was because he feared that if she were seized by Caesar, and tortured, she might reveal the plot. So taking a knife, she cut herself deeply in the thigh, and once she had mastered her pain, showed the wound to her husband, avowing that it proved her fortitude in the face of torture. Brutus, moved by the conquest of her feminine bodily weakness by her mighty will, revealed the plot to her.[4]

As history, Porcia's fear of torture seems unlikely. Julius Caesar was a man of no few vices, but torturing ladies of the Roman aristocracy is not recorded as having been among them: in fact the historical Caesar seems to have had a positively un-Roman distaste for torture.[5] Caesar, indeed, was unwisely kind and pardoning of his enemies; it was probably to avoid Caesar's mercy, not his cruelty, that Porcia's father Cato killed himself at Utica, and it was the consequence of Caesar's famous policy of clemency to his enemies that Marcus Brutus, and many other former opponents in civil war and followers of Pompey, were still walking the earth in 44 BC and able to organize a conspiracy to murder him.[6]

Porcia's fear of torture by Caesar is absent in the version of the story told by the Tiberian Valerius Maximus: there, aware of the plot, Porcia cuts herself to prove that she has the courage to commit suicide should it fail. In the second-century versions of Plutarch and Polyaenus, Porcia cuts herself merely to prove that she is strong enough to be worthy of the confidence of Brutus, worthy of being informed of the plot. And, for what it is worth, Plutarch gives a source for his version, implying that he took it from a surviving book that Porcia's son Bibulus (by a previous husband) wrote about his mother.[7] How, then, did torture force its way into the story? Torture, and not infrequently the torture of women, was entirely characteristic behavior of the tyrant of declamation: it set up conflicts about which speeches could be given. Suppose that a tyrant tortures a wife to get information about her husband, and she reveals nothing but becomes barren as a result of the torment? Then her ungrateful husband divorces her because she cannot give him children, and she sues him: a lovely declamatory scenario.[8] And the very words Cassius Dio gives to Porcia sound like they have wandered in from the peroration of a student declamation: "Neither fire, nor whips, nor spikes will make me reveal anything! To that degree I was not born a woman! If you still trust me not, it is nobler for me to die than to live! Otherwise let none think me the daughter of Cato or the wife of Brutus!"[9]

But since we can relatively easily guess at and discard from history details from declamation such as these that have found their way into the story of the killing of Caesar, our confidence in the rest is strengthened. And another way of confirming the basic soundness of the tradition is to ask why authors, if under declamatory influence, did not make a better job of it. Heavy declamatory influence on the historical tradition would encourage much polishing, simplifying, and cleaning up: not only editing out the host of unnecessary characters (all those confusing names of conspirators and their offices!), but eliminating distracting features—such as the gladiators of Decimus Brutus—that turn out to have no significant role in the story.[10] Declamation required two persons (not thirty-five persons) to dispute over the prize for tyrant slaying, or that one argue against the right of another to receive it. Declamation would have reduced that mob of eager stabbers of Caesar to one (whose claim for the prize would be opposed) or two (who would be rivals for the prize). All those ineffectual speeches mentioned in the tradition would be reduced to one or two effectual ones, written out in full. Marcus Brutus and Cassius Longinus could easily have been eased into the role of the two contenders for the prize (or either made to claim the prize, and Antony or Lepidus speak against him), but they were not.

In declamation, the tyrant-slaying plot ends with forensic—courtroom—oratory about the prize. In our later, longer accounts the authors did write speeches for the characters: Appian gives Antony a speech before the Senate in the temple of Tellus, Brutus a speech to the people on the Capitoline, and Antony a funeral oration upon Caesar, while Cassius Dio gives Cicero an interminable speech in the Temple of Tellus, and Antony a no less prodigious eulogy over Caesar. Yet these speeches refer glancingly, if at all, to the question of rewarding the assassins; they are in fact perfectly conventional speeches of political advice (deliberative) or in the case of Antony's eulogy a speech of display (demonstrative), both types of speech that throng the historians, rather than the forensic (law-court) speeches required by the tyrant-slaying theme in declamation.[11]

A rhetorical tyrant is supposed to be murdered on the *arx*, and the tyrannicides are not merely supposed to visit the *arx* after he is dead. The story of the killing of Caesar was firmly attached to the Curia of Pompey because of the irony that Caesar should die there, of all buildings, and beneath Pompey's statue, of all places. But a thorough rewriting of the story to make it accord with the declamatory tyrant-slaying plot could have wrenched Caesar loose from the Curia of Pompey and

had him murdered on the *arx*. Such a fate likely befell the early dema-
gogue and seeker after kingship Manlius Capitolinus: in Livy his story
takes place chiefly in the Forum, but by the time of Cassius Dio his
crime had shifted to an attempt to seize the Capitoline.[12] The death of
Caesar was never, however, moved to the *arx*.

A rhetorical tyrant is supposed to be protected by bodyguards, whom
the tyrannicide must often kill, sneak by, or trick. To supply Caesar with
such necessary accompaniment was trivial: the tradition could have
forgotten that Caesar dismissed his Spanish bodyguard, re-imagined his
lictors as bodyguards, or made something of the confused story that
appears in Cassius Dio that, after he dismissed his Spanish guard, Caesar
was protected by a body of senators and *equites*. Perhaps, indeed, rhetorical commonplace is the ultimate origin of that guard of distinguished
persons known only to Dio. But Dio dismisses this guard as something
that existed only "in word," and so ultimately the tradition refused to give
Caesar a tyrannical guard, and made him meet his fate undefended, in vio-
lation of the conventions of rhetorical tyrant slaying.[13]

The killing of the tyrant of declamation, moreover, is supposed to be
met with public joy, and the flight of the Senate and the chaos in the city
could easily have been photoshopped out of the story, but they were
not. In declamation the happy consequences of killing the tyrant are not
supposed to be reversed by the tyrant's surviving followers, but that is
precisely what is allowed to happen in the story that survives to us. This
all suggests that it was the historical actors themselves, more than the
later authors, who went to such pains to follow the declamatory script,
the authors having been at liberty to tidy up the story to make the events
fit the script better, but the actors not.

The core of the story, then, remains untouched: the multiple assassins, the removal to the Capitoline, the attempted speeches, the indiffer-
ence to Antony and Lepidus (the tyrant's henchmen), and most of all,
the lack of a plan for what should happen after the murder—a core that
can also be confirmed by Cicero's contemporary evidence.[14] The conspiracy ultimately failed because when the conspirators got to the end
of their declamatory script, they expected that a literary convention—
the evil henchmen vanish and the city returns to normal without any

further effort—would apply in the real world. And what really happened
is that they got to the end of their script, tried to repeat the ending several times in hope of a better result (those speeches in the Forum), and
finally fell off their script into the real world, which was inhabited by
Antony and Lepidus and their soldiers. Such might be the end of events
in the real world, but it is not a story authors massaging the murder of
Caesar into a declamatory tyrant killing would ever tell.

## Domitian and the Tyrant of Declamation

Moving forward a century and a half allows us a second crack at this
problem of the relation between literary accounts and reality, using the
example of the emperor Domitian (AD 81–96). For Domitian we rely
heavily on the surviving life by Suetonius. And here a particularly strong
case can be made that Suetonius was writing with the tyrant of declamation very much in mind.[15] Like that model, Suetonius's Domitian
is perpetually fearful and suspicious, even lining a portico with stone
polished to a mirror finish so he could see behind him when he
walked through.[16] He lives in seclusion, stabbing flies with a sharp-
ened stylus. He even questions prisoners alone, holding their chains in
his own hands.[17] Like the tyrant of declamation Domitian is avaricious
and seizes the property of others.[18] Inventively cruel, he has a critic
devoured by dogs, and is much given to torture, even of persons of high
status, and the bodily mutilation of his enemies—all set out clearly as
the particular amusements of the tyrant of declamation.[19] Also agreeable to the model, Domitian is arrogant in manner,[20] lustful, sexually
perverse, and perfectly at ease using his power to slake his evil desires.[21]
Hated and feared by all,[22] Domitian finally sweeps clean much of the
Palatine Hill to build a vast, fortified palace: the proper luxurious but
secure citadel the tyrant of declamation deserved yet Rome itself had
never possessed.[23] Pliny the Younger, relying no less on the tyrant
model to describe Domitian in his *Panegyric* on Trajan, calls Domitian's
palace an *arx*, the declamatory tyrant's bastion, and remarks upon the
security arrangements, the walls, the doors, the choke-points, the secret
rooms.[24] The only problem with dismissing this all as a purely literary

portrait is the fact that the titanic Palace of Domitian on the Palatine is, of course, *real*.

The Palace of Domitian survives in prodigious ruins—although whether the security arrangements can be detected in the archaeological record is debated.[25] The inadequacy of the Capitoline, Rome's ancient *arx*, crowded with shrines, as a proper tyrannical citadel was obvious to any observer, but especially to Domitian, who had taken refuge there in AD 69 with his uncle against the soldiers of Vitellius, and, when the hill was stormed—it was not so easy to defend as all that—had to hide and then creep away disguised as a votary of Isis.[26] Domitian took advantage of the fire in Rome in AD 80 that destroyed the smaller mansion (no more than a humble 15,000 square meters in its final stage) in which the Julio-Claudian emperors before Nero had lived. His new palace, occupying most of the Palatine Hill, spread over some 49,000 square meters.[27]

In view of such a structure, of so touchable a gigantic reality, we find our literary complacency shaken. To whatever degree the mind of Suetonius was infested with the portrait of the tyrant of declamation, it appears that Domitian's mind was similarly infested, at least to the extent of building the kind of supremely grand and impregnable edifice stipulated by the tyrant-of-declamation script. Domitian, like other Roman emperors, should be understood to have had not just a conflicted relationship with the tyrant of declamation, but a full-blown complex. All emperors, except perhaps for a few of low origins in the third century AD, were familiar with that figure from their education; all had declaimed as boys about tyrants and tyrant slaying. To teach his own children, Domitian, of course, employed none other than the great teacher of rhetoric Quintilian. And there is no reason to suppose that imperial princes had an education different from their peers, the young men who would form the Senate and the Equestrian order.[28]

All emperors knew, therefore, that their contemporaries always had the tyrant of declamation in mind and were apt to apply the model to the autocrat who lived among them.[29] All emperors knew, moreover, that being thought of in terms of the declamatory tyrant was dangerous, for by far the most common fate, indeed the main purpose, of this tyrant

FIGURE 1. Rome, Ruins of the Palace of Domitian. Etching by G. B. Piranesi, *Le Antichità Romane*. Rome, 1756 (DeAgostini Picture Library/UIG).

la *Casa Augustana*. D *Avanzi della Casa Tiberiana*. E *Avanzi della*
*ioni de Sedili del medesimo Circo*. H *Marana o sia Acqua Crabra*

Piranesi Archit. dis. einc.

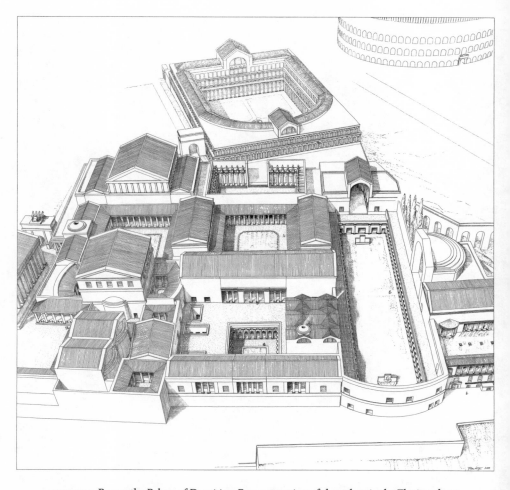

FIGURE 2. Rome, the Palace of Domitian. Reconstruction of the palace in the Flavian phase.
Drawing by J. Denkinger based on a 3d model by A. Müller according to instructions by
U. Wulf-Rheidt and J. Pflug. With kind permission of J. Denkinger and the Division of
Building Archaeology of the German Archaeological Institute.

was to be assassinated. And emperors knew that declamations on tyranny might be cloaked references to themselves. Recall that Caligula
banished and Domitian executed rhetoricians who delivered such a
declamation, although there seem to have been no broader imperial
attempts to suppress the theme.[30] Most often, emperors ostentatiously
shied away from the characteristic behaviors of rhetorical tyrants, trying

to break the connection—or at least downplay it.[31] In Domitian's case the amount of time, money, and attention he devoted to Roman religion can perhaps be understood as intended, in part, to mark this contrast—sacrilegious temple robbing being a characteristic activity of the tyrant of declamation.[32] Tyrants were generally morally wicked, and particularly in the sexual realm. Might that explain Domitian's program of moral reform, his banning of castration, his enforcement of the law against pederasty, and his punishment of naughty Vestals in the ancient, cruel fashion?[33] Similarly, while tyrants were fearful, Domitian was forever on campaign.[34] Isolation was another tyrannical habit, and something to which, if we can believe our written sources, Domitian was much given, even at meals. Might that be in part why he gave, and attended, such tremendous games in circus and amphitheater? Provided such vast public and so many private banquets in Rome? Also characteristic of the tyrant was avarice, and we hear—at least early in his reign—of Domitian refusing to accept legacies, and quashing cases at law likely to be to the advantage of the treasury, and, all through his reign, driving forward his gigantic building projects at Rome for the public benefit.[35]

But yet, but yet: if a man were sentenced by fate to spend his life in a room with a costume, would he *never* try it on? And unlike the miserable tyrant of philosophy, the tyrant of declamation—despite his continual anxiety for his life—was often a happy enough fellow: he enjoyed the luxury, the sex, the sadism.[36] Can we not imagine some emperors whom the costume of tyranny fit exceedingly well—Domitian or, for example, the isolated Tiberius—concluding sometimes that if everybody thinks he is a tyrant anyway, might he not just as well *be* a tyrant, and enjoy it? And, at a subconscious level, influenced by so powerful a literary model, might not the emperor, however much his conscious mind warned him against it, unconsciously behave like the tyrant of declamation, because it was much the most prominent model of autocratic rule he had in his head? The relationship between Roman autocrats and the tyrant of rhetoric was thus one in which we might expect to witness violent gyration between ostentatious avoidance of the behaviors of the tyrant of rhetoric and their embrace. Such seems to have been the case with Domitian—with his religious fastidiousness, his temple building, his banquets—but also his vast, tyrannical *arx*.

## Returning to Caesar

The historical Julius Caesar—to bring this chapter to a close—shows the same gyration of behaviors between attraction to and repulsion from the tyrant of declamation. One of his favorite phrases was an ironic tag from Euripides: "If one must do ill, it is fairest to do ill for the sake of tyranny."[37] But he also sometimes shied away from the tyrant's more odious characteristics.[38] Caesar possessed a bodyguard of soldiers from Spain, but this he dismissed at some point after his return to Rome for the last time—in October of 45 BC.[39] This was odd, because he would soon need a bodyguard again. Caesar did not conceal that he wished to depart from Rome to campaign in the East against the Parthians as soon as the season allowed: indeed, he had to be killed on the Ides of March because he intended to leave Rome three days later, on March 18, 44 BC, and then again he would have an armed bodyguard.[40] Nevertheless, he sent the Spaniards away, and the most plausible reason for this is that a bodyguard was firmly established as one of the indispensable appurtenances of a tyrant.[41]

That said, Caesar sometimes also seems to have despaired of escaping the tyrant archetype, and the inevitable doom it promised. After the notorious occasion when he failed to stand up and show due respect to the Senate—the moment identified in the tradition as the summit of his *hybris*—when he realized what he had done, according to Plutarch he pulled his toga from his neck and cried out that he was ready to offer his throat to anyone who wanted to cut it.[42] Suetonius reports that a strange fatalism came over the dictator as the date of his assassination approached.[43] That there were plans afoot to kill him was repeatedly reported to him (no surprise: a conspiracy so large was bound to leak) but he took no action against it, or (if Suetonius is to be believed) merely announced by a public edict that he was aware of the plot.[44] Nor did he attend to the portents of doom that stacked up before and on the day he was killed.[45] As he proceeded towards the Senate House of

Pompey a document was pressed into his hand revealing the plot; he declined to read it.[46] The evening before his murder, dining with Lepidus, when he was asked what he considered the best form of death to be, he replied, "The unexpected."[47]

It is hard to avoid the suspicion that, just as the conspirators were in some way trapped in the script of declamatory tyrant slaying, so too was Julius Caesar himself trapped therein, that "the death that befell him was very close to the one he desired."[48] It was not that he consciously desired to be murdered, but such was the psychological power of the rhetorical model that it placed him too under a psychological compulsion to follow it, and so not even to take the most obvious measures for his own protection: to act against the conspirators, or to heed two bodies of diviners, his doctors, or his wife, who warned him to take care, to beware, and to stay safe at home on the Ides of March.[49]

# Rhetoric's Curious Children

## BUILDING IN THE CITIES OF THE ROMAN EMPIRE

THE PUBLIC BUILDINGS of the cities of the Roman Empire are as familiar as the cuts of meat on the shelves of a supermarket. Where an expected item is missing, we summon the butcher with the handy bell or set out confidently with our shovels to find the structure under the earth. But why those particular cuts, why those particular buildings, and why, with broad regional variation, so similar from town to town?[1] This section examines three types of public building—monumental nymphaea (huge, spectacular fountains); city fortification walls built in time of peace; and colonnaded streets—and connects them to the rhetorical educations of the men who made the decisions to build them. These three are chosen because they appear frequently enough in rhetorical treatises and rhetorical works that despite the meagerness of those sources we can form an adequate idea of how rhetoric treated them, and also because they have excited enough interest among modern archaeologists that we can trace their chronology—less well in the case of walls, it must be admitted—and the evolution of their design. In the cases of nymphaea and colonnaded streets—neither wholly impractical, but it is unlikely that any modern cost–benefit analysis would endorse their construction—it is argued that education in the rhetoric of praise, especially exercises in encomium and comparison (aspects of the rhetoric of display, "demonstrative" or "epideictic") encouraged their building. City walls are something of a counterexample. Training in demonstrative oratory created a mild current in favor of such construction. But a stronger tradition in "deliberative" (or "symbouleutic") rhetoric, more prominent in education than demonstrative, *discouraged* the building of city walls. Nevertheless, other forces often overcame both that rhetorical dissuasion and any practical objections, and city walls were built anyway, even in places and at times when not a man alive could recall the sort of dire events for which they might be needed. Adding the oratory of display and deliberative oratory to the forensic oratory of the last chapter, we complete our circle of the three genres of rhetoric ancient theory recognized. This section concludes with an attempt to sketch the outlines of a system implicit in rhetorical training for comparing unlike buildings to one another, a system for scoring the competition in erecting rivalrous monumental buildings that cities in the Greek East undertook in the second and early third centuries AD.

# 6

# Monumental Nymphaea

A MONUMENTAL NYMPHAEUM is something essentially simple and elegant and practical—a fountain—expanded and adorned and transformed into an object, depending on your taste, either splendid in its rich luxury or revolting in its excess, the very hell of classical architecture, the perfect advertisement for its opposite, modernist brutalism.[1] In the most usual design an open basin offered water to the public, while behind it (and perhaps on its flanks) rose several storeys of columns in rare marbles—very much like the facade that backed the stage of a Roman theater—while the gaps between the columns were infested with statues. A monumental nymphaeum required a vast quantity of water, sometimes provided by a bespoke aqueduct, and wasted most of it, for water basins open to the sky ("hypaethral" is the technical term) allowed the water to evaporate. What water did not depart into the jugs of townspeople or into the sky mostly poured away (there being no way to turn off the supply), into associated sewers in towns that had them, into ornamental canals running down colonnaded streets in a few places, or simply by spilling over the lip of the basin into the street, and finding its own slick and slippery way into distant sewers or down the streets and out of the city, to us an unforgivable waste, but to the designer of the nymphaeum a spectacle of insouciance, water plentiful enough to waste.[2] The concentration of so much water in one gigantic nymphaeum came at the expense of the more convenient distribution of water through smaller neighborhood fountains (as at Pompeii), requiring those who wanted the water to carry the cumbersome fluid long

FIGURE 3. Miletus, Nymphaeum, artist's reconstruction. Th. Wiegand (ed.), *Milet, Ergebnisse der Ausgrabung und Untersuchungen seit dem Jahre 1899*. Berlin, 1919. Heft V Tafeln, Tafel 63 (Schaubild: vom Marktplatz von Norden aus gesehen).

distances.[3] For maximum visibility (and incidentally maximum inconvenience to the users), many nymphaea were set at the boundaries of cities and some, indeed, entirely outside.[4] The ultimate impracticality of monumental nymphaea is suggested by the unromantic folk of late antiquity who drilled holes into the nymphaea of previous generations and ran pipes from them into their houses and businesses.[5]

Historians of architecture naturally have their questions. Were nymphaea primarily practical or symbolic? Political or religious or secular? What was their place in city design?[6] But historians of Rome have questions of their own. Inscriptions suggest that the impetus for such projects in Asia Minor—both the origin and the center of the fashion— was primarily local (rather than directed by Rome), and that such structures were for the most part paid for by the cities themselves, or by rich donors associated with the cities.[7] But why, in a world with so many other opportunities for civic benefaction—many of which seem, to us at least, far more useful or enjoyable to the city's inhabitants—did do-nors choose to build gigantic fountains? (And let me re-emphasize: the question is not Why fountains?, for every town needed fountains, but Why did fountains grow so huge and ornate?) What prompted the in-vention of monumental nymphaea in the Flavian period and certified them as a new building type worthy to enter the canon of public build-ings that adorned the cities of Asia Minor? Why did the habit of build-ing monumental nymphaea begin when and where it did (in the late first century AD on the west coast of Asia Minor) and flourish when and where it did (through Asia Minor and points east in the second and early third centuries AD)? And why did it continue into Late Antiquity with surprising strength, with old structures repaired well into the sixth century, and new built into the fifth, in addition to the adaptation of other buildings into fountain houses (Ephesus's Library of Celsus being the most famous)?[8] Why did the habit of building monumental fountains never extend significantly into the Latin West, with the ex-ception of the city of Rome itself, its immediate region, and some cities in North Africa?[9] And why did the habit extend east of Asia Minor, into Syria and the Levant, but only to a lesser extent to the immediate west, into metropolitan Greece?[10] Finally why, most broadly, did the Romans and Greeks choose to monumentalize the structures they did, and not others?[11]

Monumental nymphaea were not an obvious or necessary develop-ment that emerged when the necessary hydraulic technology made them possible. Many depended directly or indirectly on Roman-style aqueducts, but Roman aqueducts came to Asia Minor under Augustus, while monumental nymphaea did not appear until the Flavians; Roman water technology may often have enabled, but it did not unleash, monu-mental nymphaea.[12]

Nor do the monumental nymphaea of Asia Minor seem obviously to have evolved under the Flavians from earlier local forms of fountain. Older—Hellenistic and Julio-Claudian—fountains in Asia Minor, at least those that were built with a focus on appearance, were very differ-ent. They were smaller, perhaps consisting of a statue squirting water into a pool, the pool often half-moon-shaped; or sometimes looking like a small stoa, roofed, that is, to limit the evaporation of the water, with the roof supported by a screen of columns in front; or at times like a small circular temple, again with a roof supported by columns.[13] Nor has a strong case been made that the nymphaea of Asia Minor copied Roman prototypes, because large public fountains in Rome, most famously the *Meta Sudans*, the conical "sweating turning-post," appear to have looked very different.[14]

Nor, finally, did monumental nymphaea simply echo the history of the development of other major building types in Roman Asia Minor, implying that some universal force was propelling the construction of all types of buildings willy-nilly. Certainly the second century AD witnessed a great increase in the construction of public buildings in many of the cities of the region, and monumental nymphaea shared in that rise. But some building types—such as temples to the gods—seamlessly carried Classical and Hellenistic Greek traditions into the Roman period; others, such as temples of the imperial cult, began under Augustus and continued to develop from his era. Basilicas, that distinctly Roman form, seem to have appeared in the region under Augustus as well, while baths seem to have changed slowly from Greek to Roman designs over the years of the Julio-Claudian dynasty.[15] Two classes of structures that appear to have much the same history as the monumental nymphaea in Asia Minor—a Flavian-period start, and an explosion in the second century AD—are the monumental bath and gymnasium complex, and the colonnaded street.[16] We will return to the latter below.

I argue that monumental nymphaea came to be credentialed as a new building type worthy of great and expanding expenditure by cities and benefactors not chiefly because of any superior practical usefulness or potent symbolic charge, but rather because of the peculiarities of rhetorical education. I argue that an accident in the history of education in the late first century AD led to a shift in how members of the Greco-Roman ruling class—especially the Greek-speaking ruling class—conceived of their cities and those cities' amenities. This accident led to a subtle adjustment of cities' self-conception, an adjustment evident in the public oratory and other literature of the period, with the result that their inhabitants were increasingly concerned not merely with their water supply (a perennial civic anxiety in any Mediterranean town), but especially focused on their water supply as an object of pride, of display, and especially of competition with other cities. This shift then manifested itself in a desire to show off that abundance of water, and to perform that function a new sort of building evolved, the monumental nymphaeum. And once the first monumental nymphaea came to be built, the appeal of this new civic structure was so obvious to those who shared the same education as the first benefactors that other donors and their cities quickly and naturally adopted nymphaea as suitable objects for civic and individual rivalry.[17]

## The Praise of Cities

Here we move from the forensic declamation that was the subject of the previous section to demonstrative oratory, the oratory of display, and especially its greatest part, encomium or panegyric, the oratory of praise. We do not know how (or whether) this was taught to the oldest and most proficient students. But we have ample evidence that, while working through the *progymnasmata* ("preliminary exercises"), the stage of rhetorical education that followed study under the grammarian and preceded the final stage of declamation, boys learned the techniques of how to praise or blame a man or city.[18]

No matter at what age boys were taught the elements of demonstrative oratory, the major real-world subject of such oratory was the praise of individuals, an endeavor that had frequent practical application: imperial birthdays and civic festivals of every type required speeches in praise of the emperor, while the movement of Roman governors and other great men around the provinces was accompanied by relentless speeches of praise in their honor. Such speeches also adorned the weddings and funerals of prominent personages, and, indeed, nearly any public occasion. It was natural, then, that teachers of rhetoric developed protocols for such speeches: the subjects to be treated, and the order of treatment—home city, parents, education, virtues. These protocols were taught to boys in school, and available in handbooks (some of which survive to us), if adults needed to be reminded.[19]

Persons were certainly not the only subjects of encomia. The gods demanded their praises too, at their festivals, and great human works, such as harbors and temples, merited the same. Paradoxical themes could be pursued in encomiastic form as an educational exercise or a public display of virtuosity: there were famous sophistic praises of baldness, and of a parrot.[20] But given the overwhelming importance of the praise of persons—and therefore the concentration of training upon it—it was perhaps hardly surprising that when, at some point in the second half of the first century AD, the professors set down rules about how to praise the second most common subject of panegyric, the city, it was decided that cities were to be praised according to the same formulae as individuals, adapted as necessary. Quintilian (ca. AD 95) gives the first surviving account of the method:

> Cities and men are praised similarly. For the founder takes the place of the parent, and age adds greatly to authority, as in the case of those who are said to be sprung from the soil. The virtues and vices revealed by their histories are the same as in private individuals; but the excellences related to position and fortification are proper only to cities. Citizens are an honor to cities just as children are to individuals. Public works too can be praised, in which context distinction, usefulness, beauty, and the building's creator are looked to. Temples, for example, are to be praised for their distinction, walls for their usefulness, and both for their beauty and creator.[21]

The order of topics to be addressed was still somewhat unsettled in Quintilian's day. But rhetoricians held as to a plank in a storm to the formula *laudantur urbes similiter atque homines*, and over time refined and adjusted their rules for this practice.[22] And so it was that the teachers of rhetoric came to specify that a speech praising a city should be structured as follows:[23]

- Physical position (θέσις, which took the place of "home city" for an individual)
- Origins (γένος, founding and founders, ancestors of an individual)

- Upbringing or way of life (τροφή, ἐπιτηδεύματα, moral history, just like that of a person; a city's constitution works well here)
- Actions (ἔργα, πράξεις, just like a person) under the four canonical virtues
  Justice (δικαιοσύνη)
  Self-control (σωφροσύνη)
  Wisdom (φρόνησις, σοφία)
  Courage (ἀνδρεία)

We see these protocols clearly in use in the surviving Greek speeches of Dio Chrysostom, in the same generation as the Latin Quintilian. Elements of this system go back a very long way, to the fifth and fourth centuries BC, so we are hardly surprised to see earlier geographers and historians evaluating cities according to the four canonical virtues, and showing interest in the θέσις of the city in its χώρα, hinterland.[24] But the French historian of epideictic oratory Laurent Pernot is probably right to conclude, on the basis of the broadly different themes, arguments, and organization in which cities and landscapes are praised in earlier literature (see below), that what was to become the standard formula of *laudantur urbes similiter atque homines* does not predate by too long Quintilian's description of it in the AD 90s.[25]

It should be emphasized that, however intellectually elegant and teachable the professors of rhetoric's formulation that cities should be praised as if they were persons, this rule was not without its difficulties for practitioners, who were expected to find considerable matter to include about the city under each of the required rubrics. Courage was not hard: one could list the city's victories in war before the Romans put a stop to that sort of thing.[26] But what about "justice," say, itself divided into justice towards men, justice towards gods, and justice towards the dead? Especially after the spread of Roman law had flattened much local eccentricity? An orator might find himself lauding the Athenians for their scrupulous habit of laying out dead bodies before sunrise, or, under the topic of "self-control," mentioning that women in the city were not allowed to own shops, evidently a doubtful practice, or, under "wisdom," praising the local laws of inheritance.[27]

Worse, in a speech given according to this formula there was no adequate place for the discussion of grandiose public buildings, because although this was a subject that everybody knew deserved much attention, the parallel topic in the praise of individuals—personal appearance—was not considered of much importance and was usually passed over quite quickly.[28] Much of Quintilian's early description of how to give encomia on cities (above) is spent worrying about this problem. And over time different professors urged different solutions: a city's buildings might be stuck on the front as a sort of preface, or added on the end of the speech as an epilogue.[29]

The topic of the *thesis* (physical position) of a city appears to have posed a particular problem to practitioners, because it was canonically the first topic to be addressed, and so hardly to be skimped upon, but was not one obviously rich with possibilities. Naturally the teachers of rhetoric stepped in with helpful suggestions:

> Next in order of the components of "position" is disposition in rela-
> tion to the territory round about and to neighboring territories.
> What must be looked to regarding territory round about is whether
> the city lies at its beginning, or in the middle, or at its end. If it lies
> at the beginning, it should be likened to a face, in that it protects
> the territory within, like the gate of an individual house. If it lies in
> the middle, it is like a royal residence or seat of government, or a
> shield-boss—as Aristides said—or like the mark indicating the cen-
> ter of a circle. If it is at the end, "it flees those approaching as if it were
> a girl fleeing the lustful."[30]

Is it cold or hot? Misty or clear? What produce does the land yield? Close to the sea and its cargoes? Far from the sea and its marauders? On a plain or a hill or a mountain? Near famous cities that add to its luster? Or, if a city has no advantages of place at all, the speaker may praise its folk for being such profound philosophers as to dwell in so forlorn a spot.[31]

Nevertheless, it appears that the particular crutch upon which teach-ers and orators came to lean to fill up the required topic of a city's *thesis* was water: the excellence of a city's position was illustrated by how well-watered it was. In the handbooks, water supply, and evidence for it,

assume in teachers' prescriptions for encomia on cities a role dispropor-
tionate to the other themes they discuss.[32]

> Next we have to look to the waters of the territory. Sources of water
> should be divided into three categories: either springs, or rivers, or
> lakes. These must be judged (like everything else) on grounds of
> pleasure and usefulness; a yet further division may be made in rela-
> tion to their number and whether they are natural. In some places,
> moreover, hot springs are found.[33]

And in actual surviving speeches water supply plays the same exaggerated role that it does in teachers' instructions.[34] Discussion of water
allowed a speaker to catalogue the rivers and springs that fed the city,
and tell of their shape, their modest habits (no nasty flooding), their
beauty, and their history—and to go on as long as he liked about their
myths, their nymphs, and their goddesses.[35] Water offered excellent
filler for a hard-to-fill rubric. And so it is hardly surprising that Dio
Chrysostom could mock what a hackneyed topic civic water supply had
already become in the encomia of his day.[36]

So useful, indeed, did the rhetorical use of water become, that it burst
the banks of orations in praise of cities and territories and found its way
into speeches of other sorts.[37] So the wedding guest, listening to a local
orator deliver a wedding oration, a genre in which there was considerable danger of being "tediously long-winded," might nevertheless hear
much of springs and rivers and their loves and myths.[38] But wedding
guests were tolerant: after the wedding speech there was still the orator's
*wedding chamber* speech to endure, in which he exhorted the young
couple to their amorous duty, resorting to a (rather alarming to us)
set of examples taken from war and racing, but not excluding a hymn
to the rains of autumn, should the wedding take place in that season.[39]
An important man leaving a city and delivering a "leave taking"
(συντακτικός) oration, naturally praised the city he was departing—
and its "harbors, rivers, and springs."[40] An orator delivering an oration
in praise of Apollo (Σμινθιακός) praised the region, the city, the festival, the temple, the statue of the god, and finally "the grove, the nearby
rivers, and the springs."[41]

In addition, water might seep into a speech indirectly, when the formula for encomia on cities was adapted to form a part of encomia on other subjects. When delivering an encomium upon a festival, for example, or inviting a governor to one, the *thesis* of the host city was an expected topic, and naturally the helpful professor of rhetoric drew the speaker's eye to the promising topic of the host city's rivers.[42] The most common type of encomium of all, that of individuals, also required a passage upon the individual's city of origin (and, in the case of a governor's visit, not only praise of the governor's home city, but also of the city being visited). These were shortened versions of the encomium upon a city, and governed by that encomium's rules.[43] Thus the water-sodden formula of encomia on cities, based on that of encomia upon individuals, might find itself swallowed up and regurgitated in the formula that gave it its origins.

## Flooding Interest in Water

A late first-century AD accident in the realm of education, then, teachers' decision to praise cities as if they were men, had the result of bringing civic water supply increasingly before the minds of the decision-making classes of the Roman Empire, both during their education and subsequently, during the surprisingly large amounts of time they appear to have spent giving and listening to panegyrics upon their cities, and to speeches of other types into which water themes had flowed directly by torrent or wanderingly by brook.

The wider effect of this new education can be observed and fixed approximately in time by reading works in other genres, for we witness there a transition from a literary world where water, in all its forms, appears in authors when it is somehow significant, to one where water shows up, relevant or not, because mention of it has become a required genre element of descriptions of lands and cities. Exceptional supplies or odd forms of water, or its lack, had always drawn the eye of ancient observers—in Homer, Argos already had the epithet "very thirsty"—as had water when the context demanded it: rivers tend to appear in Thucydides when they provide a useful geographical marker, or prove an obstacle to marching armies, but not where they are unnecessary for the action of the story.[44] There is mention of water and its availability (and grumpy complaint about deficiencies thereof) in the fragmentary Hellenistic travel account ascribed to Heracleides Criticus, as of the safety of roads and places to spend the night, because he is writing not least to give advice to those travelling the same routes as he did, and Athens, he felt and reported, was badly supplied with water for travellers.[45] But (for example) in Cicero's encomium upon Sicily in his second Verrine oration, despite the orator's harping on the province's fertility of grain, he mentions no sources of fresh water, no river, no spring, no fountain: such mention, evidently, was not yet expected by Cicero's time.[46] Nor was it by the early Empire. The respectively Tiberian and Claudian geographical authors Strabo and Pomponius Mela mention water mostly when there is something remarkable about it: if it is very cold, or curative, or plunges down a waterfall, or if it proves Homer wrong when he called Argos "thirsty," or is famous of old, like Corinth's Peirene fountain, or if although inland it appears to rise and fall with the tides, or if it is claimed as the birthplace of Minerva, or rejoices in a floating island, or inhabits the depths of a fathomless cave.[47]

But by the Flavian period there has been a mighty spate of interest in water, and a change in thinking about it. In the geography sections of the Vespasianic *Natural History* of Pliny the Elder, remarkable water is still mentioned, but so is unremarkable water, because water is now more closely associated with cities, and so appears as a normal part of Pliny's descriptions of them. Nor was Pliny an eccentric: civic water supply continued to be a subject of surprising concern to the second-century traveler Pausanias (somewhat unexpectedly, because his interests were primarily in other realms), and springs and rivers become a positive fixation in the—probably—third-century AD geographer and teller of wonders Solinus.[48] This last devotes no more than 225 words to the district of Boeotia in Greece, but he nevertheless manages to mention the springs Arethusa, Oedipodia, Psamathe, Dirce, Aganippe, and Hippocrene (and that poets alleged that Aganippe gave poetical inspiration to those who drank from it, and that Hippocrene was created by the stamp of Pegasus's hoof), the rivers Ismenus and Cephisus, and two other rivers, unnamed but reported by Varro, one of which turned the sheep that drunk from it dark, and the other white. A well in the same district (confused and vexed, we may guess, by the ever-changing sheep) simply killed any who drank from it.[49] Solinus is mostly rubbish, of course, and worse, derivative rubbish; but that rubbish does seem to be floating in a considerable lake of literary water.

A channel back to the schoolroom for the ever-rising water in the texts is provided by the second-century AD treatise *About Rivers and Mountains and the Things Found in Them*, which comes down in the corpus of Plutarch, although it is certainly not a work of his hand.[50] This work describes twenty-five rivers, each with an associated product (usually a plant) plus a mountain or mountains, also with products (plants or stones). It is a mass of lore, some conventional, but some silly even by the standards of ancient wonder tales and evidently intended to be recognized as such; even the most credulous reader is alerted to the joke by citations of (mostly) imaginary learned works of natural philosophy. *About Rivers and Mountains* is transparently a parody, and, judging by its repetitive structure—river, product, mountain, product— presumably a parody of a tedious school exercise, a parody of the educational practice of being obliged to memorize, for the purposes of encomium, the particular excellences of all the rivers in the known world.[51]

The same shift in attitude was also going on at the same time, at a lower intellectual level, in everyday city-management. Civic leaders and benefactors began to think about their cities differently: water-supply (always, of course, a practical necessity in any city, like the supply of grain or oil or any number of other requirements) became a larger and larger part of the self-image of the city and its citizens. The timing of this intellectual shift can be traced through the civic coinage of the Greek cities of the empire. During the reign of Nero, Smyrna was alone in putting a personification of a local river god on its coins; but Egyptian Alexandria minted coins with the Nile on them under Titus, and under Domitian Ephesus put the Marnas (a river we will meet again shortly) on its coins. This practice of putting local rivers on coins then broke its banks under the Antonines.[52] In such a way did cities advertise to the world (and boast to their rivals) how well-watered they were, just as the first great nymphaea were beginning to rise on the west coast of Asia Minor.

The sculptures that adorned these nymphaea made the same link to the abundance of local water, sometimes by including sculpted swarms of water creatures and spirits, and sometimes, it seems, even by featuring the same river gods as appeared on the city's coins.[53] One of the very first facade nymphaea of all, Ephesus's *Hydrekdocheion* of C. Laecanius Bassus (AD 79–82?), was adorned with two statues of river gods.[54] A Domitianic nymphaeum in Ephesus also had (along with a Zeus) two personifications of river gods, interpreted as the Marnas and the Klaesas, the sources of the aqueduct that fed the fountain (and one of Ephesus's aqueducts was called the "New Marnas").[55] At Perge a statue interpreted as the local river god Kestros reclined on the very lintel of the waterspout of the Hadrianic Nymphaeum F3, the fountain whose spilled water formed an artificial bubbling brook down the middle of the colonnaded main street of the city.[56]

The extent of this growing fixation upon local water supply can best be illustrated by its end, of which two striking fourth-century AD examples present themselves. One is the famous inscription recording the restoration by Constantine of city status to the small Phrygian town of Orcistus, including a paraphrase of the petition of the Orcistans. Their plea for municipal status consisted of the claims that:

- They had possessed such status in the past.
- Their town sits at a crossroad, convenient for the entertainment of public officials, and has official lodgings for them.
- There is abundant water.
- There are baths both public and private.
- There is a forum with statues of former emperors.
- There is population enough.
- There are many water mills powered by the surrounding streams.

Three out of their seven claims, in other words, touch upon their water supply. That is what they thought the emperor wanted to know when considering whether they ought to be made a municipality and is especially striking if they were also trying to show that their town met a set of official criteria for that status.[57]

But an even more dramatic, one might even say obsessive, instance of the intellectual pressure of water is the orator Libanius's speech in praise of his home city, Antioch, which merits extended examination.[58] After his proemium, Libanius proclaims his intention to discuss the city's glorious past, then its glorious present (section 11). But even before that, the city's *thesis* must be dealt with, which Libanius announces will include the fertility of the land and the water supply (12). And even before the water supply is addressed directly, the streams of the territory flow into the discussion of the quality of the land (19). Then the water supply itself: "Who could number the rivers that course the land? The greater, the lesser, the perennials, and the children of winter? They are all equally useful: those that have their sources in the mountains, and those that spring from the plains; those that empty themselves into others, those that run to the lake, and those that march towards the sea. Our springs, indeed, and their bounty, are our very emblem, and none is so bold nor so proud of the nymphs of his own city, as to boast equality with us in this realm" (27–28).

So water has performed for Libanius the gracious duty assigned it by the teachers of rhetoric: to help fill up the deep urn of *thesis*. It might be thought that water could now be set aside. Not so. The speech moves from *thesis* to the mythic history of Antioch, to Inachus, and Io, and the long-wandering sons of Heracles (44). And then comes Alexander the Great, who stopped long enough in his pursuit of the fleeing Darius to drink the delicious water of a local spring. It reminded him of the milk of his mother's breast, he said to his companions, and so he named the spring Olympias after that formidable lady and made of it a fountain in the precincts of a shrine to Zeus Bottiaeus. An earlier Darius, Libanius stops to remind his hearers, campaigning in Thrace, had deemed the river Tearos the fairest of all, and had put up a notice to that effect. Alexander was *not*, Libanius insists, entering Antioch's spring into this competition of watercourses (72–74), although he thereby reminds us that waters might always be regarded as in contention one with another.[59]

Alexander's successor Seleucus, to the modern historian the real founder of Antioch, almost failed in that act of foundation, or so Libanius reports. Seleucus was sacrificing at Antigoneia, a few miles away. But Zeus sent a gigantic bird to whisk away his burning sacrifice and drop it on the altar of Zeus Bottiaeus, right beside (as Libanius reminds us) Alexander's beloved spring (85–88). And Seleucus took the hint, and built the city of Antioch on the indicated spot (90).

Upon the death of Seleucus that king was succeeded by a train of worthy monarchs, who adorned the city with temples, theater, council house, and, naturally, water conduits. Libanius carefully specifies that some kings brought into the city water from the suburbs, while others moved spring water from parts of the city to parts less well supplied (125). Eventually the city fell peacefully under Roman rule. When a great Roman army was gathered there, the water sources of Antioch (Libanius is at pains to point out) did *not* run dry, unlike the rivers of Thrace when Xerxes marched upon Greece of old (178).

Libanius then turns from history to a physical description of the city itself (196). And here, like a stream growing into a river, the splashing of water gets louder and louder. First, we hear of the springs on the mountain that towers over Antioch (200), and the river Orontes is mentioned (202). A vast facade nymphaeum (as yet unlocated by modern archaeologists)[60] stands in the center of the metropolis (202). The Orontes appears again, making an island of the so-called "new city" (203), and the emperor can gaze down upon the river from his palace (206). Baths are spread through the city (212), some suited for winter use, and some for summer (220); there are springs in the suburbs (234); and especially glorious are the springs of Daphne, veritable "palaces of the nymphs" bringing forth the purest and clearest of waters (240), water wonderful to look at, touch, bathe in, and drink (242).[61] If the nymphs sometimes inhabit other springs, they do so only as tourists, before they return to their home in the springs of Daphne (241). And the waters of Daphne flow into the city in conduits (243). The neighborhoods of the city are friendly rivals: the eastern quarter prides itself on Alexander's Olympias fountain, mentioned yet again (250).

Libanius summarizes: "And this is the respect in which we triumph over all: that is, that our city is absolutely flowing with water. And even if someone should be impudent about our city in other respects, all must give way to us at the mention of our water. We defeat those who have beautiful water by the plenitude of ours, and those who have a plenitude by the beauty of ours, or, rather, we defeat their abundance with our plenitude, and their waters of pleasing appearance with the beauty of ours" (244). The water in public baths flows richly, that in private baths hardly less so; the neighborhoods compete in the adornment of their neighborhood baths (245).[62] Nearly every house has its private fountain, so public fountains serve mostly for display (247). Not for us, says Libanius, the shabby scrums that develop around fountains in other cities, with each inhabitant trying to draw water first, producing curses, broken jars, and broken heads (247).[63] And the water in our fountains is so clear that it is nearly invisible (248). Even now, as his speech enters the last of its many minutes, Libanius is not finished with water. The sea produces its bounty—Antioch has a splendid artificial harbor (263)—as does the lake and the Orontes, which also carries all the good things of the world to Antioch (258–260, 265). Alas the folk of Egypt, whose navigation of the Nile is often interrupted by rocks! Alas the folk of Thesprotia, whose river runs the wrong way (261–262)!

Finally the peroration: "What city is worthy to be set beside this one?" But here Libanius's enthusiasm has run away with him. For there were at least two cities that all knew to be greater: Rome and Constantinople. How to escape? How can the much-patched Hellenistic walls of Antioch compete, for example, with the magnificent fortifications of Constantinople? "If we are worsted by any city in respect of our walls, we are greater than that city because of"—what?—"the abundance of our water!" (270).[64]

If the overt mention of water in Libanius's speech were not enough, it also dominates the speech's figures and metaphors. It was not altogether necessary, in his discussion of the enormous population of Antioch, for the orator to compare the crowd in the market to a river flowing over rocks (172), the motions of crowds of shoppers and roaring rivers (when one thinks about it) being rather different; nor was it expected (nor any less contrived) for him to compare the colonnaded streets of Antioch to rivers and its side streets to torrents flowing from them, nor that a cross street connecting the side streets in turn should be compared to a canal (201), nor that the arrival of soldiers who came to Antioch to fight the Persian war beginning in AD 337 should be compared to rivers flowing to the sea (178).[65] Nor again was it strictly compulsory that the kindly wind Zephyrus should cool Antioch by "flowing" rather than "blowing" through the city (225).[66] But the orator reaches most easily for the most friendly, that is watery, metaphors.

Was Libanius simply mad? If so, he shared his madness not only with his own townsmen and but also with many or most other educated inhabitants of the Roman Empire of his day. Watery themes were common on mosaics in private houses all over the Roman world, even if they seem to have been especially common at Antioch.[67] And two centuries later John Malalas, also from Antioch, wrote a history of everything from Adam to his own day, with a good deal of emphasis on Antioch and its buildings, and especially its baths. But he also illustrates the wider late-antique interest in water, laboriously listing imperial donations of fountains and baths and waterworks in other eastern cities as well.[68] And water, both natural in springs and streams and rivers or displayed in fountains and baths, simply appears to occupy a larger place in the literature of Late Antiquity than in that of earlier times.[69]

## Competition to Build Nymphaea

In the late first century AD, a novel formula for delivering encomia upon cities had entered practice and education, and exaggerated the interest of the Greco-Roman ruling class in civic water-supply as an element of civic identity. The resulting passion for displaying civic water inspired the depiction of local rivers on coins in the late first and second centuries AD and culminated in the Orcistus inscription and Libanius's oration in praise of Antioch. And since giant fountains advertised a city's water with the greatest spectacle and insistence (splashing it around in public, rather than hiding it, as did a bath or aqueduct), that novel formula for encomia encouraged cities to build nymphaea, first in western Asia Minor, then in Asia Minor in general, Syria, and the Levant.

In its early days, the building of nymphaea maps well onto the geography of the Second Sophistic narrowly understood, that is, the normal cities of residence and performance of the orators described in Philostratus's *Lives of the Sophists*, and the cities that honored sophists and rhetors in inscriptions.[70] In such cities would the oratory that drove nymphaeum building be most frequently taught and learned, heard and valued. And the greatest of the sophists, Herodes Atticus, himself built two major nymphaea in the mid-second century, one at Olympia.[71] But nymphaea were probably not a function of, or caused by, the Second Sophistic: they resulted from changes in elite education that inspired both the Sophistic and giant fountains alike, albeit in different ways.

Once rhetoric canonized monumental nymphaea as legitimate public buildings, the building of such structures was snatched up like a feather and whirled into the vortex of one of the most powerful historical forces in the Roman Empire: the competition for status between the cities of Asia Minor.[72] Thinking of fountains as ranked against one another was old: a Ptolemaic papyrus preserves a list of the "most beautiful fountains" (κρῆναι κάλλι[σται]).[73] By Roman times, Aelius Aristides claimed, "all other competitions have been abandoned, but one competition holds all the cities: that each may appear the most beautiful and charming. And everything is crammed with gymnasia and fountains and gates and temples."[74] The nymphaeum of one city inspired the prompt building of one in the next, which might echo or strive to overtop the first in size or design or decoration, this achievement sometimes inspiring the first in turn to build another fountain to regain its lead over its rival. Indeed, cities built nymphaea near their gates or on the very roads leading to such rival cities.[75] And it was in city pairs where such rivalry was strongest that nymphaea might both multiply and wax largest: in its competition with nearby Laodicaea, Phrygian Hierapolis built the largest fountain in Asia Minor, the Nymphaeum of the Tritons, with a facade more than sixty meters long.[76] With such a structure as this functioning as Hierapolis's *second* major nymphaeum—quite aside from the city's famous hot springs, which tourists still visit today—the epigram in the city's theater that urged "Hierapolis, may you of all cities rejoice in the most outstanding land in wide Asia, O thou city of gold, mistress of the nymphs, adorned with splendid springs," was wholly jus-tified.[77] Cities, mostly in the early third century, proudly depicted their new nymphaea on their coins so that all might know and envy them.[78] And in some cities with multiple nymphaea—and especially Ephesus—it appears that the erection of such buildings also became a form of internal rivalry, not merely a contest between cities, but a contest between the benefactors of a single city.[79]

This building frenzy mates well with scholars' sense that cities' com-petition for status through construction was a habit considerably more violent in Asia Minor than in other parts of the Roman Empire. So the powerful culture of *philotimia* characteristic of the region can perhaps explain why the phenomenon of monumental nymphaea grew to its greatest proportions in Asia Minor and in Syria and the Levant, which appear to have shared that culture. In metropolitan Greece, on the other hand, competition between cities tended to emphasize their ancient monuments. So often rather than building new fountains, famous old ones could be renovated and bedizened: the most striking instance is Corinth's venerable and oft-reconstructed Peirene.[80] And a late teaching text tells us that the ancient fountains of Greece were still thought to hold their own against much later, grander structures.[81] Whence, per-haps, in addition to the poverty of the region, an explanation of the lesser extent of the building of monumental nymphaea in Greece.[82]

In the western provinces, the building of monumental nymphaea was, as far as we know, confined to the region of Rome and to North Africa. The most obvious explanation for this is climate. Competition in the display of water only made sense in arid regions. In northwest Europe, where most Roman cities were situated on rivers and where the engineering genius of the Romans was devoted to preventing flooding and draining wetlands, there was something slightly absurd about mak-ing a spectacle of the abundance of a city's cold water.[83] This more prag-matic attitude towards an abundant resource perhaps produced a com-parable outcome in the building of Roman baths, of which modest versions existed in great number in the northern provinces, but where there were few gigantic monumental baths—for baths too showed off a city's abundant water supply, as is clear from the Orcistus inscription and the speech of Libanius above. The folk of the northern provinces liked bathing as much as any other inhabitants of the empire but had less patience for gargantuan baths that displayed their water, because they saw less need to show it off. Perhaps it was therefore also to be expected that, outside Rome, it was the cities of Asia Minor that built the most monumental baths, often combining them with gymnasia into tremendous structures.[84]

But a second reason for the lack of monumental nymphaea in the Roman West was a lack of first- and second-century models, either in Rome itself or elsewhere in the West.[85] The two areas of the West that did eventually come to participate in the competition of nymphaeum building did so only belatedly. First came Rome itself, which stormed into the contest under Septimius Severus with the immense three-storied Septizodium, the biggest nymphaeum in the world, with a facade at least some ninety, and perhaps one-hundred and fifty, meters long.[86] Ammianus Marcellinus knew what to make of it (even if he thought Marcus Aurelius had built it): he called it an *operis ambitiosi nymphaeum*, a "nymphaeum of rivalrous work." This structure was patently built in imitation of, in competition with, and in triumphant victory over, the great nymphaea of Asia Minor. The Latin West, where without an earlier example from Rome the challenge to competition in building nymphaea was neither thrown down nor picked up among the provincial cities, may now have been doubly reluctant to enter into competition with Rome's monster. But North Africa was the exception. For here Septimius Severus built a large nymphaeum in his home city of Lepcis Magna—large, but hardly as unsurpassable as the Septizodium in Rome was. And so the competition in nymphaeum building that had begun in Asia Minor in Flavian times, and that tempted Severan Rome to compete and triumph, spawned a second-order competition in North Africa in the early third century AD, and rival fountains subsequently arose in far-flung North-African cities such as Timgad, Lambaesis, Volubilis, Cuicul, and Simithus.[87] In what is perhaps a parallel development, from the reign of Hadrian, but especially during the Severan period, and perhaps in part to show off their abundant water, the cities of North Africa also began to build large spectacular baths.[88]

Nor was all the world intimidated by the Septizodium: it seems to have recharged the competitive engines of Asia Minor, where Side soon began a three-storied nymphaeum looking eerily like the Roman giant, and under Gordian III (AD 241–244) a third story was added to the by-then venerable nymphaeum in Miletus.[89]

## Conclusion

The often artificial way knowledge is structured in order to teach it can have real-world consequences. There was nothing inherent in the practice of delivering encomia upon cities—or teaching boys how to deliver encomia on cities—that required civic water supply to achieve an unnatural prominence in the minds of those who received that education. It was the result of an idiosyncratic decision made and popularized by late first-century AD teachers of rhetoric whose names and works are lost to us, a decision that cities were to be praised according to the same formula, adapted as little as possible, that was used to laud prominent men. But once that rule of rhetoric was laid down and accepted, the construction of monumental nymphaea followed by a process that, although hardly ineluctable, certainly involved a more familiar logic. For the new teaching adjusted the way the rhetorically educated ruling class of the empire—at least in its drier sections—looked at their cities, and at the amenities their cities ought to possess. Water, they thought, should not merely exist, or merely be used for drinking and bathing: it should be shown off, as ostentatiously as possible. Teaching boys to mention fountains in speeches, it seems, encouraged those same boys to build fountains when they became men.

# 7

# City Walls, Colonnaded Streets, and the Rhetorical Calculus of Civic Merit

## City Walls

In his brief description of how to deliver encomia on cities, Quintilian had singled out city walls as a special topic for mention: they were to be praised for their usefulness, their beauty, and their builder.[1] With what we know about nymphaea, we might be forgiven for wondering whether rhetorical training in the demonstrative mode also encouraged the building of city walls. But in fact, Quintilian aside, we find less attention to city walls in encomia—both in theory and in practice—than we do to water supply; in some cases there seems almost a reluctance to mention city walls where they might be expected. The speculation offered here is that the building of city walls under the Roman Empire offers a counterexample to the encomium's encouragement of monumental nymphaea, that the positive influence of demonstrative oratory was confounded by another rhetorical tradition, no less strong, that had wandered in from a different branch of rhetorical schooling—deliberative rhetoric—a tradition that for centuries sharply limited mention of city walls in oratory, and thus *a fortiori* limited as well the influence of encomium on the actual construction of walls. When city walls were built, forces other than rhetoric built them. First we will

Porta nigra in Trier.

FIGURE 4. Trier, the Porta Nigra (built after AD 170), a surviving gate in the Roman walls. Wood engraving, 1864 (iStock.com/ZU_09).

examine how rhetorical training in encomium encouraged the building of walls, then how it discouraged it, and finally why walls were built anyway.

The construction of walls by cities under the Roman Empire is a well-known archaeological puzzle. We can readily grasp why cities threatened by nearby barbarians might need walls, and how, in the late third century—"In the day when heaven was falling, the hour when earth's foundations fled"—any city in the empire might yearn for mighty battlements. What is harder to understand is the practice of building city walls—the most expensive civic project known to the ancient world—far from the borders, deep in the safe interior of the empire, and during the flannelled tranquility of the Roman peace, from the reign of

Augustus through the early third century AD. On the face of it, this seems an undertaking even more perverse and impractical than building monumental nymphaea, even odder than gathering a vast volume of water in one place to evaporate in a gigantic open fountain or to spill over into the streets.[2] These mysterious walls of peace have naturally been studied mostly in the West, where brand new enceintes (often datable) attract our attention.[3] Many cities in the Greek-speaking East already had Classical or Hellenistic walls, but we are coming to suspect that the replacement or rebuilding of those walls in Roman times (sometimes after earthquakes), their periodic repair, and their elaboration and adornment with spectacular gates form part of the same perplexing phenomenon of peacetime wall building.[4] A recently discovered fresco in Jordan celebrates the founding of the Roman-period city of Capitolias (AD 97 or 98) and proudly depicts its shining circuit of walls.[5]

With walls it is harder to form an estimate of who paid for them—the town, its richest citizens, Roman officials, or the emperor.[6] But we can be quite confident that persons with rhetorical educations made the decisions. How could education in the demonstrative oratory of display encourage the building of city walls? Easily. Even if walls were not praised for their own merits, as Quintilian suggested they should be, the size of a city was an overwhelmingly common subject of rhetorical praise.[7] And it was an old convention to estimate a city's size by the circumference of its walls.[8] A speech descending in the corpus of Aelius Aristides praises the walls of Rhodes (just knocked down by an earthquake) especially for the fact that the built city itself extended all the way out to them, it being perfectly usual for ancient city walls to encompass an area far larger than the actual conurbation and so to game the system.[9] Indeed, we notice that some walls built in time of peace, especially some of those in Gaul of the Augustan period, appear to have made a point of being much larger than the cities they enclosed, rendering the actual defense of the city against a concerted attack difficult or impossible because there could hardly be enough soldiers or inhabitants to man them. Building an oversized circuit of walls was presumably intended to make the city appear bigger than it was.[10] A city's age, too, brought it prestige, so said Quintilian. So we are not entirely surprised to find Aphrodisias in the mid-fourth century AD building walls with a stonelaying technique and square towers that made them look late classical or Hellenistic.[11]

A related category under which walls might in principle have been praised was "upbringing," which was a far easier enterprise when a person, rather than a city, was the subject of encomium, cities not being "brought up" or educated in any very obvious way.[12] But like children, cities do grow in size, that growth was praised, and the noble dimensions in which that growth resulted might in principle have been attested by the noble extent of a city's walls.[13] Speakers also harped on the harmonious appearance of a city, which reflected the city's internal moral harmony, praised under the city's virtues as an aspect of justice or self-control. Here too an elegant suit of walls might have been an appropriate subject.[14]

But, for the most part, none of this happened. City walls were comparatively neglected in panegyric, both as an independent topic (as Quintilian suggested they should be treated) and as potential material to illustrate virtues under the formula *laudantur urbes similiter atque homines*. When we look into the later rhetorical manuals we find reference to walls, but more rarely than to other forms of building, and walls are often missing where we expect them.[15] Menander lists admirable buildings of a town—"colonnades, harbors, an acropolis, extravagant temples, statues . . . structures devoted to the Muses, theaters"—but not walls.[16] Although city walls are hardly left out of the surviving high-imperial encomia on cities, they are not an invariable, or even a particularly common, topic, and are completely absent in, for example, Aristides's series of speeches on Smyrna, whose walls were notable, and even in his encomium of Cyzicus, a city whose walls were positively renowned.[17] Similarly, walls can appear—but are hardly inevitable—in lists of building types admirable for a city to possess that survive in actual speeches.[18]

Just as Libanius's oration on Antioch bent itself out of shape to include water—fountains, rivers, baths—at every possible juncture, that orator seems to employ almost equal ingenuity to avoid mention of Antioch's walls.[19] Antioch had walls, labored over by both Hellenistic monarchs and Roman emperors.[20] But in his extended account of the history of the city—almost half the length of this very long speech (sections 44–130)—Libanius mentions the building of fortification walls only twice. When he founded the city, Libanius says, Seleucus set his elephants about the perimeter to help him imagine where the towers on the walls should be (90), and the expansion of the city and its fortifications, by Antiochus the Great, also merit mention in passing (119). Later in the speech, gates (presumably set into the walls, but the walls themselves are not mentioned) appear, but only to demonstrate the population of the city, which must squeeze uncomfortably through them, and wait to crush their way in (170, 172). Fortunate he who enters the western quarter, where there are gardens, fountains, villas— delightful spectacles to be seen after passing through gates Libanius does mention in walls that he does not (234). The visitor new arrived at the city sees a profusion of goods, baths, markets, flowers, trees; admires the climate, the crowds; but manages never to notice the city walls (266). Antioch is physically the largest city in the world, says Libanius— but the circuit of the walls is not introduced into evidence for this, rather the length of the great colonnaded avenues, which are given an elaborate description (196–202; cf. 218), to which we will return. When Libanius describes the New City district, the fortified island in the Orontes, he does grant it a circuit of walls, but does not mention who built them, and again the extent of this district is emphasized by describing not the walls, but yet another set of colonnaded streets (203–204).[21] In a *jeu d'esprit* Libanius imagines the various quarters of the city vying with each other—fruitlessly, because they turn out to be equal, so excellent are they all: the center, the eastern and western districts, the hill-side, and the insular New City. This last alone volunteers its wall as a particular merit—re-emphasizing Libanius's apparent failure to notice the tremendous circuit of walls that protected the city as a whole.

Why this strange reluctance to mention city walls in panegyric? Libanius was forced to admit (270) that other cities had better walls than Antioch: that may account for his particular shyness on the subject.[22] But this hardly explains the wider oratorical neglect of the subject, and it is no less likely that Libanius's coyness about the walls of Antioch reflects the wider coyness of the rhetorical tradition in general.

There was, it turns out, within rhetorical training, a potential coun-
tercurrent to the praise of walls in panegyric: the disparagement of city
walls in deliberative oratory. Deliberative oratory—simulated addresses
to sway a great man or sovereign assembly, often given in the person of
a famous mythical or historical person—was a much larger part of education than the epideictic genre that included panegyric, and was certainly practiced at the last and highest stage of rhetorical education,
declamation.[23] And what deliberative oratory had to say about building
city walls was equivocal at best, picking up from a very old antiwall
tradition. "Warlike men are the tower of the city" sang the archaic-age
poet Alcaeus.[24] By Thucydides's time this had come to mean that brave
men were a *better* defense than walls.[25] This was taken into Spartan
myth, Sparta having been so long without walls and proud of it. "Where
are the walls of Sparta?" asks a rube in Plutarch (well into the era of our
rhetoric). "*These* are the Lacedaemonians' walls," Sparta's king Agesilaus
is imagined to grunt back, pointing at his soldiers.[26] And into rhetorical
training this prejudice came with the *progymnasma* "Should one build
a wall" around one's city? The positive argument, that one should indeed build walls, survives in the *progymnasmata* of Libanius, and has an
apologetic, unconvincing quality to it, suggesting that in the schools the
"no" argument about building walls was considered stronger than the
"yes" argument. This negative argument emphasized the cost of walls and
how they gave refuge to cowards.[27] And this theme, often in the form
"When the Persians are coming, the Spartans debate whether to build
a wall [around Sparta]," was popular among adult declaimers as well as
younger students of rhetoric.[28] What would seem to us mere common
sense (helped along by our privileged knowledge that the Roman peace
would not, in fact, last forever), that a city should indeed build walls
when it was flush with cash, was thus cast into doubt by the practice of
generations of schoolboys and adult declaimers who had spent many
hours devising arguments for just the reverse.

The history and geography of the building of walls during the Roman
peace confirms our doubts about the positive influence of oratorical
training on such construction. There was great activity under Augustus
in Italy, Gaul, and Spain, and then less over time (nothing new in Italy

or southern Gaul in the second century, apparently) but a continuing trickle in Africa, Gallia Belgica, and the Germanies, and then a reignition of interest in late second-century AD Germany, and even more fierce commitment in Britain (including the fortification of many settlements beneath the level of cities, and so, one might think, less likely to indulge in competitive pride). Whatever we imagine the chronology and geography of interest in the rhetoric of encomium to be, this does not match it well: on present evidence, we must press too hard on a scattering of ornamental gates in Asia Minor and walls in the Levant to match the world of rhetoric to that of wall building, and blush at the fact that ornamental gates were also going up in cities near the Rhine (see Trier's Porta Nigra, depicted above, on page 89)—hardly, we imagine, the favorite pleasure-gardens of the Muses—at much the same time.[29]

What can account for building walls in time of peace? Those living on the borders or in ever-troubled places (such as Britain) needed walls, and so often erected them.[30] In principle even those living in the unruffled depths of the Roman Empire, although they knew they were living in an era of peace, could not be sure that the occasional outbreaks of rebellion and civil war would indeed be occasional, and that the Roman armies on the borders would in fact keep the barbarians out; walls might also protect cities against local uprisings, marauders, and bandits.[31] In prosperous times, from Augustus through the early third century, cities may also have built for protection walls they could not afford before, or repaired older circuits.[32] But against these considerations we must place the facts that the great majority of cities in the West actually remained unfortified in the first, second, and early third centuries AD;[33] that we do not see explosions of slamming-the-barn-door-after-the-horse-has-bolted wall-building after the troubles of AD 68 to 70 and 193 to 197; and take note of statements from contemporaries that show that those living under the empire knew that they lived in a time of peace and that the walls of their cities were not, in fact, needed for defense.[34] To that we must add the frequent neglect or razing of existing city walls (the latter especially accompanied, for example, the Augustan explosion of wall building, so one town might be building walls as its neighbor tore its down), and the habit of allowing private individuals to build structures over and atop walls (to enjoy the lofty views), to cut passages through them, to take stones from them to use in other structures public or private, and to lean buildings up against them, all of which compromised the defensive function of walls; in Italy especially we find stretches of wall removed because the space they occupied was deemed more useful for theaters and amphitheaters.[35] In times of prosperity, too, cities expanded far beyond their existing walls, and in most cases no efforts were made to extend those walls to incorporate the new suburbs.[36]

Ideological motives for wall building are probably thus needed to bolster the only partially adequate practical, defensive ones. The Greeks had a tradition going back to Homer that cities should have walls, and, so far as we can tell, most archaic and classical Greek cities did.[37] A city, like a man, was a thing of dignity, and a city ought to have walls appropriate to that dignity.[38] This sense that having walls was somehow "right" for a city continued in the East and spread to the Latin West: when visual shorthand was needed for a city, be it on a coin or map, that shorthand was apt to be an image of a circuit of walls.[39] The symbolic quality of walls was emphasized by the building of ornamental gates, especially in the second century AD both in the West, and in Asia Minor and further east.[40] These were usually inserted into existing wall circuits (even if the walls themselves were not in a defensible condition) but were sometimes separate from walls or built where major roads entered cities that did not possess walls at all, as symbolic proxies for walls.

The Romans, and those of, or aspiring to, Roman culture, added other reasons for building city walls. In most cities of Roman foundation (Rome itself being the exception) the fortification walls (where they existed) marked the *pomerium*, the sacred boundary of the city; the walls and gates themselves were therefore in some sense sacred; and the wish to underline the religious distinction between city and space beyond will have splashed back and encouraged the building of walls.[41] Entering and leaving a city were moments of symbolic and pyschological importance: a sharp architectural distinction—a wall—gave the Romans comfort in a way perhaps inexplicable to us.[42] Walls, finally, marked the distinction between the living and the dead (who were buried outside them), where trash could not be dumped at random and where it could, and divided an area of safety within from a dubious, dark, and dangerous beyond.[43]

There was also a second significant Roman tradition that encouraged the building of city walls. Earlier in its history, Rome's long conquest of Italy was anchored by the settlement of colonies of Roman and friendly Latin citizens in strategic places and in the territories of peoples who required watching or were obliged to be punished by having some of their land given to the colonists. These colonies were almost always set among potentially hostile folk, and they were, accordingly, usually walled.[44] So also, partially for the same reasons and now partly from custom, were many of the colonies of veterans established in Italy and the provinces during the late Republic (the most famous exception being Caesar's colony at Carthage). This habit of building a wall when founding a *colonia* continued under Augustus and into the Empire (with exceptions, and sometimes the fortifications took a century to finish or never were, or were merely gestured at with brief lengths of wall-flanking gates, or gates only).[45] This association with veteran colonies perhaps explains the striking explosion of wall building under Augustus, who, of course, scattered such colonies all over Italy, Southern Gaul, and Spain.[46] And this habit of building walls was taken up later (although, again, not invariably) by cities that were by imperial boon raised to the legal status of a Latin or Roman colony.[47] This explains much wall building in the West under the empire: colonial status demanded a wall to demonstrate and celebrate it, and colonies' walls inspired competitive wall building in a certain number of non-colonies.[48]

Enough! It is to be hoped that these explanations for the cities of the empire building warlike walls in time of peace are adequate to begin to explain the perplexing phenomenon. For the two rhetorical traditions, the demonstrative in favor of walls, and the deliberative disparaging them, crashed against and baffled each other. The result was that until the turn of the fifth century AD—unlike water supply—walls never became a secure part of the canon of expected topics for panegyric on cities, either in teaching or in practice. Reasons other than rhetorical education, reasons both practical and ideological, built walls for the cities of the empire. In the fifth century, however, the overwhelming practical necessity for walls in an embattled era, and the actual walling or re-walling of many hundreds of cities, finally twisted the arm of rhetorical teaching, and the pro-wall rhetorical tradition defeated the anti-.[49] And so, once again, like destined lovers, the worlds of reality and rhetoric inexorably came together, although in this case reality seduced rhetoric, rather than the other way round.

## Colonnaded Streets

In Libanius's praise of Antioch, colonnaded streets rather than city walls proved the city's size—that perennial topic in encomium. And not in that oration alone: Libanius does much the same in his *Monody on Nico-media*.[50] And, in fact, it is worth wondering about the influence of rhetorical education on the building of colonnaded streets in North Africa and in the Greek-speaking provinces of the empire. For a speculation presents itself that colonnaded streets assisted the orator in not one category of his encomium upon a city only, but in three, and for this reason rhetorical education might prod civic leaders and benefactors to build them.

The dates and geography of the building of colonnaded streets, moreover, unlike those of city walls, closely match those of monumental nymphaea, suggesting that their spread might have been subject to similar influences. Colonnaded buildings—stoas, porticos—had long existed in both East and West; the change was liberating colonnades from individual buildings and stretching them along both sides of the major streets of a city.[51] There may be more earlier instances of colonnaded streets than huge nymphaea: Hellenistic Alexandria may have had such streets, and we are told of an early instance in Antioch, allegedly built by Herod the Great (d. 4 BC). But neither is confirmed by archaeology.[52] Of what we can be certain are examples from the very late first century AD, and then ever more in the second and early third centuries.[53] As with nymphaea, they appear in Asia Minor, Syria and the Levant, North Africa, and Rome. The northwestern provinces for the most part lacked colonnaded streets just as they lacked nymphaea, and so did old

FIGURE 5. Palmyra, colonnaded street. W. Wright, *An Account of Palmyra and Zenobia: With Travels and Adventures in Bashan and the Desert*. New York, 1895. "Central Part of the Great Colonnade" (plate pp. 104–105).

Greece.[54] Like nymphaea, colonnaded streets seem for the most part to have been built with local money, with civic funds, or by benefactors: in Palmyra and other Syrian cities, the name of the donor—or members of an association contributing in common—might be inscribed on the stretch of colonnade donated or repaired, and the donor might be allowed a small statue (of himself, or of a man or god he chose to honor) on a perch extending out from one of the columns (the perches are visible in the photograph above).[55]

The main difference between the broad patterns of building colonnaded streets and nymphaea appears to be that, on current evidence, Asia Minor, Syria, the Levant, and North Africa began to build colonnaded streets at much the same time, unlike nymphaea, where North Africa lags.[56] And the emperor Septimius Severus plays a slightly different role: he may perhaps have built the first great colonnaded street in

Rome (it is speculated that he colonnaded the last stretches of the *Via Nova*, leading to his Septizodium), and certainly did so in his home town of Lepcis Magna. And rather than kicking off a spurt of secondary building in North Africa (where many towns already had colonnaded streets), as his nymphaeum in Lepcis did, such a spurt appears instead in the Levant. Ancient Tyre was Lepcis Magna's mother city. The emperor may have built Tyre a second colonnaded street (it already had one, it appears), or Tyre herself may have acted in rivalry with favored Lepcis; in any event, a number of the cities in the Levant seem to have built colonnaded streets in the same era, perhaps out of rivalry with Tyre.[57]

A glance through the rhetorical treatises reveals that professors of rhetoric were considerably more interested in colonnades than in city walls.[58] Indeed, in the *ecphrasis* on the Serapeum at Alexandria given in the *progymnasmata* of Aphthonius, the elaborate account of the numerous and crisscrossing colonnades renders the passage almost unintelligible.[59] And the same appetite for colonnades reappears in the surviving encomia on cities, be they colonnades as isolated structures, colonnades forming the borders of public squares, or (especially) colonnades lining streets.[60] But, although we may accept that in general the rhetoric of praise was more interested in colonnades than in walls, the textbooks do not tell us why. Dio Chrysostom, however, in the years very close to AD 100, attempted to build a colonnaded street in his native Prusa. His acrid speeches on the subject survive and can be compared to the remarks Libanius offers about the merits of the colonnaded streets at Antioch.[61]

Dio generally justifies his construction (vigorously opposed because it seems to have involved a considerable degree of destruction of existing buildings, not excluding shrines and tombs) in terms of a desire to increase the prestige of Prusa, which would result in greater respect from the Roman authorities, and specifically in terms of rivalry with other cities possessed of colonnades, those of Antioch being mentioned in particular.[62] But when he discusses the colonnades themselves, his main interest is in climate: sweeter air, shade in summer, and a roof so that the wan sun of winter might better be enjoyed.[63] We instantly recognize the encomiastic category of a city's *thesis*, so often discussed in terms of its climate. So also in Libanius, in his oration on Antioch, where in addition to proving the size of the city, the colonnades protect the inhabitants from bad weather.[64] But then Libanius makes an intellectual leap: the colonnades of Antioch also mold the character of the folk of the city. Libanius had canvassed the required topics of the moral excellences of the city, elegantly dividing the virtues among the city council (wisdom, courage, and justice) and the commons (temperance and justice), and also attributing courage to the whole, as evidenced by the city's spontaneous suppression of the rebellion of Eugenius in AD 303, and—perhaps we may forgive him—also treating the city's schools of rhetoric under the headings of wisdom and justice.[65] Right after that, Libanius says he will turn to the city's size and site (*thesis*).[66] But this is a conjuring trick. As we have seen above, he actually dealt with *thesis* at length at the beginning of the speech, in its normal place, and the theme of size turns out to be largely about . . . colonnades. Colonnaded streets indicate the size of the city; cross streets stretch from the mountain to terminate in the colonnades; the colonnaded streets are like rivers; the colonnaded streets are long enough for three cities; they connect in arches; a nymphaeum stands along one of the colonnades; the New City on the island has its own colonnades, crossing, three ending at the walls and one at the palace; the palace wall itself has columns, like a colonnade; there are more colonnades within the palace complex. There are some words about the city's shape; but, Quick! Back to the colonnades! If laid end to end the city's colonnades would take a full day to walk. Private houses and public buildings mingle along the colonnades; the doors of the former open right onto the colonnades.[67] And this is not just an orator's local-boy enthusiasm for Antioch's famous colonnaded streets. It has a point even beyond its overt one of illustrating the city's size (itself a venerable encomiastic topic, as we have seen): "Why am I doing this? Why have I gone on about the colonnades for so long?" (Libanius's reader has been wondering the same for a while.) "Because it seems to me that the most pleasant of things in cities, and I would suggest even the most useful"—the standard pairing of the agreeable and the useful—"are [people's] meetings and minglings."[68] These meetings and minglings are rendered possible by the colonnades that allow the people of Antioch to get together in all weathers: those who live in cities without colonnades are like prisoners in their houses, Libanius fantasizes, or as isolated as those who have gone on long voyages away, even though they are living at home. But the people of Antioch rub up against each other in all weathers, give each other sagacious counsel, and friendship blooms.[69]

This is not, then, a demented passage of details about colonnades, or really entirely about the city's size. This is the culmination of Libanius's account of the virtues of the Antiochenes. Mingling, "the most useful things for cities," makes the people of Antioch supremely excellent, and the colonnades create that mingling.[70] Dio's colonnade just kept off the rain; it did not make the people of Prusa better.[71] The colonnades of Antioch do. Although he is happy to let colonnades contribute to the required encomiastic subject of the *thesis* of Antioch, and praise of the city's size, the main concern of Libanius is to use colonnades to supply material for the no less obligatory subject of the moral merits of the city.[72] The eerie similarity of Libanius's thinking about how the inhabitants of a city should interact to today's notions in the field of urban planning, where the call is for "cities for people" built for pedestrians and an end to isolating modernist "towers in the park," will strike many readers.[73] And it may reassure us about the advance of mankind that we have, more than seventeen hundred years later, laboriously rediscovered by decades of disastrous architectural experiment what a mere teacher of rhetoric, Libanius, already knew.

## The Rhetorical Calculus of Civic Merit

The ruins of Perge and Side, some thirty miles apart, are today often visited together in a pleasant one-day excursion from the Turkish resort of Antalya. But in Roman times these two cities of the province of Lycia-Pamphylia, on the south coast of Asia Minor, were ferocious rivals. This rivalry took the form, as such rivalries often did, of importuning the Romans for the title of first city of the province, which the winner marked by placing an alpha (the number one in Greek) on its coins. Eventually the exhausted Romans allowed *both* Perge and Side that title.

The cities also vied for the title of "metropolis," and to be named—and named again—*neokoros*, "temple warden" of the imperial cult; and they competed for permission to hold games, and to elevate their games up the ladder of ranks that distinguished greater games from lesser.[74] An odd inscription records the folk of Perge chanting their city's claims to standing: "Up with Perge, four times *neokoros*!" "Up with Perge, which alone has the right of sacred asylum!"—unlike wretched Side, we are to understand. "Up with Perge, honored with the sacred standard"—we have no idea what this is, but Side had one too. "Up with Perge, which tells no lies: *our* rights are confirmed by the Senate!"—a low blow, insinuating that Side was guilty of the pathetic practice of granting itself titles unapproved by the Roman authorities.[75]

Perge and Side were rivals also in building spectacular structures. We can prove this—although could assume it without such proof, such contention being so usual—because they shared an idiosyncratic edifice: Perge built a colonnaded street with an ornamental canal running down the middle, a rare thing in the Roman world, and then Side emulated Perge with similar bubbling colonnaded streets, albeit with more modest canals running down the sides, perhaps rather like the charming *Bächle* of Freiburg im Breisgau (or Side may have acted first: we lack good dates). But although tit-for-tat competitive construction such as this was perfectly usual in the Roman world—we have seen it in the building of nymphaea, and Perge and Side may have also built dueling theaters and markets—cities just as frequently competed with unlike structures: between Hadrian and the Severans Perge built one colonnaded street but four nymphaea, while Side built one enormous nymphaeum but three colonnaded streets.[76]

Yet if rival cities rivalrously built buildings of different sorts, how could one tell who was winning the competition? What was the relative value of a nymphaeum, a theater, or a hundred yards of colonnaded avenue? The long-term existence, spread, and advance to full fever of competitive construction through building different structures (albeit within a narrow canon of types) seems to require some way of comparing unlikes and somehow combining those comparisons into a general ranking.

The ranking of people, places, and things within their categories was old among the Greeks: thus Achilles could be the best of the Achaeans, Sestos the best of the cities of the Thracian Chersonese, and the Lusinian snails the best in the world (for eating, one assumes, not racing).[77] Nor did rough-and-ready comparison of collections of unlikes defeat earlier men: Herodotus described Egypt as "having more wonders than any other land, and more works of man that defy description."[78] And so too the Caesarian-period historian Diodorus of Sicily, who cites the palaces, dockyards, harbors, dedications, and remarkable structures of Alexandria, "with the result that it is now usually reckoned the first or second of the cities of the *oecumene*."[79] But so crude a method could hardly guide the city fathers of Perge in deciding whether to build a second colonnaded street or yet another nymphaeum to pull past their hated rival Side.

A technique for ranking cities with unlike qualities against each other was, thankfully, implicit in encomium. For a rule of rhetoric imposed unexpected honesty on those delivering eulogies upon cities: an orator praising a city was required to cover *all* the canonical topics. Menander Rhetor says, speaking of cities' origins, "On the more glorious topics one should say more, on the less glorious less, but under all circumstances this is an *absolutely necessary* subject for an orator when he praises a city."[80] The orator was, moreover, urged to speak in such a way that he made evident that he had indeed covered all the required topics.[81] Within the set structure of required topics the orator would naturally labor to make the city he was praising appear as outstanding as possible: deficiencies could not be left out, but "it is necessary to show that these problems do not exist or that they are not serious in this case."[82] If a location is too dry, it is to be praised as "fiery like the aether and firmament (for the firmament is dry and fiery)." If a place is too hot, damn cold places; if too cold, lovingly detail the horrors of heat. A place far from the sea and hard to reach is praised as secure; a new city among the famous old is praised as their guardian, and blooming like a maiden.[83] Or vices can be counter-weighted with excellences: "The best thing to do is to show the presence of virtues, the absence of all vices, or at least that there are more virtues than vices."[84] Even if a city is small (which must be admitted), it can still be beautiful and influential.[85] If a city was founded by a great man it can be praised for that; but if it was founded by a wretch (which, again, must be admitted), his merit must lie in founding the city, or his wickedness at least offset by the founding of the city.[86] There were countless dodges, but even allowing for all the exaggeration of good qualities and minimization of bad, the requirement that all the canonical topics be covered did establish a broad league table of standing that allowed approximate distinctions between the merit of whole cities: the rules of encomium did not allow Ascra to rank with Antioch, and certainly set the rival cities of Side and Perge above their near neighbor, humble Sillyon.

But how could relative equals such as Side and Perge know where they stood and how to advance themselves in their competition? The second treatise attributed to Menander Rhetor tells its reader preparing to praise a city that "for each of the virtues" he should "work up a comparison, with one competitor city for each virtue, and then take them all together into a total, and make a comparison city to city, taking in everything . . . nature, upbringing, cultural accomplishments, actions."[87] What leaps out is the casual assumption that a synthesis of *different* civic qualities is possible and that a comparison of grand totals for each city (ἀθρόαν σύγκρισιν) can in principle be arrived at. How the orator is to do such a thing, this treatise, however, does not say.[88]

It did not need to. The orator already knew. For this technique was taught elsewhere in rhetorical training, in the *progymnasma* of comparison (*synkrisis* in Greek, *comparatio* in Latin), where instruction was given in exactly the art of evaluating objects—including cities—with different and contrasting features.[89] *Synkrisis* taught the comparison of wholes by means of comparing their parts and by creating on either side a grand summation for a final assessment—exactly what the city leaders of Perge and Side would be obliged to do if evaluating the relative contributions of their public buildings to their standing.[90] First, obvious likes were compared: for Achilles and Hector, their births (equal, both being descended from Zeus). Then, similarities that were created by the orator: pleasant noises, for example, might be used when comparing country to city living, claiming that the sounds of baby animals—calves, kids, and lambs—are superior to the man-made tunes of the cities; or beauty, claiming that the country's fair flowers and the spectacle of "cicadas sitting upon shoots" are finer than any citified daub; or learning, preferring rural knowledge of the ways of nature to overwrought urban expertise in rhetoric (that is a little joke in an ancient rhetorical treatise: treasure it).[91] When an orator needs to compare multiples to multiples (the example is comparing men to women, but it will work no less well for multiple nymphaea versus multiple colonnades), he either compares the single best item in each class, or (tacitly accepting that the classes are equal to one another per se) counts the number of items in each class, and awards the palm to the higher number.[92]

The best single item, or the largest number of them: that sounds exactly like the kind of logic that would encourage Side to build ever more colonnades and Perge ever more gorgeous nymphaea. Such thinking both gave clear instructions—build more or better—but did not deliver too precise a verdict as to who had won the contest: We have more! one city could crow, to which the other could respond, We have better! The rhetorical science of *synkrisis* offered ultimate indeterminacy within a broader determinacy, both encouraging competition and allowing near equals always to claim that they were ahead.

## Conclusion

Training in the oratory of display did not create competitive building in the Roman provinces; that titanic undertaking had many roots. But it is attractive to suppose that over time rhetorical training nudged that competition towards some structures—nymphaea and colonnaded streets—and not towards, or even away from, others, such as city walls. And it seems possible that rhetorical education also came to supply the intellectual mechanics for comparing and ranking cities by their various public works that gave a broad logic to competitive public building. If the men who made decisions about whether and what to build in their cities had not possessed, from Flavian times, a common education in rhetoric of a very particular and curious type, it is likely that the phenomenon of competitive building would itself have gone in different directions and that the cities in whose ruins we now wander would have raised buildings other than those they did, and more various from city to city. For the reality of Roman provincial building—variation within a relatively narrow canon—may also have been the creation of rhetorical training. The cities of the empire looked different in fact, but in the minds of the city fathers, they were all reflections of the perfect city they had learned to praise in school.

# Lizarding, and Other Adventures in Declamation and Roman Law

## Stellionatus

The stellion—*stellio* in Latin—is a distinguished Mediterranean lizard that can grow to over a foot long and takes its name from the star-shaped spots that adorn its back. In 2012 it was promoted from the vulgar scrum of the genus *Laudakia* and now preens itself as the sole member of the new genus *Stellagama*. The stellion sheds its skin, changes color, and is extremely modest, quick to dive into a crack in the rock if anything fearful approaches. The ancients thought it poisonous, and the sworn enemy of the scorpion. Which of these qualities recommended it to the businessmen of ancient Rome as a metaphor for a financial swindle we do not know, although Pliny the Elder implies that it was the lizard's wicked habit of devouring its shed skin to deprive humanity of its use, the skin of the stellion being a sovereign cure for epilepsy, even more efficacious than the brains of a weasel.[1] But by the second century AD *stellionatus*, acting the stellion—or, perhaps better, "lizarding"—was a recognized offense at Rome, a type of fraud having to do with pledges (*pignora*), either a debtor offering to his creditor as security something he did not actually own, or a debtor offering the same security to two or more creditors. So—probably—the jurist Marcellus had used the term in the 160s AD, so Paul—another jurist—used it at the turn of the third century, so the great Ulpian used it in the teens of the third, and so Modestinus was to use it in the middle of that century. *Stellionatus* also had the slightly eccentric quality that it could not be heard as a private suit (*privatum*) or as a regular public offense (*publicum*), but only under *cognitio extra ordinem*, the almost unlimited prerogative of an official, usually a provincial governor.[2]

But there is a competing tradition. The same Ulpian also defined *stellionatus* as a charge that could be made against someone who had done something dishonestly (*dolo*), but against whom no existing crime could be alleged. "Where, therefore, there is no name for the crime (*titulus criminis deficit*), we make a charge of lizarding."[3] And the apparent failure of connection between this formulation—the crime without a name—and the brisk alternative fraud-with-pledges definition of *stellionatus* has attracted much learned head scratching among modern students of the Roman law.[4] But even if the latter formulation was a curious one in the Roman law, it was hardly curious to Roman lawyers. For Ulpian, and indeed every educated man in Ulpian's generation, was perfectly familiar with the concept, perhaps indeed to the point of surfeit, because a popular law that governed the declamations of their teens was *inscripti maleficii sit actio* ("Let legal action be allowed for an act of evildoing not written down as illegal"), that is, essentially, that there did not have to be an existing law against a wicked deed for legal cognizance to be taken of it. The professors of rhetoric liked this law because it allowed superbly inventive and contrived cases: "A man, having been shipwrecked, and having lost his wife and three children in a house fire, hanged himself. Someone who happened along cut the noose. The savior is charged with evildoing by the man he saved."[5]

As the great civil law scholar Jacques Cujas—the teacher of Scaliger—noticed in the 1500s, this declamatory law, like many of its fellows, probably had its origins in Athenian jurisprudence of the fourth century BC, which knew a catchall law against "wrongs not written down as illegal" and "novel crimes." And in time it became both a Greek and a Latin declamatory theme, while certainly not, in the early first century AD at least, being part of the Roman law.[6] This last we know from a cruel joke the eminent advocate Cassius Severus (d. AD 32) played upon a teacher of rhetoric, summoning him before a real Roman praetor to sue him exactly for an "evildoing not written down as illegal." The teacher was so alarmed and upset that he asked for a postponement of the case. So deep was the teacher immersed in the world of school declamation and so ignorant was he of the real Roman law that he did not realize (despite what must have been the chortles of everybody standing by, including the praetor himself) that the praetor could not give such an action, because the *inscripti maleficii sit actio* existed only in the schools.[7]

But from the schools the theme had, apparently, by the time of Ulpian—the early third century AD—escaped. For the most obvious explanation for Ulpian's alternative definition of lizarding is that a litigant recalled the *inscripti maleficii sit actio* from his rhetorical training, and tried it out for real before a Roman judge, and the question of whether it should be allowed made its way to Ulpian (for that is what the jurists did, reply to questions about the law). He decided to endorse it—perhaps because in practice it elegantly restated the wide prerogative a Roman governor had anyway when judging under *cognitio extraordinaria*—and simply added it to an existing form of fraud, *stellionatus*, choosing that particular offense because *stellionatus* was a rare item handled only under the *cognitio extraordinaria* of Roman officials.[8]

This definition of *stellionatus* as an unwritten crime came into the world first, we guess, in a response to an inquirer, but it was later replicated in Ulpian's legal treatise *de Officio Proconsulis* (*On the Duty of a Proconsul*), which quickly came to be regarded as one of the most authoritative works in the Roman legal tradition.[9] This work was heavily excerpted for the sixth-century AD *Digest* of Justinian—a work that gathered the opinions of Roman jurists from the late Republic through the early fourth century AD (with a heavy emphasis on the early third century, and the works of the Severan jurists, such as Ulpian)—which is why we know of it. Inclusion in the *Digest* implies that Ulpian's definition of *stellionatus* as the nameless crime of rhetoric had achieved traction among other jurists, and, probably long before Justinian, had managed to make the transition from rhetoric to the opinion of a single legal expert to an accepted part of the formal and substantive law of the Romans.

# 8

# Rhetoric and Roman Law

THIS SECTION INVESTIGATES the influence of laws used in declamation on Roman law. If a convincing case can be made for such influence, it will imply much about the power of rhetorical training over those who wrote, studied, and commented on the Roman law—men such as Ulpian—and over the Roman mind in general.

Our process will be as follows. In this chapter the relationship between legal writing and rhetoric will be examined; then, as a class, the laws that governed declamations. Next (chapter 9) will come the reasons for possible influence of the laws of declamation on Roman law with examples (the laws of ravishment and adultery, gratitude, and revenge): the law of declamation's appeal to Roman moral sensibility was sometimes greater than that of the real Roman jurisprudence.[1] After that (chapter 10) comes the potential allure of rhetorical law to rhetoricians and perhaps jurists working through the problems in the real Roman law; and declamatory law's sometimes greater familiarity to practitioners and judges than that of the formal Roman law. Finally, we evaluate, by looking at declamatory laws that failed to penetrate the real Roman law, the degree of influence of education in declamation on the Roman law.

Such an investigation is useful because it is conventionally thought that Roman law was for a very long time uniquely resistant to the influence of rhetoric, maintaining its intellectual and stylistic independence (what its votaries call its "classicism") until late in the reign of Diocletian.[2] As rhetoric clambered over the walls and sacked every other

Roman literary or cerebral city and bastion, Roman law—such is the story—was the last castle, austere and inexpugnable. For centuries, judging by the longer passages in the *Digest* of Justinian, those who wrote on the Roman law remained precise, terse, and snappish; their style, the types of arguments they used, and their general habit of mind starkly different from that of the rhetoric-sodden world around them.[3] A jurist using a single jargon term from rhetoric can kick off two centuries of scholars' wonderment and gnawing upon each other, so rare are clear cases of the phenomenon.[4] As far back as we can see clearly, knowledge and interpretation of the Roman law was the province of a small clique of *iurisconsulti* or *iurisprudentes*, their lore, indeed, sometimes passed down from father to son. As such the classical Roman law evolved (we are told) by internal debate among a learned few, rather than by being pushed hither and thither by the great forces of the outside world. Let us devise a metaphor for this received view: the classical Roman law was worked up in a laboratory clean room in which the few meager cells of Republican or early imperial legal matter—the Twelve Tables, the actual *leges* passed by the Roman people, the Praetor's Edict—were reduced to their legal essence in centrifuges and then cultured over the centuries by the interpretations of the *iurisprudentes*. Under the Severan jurists the law reached both intellectual perfection and abundant mass, but was kept safe by airlocks that allowed no impure ingredient from the outside to enter. It is also usual to emphasize the sharp distinction between the lofty jurisconsults and the spit-stained advocates— men such as Cicero—who humbly applied to the juristic experts for advice when they had a case that raised a question of law.[5] In time some and then all responses to legal inquiries emerged in the name of the emperor, rather than those of his jurists: but even if we no longer know the names of the *iurisconsulti*, students have seen no reason to suppose that the basic structure of the profession—tiny, elite, arrogant, internally quarrelsome, and gathered near the seat of power to advise— changed significantly from the late Republic through the time of Diocletian.[6]

This story, however, has a tragic end. For in the fourth and fifth centuries AD, before Justinian's sixth-century classicizing revival effected a partial renaissance, the Roman law of that evil age—"vulgar law" was the wonderful and derisive name given to it by scholars—was seeded and soon overgrown by that "noisome weed," "a bombastic and detestable rhetoric," as well as by every other possible form of corrupting influence, especially from the Greek-speaking East and its uncleanly legal habits.[7] Just compare the sharp lucidity of the jurists in the *Digest* to the cetacean enormity of the imperial constitutions set out in the *Theodosian Code* (AD 438) with its "dismal reputation" for style, where one sometimes gropes in vain amidst the steaming blubber to find any law, any sense at all, or even a hint at what vexed the emperor and prompted his rhetoricians to vomit forth his imperial will.[8]

This vision of the conventional history of Roman law is a caricature: few of today's students of Roman law would admit to such views. They have long abandoned the story of a pure internal uninfluenced-from-the-outside march to juristic perfection under the Severans, and now, in principle, at least when anyone is watching, admit outside influence upon the Roman law at every stage of its existence. There is even a movement to read Roman law texts as literature.[9] Nor do they any longer believe in a late-antique collapse into legal decadence under the weight of revolting contagions from outside: they no longer use the term "vulgar law" (at least in print), and in what they now call "post-classical jurisprudence" they have found, despite its rhetorical mode of expression, palpable attempts to preserve the fine old mental machinery of the Roman juristic science.[10] But there is some doubt about the sincerity of this conversion, and its effects are doubtful. The old story of the rise and decline of the Roman law still invisibly undergirds much study, and although exterior influence on earlier classical law may be admitted in theory, suggestions for specific cases of influence are often still resisted, or (far more usually) simply ignored.[11]

Despite this generally hostile environment, many claims have been made for significant external influence on the Roman law,[12] from actual practice and legal custom in the *fora* and Roman courts of Italy and the empire;[13] from the opinions of working judges;[14] from every-day morality, and changes in it; from the morality of humbler people; from the pressure of those humble people who wrote to the emperor inquiring

about the law;[15] from changing economic realities;[16] from political differences among jurists;[17] from the pre-existing non-Roman laws and
legal customs in Rome's western and especially eastern provinces;[18] from
the categories of philosophy and its ways of thinking and arguing;[19] from
theories of grammar;[20] from theories of medicine;[21] from antiquarianism, and its handmaiden etymology;[22] and from Christianity.[23]

Our particular interest here is allegations of influence upon the
Roman law by rhetoric,[24] allegations that have been many, including
the influence of rhetorical theories of equity, *stasis* theory (discerning the
issue at stake),[25] the theory of topics (as in Cicero's *Topica*),[26] the influence of definition,[27] argument and proof,[28] "humane" interpretations
of the law,[29] the expression of the law in pithy maxims (*regulae*),[30] *color*,
setting the facts in an advantageous context,[31] and the habit of setting
down legal opinions in treatises.[32] Alas, the arguments that have been
made for the influence of rhetoric (and most other potential external
influences, except that of the local law of Rome's Greek-speaking provinces) on the Roman law have usually asserted it at a high level of abstraction, arguing a general effect upon juristic patterns of thought. It is
certainly possible that Roman law got, say, its notions of equity from
Greece via rhetorical training, as Johannes Stroux, who made the most
famous argument along these lines, contended early in the last century.
But it could equally have gotten them directly from Greece, from Greece
via philosophy, or simply had them of old from origins unknown and
unknowable, our grasp of early Roman society and law being so poor.
Arguments at such a level of generality are by their nature inconclusive,
and even with the best will in the world it is hard to be entirely con-
vinced by suggestions of patterns glimpsed so high among the clouds.
Nor have scholars of Roman law found such arguments worth more
than a polite nod in passing, as they proceed to seek, as they have so
long done, the history and evolution of Roman law safely within the
logic of Roman law itself.[33]

More recently arguments asserting rhetorical influence on the law
have been made at the opposite extreme from generality: minute philological examination has found rhetorical features in the writings of

certain jurists.[34] But this approach too is apt to be self-defeating. There is no arguing with results so painfully dug out of the *Digest* with broken fingernails, but the meager rhetorical gold thus mined, and the immense effort of mining it, tends to leave even a well-disposed observer wondering at the lack, not the profusion, of rhetorical influence on the classical jurists.

This section, hoping for greater conviction at the cost of a smaller reward, will seek the impact upon the Roman law of the actual laws and legal principles that governed declamations. The potential reward is smaller because laws governing declamations can only influence Roman law in the areas where declamatory laws existed. For just as declamation got on for centuries with a tiny cast of stock characters, so also it satisfied itself with no great number of laws.[35] Most of those laws concerned dramatic situations within families, and so their potential influence is primarily on the Roman law that concerned dramatic situations within families.[36] Declaimers, oddly enough, never took much interest in usufruct or rustic praedial servitudes, and so the potential influence of declamatory law on the Roman law of usufruct or rustic praedial servitudes—each of which occupies an entire book of the *Digest*—is nil.

This investigation faces other perils too. The great mass of surviving Roman law is no earlier than the late second or early third centuries AD, while most surviving Latin declamation is earlier.[37] What appears to be a law used in declamation taken into the Roman law might therefore be an early law of the Romans, of which (as so often) we lack evidence, taken in the reverse direction into declamation; indeed, Roman declaimers of the empire were particularly apt to call for inspiration not upon the Roman law of their own day, but the law of the Republic.[38] Or it might be a Greek law, old or new, taken into both the Roman law and the law of declamation alike.[39] Or since, as has been suggested, the laws of declamation often represent the *giuridicizzazione dell'etica*—the expression of everyday ethics in fictive legal terms—those same ethics might force their way into the Roman law quite independently of declamation.[40]

## The Laws of Declamation

The laws used in Latin declamation are, a few of them, clearly taken from the Roman law, and some of them—such as *inscripti maleficii sit actio*, above, and the reward given to tyrant slayers (chapter 4)—clearly from the Greek, while some are specifically identified by ancient authors (albeit sometimes wrongly) as fictional creations of the schools of declamation. But in most cases we simply cannot be sure. Once upon a time guessing at the historical origins of declamatory laws was the subject of acute scholarly interest.[41] That many of the laws of declamation were based on lost old Roman laws was the assumption of a whole tradition of scholarship—the broad trunk of all study of declamatory law—that ransacked declamation for early Roman legal matter.[42] More recent scholarship regards the whole quest for old Roman law in declamatory law as quixotic, even faintly comic.[43] But the indefatigable learned search for parallels between the law of declamation and the Roman law is highly useful if we reverse the assumptions of the old seekers: while they sought the origins of declamatory law in Roman law, we can use the similarities they discovered to examine the influence of the declamatory law, and declamatory legal concepts, on Roman jurisprudence.[44]

Certainly the overall imagined legal environment in which Latin declamation took place was not that of the Roman Forum, or of any Roman citizen court. Only a single real Roman *lex*, the *lex Voconia* of 169 BC, is mentioned by name in the preface that sets out the laws that will govern the exercise in the ample body of Latin declamation surviving to us.[45] Characters in Latin declamation calmly violate Roman law all the time with no expectation of being called on it, and not even its more obscure provisions, but those that any educated Roman would know. In fact, much the most common pairing of opponents in the imaginary courts of Latin declamation, that of the son against father or father against son, was among the least likely to occur in real Roman courts, where sons, with a few exceptions, could not sue their fathers even if they had been emancipated from their father's *patria potestas*, and where fathers could, in principle, deal with the misdeeds of sons in power (still under *patria potestas*) privately by virtue of that *patria potestas*.[46] As Livy has a character say, "Nothing could be shorter than a trial between a father and a son. These few words would end it: 'If the son doesn't obey his father, it'll be the worse for him!'"[47] Because of the concentration of declamation on disputes within families, especially surprising is the scarcity in the themes set for Latin declamation of the fundamental Roman legal principle of *patria potestas* and its tasty refinements, with their impact on so many other aspects of Roman law and life—children in or out of power; the legal disability of the former; their emancipation and its testamentary *sequellae*; *peculium* in its colorful varieties; and marriage with or without *manus*. When a father wishes to execute his son in Latin declamation (twenty-two instances have been counted), around half the time he charges him with a capital crime in court, apparently ignorant of his right to execute a child-in-power himself under the notorious *potestas vitae necisque* that *patria potestas* gave a Roman father (that right that remained powerful in the Roman imagination even if it was almost never exercised in Roman reality). And when he does wish to do the killing himself, his right to do so is not assumed, but usually has to be specified in a law governing the declamation—*indemnatos liberos liceat occidere* ("It is legal to execute [one's own] children without trial")—for reasons that will be considered below.[48]

The imagined legal environment of Latin declamation was less that of Rome, and more that of an imaginary mixed world taking some laws and ethics from Rome (mostly that of the Republic), some, including tyrants, from historical Greece, stock characters from the Greek New Comedy—the War Hero, the Rich Man, the Poor Man, the Profligate Son—and much from the obscure-to-us world of Greek folktales that blossomed into the Greek novel, especially the pirates and evil stepmothers ubiquitous in declamation.[49] But most of all, declamation took from traditions and conventions of declamation itself as they had developed and barnacled-up over the centuries, including its laws, not least because a declaimer was allowed to assume that other laws from the body of declamatory laws applied to a given case, even if those other laws were not mentioned in the formal preface to the exercise that stated the laws upon which the case turned.[50]

Insofar as the laws and legal principles of declamation represent the *giuridicizzazione dell'etica*, the potential always existed for the law of declamation to cleave closer to the moral sense and social expectations of inhabitants of the Roman empire than did the Roman law, guided as it was by jurists, intellectuals following an independent intellectual tradition with its own logic somewhat removed from an everyday sensibility.[51] And it is attractive to speculate that cases when the law of rhetoric seemed to "fit" social expectations better than the Roman law explain some of the influence of the declamatory law on Roman law. We consider such a case next, that of *raptus*, the Roman law of ravishment, a rare instance where we can see multiple stages of a declamatory law's duel with the Roman law.

# 9

# The Attractions of
# Declamatory Law

### The *Raptarum Lex*

To teachers of rhetoric and those who declaimed for show or their own pleasure, one of the most fruitful imaginary laws that launched declamations was that a girl who had been ravished had the right to require the death of her ravisher—or to marry him. (We say "ravished" rather than "raped" because the stress in both declamation and Roman law was on the abduction rather than the sexual crime, although the latter was implied.) Suppose . . . just suppose . . . a man ravished two women on the same night! And one demands his death, and the other wants to marry him! The declaimers argue for the wronged ladies' contradictory rights. Or suppose that the victim opts for marriage, but when her convicted ravisher churlishly denies his crime, she wants to change her choice to death: should she be allowed to? Or suppose the ravisher is already married, but the victim chooses marriage, forcing him to divorce his original wife, whereupon that wronged matron sues him under a second declamatory law—many declamations involved two or more laws, often in conflict—"That legal action be permitted for unjust divorce."[1] The declamatory law letting the victim of ravishment choose her assailant's fate was so well known that it could simply be referred to in shorthand as the *raptarum lex*, the "Law of the ravished."[2]

The Roman law originally knew nothing of such a choice for victims of sexual violence.[3] In fact, as far as we can tell, the Roman law for centuries knew nothing of *raptus* as a distinct crime. During the Republic and after (such is the conventional view) the doer of such a deed might be sued for *iniuria* (serious insult, perhaps with violence); later, if the deed rose to the level of *stuprum* (relations with an unmarried or widowed lady of elevated social position) without consent but also without force, and was prosecuted as an offense under provisions of the Augustan adultery law, the *lex Iulia de adulteriis coercendis* of 18 or 17 BC, the penalty was forfeiture of half the criminal's property to the state and of his right of testation, while under the *lex Iulia de vi* (violence) the penalty for forcible *stuprum* was capital.[4] But it is not until the jurist Marcian, in the early third century AD, that the word *raptus* actually appears in the law, and he wished to kick it from the realm of adultery into that of *vis*.[5] He used the term, that is, but he was not sure how it should be dealt with legally, and he did not consider *raptus* a separate crime in itself. That would only come in Constantine's day, and its coming is a puzzle, given the existing array of ways in which the offense could already be prosecuted.[6]

In that same passage Marcian stated that the penalty for *raptus*, whatever the legal category into which it fell, was capital; and this was confirmed by Constantine in AD 326, and again in AD 349 under Constantius.[7] Such reiteration of the penalty, we are entitled to suspect, suggests that in the real world something rather different was often happening, and happening over many years, and that as a result in the real world puzzled people were writing to Rome and asking the authorities what the Roman law actually said was to be done in cases of *raptus*.

What, then, was going on in the courts of the empire? In yet another reassertion that *raptus* was indeed a capital crime, Justinian adds helpfully, "nor shall it be in the power of a virgin, or a widow, or indeed of any woman, to ask that the *raptor* shall become her husband."[8] And we notice too that late-antique canon law sometimes took it for granted that *raptus* would end in marriage—indeed in marriage blessed by the church.[9] Aha! So out there in the real world, we guess, the *raptarum lex* had pushed through the doors of the schools of rhetoric and walked down to the courts—and judges were accepting it in actual cases.[10] And why not? Every educated man in the Roman Empire—be he a governor or his legate, an assessor, advocate, or litigant—was familiar with this "law" because he had declaimed and heard declamations upon it in youth.

In a traditional society a victim of sexual abduction's chances of contracting an advantageous marriage were poor, and the prospect of marriage to her *raptor*, especially were he wealthy, and likely without need for her father to offer a dowry—for such was a frequent provision of the *raptarum lex* as it appears in declamation—will in many cases have been, as dreadful as it appears to us, the best option for the victim and her family.[11] To a Roman judge, then, faced with the united pleas of victim, her family, her ravisher, and his family, and all their friends and connections, and very likely his own moral sense, itself formed by his rhetorical training, it will have been very easy and merciful to apply in his court the *raptarum lex* he remembered from his school days.

At first the authorities at Rome tried to stop this. That is why Marcian, Constantine, and Constantius, all using the word *raptus* most familiar from rhetoric (and by using that word arguably frowning specifically at the rhetorical *raptarum lex* applied in the real world), insisted on a capital penalty, Constantine adding that the subsequent pleas of the victim (as would arise from the *raptarum lex* if the victim chose marriage) were irrelevant, except to implicate her in the crime as well.[12] There was to be no choice. But eventually the central authorities weakened and yielded in part to what was actually happening in the empire. In AD 374 the emperors Valentinian, Valens, and Gratian decreed a time limit of five years for legal challenges to the validity of marriages resulting from *raptus*. If not challenged within that time, the marriage was thereafter to be considered legal and any resulting offspring were legitimate. The emperors were, in short, offering a legal passage from *raptus* to marriage, and it seems plausible that the marriages in question were those resulting from the day-to-day application of the *raptarum lex* in the courts of the empire: after five years, the rhetorical *raptarum lex* was enforceable as the Roman law.[13] Where did the idea of a five-year limit on legal complaint come from? It has been powerfully argued that the ban on bringing cases after a specific interval, the *longi temporis prae-scriptio*, was itself an import from the world of rhetoric, or imported by Roman rhetorical training from Greek law.[14]

As far as we can see, the compromise of AD 374, enshrining a law of declamation in the law of the Romans, and inserting the *longi temporis praescriptio*, remained in force until the reign of the traditional- and tidy-minded Justinian, who reasserted that a woman might not marry her *raptor*.[15] But thirty years later an older, wiser Justinian capitulated, and, in that baffling way of Roman emperors, both restated the old law and admitted that no one was paying attention to it. In a *Novella* of AD 563 he firmly reasserted that *raptus* was a capital offense, but then went on in the same constitution to complain that the ravished were still marry-ing their ravishers, and "Much do we wonder that some," necessarily judges, were, "against the sense of our law," even authorizing such women to inherit from their ravisher husbands. This was to stop: upon the husband's death his property was to go to the wife's parents, as long as they had not approved the match, or, if they were dead, was to be confiscated by the imperial fisc.[16] So, in fact, Justinian accepted that in many cases *raptores* were not going to be executed, unless their victims should decline to marry them, and so undergirded the (evidently indif-ferently enforced) capital penalty for *raptus* with a purely financial one. In other words, the *raptarum lex*'s popularity in the courts of the empire eventually wore down even the obsidian heart of Justinian. In the end, the law of declamation won, at least partially.

The incompleteness of this victory is well illustrated by the contrast-ing fates of two variations on the *raptarum lex*. "Let the ravisher perish, unless, within thirty days, he has obtained the pardon of both his own father and the father of the ravished," read one declamatory law.[17] So far as we know, avoiding punishment by being pardoned for *raptus* by the father of the victim was never sanctioned under the Roman law. But evidently it happened in practice, and it had to be stamped upon. For in the same passage of Marcian we noticed above, that third-century jurist remarks that under the Roman law ravishers should *not* escape punish-ment even if they are forgiven by the victim's father, and even uses the same rather unusual word, *exorare*, for the act of begging for pardon, a

word found in the law of the declaimers.[18] But more successful was declamation's "Let a ravisher's victim choose the ravisher's death or his
*property*."[19] Under the *lex Iulia de adulteriis coercendis* the criminal's fine
went to the state, as it did under the *lex Julia de vi publica*. But by Justinian's
time the property of a *raptor* was ideally to go to his victim, the Roman
law, it is nice to think, finally lining up with the law of declamation.[20]

## Adultery

We cannot usually see or guess so many stages of the siege of the Roman
law by a law of declamation as we can in the case of the law of *raptarum
lex*. But we can see other cases where the Roman law seems to have sur-
rendered to the declaimers, perhaps because the declamatory law appealed to the Roman moral sense better than the Roman law. Consider
adultery. The law of the late Roman Republic appears to have been that
a husband could kill his wife if caught in adultery and her lover also, as
long as he killed both of them.[21] This right he lost under Augustus's *lex
Julia de adulteriis coercendis* (18 or 17 BC), which forbade a husband to
kill his wife—it was murder—and laid down that he could only kill her
lover if the lover was of a degraded social category (a slave, a freedman,
an actor).[22] Latin declamation was having none of this, and kept to the
old law: "Who [and it is always a husband] apprehends an adulterer
with an adulteress, as long as he kills both of them, shall have committed
no crime."[23] And the old law, kept in the public mind by declamation,
appears to have exerted continuous pressure on the new. Antoninus
Pius, we read, simply used his imperial prerogative to pardon some husbands who in a fury killed wives whom they caught in adultery, and for
other such husbands he remitted the capital penalty: if they were of high
status, they were merely relegated to an island for a given period. Marcus
Aurelius and Commodus appear to have weakened the formal penalties
further. And by the reign of Majorian, at least in the West, a husband
who killed his adulterous wife was no longer punished at all, so long,
once again, as adulterer and adulteress were killed together.[24] The law
of rhetoric appears to have prevailed.[25] And it prevailed, presumably,
with the powerful help of Roman feeling in general, to which the law of

declamation represented the authentic legal tradition of the Romans, with which Augustus had meddled outrageously, and a strong moral sense that Augustus's limitations on husbands' venerable right to kill adulterous wives were unjust and unnatural.[26]

Not only the hale had adulterous wives. As we will note below, the mutilated formed an important population of the characters in declamation. Imagine a war hero, who, in the course of fighting heroically for his country, had misplaced his hands. Seeing his wife in adultery, and being incapable of killing her himself—having, you see, no hands—he bellowed for his son to do so in his stead. When the son balked at killing his mother, he was disowned by his father, and declamation inevitably followed. This contrived plot required, naturally, a special declamatory law that allowed a *son* to kill his mother if she were caught in adultery.[27] Now, such a right of sons to kill mothers caught in adultery was not, one might naïvely imagine, a law with much application in the real world; no matter: under Severus Alexander, sons are allowed to kill adulterers as their father's agents, not inconceivably as a result of the influence of the declamatory law authorizing such acts.[28]

Adultery became a public offense for the first time under the *lex Julia*, and under its provisions adulterers were to be relegated to islands—different islands, naturally, lest they continue to be naughty together—and if female the convicted lost a third of her property and half her dowry, and if male half his property: severe but not capital penalties.[29] It appears, however, that by the reign of Constantine adultery had become a capital crime, and had indeed arrived among a select group of atrocious villainies for which the normal process of appeal was blocked and which were excluded from the Easter amnesties the emperors decreed for lesser wickedness.[30] Now there are any number of possible reasons for this: Constantine was grumpy—many crimes began to be punished more severely in his reign—and somewhat given to Christianity, which discountenanced adultery even more seriously than Augustus had.[31] But it may perhaps also be worth noting that one of the atrocious crimes with which adultery was classed under Constantine and his successors, *veneficium* (poisoning; sometimes involving sorcery), had also been joined with it in declamation: there are no fewer than fourteen surviving declamatory cases mixing adultery and poison. The scenario in almost all the cases is that a mother objects violently to a match planned for her daughter, crying, "She'll die before she marries him!" And so the daughter promptly does, with signs of poisoning. A slave, upon being tortured, reveals an adulterous affair between mother and her daughter's suitor. The mother is accused of murder or poisoning and declamation ensues.[32] Might the traditional nexus between adultery and poison recited so often in the schools have suggested to Constantine or his jurists that they belonged together and that there should be such a nexus in the formal law as well?[33] It has been observed that a discussion of *veneficium* in Marcian—a jurist open, as we have seen above, to borrowing from rhetoric—seems to recall, and therefore perhaps draws from, formulations of the subject in declamation.[34]

## Gratitude and *Talio*

Seneca the Younger identified the popular declamatory general law against ingratitude—"An action at law shall lie against one who acts ungratefully" (*ingrati sit actio*)—as a denizen of the schools of rhetoric, noting in passing that in the real world only Macedonia had such a law. He was probably wrong about Macedonia, and the law is likely Attic in origin, the Athenians allowing elderly parents to sue their children for support under a similar provision.[35] And although he was right that in his time there was no general law against ingratitude at Rome, there was a provision—part of the *lex Aelia Sentia* of AD 4—that applied to freedmen who were disrespectful or undutiful to their former masters, and could be punished for it, eventually by having their manumission revoked and being hauled back into slavery (although when that penalty formally entered the law is unknown).[36] And this issue remained on the public mind: Claudius is reported to have returned "ungrateful" freedmen to slavery, presumably using his arbitrary imperial authority, and so rather implying that this was not yet the regular law, and in AD 56 the Senate debated whether masters ought to have the right to re-enslave misbehaving freedmen.[37] We can hardly be certain that the Roman law *accusatio ingrati liberti* was inspired by the more general law in declamation, but it is interesting that the charge uses the same word, *ingratus*, as the declamatory law, because while there is nothing unnatural in understanding the freedman's crime as an act of ingratitude for his manumission (rather than, for example, an act of disrespect or insult), there is also nothing inevitable about it.[38] And declamation (like Roman society in general) did take for granted the gratitude owed by freedmen to those who had freed them.[39]

The other early imperial branch of thinking about ingratitude in the world of justice concerned wills. Caligula declared invalid on grounds of ingratitude the wills of senior centurions (they were very highly paid: their retirement bonuses alone ranked them as equestrians) who had failed to number Tiberius or himself among their heirs.[40] Nero, we are told, extended the excuse of "ingratitude" to seize for the fisc the goods of any testator who caught his eye.[41] Pliny the Younger strongly implies that Domitian too had invalidated wills and seized estates because of failures of "gratitude" to him.[42] In each case the act is represented as monstrous, but in each case ingratitude is the respectable cover the emperor places over his evil deed, implying that senatorial society in general approved "grateful" wills and expected them to be so. And from the reign of Diocletian (although it might well be older) we see in the formal law the requirement that children be "grateful" if they wish to invalidate a will from which they were excluded, and that the defenders of the will can assert the ingratitude of such children in its defense.[43] As to whether the declamatory law contributed to the expectation that wills and those hoping to receive from them be grateful, we can, again, only speculate.

The declamatory law applied to any outrageous act of ingratitude, whatever the relationship of the parties. In Latin declamation we see it invoked twice by wives. In one case a wife resists the appalling tortures of a tyrant in order to save her husband, but is rendered barren by the injuries thereby incurred, and so is divorced, and sues her wretched husband for ingratitude; once it is adduced by a father-in-law against a son-in-law; and in one case by a Rich Man suing an unrelated Poor Man.[44] So too Seneca the Younger imagined it working, when under Nero he asked himself (and answered himself in the negative at painful length) whether the law against ingratitude "which operates in the schools" should be imposed in the real world.[45] His lucubrations on the subject remind us—if we needed reminding—that reciprocity lay at the heart of the Roman moral sensibility.[46] As such, any declamatory law grounded in reciprocity, or that seemed to reflect the commands of reciprocity better than the existing Roman law, would have powerful aid in pushing itself into the Roman law, supported by its deep roots in Roman moral sentiment.

It is hardly surprising, then, that eventually the Roman law of ingratitude broke free of its limitation to freedmen and wills and assimilated itself to the law as it existed in declamation. In AD 367 Valentinian, Valens, and Gratian—those emperors again—decreed that children who verbally or physically abused their parents might have their emancipation revoked and be brought back under *patria potestas*. There is no direct reference to ingratitude in the brief surviving text of the law, but the editors of both the *Theodosian Code* in the early fifth century and the Justinianic *Codex* in the early sixth classified this law under the rubric "Concerning Ungrateful Children."[47] And in that later work, Justinian in AD 530 takes it for granted that a general law against ingratitude exists, a law that applies even between persons who are not related by the parent-child or the patron-freedman bond, and lists occasions when it might be invoked and a *donatio* recovered: if the recipient has outrageously insulted the giver, or beaten him, or conspired that he should lose a large sum of money, or placed him in danger of death. All are circumstances that sound very much as though they are taken from, well, declamations governed by the law against ingratitude.[48]

Related in theme, and also grounded in an expectation of gratitude, is the common declamatory law that "Children must support their parents or be imprisoned," a law probably again of Greek origin, which can produce a fine rhetorical quandary when, for example, a father sues his son for support, the father having previously rendered such support impractical by offering the pirates who had captured that son twice the ransom they had asked for the son's freedom if instead they would cut off the son's hands (which they did), hands that son had used to kill the father's other son, who happened to be a tyrant.[49] A very similar duty for children to support their parents (albeit without the penalty of imprisonment, and with pirates nowhere in sight, but with much discussion of *pietas* and other conventional values) appears in the Roman law of the reigns of Antoninus Pius and Marcus Aurelius.[50] This is a curious provision, illustrating the force of rhetorical law upon the real law particularly strongly, because it lies athwart many established principles of the Roman law. It would seem contradictory to require a son-in-power to support his father, for several reasons: because his father owns all the son's wealth anyway; an emancipated son should not be obliged to support his father, because emancipation breaks the agnatic link; and a son in the army should not be obliged to support his father because part of the point of his *peculium castrense*—the financial proceeds of his military service—is exactly that it was protected from his father.[51] This declamatory law has been pointed out as a particularly strong case of the *giuridicizzazione dell'etica,* where the law of rhetoric expressed an accepted moral duty that for centuries no one felt needed to be incorporated into the formal Roman law.[52] But eventually, with the help of that ethical familiarity, the law of declamation forced its way into the law of the Romans.

The larger principle lying behind the rhetorical *actio ingrati* and the requirement of children to support their parents was reciprocity, and in that same realm we notice the declamatory law: "He who acknowledges a child he has exposed may claim the child back after paying the cost of the child's upbringing (*solutis alimentis*)." Example: Such a son is redeemed by his rich father but prefers the poor family that actually brought him up and proposes to marry his poor stepfather's daughter, so his rich father disinherits him. Declamation follows. This law of rhetoric seems to have made its way into the Roman law by the reign of Diocletian, using words—*alimentorum solutione*—that recall the rhetorical law.[53]

A crueler reciprocity was also popular in declamation: the *talio*—"Let there be an action for *talio*"—and especially in cases of blinding: an eye for an eye.[54] Now the *talio* was a very ancient principle of Roman law, appearing in the Twelve Tables: if you broke a man's arm, and the two of you could not agree on compensation, he might break yours in exchange.[55] But by the middle of the second century AD, by the age of the pedantic discussions depicted by Aulus Gellius in his *Attic Nights*, it could be represented (if just to make a point) that even a jurisconsult might not know the legal significance of the word *talio*, so entirely superseded was the practice.[56] Under the early Empire punishments reflecting the *talio* survived mostly as irregular one-offs, sometimes used in spectacles, as when a bandit who had ravaged the area around Aetna was placed atop an artful model of Aetna in the Roman Forum, a structure that, collapsing upon command, delivered him to the beasts that devour.[57]

But *talio*, adjusted to the needs of rhetoricians, reigned in the rhetorical schools. "Let the false accuser suffer the same penalty that the defendant would have suffered, had he been convicted," was the rhetorical law.[58] In a world where informers and greedy bringers of prosecutions (*delatores*) were so hated and feared, this pleasing idea, whether from rhetoric or elsewhere, caught the public imagination. And so Pliny the Younger imagined (or described?) those who were *delatores* under Domitian now subjected to the same punishment as their victims, being themselves sent into exile—those who survived the storms and tempests of such a journey—to "dwell on bare rocks and an unfriendly shore." He goes on, "Those islands, once mobbed with senators, were now filled up with *delatores*. . . . They took the money of others: now let them lose their own . . . the fear they made others to fear, let them fear it themselves."[59] And the application of the *talio* to false accusers eventually made it into the written law: if a person claims that a farm has been taken from him by violence (*vis*), said Constantine, but fails to prove the claim, the false accuser will suffer the penalty for *vis*.[60] If a false accusation were made for treason, *maiestas*, and the defendant tortured (and not even the highest in the land were immune from torture in cases of *maiestas*) but the accused was acquitted, then the accuser and his cronies were to be tortured in their turn.[61] Even before a formal charge was made for murder, said the emperors in AD 383, the accuser had to bind himself in writing to undergo the penalty for murder if he failed to prove his case.[62] Finally, the exact parallel to the declamatory law, that *any* unsuccessful accuser suffered the penalty for the crime he accused another of, was enunciated by Honorius and Theodosius in AD 423.[63]

Related to the *talio* are what we might call anatomically appropriate punishments that blossomed under Constantine: put a foot wrong—use it to flee over the border to the barbarians, if you are a slave—and whack! off comes the foot. Use an official hand to steal, and thwack! off comes the hand. Insult the emperor with it, and—yank!—lose your tongue. Lure a girl into the hands of a ravisher with spoken blandishments, and—gurgle! gag!—have your mouth stopped up with molten lead.[64] "That execrable blight, the single greatest evil in human life, the malicious accusor [*delator*]," ranted Constantine in the fine style of his generation, "let his very attempt be strangled in his throat as he begins! Let his envious tongue be cut from its roots and ripped out!" All jabber it turns out, because the emperor goes on to specify a (merely) capital penalty. But when the law came to be interpreted later, the strangulation and (post-mortem) removal of the tongue had become appallingly real.[65]

> My object all sublime I shall achieve in time—
> To let the punishment fit the crime,
> The punishment fit the crime.

Thus that eminent jurist, Gilbert and Sullivan's Mikado, and punishments that fit the crime are hardly uncommon in many different legal traditions, not least in the Code of Hammurabi, the Old Testament, and in Islamic jurisprudence. But, as far as we can tell, such anatomically appropriate punishments played little role in classical Roman law or its juristic interpretation.[66] Accepting that Roman punishments generally became harsher in the reign of Constantine and thereafter, it was hardly a necessary or natural evolution of the existing Roman law for punishments to become harsher *in this particular way*. But educated Romans were hardly unfamiliar with such appropriate punishments: they were a staple of declamation, a world in which the man who blinded another could expect—if he did not wish to be blinded himself—to serve as the blind man's guide for the rest of his days, he who struck his father lost the hand that administered the blow, and he who stole temple treasures lost the hands that had grabbed them.[67]

This is a case of the laws of declamation apparently providing general inspiration for the Roman law, rather than specific declamatory laws being adopted into the Roman law: for although in late Roman law hands were indeed lopped, they were not those of a son who had struck his father, nor, in the Roman law, was the blinder blinded. So what flows in from declamation is the general idea of mutilation as a punishment appropriate to the crime, and also, more broadly—and also very much against the spirit of classical Roman law—the idea that mutilation in general was something normal, something that might well happen and that could, therefore, be adopted as a judicial punishment. For in addition to mutilation being common as a punishment in declamation, the prior mutilation of a character—and especially amputated hands—was also common as part of the scenarios that gave rise to a declamation: sometimes it feels as if the whole of declamation's imaginary city was filled with persons either previously mutilated or liable to mutilation.[68]

# 10

# Legal Puzzles, Familiar Laws, and Laws of Rhetoric Rejected by Roman Law

IN ONE OF THE DECLAMATIONS recorded by Seneca the Elder the governing law is "Let there be an action for *iniuria*" (injury or severe insult). But the nature of the alleged injury is peculiarly Roman. The son of a Poor Man, who was certain that a Rich Man had killed his father but lacked the resources to take legal action against him, had taken to following the Rich Man around dressed in mourning. Because of the resulting disgrace the Rich Man had lost an election, and sued the Poor Man's son for *iniuria*: their speeches are the declamations.[1] What has attracted the attention of modern students of Roman law is the relative legal technicality of some of the arguments made: one of the declaimers who handled the subject denied that following a man around was *iniuria*: "All types of *iniuria* are included under the law [i.e., and no others]: one cannot strike a man, and you cannot shout insults at him in contravention of good morals," while another sarcastically described the accusation as creating a "new *formula* for the offense of *iniuria*: 'that he wept in contravention of good morals.'"[2] This is interesting because praetorian remedies for *iniuria*—by virtue of his slowly evolving edict the urban praetor allowed actions for offenses not comprehended under strict law—were under dispute at much the same time. One of the provisions of the Praetor's Edict read, "Let there be no reason for defamation in any respect. If anyone acts to the contrary, I shall penalize in proportion to the seriousness of the matter." But the great Augustan jurist Labeo—contemporary to the declaimers in Seneca—thought this provision "superfluous, because we can proceed under the rule against *iniuria* in the general edict."[3] Was the praetor's provision new, and was that why Labeo pointed out that it was not needed? Or was it old, and was this part of Labeo's wider campaign to fold insult into the law of *iniuria*? We cannot tell.[4] But it does seem unquestionable that the declaimers were arguing over a real contemporary legal issue in this case. Suppose the jurists noticed?

## The Slave Boy of Brundisium

In his *Lives of the Grammarians and Rhetors*, Suetonius noted that some topics for declamation were taken from real events in Rome's legal history, and instanced a case at Brundisium where, to avoid paying the high customs duty on a fresh, young, attractive—and thus valuable—slave boy, the slave trader had dressed him up in the *toga praetexta* and *bulla* of a free Roman citizen youth, upon whom no tariff was chargeable. When the boy arrived at Rome, the boy's freedom was sued for, on the grounds that by dressing him as free, and having had him act as free, the slave dealer had inadvertently indicated a will—a *voluntas*—that he should be free in fact.[5] Only one Latin declamation on exactly this topic survives, although we may guess from Suetonius's mention of the case that it was more common than it appears to us. In that declamation the law is given as "Who was freed by the will (*voluntas*) of his master, let him be free," and that law is also quoted in a second declamation.[6] Some scholars have claimed this as a quotation from the words by which the praetor protected those who had been freed informally under the Republic; others from the puzzling *lex Junia*, of 19 or 17 BC, the real Roman law that consigned some freedmen to the inferior status of Junian Latins.[7] Neither is impossible, but the dispute arises because the declamatory law does not sound particularly like what we know of either. What it does sound like is the second-century AD jurist Pomponius, explaining that inadvertent manumission (how exactly such a thing could happen we are left to guess) was invalid, and offering in an attempt at clarification that a slave "only is free by the will of the master if his possession of freedom accords with the will of the master."[8] Not only is the simplest solution that Pomponius took his wording from the well-known law of declamation, but Pomponius has wrapped himself so thoroughly up in his Latin that his formulation really makes sense only if his reader is familiar enough with the law of declamation to supply it as a gloss.[9] What appears to have happened is that the case of the Boy at Brundisium was taken into declamation, and there percolated over many decades, and that when needing to express the legal principle that that real case presented, a jurist simply adopted a formulation at which the declaimers had already arrived.

## Malleolus and the *Querela Inofficiosi Testamenti*

A few years before 100 BC, a Roman by the name of Malleolus murdered his mother. When he was convicted of that horrible crime, the strange and cruel Roman punishment for parricide was cranked into action: his head was muffled in the hide of a wolf, and special wooden shoes were placed upon his feet. He was to be drowned enclosed in a sack, but it took time to gather the small zoo of animals (a rooster, a dog, and a snake? the ancient authorities disagree) with which, according to venerable usage, he was to share the sack, so while the search for the beasts was in progress, he was confined in the *carcer*, Rome's prison. During the delay his friends rushed to the prison, bearing wax tablets: in that dark place he made his will with all legal punctilio and the necessary witnesses, disinheriting his younger brother (who had been one of his accusers). When the animals were finally found, he was conveyed to a body of flowing water on a cart drawn by black oxen, bound in the sack with the blameless smaller creatures, and there, with all due solemnity, drowned.[10]

We know this story because the will produced a famous legal controversy. The beneficiaries Malleolus had listed in his will entered upon his property, but his younger brother sued on the grounds that, despite the exquisite legal care with which it had been made, the will was nevertheless invalid. His argument appears to have been that a man who murdered his mother should be considered ipso facto mad, a *furiosus*, and that the property of a *furiosus* should be under the control of the relatives on his father's side, in short, of his younger brother. The argument on the other side will have been cheerfully to admit that Malleolus was barking mad when he did the terrible deed, but that did not in itself make his *will* invalid in those days. Such an intractable conflict of law sounds very much like the sort of thing declamation loved, and, indeed, by the time we hear the story—in the young Cicero and the anonymous *Rhetorica ad Herennium*—it has been processed into a declamatory theme.[11]

Jump ahead several hundred years. Now we can more clearly see the procedure by which Malleolus's brother challenged the will. In early imperial terms, this was the *querela inofficiosi testamenti* or "complaint of an undutiful will," which was heard before the venerable court of the *centumviri*.[12] The second-century AD jurist Ulpius Marcellus, commenting on insanity as a possible grounds for the *querela inofficiosi testamenti*, described it as a *color*, the technical term in rhetoric for the circumstances a declaimer invents to put the facts in the best light, a rare juristic use of a rhetorical term. This *color insaniae* was, or became, a legal fiction used to overturn objectionable wills even when the testator was not mad, as the third-century Marcian went on to explain, using the same word, *color* (so he probably had Marcellus's comment in mind): if the testator was in reality patently insane, his will was simply invalid, and the rules of intestacy applied.[13] Where does this *color* come from? And where did the intellectual jump to a claim of madness (perhaps the very first use of such an argument in these circumstances) come in the actual case of the will of Malleolus? Probably from the popular declamatory *actio dementiae*, a son's prosecution of his living father for madness, in order to seize his property.[14] This type of action, the δίκη παρανοίας, really existed in Greece: Sophocles, famously, was prosecuted under it. It became a law of Latin declamation, but, as we will see below, never made its way directly into Roman law proper, which never allowed a son to prosecute his living father for madness. Nevertheless it lurked in the minds of educated Romans, had its impact on the jurists who described insanity as a *color*, and influenced the way cases of *querela inofficiosi testamenti* were argued; and perhaps, many years before, had inspired the arguments of the unfortunate brother of the monstrous mother slayer Malleolus.

## The Testamentary Consequences of Suicide

We turn from parricide to suicide. Soon after the turn of the millennium, C. Albucius Silus, who had been a successful teacher and declaimer in Rome and an acquaintance of Seneca the Elder, but had retired in old age to his native Novara in northern Italy, summoned the people of the town and delivered a long speech justifying why he proposed to kill himself: he was, he explained, suffering from an incurable abscess. Having finished his speech, he went home, and starved himself to death.[15] And so he died as he had lived, because he was adapting to reality, as much as he could, the much-loved declamatory theme, "Who does not give reasons for suicide before the Senate, shall be cast out without burial."[16] Like the rhetorician mentioned at the beginning of this chapter whose ignorance of the Roman law was exploited to comic effect by the witty advocate Cassius Severus, Albucius always had difficulties keeping school and reality apart. "Swear!" he once challenged a litigant in a real-life court case, "Swear upon the ashes of your father and mother, those ashes that lie unburied!" Whereupon the litigant gleefully did just that, and won the case. Albucius had forgotten that in real Roman courts there were opponents who could respond to such windy rhetorical challenges, and was unaware that he had inadvertently offered a *iusiurandum*, a challenge to take an oath that, if accepted, won the case for the oath taker.[17]

The declamatory law requiring prospective suicides to explain themselves to a public body, and in some versions get its permission for the act to be allowed burial, was much beloved because of its potential for paradox and gaudy flights of self-pity and may have been adapted by declaimers from a real law that existed in some Greek cities.[18] But it never, so far as we know, entered Roman law. What we do have, however, are suggestions that it influenced the Roman law that concerned the validity of the wills of those who committed suicide when under legal threat.[19] In this domain the law wobbled between a position that suicide obliterated potential charges, or perhaps even those already laid—thus the frequent anticipatory suicides of those accused of *maiestas* in Tacitus—with the result that the will of such a person was valid, and the position that suicide under such circumstances constituted a confession, with the result that the will was invalid and the accused's property was seized by the state.[20]

When legal texts become available, under the Antonines, the law was leaning toward the latter, harsher position, and the Antonines proposed to soften it with a series of limitations and exceptions. A formal charge had to have been brought before the suicide for the suicide to be deemed a confession; and the charge must have been such that condemnation in that case would threaten the loss of the condemned's property. The suicide had to have occurred from fear of legal conviction, not to escape the pain of disease or *taedium vitae*.[21] Had a father killed his son, Hadrian wrote, his suicide was not to be attributed to fear of punishment, but to grief at the loss of that son—and, suddenly, we are in the world of declamation, where killing sons is exactly the sort of grounds upon which fathers, consumed by regret, inform an imaginary senate of their intention to commit suicide.[22] And the jurists took up the same theme, Ulpian considering the question of the validity of the wills of those who committed suicide after having been accused of parricide (surely not an every-day occurrence—except in declamation).[23] Marcian, glossing the merciful provisions of the emperors in this area, editorializes floridly, "And he is rightly punished who turns his hand against himself without due cause, for if he has not spared himself, how likely is he to be merciful to others?" It is as if he had just read, but not exactly remembered, Seneca the Elder: "What might he have dared who could kill—himself?" a phrase even more closely mimicked by Ulpian when contemplating the suicide of a slave.[24] It does rather appear that emperors and jurists had declamation on the mind when they pondered the legal aspects of suicide, and so we are hardly surprised to discover that, although Antoninus Pius allowed a formal hearing to the heirs of a man who committed suicide while charged with a crime, with his will to

stand if they could prove him innocent of the crime itself, by Diocletian's time the heirs had to prove merely that the suicide was not motivated by fear of punishment for the will to be valid, thus entirely over-
turning the old, harsh position on the wills of the accused.[25] Roman law
never quite arrived at the duty of the suicide to explain his motives before his death, but it got very close, by allowing the heirs to explain the
suicide's motives in his place.

## Bees and Other Instances

And there are bees, wee creatures much loved by legal thinkers in both
the common- and civil-law traditions. Bees and their sad vicissitudes
are the subject of the thirteenth pseudo-Quintilianic *Major Declamation*. A Rich Man's pretty flowers were infested by a Poor Man's bees. So
the Rich Man sprinkled poison over the flowers, and slew the bees: the
Poor Man sues the Rich Man for damages, and the Poor Man's speech
is the declamation.[26] Now, it happens that we have traces of an early
second-century AD controversy between jurists about bees and liability
for destroying them. Earlier jurists had said there was no such liability,
because bees were not susceptible of ownership, as neither tame nor in
confinement. But the jurist Celsus replied that action was allowed,
because it was the habit of bees—like doves—to return home, and one
could make a profit from them.[27] Now it turns out that the arguments
the Poor Man makes in the thirteenth *Major Declamation* (and antici-
pates from the other side) are curiously similar to those in the legal
controversy, and there are even some words in common, and verbal tics
of declamation can be found elsewhere in Celsus, and can be paralleled
in this declamation itself. Celsus, the sagacious Dario Mantovani has
suggested, was drawing on this very declamation in his legal reply.[28]

Mantovani has had intellectual children. So recently we find it argued
that from thinking in declamation came the Roman law doctrine that a
wife had a privileged right (the *favor dotis*)—before other creditors—to
get her dowry back from the remains of her husband's fortune or estate
if his debts exceeded his wealth, or if it be discovered that, being a slave
and not having admitted it, he could not legally own property at all.[29]

And also worked up in declamation was juristic thinking about the nature of the shames that might ban a rich Roman from the honorific first fourteen rows of the theater, set aside for such worthies by the *lex Roscia theatralis* (67 BC), there being a surviving declamation about whether a man who became a gladiator (an infamous profession) for the virtuous reason that he needed to raise money to bury his father, should, after acquiring a qualifying fortune, nevertheless be denied such seating.[30] Some scholars, on the basis of parallels of this sort, are moving towards a position that posits declamation as a sort of moot court, where jurists worked out their arguments in collaboration with declaimers, and tried them out against colleagues, before the jurists expressed them in the much different style of written juristic opinion.[31]

## The Power of Familiarity

Some declamatory laws found their way into Roman law because they appealed to the Roman moral sense; they "felt right," in some cases more right than the actual Roman law. Others made their way in because declaimers (with jurists perhaps among them) used declamation as a laboratory to solve legal problems, and jurists then inserted those solutions into the law. But it must finally be admitted that there are other cases, such as the possibility that Ulpian appended the *inscripti maleficii sit actio* to *stellionatus*, as was argued at the beginning of this section, for which it is hard to find a positive reason other than the greater familiarity of the law of declamation by contrast to the law of the Romans.

We just saw, in the case of Malleolus, the traditional, elaborate *poena cullei* (punishment of the sack) for the atrocious crime of parricide.[32] But during the Empire this passed out of fashion, and by the age of the classical jurists parricide was punished otherwise, by the sword or by burning alive, or by being fed to beasts—perfectly conventional forms of execution. Constantine restored the *poena cullei*.[33] Why? One place the sack and its unhappy denizens had never gone out of fashion was declamation, where it always remained the punishment for parricide, and was alway available to remind an emperor what the penalty for parricide really ought to be.[34] Nor will the Romans in general, a conservative folk if ever there was one, have been likely to object to the restoration of a hallowed, ancestral punishment. So perhaps the return of the *culleus* from rhetoric to reality had the wind of tradition at its back.

But the return of the sack under Constantine stands in contrast to legal treatment of other forms of killing within the family. It is generally accepted that the Roman father's ferocious *ius vitae necisque*—the right to kill children under the power inherent in his *patria potestas*—does not seem to have been much exercised in practice under the Empire, and that the Roman law implies that it became more usual to go to court to deal with adult children who seemed to require execution, and that it eventually became compulsory to do so.[35] We have seen above that *patria potestas* only existed in an etiolated form in declamation, and that in declamation fathers who wish to kill their sons usually go to court to do so.[36] Might the change in real-world practice and law have been a result of the influence of declamation? If so, in this case declamation pushed *against* Roman tradition, but prevailed.

There does seem to have been a weak current pressing all declamatory laws alike into the Roman law. And that current probably arose from the simple familiarity of declamatory laws, greater familiarity in most cases than people had with the Roman civil law. The Roman governors who served as judges had, in most cases, no legal training, and it was hardly invariable for them to equip themselves with advisors who did. Acting as they did *extra ordinem*, they were positively encouraged to decide legal matters in the provinces on the basis of local law or their own moral sense rather than strict Roman law.[37] If a question of Roman law arose in the provinces (not necessarily an everyday affair, since in principle and perhaps in fact the Roman law only applied to Roman citizens, and there were fewer of those with every step taken away from Italy until the emperor Caracalla made most free people in the empire Roman citizens in AD 212), written treatises by jurisconsults could be consulted if available, which they might or might not be, although a Roman official could assume that Ulpian's volumes on the duties of various Roman magistrates would be accessible in, say, great Ephesus.[38] Or a letter of inquiry might be sent to a jurisconsult at Rome, or to the emperor, which he might (or more likely not, given the press of such inquiries) answer, with a jurist looking over his purple-clad shoulder to advise him.[39] But nearly every high-status person who appeared in court in the Roman Empire East or West, be he judge—a governor or his legate—assessor, advocate, or litigant, had declaimed in school and was well familiar with the laws of declamation. Until the fourth century AD persons in the provinces of the empire who were familiar with declamatory law will have outnumbered persons trained in Roman law by a hundred to one. No wonder declamatory laws infected actual legal practice. Even if we accept the most optimistic arguments of contemporary scholars who think that Roman law spread through the empire faster than Roman citizenship, Roman law was always the purview of a few, while rhetoric, because of the conventions of education, was the common possession of the entire ruling class of the empire.[40]

## Roman Law Rejects Declamatory Law

Finally, we glance at a few significant occasions where the Roman law rejected the law of declamation. In his *Institutes*, Quintilian gives special consideration to three declamatory laws because they are very close to the Roman law, and so especially good training for aspiring advocates. These are *abdicatio* (renunciation and disinheritance of a child), the *actio malae tractationis* ("mistreatment," usually of a wife by a husband), and the *actio dementiae* (a son accusing his living father of insanity in the hope of taking over his estate). *Abdicatio*, says Quintilian, is good training for cases of improper disinheritance before the centumviral court that dealt with such matters, "mistreatment" usefully mimics the issues in divorce cases, and the accusation of insanity requires arguments similar to those used when asking for a guardian, a *curator*, to be appointed for a madman.[41] Such laws might above all be expected to make their way into Roman law. None of them did.

We are already familiar with the rhetorical *actio dementiae*, which may have inspired the frequently used argument (or pretense) that a testator had been mad, so that his will should be overturned or adjusted postmortem (the *color insaniae* of the *querela inofficiosi testamenti*). But the *actio dementiae* itself, which originated in a well-known Athenian law, and was highly popular with declaimers, crashed, we guess, into the Roman legal principle of *patria potestas*, which, although the more grotesque aspects of it had passed out of use (if acts such as executing one's children had ever been common), remained a bedrock theoretical principle of the Roman law.[42] Except under rare and extraordinary circumstances a Roman son could not sue his father. If a Roman son were disinherited, or felt otherwise ill-used by his father's will, he had to wait until after his father's death and then claim a share of the estate by making the *querela*. The praetor or a governor could, as Quintilian said, appoint a *curator* for a lunatic, but he was supposed to appoint an older relation in the male line or brother if possible and until the reign of Antoninus Pius (the change itself perhaps occurring under rhetorical influence) it does not appear that a son could even be made his father's *curator*, because "It seemed somehow unbecoming for a son to rule over his father." Even were a son appointed, when it became allowed, the powers of the *curator* over an estate were quite limited, and his financial peril if he did not act in the best interests of the madman severe.[43] A more direct transfer of authority from father to son would appear to be conceptually extremely difficult if *patria potestas*, and all the moral assumptions that surrounded it, were to be respected.

The acceptance of the *actio malae tractationis* in the Roman law was probably blocked for a whole series of reasons.[44] Despite Quintilian, the most common use of the *actio malae tractationis* in declamation is for a wife to sue her husband because he had killed one of their children, an act that *patria potestas* set beyond the rights of a wife to litigate.[45] The *actio* also complained of some of the deeds the Roman law classed as *iniuria*, and was thus in part superfluous.[46] Nor could it easily replace the *actio rei uxoriae* of the Roman law, a suit to recover a dowry upon divorce, for which Quintilian identified it as good training. For the Roman law of reclaiming a dowry upon divorce was extremely intricate; in 1899 a learned book on Roman law of 466 pages could be consecrated to that subject alone.[47] And declamation was impatient of technicality. Its laws, after all, had to be but a single sentence long. So when the law of declamation threatened to impinge upon a complicated region of the

Roman law, the Roman law and its practitioners were, we guess, apt to push back. Declaimers could not handle anything as hellish as the historical *lex Iulia et Papia* (18 BC and AD 9), which regulated the size of the legacies persons could receive from those to whom they were not closely related on the basis of whether they were married and had children. And so declamation could have no influence upon such laws.[48]

Far the most puzzling, however, is the firm denial, by Diocletian and Maximian in AD 287, of the legality of the declamatory legal practice of *abdicatio*, "repudiation," the banishment from the household and disinheritance of a child, an act that, in declamation, was subject to an automatic trial in which the justice of the act was argued by the father and the banished child (impersonated, naturally, by declaimers).[49] Some such repudiation of a child (but without much trace of the immediate legal hearing) always seems to have been possible in the Greek world under the name ἀποκήρυξις, and some warm testimonials to it survive from late Roman Egypt: "I reject and abhor you from now on to the utter end of all time as outcasts and bastards and lower than slaves . . . [let] ravens . . . devour your flesh and peck out your eyes," and, "I declare, taking the most terrible oath on all the Principalities, Powers, Thrones, and Dominions, that I expel you, that you have been renounced, and that I have already disowned you in every legal way today for all the course of the sun, from now on, for centuries of centuries and for unlimited time."[50] The emperors helpfully gloss the term *abdicatio* by the Greek ἀποκήρυξις.[51] In fact a Roman father could accomplish much the same end as *abdicatio* with a pair of legal acts, *relegatio*, formal expulsion of a child-in-power from the household (although a simple chucking-out by burly slaves would also work) followed by disinheritance by name of the child in his will; nor did he have to go to court against his child to do either.[52] Quintilian, moreover, makes the connection between the real Roman legal process of disinheritance and *abdicatio*, but makes clear that *abdicatio* was a term limited to "the schools"—of rhetoric, that is—for the process known in the real world as *exheredatio*.[53] And he was probably right, for the word *abdicatio* never appears in the *Digest* in that sense, while *exheredatio* and related words formed from it appear more than three hundred times.

But if the term *abdicatio* was limited to the schools, it was over-whelmingly common there, for the automatic referral of an *abdicatio* to court was the single most frequent pretext for the Latin declamations whose themes survive to us (although, as mentioned above, a legal case that set a son against a living father was exceedingly unlikely in Roman reality).[54] Many odd accidents and cruelties—some of them highly contrived, in the way of declamation—could lead to *abdicatio*, but most commonly a son refuses to obey a monstrous or impossible command of his father, is repudiated, and then the declaimers representing the father and son give speeches to the court that decided whether the *abdicatio* should stand. Example: A young man is captured by pirates. He writes asking his father to ransom him, but his miserly papa refuses. The pirate captain's daughter makes the young man swear to marry her if he is released without ransom. He does and is, and the happy couple returns to the young man's city. His father now produces a rich orphan and requires that his son divorce his savior and marry that heiress in-stead. He refuses. His father repudiates him.[55] Alternatively, in a decla-mation famous because an account survives of how the young Ovid approached it, a husband and wife swear that if either should die the other will commit suicide. The husband, away on a trip, sends word to his wife—for reasons upon which the declaimers are left free to speculate—that he is dead. The wife loyally throws herself off a cliff to kill herself but fails to expire. Her father orders her to leave her husband, who has now returned in the bloom of health. She refuses, and her father repudi-ates her.[56] Or, finally, in the Greek tradition, where repudiation themes were often mined for comic effect, a grumpy man falls down and repudi-ates his son for laughing, or a miser, whose son has vowed a talent of silver to Asclepius if his father recovers from an illness, does indeed recover, and then repudiates the son for wasting the silver.[57]

What is striking—to return to AD 287—is that in their constitution Diocletian and Maximian do not use the terminology of the Roman law, *exheredatio*, but the term of the rhetorical schools, *abdicatio*. The em-perors chose to forbid in the real world a practice comprehended by the jargon of declamation. Evidently, cases of *abdicatio* were being heard in the courts of the empire, and (whether in this case or others) the emperors' subjects were writing to find out whether *abdicatio* was legal. The most likely reason, indeed, for Hermogenes, the recipient of Diocletian's response, to write to the emperor was that he wished to repudiate one of his children or had been the victim of such a repudiation and wanted a share of the estate. Here again a law of declamation had made inroads on legal practice, and the emperor wished that to stop.[58]

*Abdicatio* butted against legal reality for centuries. For although the term does not appear in the jurists, it does appear occasionally in works in other genres. Both Pliny the Elder and Suetonius say that Augustus subjected his adopted son Agrippa Postumus, who turned out to be "defiant," to *abdicatio*.[59] Whether these authors are simply borrowing a term from rhetoric as a metaphor to describe a particularly violent parting between a father and son, or whether the term described a wrathful and essentially extralegal act that would have to be formalized after the fact by *exheredatio*, or whether *abdicatio* had real legal existence in some form before Diocletian and Maximian banned it, are all positions that have been held by reputable scholars.[60] I suspect that the last is the least likely: no matter. But all the possibilities illustrate in common how the concept was metastasizing out of rhetoric (its most frequent resort) into the wider Roman world, and all help to explain how someone could attempt to undertake an *abdicatio* in the real world just before AD 287, and thus draw the scowls of Diocletian and Maximian.

Why did the Roman law not simply admit *abdicatio*, or, more likely, a slightly adjusted version—eliminating declamation's immediate lawsuit between the son and father (that being nearly impossible in the Roman legal tradition)? The immediate court hearing aside, *abdicatio* seems to agree very well, rather than conflict, with Roman legal culture—especially the mighty *patria potestas*—and would have been useful in dealing with that figure so dreadful to Roman lawyers, the profligate son, so often subjected to *abdicatio* in declamation, but who in the real Roman law had to be restrained by elaborate legal workarounds.[61] In a world where fathers no longer executed their children, and *abdicatio* was described by a declaimer as "the ultimate thunderbolt of *patria potestas*," the adoption of *abdicatio* into the law might even seem positively necessary.[62] Nevertheless, *abdicatio*, despite being overwhelmingly common in rhetoric, failed to establish itself in the substantive Roman law, and we can say only that the Roman law had its own traditions, Roman jurists liked the way they did things, and that in this case those traditions prevailed over the influence of rhetoric.[63]

## Conclusion

How did the law of rhetoric exert influence upon—and sometimes force its way into—the Roman law? There are some instances, as in the case of Celsus and his opinion about bees, where verbal echoes of a declamation in a legal opinion suggest that a jurist may have borrowed directly from his own declamatory education or experience. And some jurists—such as Marcian—may have been more amenable to such influence than others. But in most cases, we guess, the application of rhetorical law to a real case will have occurred first in a provincial court, where such law was more familiar than real Roman jurisprudence. To noncitizens (the great majority before AD 212), provincial courts were supposed to do justice on the basis of local law. It has recently been suggested that they actually often used Roman law, granting noncitizens a fleeting fictive citizenship for legal convenience. Taking, as I do, a minimalist view of the knowledge of Roman law outside Italy, I am inclined to doubt that.[64] It is rather my suspicion that in provincial courts litigants, advocates, and judges often in practice simply used what they knew best: declamatory law, Latin in the West, Greek in the East. In a fraction of such cases someone—presumably often someone who had lost according to the law of declamation—wrote to Rome to inquire about whether it was correct to apply such a law, and then a jurist (under his own name or, later, the emperor's) will have decided, in full knowledge of what he was doing (for he too had a rhetorical education) whether or not to admit the declamatory law or legal concept to the jurisprudence of the Romans. If it was refused (as it usually was, we guess), it might come knocking again and again until at last, as we saw in the case of *raptus*, it was allowed within the hallowed doors.

The declamatory law of *raptus* battled long for entry into the Roman law, and eventually forced a passage in. More successful invasions were launched by the declamatory laws that treated adultery, manumission, redeeming exposed children, requiring children to be grateful to and support their parents, condemning a false accuser to the punishment for the crime he asserted, and the law against unwritten evildoing. And where no full laws entered, some notions from rhetorical law found homes in the Roman law as well: anatomically appropriate punishments for crimes, the revival of the odd, old punishment for parricide, the weakening of the father's right to execute his children-in-power, legal treatment of suicide, the perplexing legal treatment of bees, recovery of dowry, and who got to sit where in the theater. But in most cases, of course, the law of the declaimers did not gain entry. The surviving corpus of Latin declamations knows of some one hundred and sixty laws. Of those perhaps half were amenable to be included in the Roman law.[65] Our survey has turned up about twenty declamatory laws that can plausibly be suggested to have made their way into the Roman law or had some effect upon it: one-fourth. Such a number is hardly to be relied upon strictly. There are no doubt possible cases of influence that I (and the scholars I have drawn so heavily upon) have missed that would add to the count. And on the other hand, not one of the cases I have adduced can be regarded as certain, and the more moss-backed sort of scholar of the Roman law might well reject a good number—or most, or all—of the instances of influence here suggested. But let us suppose for the sake of argument that one-fourth is not an impossible distance from the real proportion. That means that not merely the three laws I adduced as rejected, the *actio dementiae*, the *actio malae tractationis*, and *abdicatio*, were resisted by the Roman law, but nearly sixty others. The assault upon the Roman laws by the laws of declamation was not a total failure, but mostly a failure. Overall, so far as we can see, for the most part, the law of the jurists resisted the law of the declaimers. And this should come as no surprise. The long resistance of Roman law to rhetorical style alerted us to the fact that the Roman law would be hard for rhetoric to conquer, and hard it turned out to be. But in a few cases, possible.

# Conclusion

## RHETORIC, MAKER OF WORLDS

THE MOST CELEBRATED TRIAL of the second century AD unfolded in the mid-170s at Sirmium, in chilly Pannonia, where the Emperor Marcus Aurelius was resting from his long, low-feverish wars against the rude Germans over the Danube. Hailed before the imperial tribunal in that dismal place—one of the towers of the town was struck down by lightning the day before the proceedings—was none other than Herodes Atticus, once consul at Rome, but even better known as one of the richest men in the empire. Herodes was a public benefactor on a titanic scale—we have noticed his nymphaeum at Olympia in a previous chapter, and even today we can attend the opera in his Odeon at Athens—and also the most famous Greek sophist, show rhetorician, and teacher of rhetoric of his time.

It appears that, among other dubious deeds, Herodes had been trying sneakily to increase his already overweening influence over his home city of Athens by contriving to insert the sons of his freedmen into the governing councils of the Athenian republic, a desecration of those hallowed bodies for which he was sued and that Marcus Aurelius reaffirmed was forbidden. But the emperor punished only the freedmen, and not Herodes himself, despite the sophist's abusive oration openly attacking Marcus (the orator was unhinged by the fact that two favorite servants had been killed by the lightning strike the night before, and so failed to employ tactful "figured speech," see chapter 2). The orator unleashed an unrestrained hurricane of words that startled the Praetorian Prefect into blurting out that Herodes evidently wished to die. "An old man fears little," grumped Herodes as he stomped out of the emperor's court, his opponents unheard. It was left to the cultured emperor to restore the nimbus of elegant antiquity that was supposed to surround a Greek sophist. "Happy those who died in the plague!" he sighed, when the charges against Herodes were detailed by the advocates for the Athenians: he presumably meant the Athenian plague of 430 BC.[1]

As students of the influence of rhetorical education our notice is naturally drawn to the detail that the many and various charges against Herodes seem to have been wrapped up in the general accusation that the sophist was conducting himself as a tyrant at Athens.[2] Nor was this the first time his family had faced such an accusation: Herodes's grandfather, with the unfortunately suggestive name of Hipparchus, had been convicted "on charges of tyranny" and his estate confiscated.[3] Given the ubiquity of tyrants and tyranny themes in ancient education, and what we know of the influence of that education on Roman justice, it is wholly unsurprising that such charges should make their way into court in the real world: the trial before Marcus Aurelius was merely a gentler reverberation of the same declamatory tyranny themes that guided the assassins of Julius Caesar.

The abusive term "tyrant" was, in fact, thrown around ceaselessly in invective, both Latin and Greek, and in Roman-period papyrus petitions in Egypt; even the losers of small-town rumbles accuse those who have thumped them of acting like tyrants.[4] But surprising is the *rarity* of legal charges of tyranny, and the scarcity also, in the Roman empire, of even bland, unangry, factual statements that a man ruled over his city as a tyrant.[5] We can identify what seem to have been monopolized towns, such as early imperial Sparta under C. Julius Eurycles and his family, where an individual or family appears to have enjoyed so predominant a place that we are entitled to guess that little happened without their nod.[6] But such men of preponderant local power were not soberly described as tyrants.

If we are not in fact surprised by this lack of obvious, identified tyrants in the cities of the Roman Empire, that is because we take it for granted that, although the empire was an autocracy at the levels of the emperor and provincial governor, the individual cities of which the empire mostly consisted operated as constitutional republics where decisions were made by consultation and voting, and where officials were chosen by annual election. The degree to which these republics were in practice dominated by the semihereditary oligarchy of rich men who made up the city council, the *curia* or *boulē*, and the extent to which their power was balanced by that of the rest of the male citizenry, acting in the assembly, is controversial and likely to remain so.[7] But it does not matter to us: we notice merely that open and overt leadership of a city by an individual or a single family, however described, seems to have been nearly unknown (the operation of conventional civic mechanisms concealing such domination even in the few monopolized cities). Not only, indeed, were the cities of the empire administered as constitutional republics, they were proud of the fact, in the East even placing personifications of their official bodies on their coins, a mature bearded *boulē* for the council and an unbearded young *demos* for the assembly.[8]

Our overfamiliarity with Roman rule and its ways tends to conceal from us the fact that the chasm between the two ways the empire was administered—an autocracy at the top, and the cities of the empire working as consultative republics beneath—is actually a puzzle. For such an arrangement was hardly inevitable: the Greeks, of course, had the powerful tradition of the self-governing polis to look back upon and preserve, but the Romans could have imposed upon the cities of the East imperial supervision at the city level (as their predecessors the Hellenistic kings sometimes did, and as the Romans were to do, fitfully, under the high Empire and more commonly in the late).[9] Nor did all towns work as free republics: in teeming Egypt formal, autonomous cities with their republican institutions were rare, and most places were ruled by appointed officials. This top-down model could have been expanded outside Egypt, but, for the most part, it was not. In the West, it was perhaps not unnatural for the Romans of the Republic to gather their conquered peoples into cities that were miniature, simplified models of free Rome. But when Rome shifted from Republic to Empire, that shift was not echoed at the city level, a more autocratic Rome by and large leaving city governments alone, and under the Empire cities in the

West continued to be established and to be governed on the Republican model. In the West, too, cities could have been administered by appointed Roman officials, rather than by councils of local notables from whom the two town mayors-cum-judges and other local officials were drawn, but for the most part they were not. Historical comparison to other societies yields parallels pointing both ways: in some monarchies (as often in Asia) the monarchical principle was reproduced down to the village level, while in other places rich established parcels of a monarch's realm might be governed internally in a wholly non-monarchical fashion. Think of the proud, free, chartered cities of the European Middle Ages, and the uncooperative torment they were to the kings who claimed sovereignty over them.

It is appealing to suppose that rhetorical education had something to do with the continuing strength of republican institutions at the city level under the Roman Empire. The actual themes upon which young men declaimed, the laws and characters and details of the cases, were perhaps less important than the ideological assumptions that lay behind rhetorical education, picked up unconsciously by students of rhetoric. Rhetoric assumed not only that the man who killed a tyrant (tyranny, where such institutions and rights were in abeyance, was always exceptional and bad) would receive a reward, but that he lived in a city as free to make decisions about that reward as it was about the rest of its internal affairs, a city where civic decisions were made by consultation.[10] The experience of rhetorical education rendered any other form of organization at the city level nearly unimaginable to the ruling class of the Roman Empire, and, by rendering it nearly unimaginable, in practice constituted a bulwark protecting the traditional *polis* or *civitas* structure.[11]

Levels of government above that of the city—province, kingdom, or empire—were, by contrast, invisible in forensic declamation, but instruction in deliberative oratory consisted in large part of giving advice to monarchs and potentates (and training in demonstative oratory, although we see it less clearly, will have consisted mostly of training in praise of just such persons).[12] And so, above the level of the city, rhetorical education created no expectations that posed an obstacle to autocratic rule; indeed, if anything, it created a certain expectation or at least acceptance that rule at the highest level would be autocratic. The ideological assumptions rhetorical education created in the heads of young men about how the political world would be structured at its different levels helped the curious superimposition of different regimes that was the Roman Empire to subsist. It was not intended that way—rhetorical education was not a devious program of propaganda unleashed by some imperial office: the imperial authorities took almost no interest in such things. But that was the way it worked.

More widely, the real Greeks and no less so the real Romans were legally minded folk. They considered that they lived in societies governed and defined by law, that adherence to law was important and natural, and that it was right and proper and normal to settle their differences by litigation according to law.[13] That they did so in fact is another thing we take for granted about the Greeks and Romans, but that actuality is a puzzle. In a world without police, and where the commoners had families equipped with flails and wolf spears and the great had swarms of slaves that could easily be turned into armed retinues, why did they bother with litigation? Why did they not depend instead on what is so charmingly called "self-help"? It is true that we see enough violence in the ancient evidence—especially in the papyri from Egypt—to grasp that the Greek and Roman reliance upon going to court to resolve disputes was hardly inevitable.[14] And for serious matters, relying on the formal machinery of Roman justice might be regarded as positively perverse. Important legal affairs—serious crimes, high-value suits over money and property—had to go before Roman judges, the governor or his handful of designates, and a vast number of would-be litigants pursued a tiny number of exhausted officials. The single document we have offering a number reveals the Prefect of Egypt receiving 1,804 petitions— most of which will have been requests for hearings—in slightly over two days.[15] And even if we lacked that papyrus document, we could tell from official scrawls on countless other papyrus petitions that by far the most usual official disposition of petitions in Egypt (when they were not simply thrown away) was to forward them to another official—higher or lower or of equal rank in the system, which was far better manned in Egypt than elsewhere in the empire—thus casting them into a vast, slow-swirling Sargasso Sea of pleas for hearings never likely be heard, or, if by some chance or miracle of influence they were successful, likely to secure justice very slowly, perhaps in a matter of generations rather than years.[16]

Given the existence of speedier alternatives, and the foreseeable frustrations of Roman justice, at least at the level of the provincial governor, the practice of justice by litigation probably needed ideological help. And it is very tempting to guess that the continued belief in a world of laws and litigation was strongly reinforced by the relentless forensic declamation that dominated the last years of Greco-Roman education.

Even more widely, competition between members of the rhetorically educated classes was fundamental to the working of the Roman Empire, and upon exploitation of that competition the ruling of the empire and the finances of the empire's cities largely depended: cities relied as much on gifts from the rich as they did on taxes, and cities' officials were local notables who often paid for the right to serve, in order to surpass their rivals in distinction. Competition between the rich of Asia Minor in public benefaction—games, handouts of food and money, buildings—under the High Empire became so extravagant, so much like a potlatch, as to ruin some competitors; governors were consequently required to approve major public benefactions. Competition, even self-destructive competition, was, of course, deeply rooted in the culture of the ancient Greeks and Romans (think of Hector's decision to come out and fight Achilles, who, he knew, would kill him). And it is perhaps superfluous to suggest either ideological accelerators to, or brakes on, this, perhaps the most powerful and creative force in the Roman Empire. Still, the common culture created by rhetorical training, and especially by forensic declamation, was not one of cooperation and solidarity, but of discord and rivalry: "School is like a gladiator school: the forum is the arena itself," said the Elder Seneca.[17] Rhetorical education taught its students not to hold hands but to scrap, to seek out arenas in which to struggle against each other.[18] More tangibly, it was rhetorical education that defined the arenas in which competition between its students should be carried on—in the council house (as the deliberative genre covertly taught), the courts (forensic declamation), and public benefaction (demonstrative oratory). Although each of those competitions had deep historical roots, the rich of the empire might at any stage have adopted other competitions (as eventually they did, when they took up being quarrelsome bishops) or elevated less prominent competitions (athletics, say, or music) to the first rank. That the great men of Greece and Rome so long confined themselves to the same competitions may be in large part the consequence of their educations, which formed a feedback loop with their deeds as adults: for what adults competed in, teachers were encouraged to teach their sons to speak about, and what sons were taught to speak about, adults often competed in.

So much, then, for possible large-scale ideological functions of rhetorical education. But rhetoric had effects beyond ideology. It is conventional to note that rhetorical education created for the ruling class of the empire a fully worked-out imagined community—a parallel universe, if you like—an ideal city with characteristic institutions, ways of doing things, and structures, where people spoke and behaved just so.[19] But this complete, seamless city imagined by rhetoric, this "Sophistopolis" in the happy coinage of Donald Russell, defeats the category into which our contemporary thinking would urge it.[20] For it is not a thing of ideology—or, in the more up-to-the moment term, an "imaginary"— because everybody knew, and critics of rhetorical education relentlessly complained, that the highly elaborated world that was used in rhetorical education *was not real*.[21] Petronius writes, "Our young men in school become complete idiots, I think, because they never hear or see anything that happens in real life!"[22]

This understood-by-contemporaries artificiality of the world of rhetoric allowed ancient people the critical distance to use Sophistopolis to think about their own lives and cities. Enabled by an awareness of this artificiality, this critical distance, "Rhetoric . . . was an interpretive scheme. It framed Romans' understanding of human motives while it also provided templates for discussing the nature and operations of government, religion, and social institutions."[23] The historical significance of rhetorical training consisted in part of its unconscious, ideological power over its students—thus the story of the killing of Caesar. But holding the artificial ideal of Sophistopolis in his mind, and comparing it to his own city, a student of rhetoric could *consciously* grasp, and *consciously* imagine, what his city should be like. How the city should be ruled, and that no one man should be allowed to rule it. How justice should be done. The buildings it should build. How a man should speak, carry himself, and behave. Perhaps rhetorical education was as much a thinking machine as it was an ideological machine.

This known artificiality of the world of rhetoric—of Sophistopolis—lets us account for one of the most interesting aspects of the influence of rhetorical education: its moments of weakness. Given the universality of rhetorical education and the literary study upon which it was based, we wonder why it did not take over the whole world of thought. And in relatively shallow-rooted realms of the intellect, such as Latin poetry, rhetoric indeed blew down the trees: read Ovid or Lucan or Statius. But rhetoric could give conflicting orders (as we saw in the case of rhetoric's views of city walls); and it could crash into reality and be defeated or resisted by deeper-rooted intellectual forces. So, while every upper-class boy praised the water supply of his city, those who did so while shivering from the perpetual damps and downpours of the northwestern provinces did not, when they came of age, and unlike their brothers in dry provinces, seek to embody that praise by building gigantic fountains. Here wet and bone-chilling reality defeated rhetoric.

As we have seen with the Roman law, moreover, when faced with an older, well-established, and well-defended intellectual tradition that thought and spoke differently, rhetoric was for centuries thrown back. The law of rhetoric gnawed at the boundaries of the Roman law, while never touching Roman law's fundamental assumptions and dogmas, and, even in the limited areas of jurisprudence in which the law of rhetoric interested itself, rhetorical laws often found themselves resisted by the Roman law, although in some cases they triumphed after a dogged, centuries-long assault. And if Roman law resisted taught rhetoric, so might have other strong, venerable, self-conscious literary and intellectual traditions—that of Greek technical manuals, for example, or medicine, philosophy, and history—traditions in some cases older than rhetorical education becoming nearly universal among the upper classes, and which are at least as likely as the Roman law to have maintained their intellectual integrity and independence.[24] The *stylistic* independence from rhetoric that the Roman law preserved until around the year AD 300 few other Latin genres can claim, as a dip into Tacitus or Frontinus's *On Aqueducts* quickly shows.[25] But regardless of these genres' styles, their deeper logic and rules also proved resistant, just like Roman law, to the sway of formal rhetoric. Thus was limited what in an older, grouchier age was termed "the unwholesome *rapport* between the rhetorical schools and the literature of the empire."[26] We should imagine rhetoric as a vast, permanent cloud shaping and obscuring the sharp edges of Roman civilization at a certain level. The poor, living in the terrible clarity down where the cloud did not reach, were fated to live in reality: such has always been the fate of the poor. But the leaders of society lived within the cloud, and around their lives and thinking that cloud swirled. But not all of them and not all the time. For from the top of that cloud some mountains emerged—we have looked at the Roman law—oddly and interestingly impervious, because they operated upon a logic too alien to that of taught rhetoric to be replaced by the logic of taught rhetoric.

Let us, finally, celebrate the conscious artificiality of the world created by rhetorical education. Let us admire Sophistopolis: as the work of millions of mouths over centuries, the labor of teachers, students, and adult rhetoricians, it was perhaps the single greatest collective work of art, the greatest common act of the imagination, in the history of mankind. We must stand in awe of its centuries of longevity: with no master artist, no curator, no guidance public or private, it was kept gleaming and nearly unchanged for centuries. It hung over Mauretanian Volubilis just as it hung over Athens, over Jordanian Petra as it did over Rome, over Spanish Italica as it did over Ephesus. And if the real buildings at real Volubilis look rather like cousins of those at Athens, and those of Italica look like the stiff uncles of the buildings at Ephesus, and if those at Petra look like the unsuitable boyfriends of the buildings at Rome, this was so not from the homogenizing effect of mass media or the conveniences of mass production (neither of which the ancients knew), but from having, for centuries, all alike been in thrall to that tyrant, Persuasion.

# NOTES

## Preface

1. Wilde 1921 [1889], 30.

2. Twain 1982 [1883] quoted 502. On the influence of Walter Scott in the US South, Wyatt-Brown 2001, 138–139, 181.

3. Twain 1982 [1883] quoted 468, 500, 501, on which see Orions 1941 and Seelye 2001.

4. Leonard 1949, esp. 25–65; adopted by H. Thomas 2014 esp. xv-xvi.

5. Cf. Griffin 1985 [1976], 3–4.

6. Rogers 2009.

7. Champlin 2013.

8. Turner 1974, 60–155, quoted 64, and for acting against one's interests (123); Turner and Turner 1978, 248–249.

9. See Lehnert 1920, 223–226, 230–232, 250–255 for pre-1914 work tracing the influence of rhetoric on Latin poetry and other nonhistorical writing. For more recent work on Latin, Lentano 1999, 600–605; Berti 2007, 265–358; and the appropriate essays in Dominik and Hall 2007; Poignault and Schneider 2015; and Lentano 2015a. Cairns 1972 was especially influential. For rhetorical influence on Greek writing, see Fernández Delgado 2007 and the appropriate essays in Porter 1997 and Worthington 2007. For both Greek and Latin, see the essays in Richter and Johnson 2017.

10. See Higham 1958 (cf. Schiesaro 2002, 70–74) for the perplexities presented in trying to make a case *against* overwhelming rhetorical influence in Ovid, who is an especially interesting case, because Seneca the Elder identifies him as a declaimer in his youth (*Contr.* 2.2.8–12, 9.5.17, with Fantham 2009, 27–29). Williams 1980 tried to argue for a period of Latin poetry free of rhetorical influence; and Griffin 1985 [1981]) made an indirect attack on Cairns 1972. But going the other way, Gunderson 2016, 186–190 has no better luck denying the influence of drama on declamation.

11. So this author has argued about Latin history-writing in Lendon 2009, with literature. For tracing the influence of taught rhetoric in (mostly) Latin historians, and the controversy before 1914, Lehnert 1920, 218–223.

## Section I: The Strange World of Education in the Roman Empire

1. Just as the older histories of education—gathered by Vössing 1997, 10–11 nn. 6–7, 12 n. 9, and passim for the older scholarly literature—were superseded by Marrou 1971 [1948] = 1956; Clarke 1971; and Bonner 1977; so those later treatments, although still valuable, are now in large

part superseded by Cribiore 2001 and Wolff 2015; augmented by Morgan 1998, on Greek education for younger pupils; Bloomer 2011a on Roman education with attention to modern educational theory; and the essays in Bloomer 2015a for up-to-date accounts of ancient education in
all its aspects.

2. For general histories of rhetoric in the Roman centuries, Clarke 1996 [1953]; Kennedy
1972, 1983; and Pernot 2000 [2005], 115–263. For a taxonomy of mature ancient rhetorical theory,
Lausberg 1998 [1973]; Martin 1974. For lack of change in rhetorical teaching over time and
distance, passim in the scholarship, but see esp. Cribiore 2007, 147–148; Barrow 2015; and
Keeline 2018, 15. Note especially the Hermogenic corpus, which came together in the late
second or early third century AD, and remained standard until the fall of Byzantium (Heath
2002, 424), which, at over a thousand years, is a pretty good run for a set of textbooks.

## Chapter 1: Education in the Roman Empire

1. The first teacher was usually called the *ludi magister*—in Greek *grammatistes* or
*grammatodidaskalos*—and his (or occasionally her) school the *ludus* or *grammatodidaskaleion*,
Cribiore 2001, 19, 36–44, 50–53, 160–184. For the various titles held by teachers at all levels in
both Greek and Latin, Kaster 1988, 443–452. For teaching arithmetic, Vössing 1997, 317–318;
Cribiore 2001, 180–183; Sidoli 2015, 389–390. Cribiore 2001, 74–101 also finds abundant evidence
for the education of girls, but mostly at this elementary level.

2. Poetry, North 1952; Cribiore 2001, 53–56, 185–219, and esp. 140–142, 179 (cf. Morgan 1998,
69, 71, 313, 320–322) for the *Iliad*, with a strong emphasis on books 1 and 2. For the *Aeneid*,
Winterbottom 1982 [2019], 243, 246; Vössing 1997, 371 n. 1276; Morgan 1998, 317 (cf. 71). In the
*Ars minor* of Donatus, Virgil is cited 122 times (with a strong emphasis on *Aeneid* book 1, which
is also confirmed by the graffiti from Pompeii, 106), and the next most frequent author, Ennius,
only eight; Virgil was also the basic text when Latin was taught to Greek-speakers, Rochette
1997, 188–198, 263–279. For the *Aeneid*'s ubiquity in the empire, see also Hedrick 2011, 167–170.

3. Cribiore 2001, 56–59, 220–244. Several years: Petit 1957, 65 deduced that three years was
the normal course in Libanius's school in fourth-century Antioch, but Cribiore 2007, 31–33,
174–183 makes trenchant criticisms of Petit's method, suggesting that there was no standard
period of attendance.

4. Topics similar or identical over time: letting us pass by the question of the exact dating
of the declamations coming down under the name of Calpurnius Flaccus (Sussman 1994—early
second century AD, with earlier literature; Balbo 2016, third century AD or later; Santorelli
2017a second half of the second century AD); and the pseudo-Quintilianic *Major Declamations*
(= *DM*), which scholars string out in packets from the first century AD through the fourth
(without any agreement as to which should go when). For the older scholarship, Brescia 2004,
23–26 with a convenient table (25), revealing the extent of disagreement; the major recent contribution is the posthumous Håkanson 2014, summarized by Santorelli 2014, 38–45, with all of
the *Major Declamations* finally gathered into a collection in the late fourth century, Schneider
2000. None of the suggested dates for individual *Major Declamations* are to be relied upon. In
contrast to the wrangling over the *DM*, scholars seem content to date the pseudo-Quintilianic
*Minor Declamations* (= *DMin.*) to around AD 100, because they adhere so closely to Quintilian's

teaching, e.g., Winterbottom 1984, xv. We are also delighted to be able to walk around the question of the spuriousness of some (but which?) of the declamations of Libanius, Najock 2007: real or spurious, they are much the same.

5. Tac. *Dial.* 35.4; Quint. *Inst.* 2.1.2–3. The Latin *declamatio* was simply *meletē* ("exercise") in Greek, but the word *declamatio* may have started meaning something closer to "voice exercise" (Stroh 2003).

6. On the *progymnasmata*, Webb 2001; Kraus 2005; Berardi 2017, 228–256 et passim; and Chiron 2017, a magificent commented bibliography covering works back to the 1500s. For English translations of the surviving textbooks, Kennedy 2003, and for collections of such exercises attributed to the fourth-century Libanius, Gibson 2008 (for the actual authorship of the Libanius collection, to which we are indifferent, see xxiii-xxv) and Ureña Bracero 2007. The pseudo-Aristotelian *Rhetorica ad Alexandrum* (ca. 340 BC) knew the term *progymnasmata* (1436A); Cicero's *de Inventione* (ca. 91–88 BC) and the *Rhetorica ad Herennium* (ca. 88–82 BC) were familiar with the practice, Kennedy 2003, xi. For the dates of these Latin works, Gaines 2007, 169–170, and Frazel 2009 finds extensive traces of the *progymnasmata* in Cicero's Verrine orations (70 BC), implying that they were present at Rome at the time of Cicero's education in the 90s (on the early history of the *progymnasmata*, Frazel 2009, 26–28). Dating the earliest surviving textbook of *progymnasmata* depends on the date of the *Progymnasmata* of Theon, which is disputed. It is traditionally dated to the first century AD (Kennedy 2003, 1), although Patillon prefers the first half of the second century AD (Patillon and Bolognesi 1997, viii-xvi), Chiron 2017, 17 either the first or second century, and Heath 2002–2003, 158 would move the work to the fourth or fifth century AD. *Non liquet*, and I do not depend on Theon's date in my arguments.

7. Variety, Kaster 1983; Cribiore 2001, 18; Maurice 2013, 2–10.

8. Booth 1979a and 1979b—endorsed by Kaster 1983, emphasizing the likelihood of variation over place and time—argued for the social differentiation of primary teaching, with the poor free and slaves going to the *ludus* while the children of the wealthy were taught the basics at home. But in North Africa, at least, even the children of the well-off attended the *ludus*, Vössing 1997, 317, 563–567. For tutoring at home we know most about the imperial family, Parker 1946; Rawson 2003, 162; which may, of course, have been somewhat unusual.

9. Marrou 1971 [1948], 374–388 = Marrou 1956, 255–264; further, on Greek in the West, Vössing 1997, 375–377. Greek aspired to but hardly invariably learned, or learned to a good standard, by Latin speakers of high station: Horsfall 1979 and Adams 2003. On Latin in the East, Gaebel 1969–1970; Rochette 1997, 165–210, 257–319; Eck 2000 and 2009; Dickey 2012–2015, 1.4–6.

10. *Progymnasmata* varying in number and order, Suet. *Gram. et Rhet.* 25.4 (Kaster); Patillon and Bolognesi 1997, xiii-xv; Kennedy 2003, xiii; and Pernot 2008 suspects an even larger degree of variation. Who teaches which? Quint. *Inst.* 1.9, 2.1–4 (and grammarians might even teach *suasoriae*, the next stage after *progymnasmata*), with Kaster 1995, 279–280; Cribiore 2007, 143–144; Penella 2015, 161.

11. Free education unknown: notice the mention of paying the teacher in the "glossaries," a genre intended for young children, Dickey 2012–2015, 2.22, 2.96. Harris 1989, 130–135, 244 gathers Hellenistic and Roman inscriptions recording foundations established to pay teachers—on which Ziebarth 1914 is still well worth consulting—but the number of cases where a foundation

provided for free education is tiny, and only one is known from the Roman period. Teachers under the Roman Empire who received imperial or civic salaries, or rent-free classrooms, or enjoyed immunity from civic burdens (see esp. *CTh.* 13.3), nevertheless charged fees (Laes and Strubbe 2014 [2008], 82–85). On teachers' fees, salaries, and other emoluments, Kaster 1988, 114–123; Vössing 1997, 335–339.

12. *Calculator,* and also the *notarius,* the teacher of shorthand writing (Mart. 10.62.4; the pair appear again in the glossaries, Dickey 2012–2015, 2.170–171; cf. Vössing 1997, 577), probably teaching very humble students, Booth 1979a. In Egypt the functions of *notarius,* and the teacher of bookhand, and the *calculator* were combined in a scribal school, which also taught more complex math, Cribiore 2001, 182–183; and elsewhere primary-school teachers could also teach shorthand, Kaster 1988, 45. For apprenticeship, Laes 2015 with literature.

13. For various versions of the list of Greek writers read in the rhetor's school under the Roman Empire, Rutherford 1998, 37–63; Patillon 2007; and Vix 2010, 345–365, who demonstrates the primacy of Homer, Demosthenes, and Plato. For younger children, Cribiore 2001, 142–143, 179, 194–204. For Latin authors, Vössing 1997, 371 n. 1277; 513 n. 1711; Morgan 1998, 97, 317, for authors referred to in Quintilian (Cicero: 802 instances; Virgil: 156; Horace: 26; then others with fewer). For the canonization of Cicero, Winterbottom 1982 [2019]; Kaster 1998; Keeline 2018; and La Bua 2019; and Cicero was used alongside Virgil (for whom see this chapter n. 2) when Latin was taught to Greek speakers, Rochette 1997, 188–198, 279–286.

14. Those growing up in smaller places would thus have to lodge (presumably with friends of their parents) in larger towns, perhaps for years, Kaster 1988, 21–22; Cribiore 2001, 54, 57–58; Cribiore 2007, 117–118. The implication of Kaster 1988, 20, 106–107 is that it was towns large enough to be the seats of bishops in late antiquity that could command the services of grammarians, and that sounds about right.

15. Architecture, Hadot 2005 [1984], 449–451; Capriglione 2007; Pollitt 2015, 379–380; and esp. Vitr. *de Arch.* 1.3–18 (an aspirational, rather than actual, education: Romano 1990, 47–141). Medicine, Marrou 1971 [1948], 288–291 = 1956, 192–193; Hadot 2005 [1984], 456–467; Laes and Strubbe 2014 [2008], 184–186, 188; Boudon-Millot 2008, with literature; Bannert 2015; and esp. Lucian, *Abdicatus* 4.

16. See Lib. *Ep.* 1208 (= Cribiore 2007, 252 nr. 45 for English translation) for a student of Libanius who pursued medicine after his rhetorical training, and such was necessarily the case for the somewhat mysterious *iatrosophistai,* medical rhetoricians of late antiquity, Eunap. *VS* 497–499; Cracco Ruggini 2003, 197–199; Hadot 2005 [1984], 463–464; and similarly the doctors told of in Ausonius, Cracco Ruggini 2003, 207 n. 36, with 207–210 for other highly educated doctors in the West.

17. On Galen's education (Mattern 2013, 29–80 and Petit 2018), a course of education that also seems to be envisaged in the educational works of Plutarch and pseudo-Plutarch (Morgan 2007, 313; Xenophontos 2015, esp. 336–337), and, at least as a debating point, in Sen. *Ep.* 88 (with Keeline 2018, 216–217). But the great physician may have had a fuller rhetorical education than he admits to (Petit 2018, 8–12).

18. General, but not universal, especially for curial families in financial difficulties, such as that of St. Augustine, Kaster 1988, 23 and 25. Cf. Apul. *Apol.* 98.6–9 for a boy from a wealthy family in North Africa who "speaks nothing but Punic, and although he has picked up a bit of Greek from his mother, he will not and cannot speak Latin."

19. I have tried here to give a fair portrait of current majority thinking about the history of ancient rhetorical education, without the obnoxious insertion of too many of my own notions.

20. Assemblies in Homer, Christensen 2015 for literature. Heroic speech-giving in Homer, Schofield 1986; Roisman 2007 with literature. Heath 2002, 419–421 draws the link between Homer and later rhetoric.

21. *Il.* 3.222–223.

22. Contrast the traditional "early origins" (fifth-century BC) theory of Marrou 1971 [1948], 92 = Marrou 1956, 53 or Grimaldi 1996 with the "late origins" (mid-to-late fourth-century BC) theory of Cole 1991, who thinks that attestation of the earlier systemization of rhetoric, found in Plato and Aristotle, is their retrospective invention. Kremmydas and Tempest 2013, 2 n. 6 collect the literature.

23. On Gorgias, Bons 2007.

24. Gorgias, Pl. *Meno* 70. Sparta, Schmitz 2006; Lendon 1997a, 122–123.

25. *Il.* 3.213–215. In rhetorical theory of the Roman period, Menelaus and Odysseus were to become emblems of plain and grand style, along with Nestor for the middle style, Penella 2011, esp. 98–99.

26. The *Rhetoric to Alexander* dated to *ca.* 340, Chiron 2007, 101–102; Aristotle's *Rhetoric*, different parts of which are dated from the mid-350s to the late 340s (Fortenbaugh 1996), with proto-*idea* theory clearly visible in Book 3; the theory of style would be developed further under Aristotle's successor Theophrastus, Innes 1985. For the history of *idea* theory, Rutherford 1998, 6–36; Patillon 2002a, xxiii-lxiv; 2012, xxv-xxxiii.

27. For Hellenistic developments in rhetorical education, Pernot 2000 [2005], 82–114; Vanderspoel 2007, with 128 for standardization; Kremmydas 2013, 148–152. For Hermagoras and *stasis* theory, Patillon 1988, 56–70; Woerther 2012, xiii-xxv, lv-lxxii. For the later history of *stasis* theory, Heath 1994. For a gentle introduction to how *stasis* theory might be used in speeches (real-world or declamatory), Berry and Heath 1997.

28. Origins of declamation, Russell 1983, 15–20; Brink 1989, 500–502. Two different ancient traditions (neither of them worth much) associated the birth of declamation with Aeschines in exile (330–315 BC) or Demetrius of Phaleron (after 297 BC?).

29. Late arrival of the science of the *grammaticus* (grammar), Morgan 1998, 57–58, 63, 152–156, 290–291; Booth 1978 dates this victory around 100 BC. And the teaching of grammar appears only to have been standardized in late Roman times, Kaster 1988, 139; Cribiore 2001, 211–212. What the grammarian taught: Bonner 1977, 189–249; Kaster 1988, 11–19; Atherton 1996.

30. Traditional Athenian education, Pritchard 2015 with literature.

31. For musical education in general, Hagel and Lynch 2015. For Hellenistic instruction in music and poetry (and inscriptions suggesting instruction in drawing and calligraphy), Marrou 1971 [1948], 205–217 = Marrou 1956, 133–141; Nilsson 1955, 45–47; Del Corso 2007, 165–176.

32. Gymnasium and *ephebeia*, Kennell 2015 with literature; for the origins of the *ephebeia* and its Hellenistic *floruit*, Chankowski 2010. The *ephebeia* is now known in almost two hundred locations (Kennell 2015, 172); for its length, Chankowski 2010, 242–249 gives a range, although Kennell 2015, 174 thinks one year was normal. On the gymnasium, Delorme 1960 is the classic study, and see the essays in Kah and Scholz 2004.

33. Zanker 1993, 220. I thank N. Lindberg for directing me to this paper.

34. Pl. *Resp.* 525C-531C, 536D.

35. Kühnert 1961 is the standard treatment.

36. Hadot 2005 [1984]; and for *enkyklios paideia* and *artes liberales* meaning "the common education" cf. Lausberg 1998 [1973], 9.

37. Disappearance of Greek music and athletics in the spread of Greek education to Rome, Marrou 1971 [1948], 363–366 = 1956, 247–249. But they remained popular outside the curriculum, Rawson 2003, 170–173. Despite its increasing professionalization, athletics remained an important upper-class pursuit in the Greek world under the Empire, van Nijf 2001. No regular Roman military training until Augustus, Bannard 2015, 485–493.

38. Puech 2002 reflects on, and De Hoz 2007 describes, the evolution of Greek inscriptions touching on educational matters from the Hellenistic to the Roman imperial age.

39. Possible decline of athletics and music in the East, Marrou 1971 [1948], 201–204, 212–217 = 1956, 130–132, 138–141. In principle the schoolroom papyri and ostraca from Ptolemaic Egypt—on which Cribiore 1996; Morgan 1998, 275–322—should help us follow any narrowing of Greek education, but they taper in number sharply as the sophistication of the lessons increases, being for the most part products of small-town primary schools, or, to a lesser extent, of the schools of grammarians.

40. Expulsion, Suet. *Gram. et Rhet.* 25.2 (Kaster) with Kaster 1995 ad loc. Advent of Greek rhetoric at Rome, Connolly 2007a; Stroup 2007. Bloomer 2011a, 17–36 catalogues what little can be known or guessed (or was later imagined) of Roman education before the first century BC.

41. Military service, McCall 2002, 116–117; many aristocrats continued to serve when no longer obliged to, Suolahti 1955, although the higher levels of aristocracy—the sons of senators—less frequently.

42. *Tirocinium fori,* Richlin 2011 (cf. David 1992, 334–341), who can find no ancient attestation of the phrase, but the practice certainly existed: Cic. *Cael.* 9–11, the 60s BC (p. 94); the 40s BC (pp. 100–101), gathering hints from Cicero's letters. Quintilian, Tacitus, and Pliny refer to it as an extinct habit by the late first or early second century AD (Richlin 2011, 96–98), but there are traces of survival in the period of the Empire (Richlin, 2011, 97–98); van den Berg 2014, 72–75, 183–184. Also possible: just hanging around the courts and assemblies and listening, as Cicero did (Cic. *Brut.* 304–305), or listening to jurisconsults and philosophers (Cic. *Brut.* 306–309).

43. Censors' disapproval in 92 BC, Suet. *Gram. et Rhet.* 25.2 (Kaster); Aul. Gell. 15.11.2; cf. Cic. *de Or.* 3.93–95 (probably getting the facts wrong) with Pina Polo 1996, 81–88; and Calboli 2016, 808 for literature on this much-discussed incident. Treatises: the *Rhetorica ad Herennium* and Cicero's *de Inventione*, and see n. 6, this chapter, for their dates. Same or similar declamatory themes, Cic. *Inv. Rhet.* 1.17, 1.102–103, 2.144; *Rhet. Her.* 1.19, 2.49, proving false, as Fairweather 1981, 124–131 and Berti 2007, 110–114 noted, Seneca the Elder's claim (*Contr.* 1.pr.12) that declamation at Rome was no older than he. For what it is worth, Cicero also imagines declamatory themes in use in 91 BC (*de Or.* 2.100), and himself recalls declaiming in his youth (*Brut.* 310; *Tusc.* 1.7; *Q Fr.* 3.3.4). For the use of *progymnasmata* at Rome in the 90s and 80s BC, see n. 6, this chapter.

44. For Romans who travelled to Greece to finish their rhetorical training—remarkable because we know of so many, implying many more we do not know—Rawson 1985, 9–12; David 1985, 346. Great Romans might also keep Greek rhetoricians in their retinues, David 1992, 348–349.

45. Cicero went to Greece at age twenty-seven or twenty-eight while his son Marcus went at fourteen (and back again at nineteen, when he got into so much trouble) and his nephew Quintus at sixteen, Treggiari 2015, 244, 247, 249. For others, displaying the same changing pattern, Daly 1950.

46. The sense that rhetorical education at Rome was unsatisfactory in the 80s and earlier dovetails with the fact that in the 90s Cicero was dissuaded from going to Plotius Gallus's school of Latin rhetoric (Suet. *Gram. et Rhet.* 26.1 [Kaster]).

47. For complaints about the decline of oratory, e.g., Cic. *Tusc.* 2.5; *Brut.* 22; and Kennedy 1972, 446–464 and Williams 1978, 7–51 gather the later ancient material.

48. Latin "Atticism" vs. "Asianism," see Fairweather 1981, 243–303; and Kim 2017, 61 for literature.

49. On the Hermogenic *corpus*, Patillon 1988, 8–12; growth, Rabe 1931, xix-xxiii; importance, Heath 2002, 424. Minucianus, Heath 1995, 243 with literature.

50. For an introduction to demonstrative oratory, Pernot 2015, with Dugan 2005, 24–31 for demonstrative's uncomfortable place in rhetorical theory and Roman practice.

51. Encomium in the *progymasmata*: Theon, *Prog.* 109–112 (Spengel); [Hermog.] *Prog.* 14–18 (Rabe); Aphthonius, *Prog.* 21–27 (Rabe); Nicolaus, *Prog.* 47–58 (Felten—these are all the numerations used in the English translations of Kennedy 2003); Lib. *Prog.* 8.209–328 (Foerster) = Gibson pp. 197–319 (English translation). Returned to after *progymnasmata*: Theon, *Prog.* 61 (Spengel); not, Nicolaus, *Prog.* 47 (Felton).

52. Pernot 1993, 60–62 finds encomium in surviving speeches of other types, and the second-century AD Fronto (Fleury 2006, 101–134, 221–281) implies a rhetorical education with more emphasis on epideictic than the first-century AD Quintilian.

53. See Cribiore 2001, 228 for the "lion's share" of surviving rhetorical exercises on papyri being those of *ethopoiiai* (with Heusch 2005) and *encomia* (with Pordomingo 2007, 416–435).

54. Rabe 1931, 171; on this Athanasius see Heath 2002–2003, 139. Pernot 1993, 59–60 discusses the invasion of other *progymnasmata* by encomiastic elements; cf. Webb 2009, 78–80. Students who had recently left Libanius's school were certainly capable of giving encomiastic speeches, Cribiore 2007, 146; cf. Dickey 2012–2015, 2.99; and Aristid. *Or.* 31.10 (Behr) with Vix 2010, 51–65 for a student of Aristides who dropped down dead while pronouncing a panegyric.

55. Thus Heath 2004, 277–279, against earlier scholars (including Pernot 1993, 55–105) who proposed a more thorough-going colonization of imperial-period education by epideictic. For general introductions to Latin declamation, Bonner 1949; Lentano 2017a; for Greek, Russell 1983; Guast 2019; all of which offer direction to the sources. Latin declamation has been fortunate in a series of bibliographical review articles surveying the scholarship from 1881 to 2016: Tabacco 1980; Sussman 1984; Håkanson 1986; Lentano 1999; Hömke 2002, with earlier lists at 338; Lentano 2017b. Vössing 1995, 92 lists the 388 Latin declamations and declamation-like poems surviving, while Santorelli and Stramaglia 2015 and Stramaglia 2015 gather declamations mentioned in other sources but which do not survive, the latter with a list of papyri. Another help is the list in Kohl 1915 of over four hundred declamatory themes featuring named persons from myth or history (many of the themes deliberative, in which branch of declamation giving advice to such figures, or in the voice of such figures, was usual).

56. Agamemnon, Sen. *Suas.* 3.pr.; Sulla, Quint. *Inst.* 3.8.53 (cf. Juv. 1.15–17). For deliberative declamation, Lausberg 1998 [1973], 97–102; Bonner 1977, 277–287; Migliario 2007, 33–50;

Feddern 2013; Kraus 2016. For deliberative themes in Latin see Seneca the Elder's *Suasoriae*; Kohl 1915 for Greek.

57. Quint. *Inst.* 3.8, but note that Quintilian does not always agree with this standard account.

58. Generally on forensic declamation, of which much more survives than deliberative, see Parks 1945, 67–85; Bonner 1949; Lausberg 1998 [1973], 63–97; Bonner 1977, 288–325; Lentano 2014a.

59. Sen. *Contr.* 4.4, slightly simplified.

60. *DM* 1.*pr.* For evil stepmothers (*novercae*) see chapter 8 n. 49.

61. Cases should be balanced, Hermog. *Stat.* 33–34 (Rabe); Anon. Ἕτερα προλεγόμενα τῶν στάσεων (Walz, *RG* 7.1 p. 49); Sen. *Contr.* 10.5.12, which is not to say that one side could not by design be stronger than the other, or more popular with declaimers: Brightbill 2015, 27–72. No homicide victim alive, Kaster 2001, 320, although unauthorized facts were indeed sometimes introduced, Brightbill 2015, 73–124, and minor characters as well, to Quintilian's disapproval, *Inst.* 7.2.56. No real-world laws (or contrary laws made up by the declaimer) or "inartificial" proofs, Bloomer 2007, 298, 300; 2011a, 177; that and emphasis on ethos and plausibility, Bernstein 2013, 77. On witnesses, Brightbill 2015, 92–97, who, however, finds some, 94. On *sententiae*, Berti 2007, 155–182. For torture, see chapter 5 n. 19. No sex, Walters 1997, 111; but allusion and innuendo were allowed, Adams 1982, 223. No regional accents, Sinclair 1995, 97; voice and diction, Gleason 1995, 82–130; Connolly 2001b, 84, 88. Atticism, Swain 1996, 17–64; Schmitz 1997, 67–96; Kim 2017, 43–53; and Strobel 2009 for the lexicons and guides to Attic usage that supported this linguistic archaism. Purity of Latin: Adams 2007, 16–17, 114–275; Bloomer 2017. Gestures, bodily deportment, Gleason 1995; Richlin 1997; Connolly 1998, 2007b; Wülfing 2003; Hall 2014.

62. Complaints about themes of and style in declamation, Petron. *Sat.* 1–6 (with Breitenstein 2009); Quint. *Inst.* 2.10, 5.12.17–23, 7.2.54–56, 12.11.15–16 (with Calboli 2010); Tac. *Dial.* 31.1, 35.3–5; Juv. 7.150–170; with Kaster 2001, 323 n. 14 gathering those in Seneca the Elder. Bonner 1949, 71–83; Vössing 1995, 94–102; Hömke 2002, 44–82; and Berti 2007, 219–247 discuss these criticisms; Bloomer 2011a, 240 n. 1 collects more modern writings; and see esp. Fantham 2002 [2011] and Gunderson 2003, 10–12 on how such criticism is to be understood. For discussions of criticism of style, see esp. Brink 1989, 477–482 for Quintilian; and Gleason 1995, 114–121 gathers Quintilian's passages of complaint about incorrect teaching of physical carriage in the rhetorical schools.

63. Imber 2001, drawing on studies of oral traditions in other societies, points also to the orality of declamation as a force for conservatism in teaching.

64. Institutional training in Roman law under the empire and its locations, Ducos 2008, 21–28; for Beirut (the most famous school), McNamee 1998; Jones Hall 2004, 195–220. Schools of Latin in the East, Rochette 1997, 165–177. Libanius's fears (collected at Van Hoof 2010, 221 n. 76) of competition with Greek rhetoric education from schools for *notarii*, Latin, and Roman law were recognized as exaggerated by Liebeschuetz 1972, 242–246, 252–254, and this has since been confirmed: for the continued prevalence of rhetorical education, Heath 2004, 295–299; Cribiore 2007, 207–213; and Van Hoof 2010, 221–223 with literature. Rhetoric prior to study of law: Liebeschuetz 1972, 243 n. 10, 253; Heath 2004, 293–299; Cribiore 2007, 75; Kraus 2013, 129. Students' time split between Greek and Latin rhetoric, Liebeschuetz 1972, 246. Training in

shorthand, Teitler 1985, 24–25, 27–28, 34, 68–69 with former students of Libanius becoming *notarii* after their rhetorical training (66); cf. Kaster 1988, 47–48.

## Chapter 2: The Social and Historial Significance of Rhetorical Education

1. Schmidt 1847, 423–448, 455–456.

2. Caligula, Cass. Dio 59.20.6 with Juv. 7.203–204 (Schmidt 1847, 435); Domitian, Cass. Dio 67.12.5 (Schmidt 1847, 444).

3. Boissier 1875, 99–102 and MacMullen 1966, 35–37; Schmitz 1999, 85 n. 56 gathers other writings. Long ago Schamberger 1917, 60–76 attempted to find in the Latin declamations allusions to contemporary events, a project that, if found compelling, could argue along the same lines.

4. Juv. 7.150–154, *o ferrea pectora Vetti / cum perimit saevos classis numerosa tyrannos. / . . . occidit miseros crambe repetita magistros.* In surviving Greek declamation and Greek works of rhetorical theory, Patillon 2002b, xcv counts eighty-four themes involving tyrants (see also section ii below), making tyranny the third most popular theme after murder (157) and adultery (98). Awareness that the regime did not normally object to declamations about tyrannicide goes back at least to Burckhardt 1949 [1853], 217. For thoughts on the shifts of intellectual category that allowed declamations on tyranny to be safe from imperial disapproval, Vössing 2010.

5. Usurpers, Neri 1997; Haeling 2000, 28–30; Malosse 2006, 172–176; and Swist 2017, 443 n. 42 gathers more discussions.

6. De Salvo 2001.

7. Moral improvement, esp. Quint. *Inst.* 1.pr.9–12, 12.2.27–31; Tac. *Dial.* 31.1–2; Patillon and Bolognesi 1997, xix-xx for passages in the *progymasmata*; and see MacMullen 1976, 27, 277 nn. 17–18; Anderson 1995; Winterbottom 1998 [2019]; Atherton 1998, important on the teaching of grammar; Morgan 1998, 120–151, 226–234; Kaster 2001, important, not least on the "the ability to strut and grovel at the same time" (333); Reinhardt and Winterbottom 2006, xlii-xlix; Pérez Galicia 2011; Gibson 2014; Connolly 2016 and Swist 2017, 442 n. 37 gather more. For confirmation from outside rhetorical authors of the connection between rhetorical education and moral excellence in the ancient mind, Vössing 1997, 605; Schmitz 1997, 136–146.

8. Van der Poel 2007 with literature; Bloomer 2011b, 109 n. 3 with literature; and the essays collected in Galand, Hallyn, Lévy, and Verbaal 2010, 155–396.

9. Contributions are usefully summarized by Breij 2006a, 61–62; Corbeill 2007; Dugan 2007, 16–18; and Lentano 2017b, 148–154.

10. Quoted, Morgan 2007, 317; cf. 197 for those who learned rhetoric but had no professional use for it, and Bloomer 1997b, 62. As a flat-footed historian, I thus pass by, with a respectful nod, (a) primarily literary readings of the declamations, such as Gunderson 2003 and van Mal-Maeder 2007; cf. Connolly 2016, 201 and Lentano 2017a, 62–63 for this trend; (b) readings whose purpose is primarily psychoanalytic, Kennedy 1972, 336–337; Sussman 1995; Gunderson 2000; Schneider 2016; Pasetti 2016; (c) primarily anthropological readings (see this chapter n. 31), another strong tendency currently; and (d) abstract readings such as Schmitz 1999: about rhetoric creating history (an important piece); Goldhill 2009: *Selbstdarstellung*; Morgan 1998, 241, 262–270 and Bloomer 2011a, 7, 117, 134, 195: agency. For other possible approaches see the conclusion to this book. The declamations that survive to us are not, of course, for the most

part, straight from the classroom, and so we must admit the possibility, with Hömke 2007, that many of them were given purely to entertain.

11. Social marker, primarily from Latin evidence: Bloomer 1997b, 62, 66; Atherton 1998, 222–224 (on way of speaking); Connolly 1998, 134–136, 149; 2007b (on deportment); in general, Vössing 1997, 600–604; and this was all to a degree anticipated by Sinclair 1993. Chiefly from Greek evidence, Gleason 1995, esp. xxi-xxvii, 159–168 (on deportment); and generally, on the socially distinctive quality of *paideia*, Brown 1992, 35–47; Schmitz 1997; Morgan 1998, 74–83, 235–236, 243, 270; Connolly 2001a, 349–351; Whitmarsh 2001, 5, 96–130, but admitting that this was not the purpose of *paideia* avowed by the ancients, 129–130. All of this was anticipated by MacMullen 1976, 200. Bloomer 1997a and 1997b, 59 also argued that this education served as a form of acculturation for non-Romans; cf. Vössing 1997, 596–600; Schwartz Frydman 2016; for non-Greeks, Morgan 1998, 74–79, 110, 118, arguing that, because it was laborious and expensive, the numbers of the outsiders so acculturated was limited, which was no doubt true in the minority of cases where students were not already culturally Roman or Greek.

12. Lib. *Or.* 35.15 (= Festugière 1959, 488) with Gleason 1995, 164; cf. Iambl. *VP* 44 with Whitmarsh 2001, 90–91.

13. See Edmondson 2008 on dress. Slaves: even a schoolboy of the Roman period, if upper-class, would be accompanied to school by at least two slaves, his *capsarius/scrinarius* (Dickey 2012–2015, 1.105, 2.169, 2.171 with Rawson 2003, 166) and his *paedagogus* (Dickey 2012–2015, 1.105, 1.110, 1.226, 2.169, 2.173, 2.179); see Suet. *Nero* 36.2 for the pair. Cf. Lucian, *Amores* 44, who describes a "chorus" following the schoolboy. For the luxurious clothing worn by wealthy residents of late-antique Antioch, the crowds of slaves who accompanied them, and the anxiety of the wealthy not to be seen in public without them, Leyerle 1994, 32, 41; 2018, 270–271 gathers the *testimonia* in John Chrysostom.

14. Open to the same question of significance in so hierarchical a society is the social—or political—"legitimation" variation sometimes offered on the social-distinction interpretation: Brown 1992, 41 refers to the "delicate task of making this social superiority appear 'natural' because [it was] rooted in personal skills appropriate to superior persons"; cf. Corbeill 2001 esp. 262–263, 283; Morgan 1998, 270; Schmitz 1997, 44–50; Stenger 2009, 211–217. Against legitimation as an interpretive tool, Lendon 2006, 58–62.

15. Slaves must talk properly, Quint. *Inst.* 1.1.4–5, 8, 11; [Plut.] *Lib. Educ.* 4A; Sor. *Gyn.* 2.19. Parents must model good speech, Atherton 1998, 228; sometimes teach their young children themselves, Cribiore 2001, 105–108; Greschat 2018.

16. Tac. *Dial.* 28.5 with Mayer 2001 ad loc.

17. In primary school, Tert. *Pal.* 6.2, where a Roman student met with what the author ironically calls the *primus enodator vocis*, the "first 'untangler' of the voice." Voice in the school of the *grammaticus*, Clarke 1968, 19–20; for voice in the school of the *rhetor* see chapter 1 n. 61.

18. Vössing 1997, 604–605; Morgan 1998, 74, 79–85, 169–171, 270 for so elaborate an education ranking those *within* its circle. Appetite for competition, Lendon 1997b; Schmitz 1997, 97–135; a tendency revoltingly illustrated, for example, by the competitive displays of doctors, Gleason 2009.

19. E.g., Quint. *Inst.* 1.1.20, 1.2.22–25, 1.2.29, 1.3.11, 5.12.22; Clarke 1968, 19; Morgan 1998, 79–85; Vix 2010, 321, 327–328.

20. *Harenarius*, Tertullian, *Pal.* 6.2 with *OLD* ad loc. and Vössing 1997, 318 n. 1147. This is a *harenarius numerorum*, a low-level instructor in arithmetic. Cf. Sen. *Contr.* 3.pr.13, *scholam quasi ludum esse, forum arenam.* Corbeill 2001, 277–278 gathers speculations as to the etymology of *ludus.*

21. Plut. *Cic.* 2.2; cf. Nepos, *Att.* 1.3.

22. Schmitz 1997, 97–135; Vössing 1997, 435–467, 494–541, 605–613; and esp. Lib. 55.32 (= Festugière 1959, 440). Competitive among adults who were not teachers, cf. Berry and Heath 1997, 408; Quint. *Inst.* bk. 10. And see Zadorojnyi 2019 for the way Pollux's dictionary of Attic words assumes competitiveness among its users.

23. Cribiore 2007, 84–88.

24. For sophists, see especially Philostratus's *Lives of the Sophists*, and for general introductions, Bowersock 1969 (still the best); Anderson 1993; Whitmarsh 2005; with Janiszewski, Stebnicka, and Szabat 2015 for prosopography. For competition among sophists, Bowersock 1969, 89–100; Anderson 1989, 159–165; Sinclair 1995, 98–103; Schmitz 1997, 97–135; Whitmarsh 2005, 37–40; König 2011, 283–293—emphasizing the rules of, and limitations on, such competition; Fron 2017; Schmitz 2017.

25. Kohl 1915 collects the themes, and Schmitz 1999 discusses this habit. The two themes are from Choricius of Gaza X (*Dec.* 1) and XVII (*Dec.* 4). For Greek Atticism see chapter 1 n. 61.

26. For the power sophists exerted in society, Bowersock 1969, followed by, e.g., Schmitz 1997 15, 44–66; Puech 2002, 23–35, Flinterman 2004, and others listed by Drecoll 2004, 404. The degree to which sophists in the fourth century AD continued to exert such power is controversial: see Van Hoof 2010, 213, 217–220. And Bowie 1982 doubted that sophists ever exerted significantly more power in the public realm, and especially in dealing with the Romans, than other members of the elevated class from which they were drawn; cf. Anderson 1989, 146–152.

27. Role-playing in declamation: Bloomer 1997a, 212–214; 1997b; 2007; 2011a, 7, 178–190; Schmitz 1999; cf. Friend 1999; Kaster 2001, 325, 328, 335; Imber 2001, 208–212; 2008; Breij 2009; Bernstein 2013, 78–113; Lentano 2013–2014. Pretexts by which those normally not allowed to speak for themselves might do so: Russell 1983, 14; Bloomer 2011a, 243 n. 25. The most common way of introducing another voice was *prosopopoeia* or *ethopoeia/sermocinatio* or *fictio personarum*, for the declaimer to "imagine" what that person might say, producing a speech within a speech (a practice much discussed: see Amato and Schamp 2005).

28. Quoted, Bloomer 2011a, 188.

29. Bloomer 2011a, 188 goes on to say that "growing mastery of speech depends on the exclusion of any speaker not of the status or gender of the young practitioners." Connolly 2016, esp. 193–194, 203–204 also flirts with the humanistic view that Bloomer rejects, but cannot finally drag herself away from "training young men to rule" (191, cf. 192), hardly surprising if she relies on Althusser (193–194). But note Friend 1999, 308 (a non-classicist, in an article full, alas, of errors of fact) who had the courage to take the implication of role-playing to its natural conclusion: "it created opportunities for both students and teachers to use their rhetorical skills in discussing important issues of the day and considering the positions of those who had no official voice in them." Cf. along the same lines, Breij 2009 = 2011. Note also the suggestion that declamation taught "difficult ideas" such as that torture was acceptable, Pagán 2007–2008, 166, 180.

I doubt that torture was a "difficult idea" to the Romans—who seemed generally to have enjoyed it when it was applied to the right sort of people—but the general idea is attractive.

30. Imber 2008, in the context of role-playing, "In declaiming, young Roman boys learned that these Roman categories of gender, class, and status naturally and absolutely divided society into a hierarchy of power. At the top of the ladder stood the *vir bonus*, the *civis* and *pater* the student would one day become" (164; cf. 2001, 211). Lentano 2009 [2005], 65 nn. 47 and 49; 2011 [2009], 227 n. 35 and 2017a, 79 collects the literature, and see esp. Bloomer 1997b, 60–65, 68–71, 74, 77 with emphasis on role-playing; Richlin 1997 on male versus female, effeminate versus masculine, East versus West; Connolly 1998, 145–149 for women, slaves, freedmen as disruptive; Habinek 2005, 65–71, for instruction in masculinity.

31. Although Geertz, Foucault, and Bourdieu wrote at much the same time, Geertz was picked up in classics later and to a much lesser degree than Judith Butler—and through her Foucault (Richlin 1997; Gunderson 2000 and 2003) and Bourdieu (Schmitz 1997; Gunderson 2003). The various tentacles of the shared assumptions of the 1990s classicists with theoretical interests can be traced through Gunderson 1998. A Geertzian position is approached by Beard 1993, 55–62 on declamation as mythmaking; by Langlands 2006 on declamatory treatment of *pudicitia*; and also by the anthropological methods of contemporary Italian scholars, e.g., Brescia and Lentano 2009; Lentano 2015b with literature.

32. From many good accounts of this intellectual tendency, I select nearly at random Johansson and Lalander 2012 and Vinthagen and Johansson 2013. A mocking passage in an after-dinner speech given by Marshall Sahlins in 1993 amply refutes the more radical versions of this approach (Sahlins 1996, 16–18).

33. We set aside, because "the debate has been conducted in terms too vague to permit any useful, or at least verifiable, answers" (Jones 2004, 14), the question of whether Greek declamation, and, indeed, all Greek high culture under the Roman Empire generally, was somehow subversive of Roman rule: see Bowie 2009 for the state of the question. We also pass by with respect but relief the argument that the whole of Greek education and literature under the Roman Empire was in some sense a psychological mechanism for coping with Roman rule, Bowie 1970 [1974], esp. 36–41; cf. Cribiore 2001, 239. The contrary position is just as compelling, Millar 1969; Anderson 1989, 142–143.

34. Weak more frequently spoken for, Quint. *Inst.* 6.2.36; sympathy with children against fathers, Russell 1983, 31. Rich man versus poor man, and abuse of the rich therein, see Tabacco 1978; Krapinger 2005, 67–68; Santorelli 2014, 16–26; Breij 2016, 276–283. Fathers versus sons, Sussman 1995; Gunderson 2003, 59–79; Brescia and Lentano 2009, 69–94; Lentano 2014a, 33–83; Breij 2016, 283–288; Rizzelli 2017; Lentano 2015c, 133–134 nn. 1–2. Brescia 2016, 344 n. 82, and Lentano 2017b, 175–181 gather further literature. Thomas 1983, 125 notes that, of the ninety declamations of pseudo-Quintilian that present a conflict within a family, fifty-four oppose a father to a son; in Seneca the Elder it is thirty-seven of fifty, and twenty-one of thirty-three in Calpurnius Flaccus; cf. Breij 2009, 360 = Breij 2011, 338 who counts 125 father-and-son cases in all surviving Latin declamation, only ten of them displaying good relations between the parties. Men versus women, Hawley 1995; van Mal-Maeder 2003 [2007]; Fernández López 2005; Langlands 2006, 247–280; Lentano 2012a; 2014a, 85–104.

35. Migliario 1989; literature collected by Lentano 1999, 610–616 and 2011 [2009], 222 n. 28; Connolly 2001b, esp. 77, 93–95; Bernstein 2013, esp. 13, 42, 77; Corbeill 2016—limiting his

argument, however, to a single unusual declamation. This is an argument with old antecedents, e.g., Tivier 1868, 121–122. Cf. Korenjak 2000, who identifies the product of the interaction of speaker and audience as potentially subversive.

36. On figured speech, Franchet d'Espèrey 2016 gathers the ancient evidence and modern scholarship. Classic discussions are Ahl 1984 and Desbordes 1993.

37. Connolly 1998, 148, "These speeches were not simply copied out and reread, like similar exercises in nineteenth-century American composition classes . . . but vocally and dramatically delivered with all the passion and conviction the student could possibly muster." Imber 2001, 211–212: education by declamation "was dynamic and interactive. Student declaimers actively contributed to the ideological tradition that was itself shaping their own identities." Which is not to say that, by modern Western standards, instruction in rhetoric was not also highly repetitive: Stramaglia 2010.

38. Quint. *Inst.* 2.2.9–10.

39. See preface n. 9.

40. Marrou 1938, with his description of the consequences of late-antique education at 85–157; *sclérose sénile*, 543. This view was much criticized and Marrou himself partially abandoned it, Marrou 1949 with Inglebert 2004.

41. Alföldi 1952, esp. 85–124; circumstances of writing (vi). For imperial decisions as the result of rhetorical education, cf. Millar 1977, 8, who attributes to this factor imperial favor towards the Greek East.

42. MacMullen 1976, 24–31, 48–70, 199–201; and he returned to a similar idea—rhetorical education as a factor rendering late-antique law obscure—as a contributor to the problems in the fourth and fifth centuries, 1988, 142–143. For the group-think, and neglect of practical learning, produced by rhetorical education, see also Vössing 1997, 605–609.

43. Mattern 1999, 2–3, 15–16, 25, 65, 71–80.

44. Lendon 2005, 261–289; for this "telescoping" of the past, cf. Anderson 1989, 140.

45. Portmann 1988, 215, 343–345 and Wiemer 2003, 467 note that late-antique Greek authors tended to be ignorant of the history of the period after Alexander. See Kohl 1915 for the vast number of declamatory topics set in the period before before the death of Alexander (and especially in the period of Demosthenes, Philip, and Aeschines—Demosthenes being Greek's most admired stylist and the Greek author most intensely read) and the near total lack of any after. Even those who did seek out historical works to read would find that such works too were apt to stop at the death of Alexander, Bowie 1970 [1974], 12–16.

46. Kohl 1915, 90–107.

47. Isaac 1993, 372–418; *sed contra* Wheeler 1993; with Lendon 2002, 378–379.

## Chapter 3: The Carrion Men

1. Sordid, a wrangle between Antony and Dolabella, Cic. *Phil.* 2.88; cf. 79–84; Plut. *Ant.* 11.2–3; with Dettenhofer 1992, 165–183. Late, Suet. *Jul.* 81.4; Plut. *Brut.* 15.1; Cass. Dio 44.18.1; with Ramsey 2008, 352, 361–362. For the conspiracy against and the murder of Caesar the fullest collection of ancient sources (I cite only the major *testimonia*) remains Drumann and Groebe 1906 [1837], 624–657; for the murder itself and the period after, Becht 1911. Gesche 1976, 172–175, 304–305 gathers much older scholarly writing on the conspiracy; see also Jehne 2005 and Meier

2014 for the more recent. For discussion of the German scholarship, Christ 1994 and Kolb 2015. Good, recent accounts of the assassination in English are Lintott 2009 and Strauss 2015; in German, Jehne 1998 and Meier 2012; and for the period after the murder, Gotter 1996; in Italian, Cristofoli 2002; and Ver Eecke 2008, 437–444 gathers the French tradition of scholarship. For discussion of the ancient sources and their relationship to one another, Gesche 1976, 8–9 gathers the older writing; Rawson 1986 [1991] is a classic treatment; Donié 1996 collects more recent literature; and see also Wiseman 2009, 211–234.

For the works of Plutarch and Appian the Loeb numeration is used here, while for Nicolaus of Damascus the subsection numbers of Jacoby *FGrH* 90 F 130 ( = vol. IIA pp. 397–420) are used, as in the convenient editions of Toher 2017 (with English translation) and Malitz 2003 (with German translation).

2. For the Curia, Portico, and Theater of Pompey, Horsfall 1974, 194–196; *LTUR* 1.334–335, 4.148–150, 5.35–38; Matijević 2006, 41 n. 55; Carandini 2017 [2012], 1.505. Gladiators, Nic. Dam. 98; Plut. *Brut.* 12.5; Cass. Dio 44.16.2; cf. App. *B Civ.* 2.122, Horsfall 1974, 195; for other reasons that delay was impractical, 191–192.

3. Caesar extracted from his house over objections, Nic. Dam. 83–84; Suet. *Jul.* 81.3–4; Plut. *Caes.* 63.5–64.4; Plut. *Brut.* 15.1; Cass. Dio 44.18.1–2. I am required to cite both Plut. *Caes.* and *Brut.* because either Plutarch used different sources, or, as Pelling 2011, 22, 37, 459–460, 484 (cf. Moles 2017 [1979], 11, 184 and Toher 2017, 266) argues, he carefully divided his material about the conspiracy between his *Lives* so as to avoid repetition. But I share Dobesch's 1979 [2001] 100–107, 118–119 doubts about Plutarch's using the same source for his lives of Caesar, Brutus, and Antony.

4. Caesar from home to the Curia of Pompey, Nic. Dam. 86–88; App. *B Civ.* 2.115–116, 153; on foot, Plut. *Caes.* 64.4, or on a litter, Plut. *Brut.* 16.1 (Plutarch cannot decide). A majority of the conspirators opted for killing Caesar in the Senate because he would be "alone" there (Nic. Dam. 81; cf. Plut. *Syn. Dion/Brutus* 4.5; Horsfall 1974, 194), and surprised (Cass. Dio 44.16.1). In fact (Nic. Dam. 96 with Strauss 2015, 138–139; Toher 2017, 354), two senators may have tried ineffectually to protect Caesar when he was attacked.

5. Antony kept outside, Cic. *Phil.* 2.34; Cic. *Fam.* 10.28.1; Plut. *Brut.* 17.2; *Caes.* 66.3 (the contradiction between Plutarch's two versions about who exactly detained Antony tells against Pelling's argument, see this chapter n. 3, that Plutarch used the same sources in both lives); *Ant.* 13.2; App. *B Civ.* 2.117; Cass. Dio 44.19.1. No source mentions any intervention by twelve lictors to which, as consul, Antony had a right, or the twenty-four (or perhaps more, Cass. Dio 43.14.3) to which Caesar, as dictator, was entitled (and who escorted him to the Senate on that day, App. *B Civ.* 2.118; cf. Nic. Dam. 87 with Toher 2017, 338). Without mentioning the lictors Appian says that Caesar's escort fled, perhaps regarding themselves as mere "civil attendants" (μετὰ τῆς δημοσίας ὑπηρεσίας; App. *B Civ.* 2.107). But there was a crush of people around Caesar as he went from his home to the Curia of Pompey (Plut. *Caes.* 65.2 [with Pelling 2011, 473]; App. *B Civ.* 2.118).

6. Cimber, Nic. Dam. 88; Suet. *Jul.* 82.1; Plut. *Caes.* 66.3–4; *Brut.* 17.3; App. *B Civ.* 2.117. Strauss 2015, 133 notes the similarity of this plan to the failed attempt to murder Q. Cassius Longinus (a brother of Cassius the conspirator) when he was a governor in Spain in 47 BC ([Caes.] *B Alex.* 52; *B Hisp.* 42; Val. Max. 9.4.2).

7. Fight, Nic. Dam. 88–90; Plut. *Caes.* 66.4–5; *Brut.* 17.3–5 with Wiseman 2009, 211–215 on the sources. Suet. *Jul.* 82.1 has Caesar run P. Casca through the arm with a stilus and App. *B Civ.* 2.117 adds a stab in the back by one Bucolianus: the five surviving accounts of the murder of Caesar and the events after vary in many small, unimportant ways. Doughty officers: Cassius was himself a war-hero, having distinguished himself in the aftermath of Carrhae, Dettenhofer 1992, 125–127, and Decimus Brutus had been an officer in Caesar's wars, Dettenhofer 1992, 75, 186–190; likewise others, Drumann and Groebe 1906 [1837], 627–631; Étienne 1973, 153–156; and others still had, naturally, fought against Caesar in the Civil War, Drumann and Groebe 1906 [1837], 632–639; Étienne 1973, 157–159. Strauss 2015, 90–95 offers a catalogue of conspirators in English.

8. Caesar fights back, Plut. *Caes.* 66.4–6; *Brut.* 17.

9. Brutus's blow, Plut. *Caes.* 66.6. App. *B Civ.* 2.117 has Brutus stab Caesar before he veils himself. "You too, my son," καὶ σύ, τέκνον, Cass. Dio 44.19.5; Suet. *Jul.* 82.2 (with Pelling 2011, 482–483, discussing also other interpretations of the phrase, perhaps insulting), although Dio does not believe the story, and Suetonius will not commit himself. Protégé: Plut. *Caes.* 62.1–2; *Brut.* 6–7; *Syn. Dion/Brutus* 3.4; App. *B Civ.* 2.111–112 for Caesar's kindnesses to Brutus; he may have suspected Brutus was his natural son, Plut. *Brut.* 5.1–2; App. *B Civ.* 2.112. Alföldi 1985, 345 n. 1084 gathers the literature on M. Brutus through 1981, and see now Tempest 2017.

10. Thirty-five wounds, and stabbed by all, Nic. Dam. 90; in a later tradition, twenty-three wounds, Suet. *Jul.* 82.2; Plut. *Caes.* 66.7; Florus 2.13.95; App. *B Civ.* 2.117, 147. There is no strong reason to prefer the later, lower number to the earlier, higher one: Toher 2017, 345.

11. Fuficius Fango, Cic. *Att.* 14.10.2 (but there is a textual problem).

12. Flight of senators, Nic. Dam. 91; Plut. *Brut.* 18.1; App. *B Civ.* 2.118. Expecting to suffer the same fate, Nic. Dam. 91; Plut. *Caes.* 67.1; Cass. Dio 44.20.1. For Caesar's new senators, Cic. *Div.* 2.23; Cass. Dio 43.47. 3; Syme 1939, 78–96.

13. Decision to kill no one else, Nic. Dam. 93; Vell. Pat. 2.58.2; Plut. *Brut.* 18.1–3, 20.2; *Ant.* 13.2; App. *B Civ.* 2.114; and see chapter 4 n. 9; Gelzer 1918, 990.

14. Antony's physical strength, Cic. *Phil.* 2.63; Plut. *Caes.* 66.3; *Ant.* 13.2. Cicero (*Phil.* 2.89), not part of the plot, claims that when he met the conspirators on the Capitoline he warned them once again against Antony.

15. Brutus tries to speak, Plut. *Caes.* 67.1; *Brut.* 18.1 (cf. 14.1); App. *B Civ.* 2.119. For the expectation that the Senate would receive the murder of Caesar with joy, App. *B Civ.* 2.114.

16. Chaos in the streets, Nic. Dam. 92; Plut. *Caes.* 67.1; App. *B Civ.* 2.118; Cass. Dio 44.20.

17. Lepidus, force on Tiber Island, App. *B Civ.* 2.118 (Cass. Dio 44.19.2 has Lepidus already set out for campaign, and in the suburbs; for Lepidus's actions during these days, Hayne 1971). Appian describes Lepidus's force as a τέλος, which can mean "legion" (LSJ ad loc. τέλος 10), and has been so interpreted by many, e.g., White's Loeb translation; Seeck 1902, 26; Hayne 1971, 110; Pelling 2011, 485–487. But despite Appian's regular use of τέλος to mean "legion" (Becht 1911, 76 with argument in favor), this must have been a far smaller force (τέλος can also just mean "military unit" [LSJ ad loc. τέλος 10], or, more probably, Appian was simply wrong) to have been camped on an island 270 m by 70 m, already occupied by a substantial temple to Asclepius and at least five smaller shrines (for the island and its buildings *LTUR* 3.99–101; Carandini 2017 [2012], 1.552–554; for the size of the military unit cf. Schmitthenner 1958, 23, 169 n. 9

with Botermann 1968, 197–199 and Matijević 2006, 58 n. 76 for discussion and literature; Strauss 2015, 119 tries to have it both ways and posits an *under-strength* legion; if so, very much so). Since Lepidus was about to depart from Rome to take up his proconsular command in Gallia Narbonensis and Hispania Citerior (Cass. Dio refers to the forces attached to those commands at 44.34.5: they were also not in the city), this may have been his praetorian cohort (Toher 2017, 365). The course of events also implies that Lepidus had only a small force, for why otherwise wait for Caesar's veterans to gather before advancing into the Forum? In Cic. *Fam.* 11.1.1, dated very soon after the Ides of March, Decimus Brutus also implies that the forces opposed to the conspirators were not overwhelming, and that *si mediocre auxilium dignitatis nostrae habuissemus*, the conspirators would control the city. For what it is worth, Nic. Dam. 91–92 identifies as fantasies the terrors that either the conspirators were backed by a στράτευμα μέγα or that a στρατία of Caesar's was sacking the city. By Nic. Dam. 103, when the veterans and others had gathered, Lepidus did indeed have a μέγα στράτευμα.

18. Public panic, Forum, Capitoline, Nic. Dam. 92, 94; Vell. Pat. 2.58.2; Plut. *Caes.* 67.1–3; Plut. *Brut.* 18.7–9; App. *B Civ.* 2.119–120; Cass. Dio 44.20.3–21.2; with Dettenhofer 1992, 263–266 for discussion. Gladiators, App. *B Civ.* 2.118. Malitz 2003, 169, 172 does not believe in the slaves, thinking them *"vermutlich eine propagandistische Erfindung Octavians."* The sources disagree on whether the conspirators gave, or tried to give, formal speeches in the Forum before they mounted the Capitoline, Moles 2017 [1979] 192.

19. Thanks to the gods, Cass. Dio 44.21.2. That ascending the Capitoline was always part of the plan is implied in Plut. *Caes.* 67.2–3. Motivated by fear of Caesarian soldiers, Nic. Dam. 94; App. *B Civ.* 2.119–120; fear of Caesar's veterans, Florus 2.17.2. But App. *B Civ.* 2.114 also says that the conspirators expected the soldiers to understand that they had acted in the public interest, and so not oppose them, and at 3.15 Octavian is represented as unsure why the conspirators ascended.

20. Cicero's suggestions, Cic. *Att.* 14.10.1, 15.11.2. At some point Brutus did deliver a speech on the Capitoline, Cic. *Att.* 15.1a, *orationem . . . in contione Capitolina* (cf. Plut. *Brut.* 18.10) but it may have been on March 17, App. *B Civ.* 2.137–142; Cass. Dio 44.34.2 with Sumi 2005, 76–78, 93–95, and see chapter 5 n. 11.

21. For Antony moving Caesar's treasure, Ürögdi 1980; Matijević 2006, 61–64.

22. The chronology of events after the conspirator's ascent to the Capitoline on March 15 and through March 17, 44 BC presents a notorious puzzle, given contradictions between the sources (see Becht 1911, 6–27, 73–76 and Moles 2017 [1979], 198–206 for full discussions, and Toher 2017, 357–358 for a concise exposition of the issues). Partly from perversity and partially because I do not think that recent scholars have given sufficient weight to Nic. Dam. 49 (cf. 39)—stating that people were still joining the conspirators on the sixteenth and that the Caesarians were still in confusion on that day (cf. Cic. *Phil.* 2.89)—I have in my account preferred the nineteenth-century chronology (see Becht 1911, 73 for literature; and Dahlheim 1996 [2005], 55 for a recent adherent) that places the sequence of speeches by Brutus, Cassius, Cinna, and Dolabella in the Forum on March 16, described as either the day after the murder (Plut. *Caes.* 67.4) or the day before the meeting of the Senate in the Temple of Tellus (Plut. *Brut.* 19.1; App. *B Civ.* 2.126; Cass. Dio 44.22.2–3), which was on the seventeenth (although most of the ancient authors who placed the speeches on the fifteenth thought the Senate meeting was on the sixteenth). This chronology is in contrast to most contemporary scholars who place those

speeches on the fifteenth itself with Nic. Dam. 94–101; Plut. *Brut.* 18.7–13; Cass. Dio 44.22.1 (although he only mentions the speech of Dolabella) and, by implication, App. *B Civ.* 2.121. It also seems unlikely to me that bribes could be so quickly distributed as to gather a friendly crowd (App. *B Civ.* 2.120) on the fifteenth, given the chaos in the city, nor that, given their experience of that chaos, the conspirators would try their luck in the Forum again so soon. By pushing nearly all known events onto the fifteenth, recent commentators also leave the sixteenth a historical blank, when we would expect events. But which chronology is used is immaterial: none of the possible chronologies has an impact on the overall argument made here.

23. Dolabella makes himself consul, Vell. Pat. 2.58.3 (with Woodman 1983 ad loc.); App. *B Civ.* 2.122; Cass. Dio 44.22.1. For the controversy about Dolabella, see this chapter n. 1. Syme 1980 [1984], 431–437 and Gotter 1996, 268 think that the age (twenty-five) that Appian (*B Civ.* 2.129) gives for Dolabella cannot be right: no matter, Appian's giving an age at all only makes sense if Dolabella was legally too young for the office, as Appian says he was.

24. Speeches given in the Forum, App. *B Civ.* 2.120–123 (with bribery of the commons, and whose order of the speeches I have accepted); Plut. *Caes.* 67.4 (silence when Brutus speaks); *Brut.* 18.12–13 (Cinna shouted down; see Moles 1987); Nic. Dam. 99–100; for discussion (but the muddle, especially about the order of speakers, is irremediable), Morstein-Marx 2004, 151–157; Sumi 2005, 80–89; Pelling 2011, 488–489.

25. Caesar's veterans, Nic. Dam. 49, 103; Cic. *Att.* 14.14.2; Florus, 2.17.2; App. *B Civ.* 2.119, 120 (Caesar's veterans in sanctuaries), 125, 133–135, 139; cf. Nic. Dam. 91–94; Plut. *Brut.* 21.2, 22.2; App. *B Civ.* 2.94, 2.139–141; Cass. Dio 44.34.1–4, 44.51.4; see Matijević 2006, 58–60.

26. Antony and Lepidus lead troops into the Forum, Nic. Dam. 103 (on the sixteenth); night of the sixteenth to seventeenth, Cass. Dio 44.22.2–3 (placing it the night before the meeting of the Senate in the Temple of Tellus); necessarily after the conspirators' speeches in the Forum, impossible if the Caesarians had already occupied the Forum. See this chapter n. 22 for the "late" chronology, supported in this case by the fact that Antony would still have been busy moving Caesar's treasure long into the day of the sixteenth. Siege, Cass. Dio 44.25.2.

27. Trimmers and influential men join Antony and Lepidus, Nic. Dam. 103–104. Avenged in blood, Nic. Dam. 104, 106; App. *B Civ.* 2.118, 124.

28. Negotiations, Cic. *Phil.* 2.89 (consulars); Nic. Dam. 101, 106; App. *B Civ.* 2.123–125. These may have begun on March 15 with the conspirators sending emissaries inviting Antony and Lepidus to a meeting on the Capitoline (to which offer the Caesarians pledged to reply the next day), and may have continued on March 16, or they may have begun on the sixteenth. In any event they concluded with an agreement to place the matter in the hands of the Senate, which met on the seventeenth.

29. Antony versus the followers of Dolabella in 47 BC, Livy, *Per.* 113 (800 killed); Plut. *Ant.* 9.1–2, 10.1; Cass. Dio 42.29–32, 46.16.2, with Strauss 2015, 157; the commons still in play, Morstein-Marx 2004, 157–158.

30. Fear of Decimus Brutus and his army, App. *B Civ.* 2.124.

31. Senate called to Temple of Tellus, Plut. *Brut.* 19.1; App. *B Civ.* 2.123–126 (breastplate, 130). Sp. Cassius, see chapter 4 n. 45. His house, Dion. Hal. *Ant. Rom.* 8.79.3; Val. Max. 6.3.1b with Strauss 2015, 158. Soldiers around temple, Cic. *Phil.* 2.89.

32. Debate in Senate, Antony and Lepidus address the people, App. *B Civ.* 2.127–135 (for the addresses, Sumi 2005, 91–93); rewards proposed, see also Plut. *Brut.* 19.

33. Reading of Caesar's will, properties, Plut. *Brut.* 20.1–3 (Plutarch's 75 drachmas = 300 Roman sesterces; cf. *Ant.* 16.1); Suet. *Jul.* 83.2 (300 sesterces); App. *B Civ.* 2.143 (75 drachmas); Cass. Dio 44.35.3 (120 or 300 sesterces). Funeral, Plut. *Brut.* 20.2–4; *Caes.* 68.1; Suet. *Jul.* 84; App. *B Civ.* 2.143, 147–148; Cass. Dio 44.50.2–3. Antony's funeral eulogy, Cic. *Phil.* 2.91; *Att.* 14.10.1; Plut. *Brut.* 20.2, 20.4; *Ant.* 14.3–4; App. *B Civ.* 2.144–146; Cass. Dio 44.35–49; *pace* Suet. *Jul.* 84.2, who denies that Antony gave a eulogy at Caesar's funeral, all with Sumi 2005, 98–112 with literature; Moles 2017 [1979] 217–220.

34. Attacks on the conspirators' houses and killing of Helvius Cinna, Cic. *Phil.* 2.91; Plut. *Caes.* 68.1–4 (with Moles 2017 [1979], 224–229; Pelling 2011, 492–493); *Brut.* 20.7–11; *Ant.* 14.4; Suet. *Jul.* 85; App. *B Civ.* 147; Cass. Dio 44.50.4. The Cinna incident is famous, of course, from Shakespeare's *Julius Caesar*, III.3. Flight of conspirators from the city, Plut. *Brut.* 21.1; *Caes.* 68.4; *Ant.* 15.1; App. *B Civ.* 2.148.

## Chapter 4: Puzzles about the Conspiracy

1. Cicero's evaluation, Cic. *Att.* 14.21.3, *animo virili, consilio puerili*; cf. 15.4.2; *Phil.* 2.34; Nic. Dam. 105; Plut. *Brut.* 20.1–2. And most moderns have agreed, at least as far back as 1837: Drumann and Groebe 1906 [1837], 648.

2. Nic. Dam. 90, all the conspirators stabbed the corpse of Caesar "so that each would seem personally to have shared in the deed" (ὅπως ἂν καὶ αὐτὸς δοκοίη τοῦ ἔργου συνῆφθαι); Plut. *Caes.* 66.6, "for all needed to participate in the sacrifice and taste of the murder" (ἅπαντας γὰρ ἔδει κατάρξασθαι καὶ γεύσασθαι τοῦ φόνου), with Pelling 2011, 482 for the sacrificial metaphor (also in *Brut.* 10.1 with Moles 2017 [1979] 131). Pelling 2011, 482 and Toher 2017, 345 also note the parallel with the body of Hector at *Iliad* 22.371, where all the Achaeans present stab the corpse. Caligula, similarly, ended up with thirty wounds when assassinated (Suet. *Calig.* 58.3; cf. Joseph. *AJ* 19.105–114).

3. Matijević 2006, 40 n. 53 lists ancient complaints and modern expressions of wonderment that Antony was spared; e.g., Rice Holmes 1923, 3.341, "one may well be astonished that it did not occur to them that to kill Caesar would be useless if Caesar's partisans were allowed to live."

4. Stewens 1963, 59, "*Was hatte Brutus erwartet?*"

5. Or the afternoon of March 15, for those following the "early" chronology, see chapter 3 n. 22.

6. Drumann and Groebe 1906 [1837], 648, "*Die Zukunft berührte sie nicht, mit dem Dolchstoße, glaubten sie, sei alles getan.*" "They had no further plans—the tyrant was slain, therefore liberty was restored," Syme 1939, 97. Matijević 2006, 40 n. 53 collects scholars who have noted the *Planlosigkeit* of the conspirators.

7. Legal rigorist, Gelzer 1918, 989–991; Seel 1939, 11; Stewens 1963, 54–69, "*Brutus setzte seinen Kampf für die Legitimität in legitimer Weise*" (60); with Cristofoli 2002, 27 n. 73 for Italian concurrence; elegantly discussed by Gotter 1996, 212.

8. "The assumption of a Dictatorship for life seemed to mock and dispel all hope of a return to normal and constitutional government," Syme 1939, 56; cf. Meyer 1922, 534. Suet. *Jul.* 76 lists Caesar's lawless deeds. In retrospect Cicero solved the legal conundrum somewhat along these lines, *Off.* 3.32, 3.83.

9. Nic. Dam. 93 puts Brutus's refusal to countenance killing anyone other than Caesar in terms with a legal flavor to them: "Marcus Brutus, they say, held them back, saying that it was

not just (οὐ δίκαιον) to cut the throats of persons, against whom there appeared to be no complaints/charges (ἐγκλήματα) laid down, on the basis of unclear suspicions." Cf. Plut. *Ant.* 13.2, "Brutus forbade this, saying that the deed boldly attempted for the sake of the laws and justice must be clean of injustice" (κώλυσε δὲ Βροῦτος, ἀξιῶν τὴν ὑπὲρ τῶν νόμων καὶ τῶν δικαίων τολμωμένην πρᾶξιν εἰλικρινῆ καὶ καθαρὰν ἀδικίας εἶναι). For weaker formulations that can be construed as regarding the matter in legal terms, Plut. *Brut.* 10.1, 18.2, 35.4–6; *Syn. Dion/Brutus* 3.6; App. *B Civ.* 2.111, 119.

10. App. *B Civ.* 2.114. Drumann and Groebe 1906 [1837], 627–640 and Étienne 1973, 153–159 count seven conspirators likely to have been followers of Caesar and nine of Pompey before the battle of Pharsalus.

11. Praetors, Dettenhofer 1992, 16–22. Was Tillius Cimber praetor in 44 BC? See Toher 2005, 185–187 versus Pelling 2011, 480. Tribunes, *MRR* 2.324–325.

12. Seeck 1902, 23; Walter 1938, 139–140; Syme 1939, 99; Stewens 1963, 59–61.

13. Rossi 1953, 46, "*mania di legalità.*"

14. *Ad Brut.* 1.16 and 1.17 (quoted *ad Brut.* 1.16.5; cf. 1.17.6) spurious, Shackleton Bailey 1980, 10–14; Gotter 1996, 286–298 (with literature, arguing that they are nevertheless nearly contemporary and historically useful; for earlier literature, Ortmann 1988, 15–16 n. 3); *sed contra* Moles 1997; belated, and so a *post eventum* justification, Bengtson 1970, 16.

15. Suet. *Jul.* 82.1, *ista quidem vis est!* And the conspirators may later have been accused in such legal terms by Octavian, Plut. *Brut.* 27.4. Cass. Dio 44.1.1 refers to the killing of Caesar as an "unlawful" act that "scattered the decrees." For the murder of Caesar as unlawful, Wiseman 2009, 203–207. Exactly which Roman law was involved, given that there were a number of poorly reported and dated Republican laws against *vis*, is not susceptible of certainty: see Lintott 1968, 107–124; Bryen 2018, 22–27.

16. Seeck 1902, 23, 27 for this contradiction.

17. Mommsen 1887–1888, 2.129–130. Mommsen (2.130 n. 3), citing Cic. *Man.* 58, argues that a consul could, by an *intercessio*, prevent a praetor from summoning the Senate, but the passage could refer equally well to obstruction by a tribune as by a consul; and even if true, Antony (in flight and hiding on the fifteenth, Plut. *Caes.* 67.2 with Pelling 2011, 486–487 and Moles 2017 [1979], 189–191) was in no position to enter such an *intercessio*. Moreover, if it was indeed the law that a praetor could not summon the Senate if a consul were available, that created yet more motivation to kill Antony, to leave the field clear for the conspiring praetors (Dettenhofer 1992, 254).

18. For "that influence most obvious in all the accounts, love of freedom," MacMullen 1966, 13 (with 14–16) and we note also, for the general motive of "liberation," e.g., Cic. *Phil.* 2.27; Plut. *Brut.* 18.2, 18.4, 28.4, 29.4, 39.4; *Syn. Dion/Brutus* 3.4; App. *B Civ.* 2.112. Philippi, Cass. Dio 47.43.1. For discussion of this motive see also Stevenson 2015, 153–165. Brutus and *libertas*, Ortmann 1988, 466–472; for the coins, *RRC* nrs. 498–502, 506; p. 741; Brutus had also depicted *libertas* on his coins when he was a *triumvir monetalis* in the 50s, *RRC* 433 with Tempest 2017, 268 n. 32 for the date when he held this office. For *libertas* in the late Republic, and its various meanings, Wirszubski 1950, 1–30; Arena 2012.

19. Number of conspirators: more than eighty, Nic. Dam. 59; more than sixty, Suet. *Jul.* 80.4, and no strong reason not to prefer the earlier, larger number, Toher 2017, 270. Brutus's leadership, and its recruitment of others to the plot, Plut. *Brut.* 10–12, "for the business did not so much

need violence and bravery, but the reputation of a man like him, whose act of sacrificing would ensure by itself that the deed was just" (10.1). But if Canfora 2007 [1999], 306–313 is right to detect a tradition that made Cassius the prime mover of the plot, or Strauss 2015, 67–68, 81–86, 253–254 is right to follow our earliest source, Nic. Dam. 59, in giving Decimus Brutus a role equal to that of Marcus Brutus and Cassius, then arguments stressing the motivations of Marcus Brutus in particular lose considerable force. For increasing scholarly emphasis on the role of Decimus Brutus, see also Billows 2009, 249–250; Tempest 2017, 278 n. 87.

20. Optimism about Antony, Plut. *Brut.* 18.5.

21. "Old" Academy, Plut. *Brut.* 2.2 with Moles 2017 [1979], 61–65, noting that Brutus's Platonism was heavily tinged with Stoicism (cf. MacMullen 1966, 298 n. 13), which is to be expected, because so were the teachings of the school's prime mover, Antiochus of Ascalon, on whom see Barnes 1989 [1997]; Tarver 1997, 138–145; and the essays in Sedley 2012.

22. For Cassius's Epicureanism as hard to reconcile with his participation in the conspiracy, Sedley 1997, 46–47 and Valachova 2018, 156–159; cf. Dettenhofer 1992, 220–222 and Moles 2017 [1979], 127; Tempest 2017, 277 n. 66 with more literature. But Momigliano 1941 claimed that Cassius's Epicureanism positively drove him and others into the plot (cf. Fiori 2011, 19–41), and some recent scholars have argued more weakly that quietism was not compulsory among Epicureans, Roskam 2007 and Fish 2011; and Canfora 2007 [1999], 296–305 was inclined to doubt whether Cassius was an Epicurean at all. For Stoic political quietism (or not, and its extent), Brunt 1975 [2013], 9, 18–21, 27; Griffin 1976, 315–366; and Schofield 2015, 77–80. Plutarch has Brutus reject a Stoic and an Epicurean from participation in the plot because of their philosophical quietism (*Brut.* 12.3).

23. Sedley 1997, with references to Brutus's Platonism gathered at 42 n. 7; Lévy 2012, 300–303. Following Sedley, contemporary scholars writing in English often stress Brutus's Platonism as a motive: Tatum 2008, 159–164; Lintott 2009, 74; Corrigan 2015, 74; Tempest 2017, 94–97; and cf. Malitz 2003, 146 in German, and, apparently independently, the epigrammatic Wylie: "Steeped in Academic philosophy, Brutus lived in a cloud of abstract moral principles which governed all his decisions, at times with doubtful relevance to their practical implications" (1998, 169). But Syme 1939, 57 *avant la lettre* dismissed explanations relying on Brutus's philosophical interests; Pelling 2011, 421 notes how poorly Caesar fits the Platonic model of a tyrant; and Griffin 1989 [1997], 32 warns against trying to connect specific political decisions with the philosophical positions of Romans who made them.

24. Platonist tyrants and tyrant-expellers and -killers, Ath. *Deip.* 11.508E–509B; Plut. *Adv. Col.* 1126B-C; Philostr. *VA* 7.2; and esp. for Dion, Diod. Sic. 16.5–6, 9–13, 16–20, 31, 36; Plut. *Dion* (both also representing Dion as an opponent of tyranny, rather than a tyrant); Nepos, *Dion*; Ath. *Deip.* 11.119, with Westlake 1994, 693–706; Clearchus, Chion, and Leonidas, Just. 16.5; Memnon *FGrH* 434 F 1.1–2 with Lewis 2009, 98–100. Ironically, enough students of philosophy became tyrants to warrant a book on the subject by the third-century BC Hermippus (Griffin 1989 [1997], 2).

25. Sedley 2010, 702 speaks of the "feverish interest shown by leading Romans of Cicero's day in acquiring a philosophical education and allegiance"—a conclusion we draw from the letters of Cicero, which may, of course, lead us astray, given the orator's own philosophical interests. For philosophy among the ruling class at Rome, see generally Griffin 1989 [1997].

26. Neither the tyrants of Greek philosophy nor the tyrants of rhetoric (see below) were the Romans' first introduction to Greek conceptions of the tyrant, which will have been translations into Latin and adaptations of Greek tragedies, beginning in the mid-third century BC: Dunkle 1967, 153–155; and for the portrayal of tyrants in Greek tragedy, Fleskes 1914, 7–16, 70.

27. Tyrannical souls, Pl. *Resp.* 574D-575D; cf. Xen. *Hier.* 5.2. For the tyrant in Plato, Heintzeler 1927; Boesche 1996, 25–48; Turchetti 2001, 74–83 with literature (82–83); and especially enjoyable is Meulder 2008 who, noting that Plato depicts the tyrant as a werewolf (*Resp.* 565D), suggests that he might be connected, as an Indo-European survival, to the wolf Fenrir of the Norse Eddas, who will devour Odin and harry the world at the end of time. Tyrants and persons with tyrannical souls "incurable," Pl. *Grg.* 525C-D with Dodds 1959, 380–381; *Resp.* 615D-E; cf. *Phd.* 113E (but other passages suggest that no soul is entirely incurable, Giorgini 2009). It is thus unlikely that a Platonist such as Brutus would ever have believed that Antony might reform, as Plut. *Brut.* 18.4–5 suggests.

28. Quoted, Plut. *Brut.* 2.2; cf. 24.1.

29. Result unpredictable, Arist. *Pol.* 1316A.

30. Tyrants divide men, Arist. *Eth. Nic.* 1161A; *Pol.* 1313A-1314A with Boesche 1996, 70–75; Nippel 2017, 256. For Aristotle on tyranny and his "handbook for tyrants" at *Politics* V (1313A-1315B), urging such division as a strategy of rule, Heuss 1971; Kamp 1985; Keyt 1999, 168–181; Turchetti 2001, 83–95 and 96 for literature; Jordović 2011, with 36–37 n. 5 for literature. Division of many possible types among citizens manifests in *stasis*, *Pol.* 1302A-1307B.

31. For the tyrant in the Greek philosophical tradition other than Plato and Aristotle, Fleskes 1914, 17–25, 28; Berve 1967, 1.493–498, 2.747–750.

32. Brutus's family tradition, Cic. *Att.* 13.40.1; *Phil.* 2.26 (with Decimus); Nepos, *Atticus* 18.3; Plut. *Caes.* 62.1; *Brut.* 1.1–8 with Moles 2017 [1979], 41–42, 54–58; App. *B Civ.* 2.112; with Tempest 2017, 264 n. 18 for literature.

33. *RRC* nr. 433; and see this chapter n. 18.

34. For Roman attitudes towards kings, Martin 1982–1994, 1.323–366, 2.14–184; Sigmund 2014 with recent literature, and for the *Regifugium*, 26–31.

35. Messages, Plut. *Brut.* 9.5–7, 10.6; Plut. *Caes.* 62.4 (cf. 61.5); Suet. *Jul.* 80.3; App. *B Civ.* 2.112–113; Cass. Dio 44.12.1–3; posting messages versus scrawling on statues, Pelling 2011, 462–463.

36. Popular views of Caesar and potential influence on the conspirators, Jehne 1987, 303–326; Morstein-Marx 2012, 211–213; Tempest 2017, 85–87. The graffiti, of course, could have been the work of the highly placed or their minions (thus Cassius in App. *B Civ.* 2.113; Plut. *Brut.* 10.6), but Hillard 2013 gathers the evidence that such graffiti were usually accepted to represent the authentic views of the lowly.

37. Gestures towards kingship, Cic. *Phil.* 2.85–87; Nic. Dam. 69–75; Plut. *Caes.* 60–61; *Brut.* 9.8; *Ant.* 12.2; Suet. *Jul.* 79; App. *B Civ.* 2.107–110; Cass. Dio 44.9–11. And esp. Plut. *Caes.* 60.1, "The most overt and deadly hatred towards him [Caesar] was generated by his desire for kingship (ὁ τῆς βασιλείας ἔρως)," with Pelling 2011, 445–446. On Caesar and kingship, Felber 1961; Kraft 1969; and Rawson 1975 [1991] are the classic discussions; Gesche (1976, 154–158, 298–300) gathers the older scholarship; Ver Eecke 2008, 408–422 and Pelling's additions to Moles 2017 [1979] 130 bring the literature up to date.

38. Killed a king, App. *B Civ.* 2.119; cf. Cic. *Phil.* 2.29, 34, 87, 108, 114; Florus 2.17.1, *Brutus et Cassius sic Caesarem quasi Tarquinium regem depulisse regno videbantur*; App. *B Civ.* 119–120, 122.

39. Force of family tradition, Cic. *Phil.* 2.26; Plut. *Brut.* 1.1–8; App. *B Civ.* 2.112; Meyer 1922, 534; MacMullen 1966, 7–10, noting also the story that Cato, Brutus's uncle and father-in-law, had offered as a boy to kill Sulla (Val. Max. 3.1.2b; Plut. *Cato Min.* 3.3–5); Alföldi 1985, 361–367; Gotter 1996, 213.

40. Nic. Dam. 61; and see especially Martin 1988.

41. Expulsion of Tarquins a poor model, Pina Polo 2017, 21–22; Tempest 2017, 94.

42. In Cicero's mind, Spurius Cassius, Spurius Maelius, and Marcus Manlius formed a trio of men killed for trying to seize despotic power at Rome (*Dom.* 101; *Rep.* 2.49; *Phil.* 2.87, 114). For discussion and further literature, Lintott 1970; Pina Polo 2006, 80–87; Smith 2006; Mastrorosa 2013, 127–137; Sigmund 2014, 47–48; and Pina Polo 2017, 22–27. The often-impugned historical truth of these stories is, of course, beside the point here.

43. Sp. Maelius and Servilius Ahala, Dion. Hal. *Ant. Rom.* 12.1–4; Livy 4.13–16 with Ogilvie 1965 ad loc. with other sources. Brutus, on his mother's side, Cic. *Att.* 13.40.1; *Phil.* 2.26; Plut. *Brut.* 1.5. The Casca brothers, Cic. *Phil.* 2.27. Brutus's Ahala coin, *RRC* nr. 433.

44. Cic. *Senec.* 56, *cuius dictatoris iussu magister equitum C. Servilius Ahala Sp. Maelium regnum adpetentem occupatum interemit*; Livy 4.14.3–6; cf. Dion. Hal. *Ant. Rom.* 12.2.4–8.

45. Spurius Cassius, Cic. *Rep.* 2.60, *Sp. Cassium de occupando regno molientem, summa apud populum gratia florentem, quaestor accusavit, eumque, ut audistis, cum pater in ea culpa esse conperisse se dixisset, cedente populo morte mactavit*; Livy 2.41; Dion. Hal. *Ant. Rom.* 8.69–80; Pliny, *HN* 34.15. The conspirator Cassius Longinus's descent, Cic. *Phil.* 2.26. Manlius Capitolinus, Livy 6.11, 6.14–20, his condemnation at 6.20.11–12. For this trio as poor precedents for late-Republican political violence, Wiseman 2009, 185; Tempest 2017, 94.

46. A possible exception is the story that Romulus was killed by the senators in the midst of the Senate, Livy 1.16.4; Dion. Hal. *Ant. Rom.* 2.56.3–4 (in the Curia); Plut. *Rom.* 27.3–5 (by the Senators meeting in the Temple of Vulcan); Val. Max. 5.3.1 (in the Curia), connected to the killing of Caesar by App. *B Civ.* 2.114, which Gelzer 1968 [1960], 324–325, followed by Ver Eecke 2008, 222–239, 425–442, argues that the conspirators were imitating in their killing of Caesar. But the rarity or absence of this episode in Cicero (the possible allusions, *Att.* 12.45.2 and *Rep.* 2.20 [but see 2.52], are weak) suggests that it was not much on the minds of contemporaries, if it was yet known at all. Perhaps influence went the other way: "After 44 B.C. the accounts of the death of Romulus are modeled on the murder of Caesar," Ogilvie 1965, 85. By contrast, the more benevolent story of Romulus's end—that he was snatched up into heaven—is certainly old, Ennius, *Ann.* 54, 110 (Skutsch); Cic. *Rep.* 1.25, 2.17.

47. For political murders in Rome 133–52 BC, Sigismund 2008, with emphasis (530–533) on the quest for legality, even if ginned up after the fact.

48. For the conspirators' discarded plans—killing Caesar on the *Via Sacra*, or during a *comitia*, or at the theater—Nic. Dam. 81; Suet. *Jul.* 80.4 (on which Horsfall 1974, 192–194). Harmodius and Aristogeiton, Thuc. 6.54–59 with Alföldi 1985, 321. Knowledge of historical Greek tyrant slaying—Friedel 1937, 27–72, 98–103; Berve 1967, passim with 2.742 for literature—may have been another motive of the assassination, but the details of such acts are too diverse to have provided the conspirators against Caesar with a useful model.

49. "All that one can say with certainty is that the motives of so many men must have been manifold," Rice Holmes 1923, 3.341. Nor, of course, to be discounted as motives are frustrated ambition, Storch 1995, or personal grudges against Caesar that many of the conspirators treasured, which are emphasized by Nic. Dam. 59–60 (with Toher 2006, 35–36), our earliest authority, and discussed by Epstein 1987, but these provide no explanation for their actual plan, except perhaps for the eagerness of many to stab the dictator. Cristofoli 2002, 13–35 summarizes the scholarship on the motives of the conspirators; Gesche 1976, 172–175 gathers older literature.

50. Brutus as an orator, Plut. *Brut.* 2.4–5 (cf. 52.6) with Moles 2017 [1979], 66–68, but I evaluate Brutus' eloquence more positively than Moles (to have one's speaking criticized by Cicero, as Brutus's was—Cic. *Att.* 15.1a; Tac. *Dial.* 18—hardly excludes an orator from the first rank). Brutus's oratory praised, Cic. *Brut.* 21–22, 331–2; and see Clarke 1981, 23–27; Balbo 2013.

51. For the ages of the conspirators, and the evidence and literature, Dettenhofer 1992, 14–27, 73 (Decimus Brutus); 100–101 (M. Brutus—see also Tempest 2017, 262–263 n. 28); 123 (Cassius). C. Trebonius, who appears to have held the offices of quaestor (60 BC), praetor (48 BC), and suffect consul in 45 BC, all *suo anno* (Drumann and Groebe 1906 [1837], 630–631) is the oldest conspirator of whom we know, born in 87 BC.

52. For previous, less developed suggestions of the role of this declamatory theme in motivating or guiding the killing of Caesar, Seeck 1902, 12–13; Gelzer 1918, 988; Schmitthenner 1962, 690; Meier 2012, 15; Tempest 2017, 27–28, 96.

53. On the tyrant in declamation, Fleskes 1914, drawing on both Greek and Latin materials; for Greek, Russell 1983, 32–33, 48–50, 123–128; Berve 1967, 1.498–507, 2.750–753; Malosse 2006, 164–171; Tomassi 2015; for Latin, Tabacco 1985—the most important discussion, and listing the instances of the reward for tyrant slaying in Latin (10 n. 23). More briefly on the Latin tradition, Berti 2007, 99–110; Cogitore 2013; and Schwartz 2016. Popularity: in surviving Greek declamation and Greek works of rhetorical theory Patillon 2002b, xcv counts 84 instances, making tyranny the third most popular theme after murder (157 instances) and adultery (98 instances). While many of the laws that governed declamation were fictional (see chapter 8 below), the law of the tyrannicide's reward did exist in many Greek cities, and has its roots in the Decree of Demophantus at Athens in 410 BC (Andoc. 1.96–98). On these historical laws on tyrant slaying, Friedel 1937, 72–97; Teegarden 2014. The tyrant of rhetoric, his slayer, and their associated law appear as entirely familiar in Cicero's *de Inventione* (2.144; cf. 1.102) and the anonymous *Rhetorica ad Herennium* 2.49, showing that they were well known in Rome at the latest by the early childhoods of the conspirators at whose names we can guess, and I suspect that they were well known at Rome considerably earlier than that.

54. *Prob. Rhet.* 30 (Walz, *RG* 8.407) with Lucian, *Cataplus* 28–29; *Dial. Mort.* 450 for the punishments a tyrant might expect in Hades (presumably drawing on Pl. *Grg.* 525D; *Resp.* 615D); cf. *RLM* 378; Hermog. *Stat.* 59–60 (Rabe) with Patillon 2009, 40 n. 1 for a philosopher who convinces a tyrant to abdicate and then claims the reward. For "tyrannicide by proxy" see this chapter n. 59.

55. *Theses* about tyranny, Cic. *Att.* 9.4.2–3: *et abduco parumper animum a molestiis et* τῶν προὔργου τι *delibero* (March 12, 49 BC); cf. 9.9.1; with Gildenhard 2006; for arguing *theses*, see Clarke 1951; Pasetti 2008. See Wiseman 2009, 193–196 n. 103 for letters of Cicero from before the Ides of March in which he describes Caesar as a tyrant (Cicero, naturally, did see Caesar's

tyranny in philosophical terms as well, *Att.* 10.8.6; cf. 9.13.4, and the argument of *theses* could be a philosophical as well as a rhetorical activity, Griffin 1989 [1997], 15, 34). It was claimed that Cicero was first to detect Caesar's tyrannical ambitions (Plut. *Caes.* 4.4). For Caesar as a tyrant in Cicero's philosophical works 46 to 44 BC, Wassmann 1996, 139–216; for the *Tusculan Disputations* (summer of 45 BC) in particular, Lefèvre 2008, 225–238. For Caesar as a tyrant in Cicero after the Ides of March, especially in the letters and the *de Officiis* and in large part trying to justify the murder, Sirago 1956; Strasburger 1990; Pina Polo 2006 with literature (and Alföldi 1985, 280 n. 693 for more); Wiseman 2009, 201 nn. 144–145; all in the wider context, naturally, of a perfect blizzard of invective calling Caesar everything wicked in the Roman lexicon, Strasburger 1968 [1953], 41–64. To call someone a tyrant was a perfectly standard piece of abuse that could be thrown at anyone, Pina Polo 2006, 73; for Cicero describing Antony as a tyrant, see esp. May 1996, 152 n. 30. Generally for Cicero's use of tyrants in rhetorical invective all through his career, Haehling 2000, 19–21; Luciani 2009, 153–156; Gildenhard 2011, 88–92, 173–175; Sigmund 2014, 89–97 with literature. Nor was Caesar the first figure to be so termed: both Cicero and others had long been working hard to fit Sulla into the tyrant-of-rhetoric mode, Lanciotti 1977–1978.

56. Conspirators shout, Nic. Dam. ὡς τύραννον κτείνειαν (92), τυράννου (96); App. *B Civ.* 2.119 βασιλέα καὶ τύραννον; Moles 2017 [1979], 181 suggests that Casca's shout to his brother in Greek during the murder itself (Plut. *Brut.* 17.5) may mean that "possibly here he was acutely conscious of his Hellenic tyrannicide-*persona.*"

57. Cinna, App. *B Civ.* 2.121, τύραννον, τυραννοκτόνους. In the Senate, App. *B Civ.* 2.127, τοὺς ἄνδρας ἐκάλουν τυραννοκτόνους καὶ γεραίειν ἐκέλευον . . . Καίσαρα τύραννον προαποφαίνειν; cf. App. *B Civ.* 3.15 (and in general for tyrannical terms applied to Caesar in Appian, Welch 2015, 283–284); Suet. *Tib.* 4.1, *etiam de praemiis tyrannicidarum referendum censuit.* Cass. Dio 44.21.3 has nonparticipants in the conspiracy join the conspirators on the Capitoline in hope of the ἆθλα, prizes. See Cic. *Mil.* 79–80 for the tyrant slayer's reward adduced earlier in Latin rhetoric; and Joseph. *AJ* 19.182–84 for a similar proposal for prizes after the assassination of Caligula.

58. Vell. Pat. 2.58.2 says that Brutus's use of the term "tyrant" was mere expedience, *ita enim appellari Caesarem facto eius expediebat* (with Woodman 1983 ad loc.), but in so doing he, a Latin author, tends to confirm that he was in receipt of a tradition in which the word "tyrant" was used. I do not adduce the great number of instances where our Greek sources (or characters in them) refer to Caesar or others as "tyrants" but not apparently in direct quotation.

59. Sopater, *Diar. Zet.* (Walz, *RG* 8.98 = Weißenberger XVI pp. 66, 336) = *RLM* 338. On themes of this sort see esp. Quint. *Inst.* 7.7.3, and the very popular but more involved theme of two doctors disputing which of them had poisoned a tyrant: Gibson 2013, 542–545 and Pasetti 2015, 186–187 gather the attestations and variants. For disputes over the prize, cf. *DMin.* 345, 382 (with Schwartz 2016, 268–271); Sopater, *Diar. Zet.* (Walz, *RG* 8.317 = Weißenberger LX pp. 202, 482), where the prize is shared by nine young men. Heath 1995, 103–104 gathers cases of "tyrannicide by proxy," which often generated controversies about to whom the reward was owed. War heroes who get to choose their prize for heroism (a very usual parallel theme) must sometimes fight each other if there is more than one claimant (Winterbottom 1984, 597, adding Calp. Flacc. 21 with Sussman 1994, 158) or must litigate, like multiple claimants to tyrannicide, Sen. *Contr.* 10.2.*pr.*

60. Glory of the tyrannicide of Caesar, Cic. *Phil.* 2.25, 27–28, 32–33, 114, 117 (*haec non cogitas . . . fama gloriosum tyrannum occidere*); Plut. *Caes.* 67.3; App. *B Civ.* 2.114, 119; Cass. Dio 44.21.3–4. The habit of historical authors reporting who was first to stab a person considered a tyrant is presumably related to the desire for prizes or glory: Malitz 2003, 165–166. This desire for wide participation in the act of killing also helps to explain why a meeting of the Senate was chosen as the occasion to kill Caesar: he needed to be separated from his retinue, and as many members of the conspiracy as possible needed access to him.

61. Partially distinct: a number of differences between the topoi of the tyrants of rhetoric and philosophy are pointed out in this chapter, nn. 63–64, 67–69, 77, and chapter 5 n. 16. To what degree did the ancients distinguish these various figures? If we look at Themistius's abuse of the usurper Procopius—whom he reproaches with the topoi of the tyrants of rhetoric and philosophy, compares to historical Greek tyrants, the Great King of Persia, evil Roman emperors, and the mythical wicked giant Typhon (Raschle 2011)—we might think they did not. But Amande 1993–1994 showed that although the sophist Libanius (naturally) used the topoi of rhetorical tyranny in his declamations on tyranny and tyrannicide, when he compared actual Roman officials to tyrants in his nonimaginary speeches, it was to the tyrant of Plato. The ancients could, in other words, distinguish the different tyrant types when they wanted to. But Reeves 2014, esp. 18, 107, 147 is inclined to think that they rarely did so.

62. Rich man aspires to tyranny, Fleskes 1914, 59–60; Tabacco 1985, 27–33. Winterbottom 1984, 355 and Tabacco 1985, 18–27 note that he is also conventionally youngish, an *adulescens*. And it is natural too for tyranny to run in families, Apth. *Prog.* 35 (Spengel); Apsines, *Rhet.* 1.95 (Patillon) with Patillon 2002b, 23 n. 117 for more examples. Attempting to establish a tyranny (τυραννίδος ἐπίθεσις / *adfectatio tyrannidis*) is a recognized crime, Fleskes 1914, 56; Tabacco 1985, 9 n. 20; but the acts that bring on a prosecution for attempting tyranny can naturally, to allow for compelling declamations, be equivocal, such as looking up at the acropolis and weeping (*DMin.* 267 with Winterbottom 1984, 354–355 for parallels; Hermog. *Stat.* 49–50 [Rabe] with Heath 1995, 88 for parallels; Apsines, *Rhet.* 2.3 [Patillon] with Patillon 2002b, 25 n. 127 for more parallels; Nocchi 2019).

63. Arms, *DMin.* 267.8, 322.7, 9–10; Lib. *Decl.* 37.26, 44.55; Hermog. *Stat.* 51 (Rabe; with Heath 1995, 90; Sopater, *Diar. Zet.* (Walz, *RG* 8.9 = Weißenberger I pp. 12, 276), and men to use them; cf. Lib. *Decl.* 37.19–22; Hermog. *Stat.* 47–48 (Rabe; with Heath 1995, 83), in which the rich young man is charged with attempting tyranny for supporting sons disinherited by the process of *apokeryxis* (see chapter 10 nn. 49–62). *Apparatus tyrannidis, DMin.* 322.pr., 7, 10; practicing with arms is also grounds for suspicion, Lib. *Decl.* 37.3. By contrast the tyrant of philosophy is sometimes a financially ruined man, Pl. *Resp.* 573D-575E; Arist. *Pol.* 1305B with Tabacco 1985, 29, and philosophical tyranny often has leveling ambitions to help the poor, Pl. *Resp.* 565C-D, 566A, D; Arist. *Pol.* 1305A; 1310B, a theme that is very rare in declamation (but see *DMin.* 267.8), although prospective tyrants may use the humble or wretched (e.g., the imprisoned) to be made tyrant, or be suspected of it, Hermog. *Stat.* 47–48 (Rabe); Lib. *Decl.* 37.pr., 19; [Lib.] *Decl.* 43.10. Indeed, in declamation equalization of property in the state can be a means to *forestall* tyranny, *DMin.* 261 with Asheri 1971 and Tabacco 1985, 28, because doing so eliminates the rich men who naturally become tyrants, and so throwing your wealth into the sea is a means to avoid suspicion of aiming at tyranny, Apsines, *Rhet.* 1.25 (Patillon); Sopater, *Diar. Zet.* (Walz, *RG* 8.161 = Weißenberger XXIV pp. 104, 377).

64. Citadel: *arx* or acropolis, Tomassi 2015, 252; and see Mayor 1878 ad loc. Juv. 10.307 for parallels from all genres, noting that to "seize the *arx*" (*occupare arcem*) is shorthand for becoming tyrant; cf. Tabacco 1985, 15, 42–44; Sussman 1994, 94. So deep is the association of tyrant and *arx* that "look at the acropolis" (Lib. *Decl.* 37.24; Syrianus, *in Hermog.* 2.108 [Rabe]) or even "look upwards" (Lib. *Prog.* 8.198 [Foerster] = Gibson p. 183) can be taken to signify ambitions to become tyrant (and see this chapter n. 62 for the suspicious practice of weeping near the *arx*), while ἄνειμι or *escendo* ("go up") can be shorthand for "kill the tyrant," Tabacco 1985, 43. By contrast the residence of the tyrant of philosophy is rarely marked, and, when mentioned, may merely be a nondescript "house" (Plat. *Rep.* 579B ἐν τῇ οἰκίᾳ, Xen. *Hier.* 2.10 εἴσω τῆς οἰκίας; cf. 11.2). For more stock tyrannical qualities see this chapter n. 65, chapter 5 nn. 16–21.

65. Luxury, Sen. *Contr.* 2.5.7; Lucian, *Cataplus* 8–9, 14, 16; Choricius, XXVI (*Decl.* 7).47 (on which Tomassi 2014; 2017), XXXV (*Decl.* 9).10–13, 82, 95 (Foerster and Richtsteig); cf. Sen. *Contr.* 1.7.4; Lib. *Prog.* 8.191 (Foerster) = Gibson p. 175; and Sopater, *Diar. Zet.* (Walz, *RG* 8.96 = Weißenberger XV pp. 65, 334) for his wealth. See Bouyssou 2013 for over-the-top tyrannical banquets, although the examples are philosophical and historical; and Alföldi 1955 for tyrannical dress, although again most of the examples are not from declamation.

66. Torture, chapter 5 n. 19.

67. The tyrant of rhetoric is sometimes happy and enjoys his sexual license, luxury, and cruelty, Sen. *Contr.* 2.5.6–7; DM 16; Lucian, *Cataplus* 3; Choricius, XXVI (*Decl.* 7).75 (Foerster and Richtsteig). This happy tyrant may have some connection to the tyrants of archaic and classical Greece (Trampedach 2006, 5–10; Jordović 2019, 74, 78), whom the tradition represents in some cases as envied and pleased by their lot. By contrast the tyrant of philosophy is supremely miserable, Pl. *Grg.* 469A; *Resp.* 567B; 576C, 578B, 579A-C; 579D-580C with Parry 2007; Xen. *Hier.* 1.8, 7.10 et passim with Arruzza 2019, 48–50; and see Luciani 2009, 160 for Cicero's philosophical works. The tyrant of philosophy is unhappy because he is ruled by desires that can never be satisfied, Pl. *Resp.* 573A, D-E; 577D-578A with Johnstone 2015 and Arruzza 2019, 139–143, 164–183; and with Lanza 1977, 49–53 for anticipation of this theme in tragedy, and because of his fear of murder or expulsion, Pl. *Resp.* 578A, D-E; 579B-C with Arruzza 2019, 222–226; Xen. *Hier.* 1.11–12, 2.8–13, 18, 4.2, 6.6–8; Arist. *Pol.* 1311A-1312B; 1315A; Cic. *Off.* 2.24–25; with Lanza 1977, 45–49 for anticipation of this theme in tragedy. The philosophical line was presumably intentionally polemical against the position that the unrestrained life of a tyrant was supremely blessed, Lewis 2009, 82–84. More broadly, philosophy is naturally far more interested in the inner life, and the nature of the soul, of the tyrant.

68. Esp. Lucian, *Tyr.*, where Lucian jokes about the inevitability of this fate by having a tyrant cry τετυραννοκτονήμεθα, coining a nonce word "We-are-tyrannicided" (20). On this declamation, Guast 2018, 195–203. "*Für die antike Anschauung war der natürliche Tod eines Tyrannen fast undenkbar,*" Fleskes 1914, 46. On the character of the tyrant slayer, Tabacco 1985, 12, 60–61, 83–87; and note (Sen. *Contr.* 1.7) that the tyrannicide even commands the respect of the other stock villains of declamation, pirates. The tyrannicide is similar to the stock character of the *vir fortis*, Lentano 1998, but Tabacco 1985, 64–65 points out that the *vir fortis* can also seek to become a tyrant himself (*DMin.* 293). By contrast the tyrant of philosophy is killed chiefly because of his acts of *hybris*, not because his killers seek a reward (although that is not unknown): Arist.

*Pol.* 1311A-1312B; Jedrkiewicz 2002. Motives for killing the tyrant other than the reward do exist in declamation but take second place to the reward, Tabacco 1985, 53–57. Rhetorical laws in force even if not mentioned, Winterbottom 1984, 313.

69. Rhetorical tyrant's fear, chapter 5 n. 16. Tyrant abdicates, *DMin.* 267; Sen. *Contr.* 5.8; Hermog. *Stat.* 59–60 (Rabe); Choricius, XXVI (*Decl.* 7).74, 79–80 (Foerster and Richtsteig); Anonymous Seguerianus 217 (Dilts and Kennedy); Sopater, *Diar. Zet.* (Walz, *RG* 8.95 = Weißenberger XV pp. 65, 334); *Prob. Rhet.* 68 (Walz, *RG* 8.413); *RLM* 378; Fleskes 1914, 53–54; Winterbottom 1984, 355; Tabacco 1985, 10 n. 25, 60–62, noting that by contrast the tyrant of philosophy does not have the option of stepping down, although historical tyrants did do so.

70. Escorted in glory, Sen. *Contr.* 9.4.4, 17. Return to previous regime, *DMin.* 253, 267; Lib. *Decl.* 14.8; [Lib.] *Decl.* 43.7, 19; Choricius, XXVI (*Decl.* 7).20 (Foerster and Richtsteig); and above all Lucian, *Tyr.* esp. 9–10; quoted 6. On the thematic opposition of the tyrant to the *res publica*, laws, *ius, libertas*, etc., and their restoration when the tyrant is slain, Tabacco 1985, 14–27.

71. Dominated their minds: to a greater or lesser extent. Lesser, probably in the case of Decimus Brutus who did, after all, gather gladiators, and lure Caesar out of his house, neither of which was part of the script. Schmitthenner 1962, 692 describes the image of Decimus Brutus given by Cicero's letters as *"eines energischen, klarblickenden, nüchtern-, am Ende grimmig-realistischen Soldaten."* Similarly, different conspirators will have followed the declamatory story more or less literally: although a declaimer could not change the facts of a declamatory scenario (thus the conspirators' being roped to the same basic narrative), there was much art in devising a favorable context—a *color*—for that scenario.

72. Cf. Syme 1939, 99; Drossart 1970, 381; Moles 2017 [1979], 192–193; Gotter 1996, 22 n. 62.

73. For versions of the story in which the conspirators are escorted down from the Capitoline, chapter 5 n. 1.

74. Lucian, *Tyr.* 10; *Dial. Mort.* 375; Lib. *Decl.* 44.3, 17; [Lib.] *Decl.* 43.47.

75. *"Diese Überlegungen waren zwar logisch, bildeten aber einem Schönheitsfehler in der reinen Tyrannenmordideologie"* (Dettenhofer 1992, 255).

76. App. *B Civ.* 2.114; cf. Cass. Dio 44.19.2.

77. We do see enough to grasp that a tyrant has guards, usually δορυφόροι in Greek (Tomassi 2015, 252) and minions, ὑπηρέται in Greek, e.g., Lib. *Decl.* 37.34. In Latin, *custodes* are found, but rare (Sen. *Contr.* 2.5.4), while usually the overwhelmingly common *satellites* serve both functions, on whom Winterbottom 1984, 357 and Tabacco 1985, 21–22, 38–39, who notes the lack of emphasis on such creatures, in contrast to the much-emphasized armed retainers of the tyrant of philosophy, on whom Pelling 2011, 429. Lib. *Decl.* 44 is unique, so far as I know, in imagining that a tyrant might have powerful collaborators (23–27, 62 συνεργοί) and noting that after the fall of the tyranny the tyrant's collaborators flee into exile (65–66). Lib. *Prog.* 8.203 (Foerster) = Gibson p. 189 tells us that an ex-tyrant's humble supporters are executed (cf. Lib. *Decl.* 44.49), but that usually *"leur sort lors de la chute de la tyrannie est passé sous silence"* (Malosse 2006, 169).

78. Quoted, Lucian, *Tyr.* 9–10; cf. *DMin.* 267.

79. Cf. Tabacco 1985, 132; Seeck 1902, 28; Stewens 1963, 59–60. Thus also when Antony, having fled, realized that he was not being pursued, he—with the same education as Caesar's killers—will have recognized the rhetorical plot the conspirators were following, realized that

he was in no danger, and, regaining his courage, moved to avail himself of Caesar's treasure (chapter 3 n. 21).

80. Nabis, Livy 35.36.4, *nec movisset se quisquam, si extemplo positis armis vocata in contionem multitudo fuisset et oratio habita tempori conveniens*; 35.37.2, *evocatis principibus et oratione habita qualis habenda Alexameno fuerat.*

81. Senate summoned (cf. Cic. *Att.* 14.10.1 [19 April, 44 BC]) and speech to the people, Cic. *Att.* 15.11.2 (ca. June seventh, 44 BC), *populum ardentem studio vehementius incitare*; on this diagnosis of what should have been done, Cicero says *nec vero quicquam novi sed ea quae cottidie omnes.*

82. Cicero's own flight prevented him from giving such speeches, although Cicero himself tells us (Cic. *Phil.* 2.28, 30; cf. Cass. Dio 44.20.4, 46.22.4) that Brutus called out for Cicero right after the killing of Caesar.

## Chapter 5: Who Was Thinking Rhetorically?

1. Brutus escorted from the Capitoline, Plut. *Brut.* 18.11 (with Pelling 2011, 488–489; Moles 2017 [1979], 195–196) versus Cic. *Att.* 15.11.2 (cf. 14.10.1 for the location). Nic. Dam. 99 has the descent of Brutus and Cassius escorted not by distinguished persons, but only by gladiators and slaves. Procession from the *arx* in declamation, chapter 4 n. 70. Nor is the contamination of older stories of political murder or expulsion at Rome impossible, although whether they were contaminated by a generic Greek tradition of tyranny, the tyrant of philosophy, or the tyrant of rhetoric is hard to tell. For Tarquinius Superbus portrayed as a Greek tyrant, Ogilvie 1965, 195; Dunkle 1971, 16; cf. Cic. *Rep.* 2.44–49 with Michelfeit 1964, 276, 279–281, and expelled as such by L. Junius Brutus, Alföldi 1985, 281, 295. For the similarity of the stories of Spurius Cassius and Spurius Maelius (see chapter 4 nn. 42–45) to the τυραννίδος ἐπίθεσις / *adfectatio tyrannidis*, the declamatory theme of the rich man trying to become a tyrant, Fleskes 1914, 56–58. The murky story of the killing of Romulus by the Senate (see chapter 4 n. 46), which Appian claims the conspirators also had on their minds, had also been transformed into a tyrant slaying (App. *B Civ.* 2.114).

2. Cass. Dio 44.16.1. Smuggling daggers/swords and the difficulties thereof in declamation, Sen. *Contr.* 4.7; Lib. *Decl.* 14.8 (= [Lib.] *Decl.* 43.18); Lib. *Prog.* 8.205 (Foerster) = Gibson p. 189; Choricius, XXVI (*Decl.* 7).8 (Foerster and Richtsteig). Or, of course, a Roman as late as Dio may have been unable to imagine anyone being allowed to approach Caesar unsearched.

3. Porcia, Val. Max. 3.2.15; Plut. *Brut.* 13 with Moles 2017 [1979] 153; Polyaenus, *Strat.* 8.32; Cass. Dio 44.13; Tempest 2017, 89 with literature.

4. Dio's version, Cass. Dio 44.13; cf. Plut. *Brut.* 13.2–11 (without mention of her fear of torture).

5. Caesar dislikes torture, Suet. *Caes.* 74.1. For this episode Pagán 2004, 119–122, with the unlikelihood that Porcia would actually be tortured noted on 122.

6. Caesar's desire to preserve Cato, Plut. *Caes.* 54.1. His clemency to former enemies, Suet. *Jul.* 75.4; Plut. *Caes.* 57.3–4; Plut. *Brut.* 6.2; App. *B Civ.* 2.146, 4.8; Cass. Dio 43.50.1–2, 44.39.4–5, with Alföldi 1985 and Flamerie de Lachapelle 2011, 45–119 with literature.

7. Bibulus's book, Plut. *Brut.* 13.3.

8. The tortured wife, Sen. *Contr.* 2.5 with Pagán 2007–2008; and, for torturing women, Fleskes 1914, 47–49; Ash 2018, 260–261. On torture in declamation in general, see this chapter n. 19.

9. Speech of Porcia, Cass. Dio 44.13.4, described by Moles 2017 [1979], 153 as "a standard rhetorical piece."

10. Such a process of simplifying the tradition in the direction of the stock tyrant-slaying plot may be evident in the tale of the killing of Spurius Maelius, about which an alternate version survives in which his killer, Servilius Ahala, is not master of horse, but a private citizen: Dion. Hal. *Ant. Rom.* 12.4.2–5. Servilius is chosen to be the assassin: νέον ὄντα καὶ κατὰ χεῖρα γενναῖον, i.e., as a *vir fortis*, and after his deed he runs back to the Senate ἔχοντα τὸ ξίφος ᾑμαγμένον κεκραγότα πρὸς τοὺς διώκοντας, ὅτι κελευσθεὶς ὑπὸ τῆς βουλῆς ἀνῄρηκε τὸν τύραννον. See Pina Polo 2006, 84.

11. Speech of Antony in Senate, App. *B Civ.* 2.133–134; of Brutus on Capitoline, 2.137–141 (on these speeches Balbo 2011); Antony's eulogy over Caesar, 2.144–146. Cicero, Cass. Dio 44.23–33; Antony, Cass. Dio 44.36–49. Also, Nic. Dam. 100 had in his *Assembly Speeches* (lost to us) an oration—presumably of the historian's own composition—that Brutus gave when he came down from the Capitoline to address the people. The competing funeral speeches of Brutus and Antony in *Julius Caesar* are a creation of Shakespeare's, but they give rise to exactly the sort of scenario that the ancient literary tradition might have invented under the influence of declamation, but did not.

12. Capitolinus, Livy 6.11, 6.14–20; Zonaras 7.23.10 and Cass. Dio 7.26. There was material to work with: even in Livy Capitolinus harangues the plebs in his own house, 6.14.11, which was on the Capitoline, 6.19.1; and in the wake of his execution patricians were forbidden to live on the Capitoline, 6.20.13. Cf. (perhaps) Plut. *Ti. Gracch.* 17; App. *B Civ.* 1.32, and also, for the reported plans (not carried out) to kill Caligula on the Capitoline, Joseph. *AJ* 19.71. Roman grasp of the association of tyrant slaying with the *arx* is confirmed by the placement of a Harmodius and Aristogeiton statue group (the latter statue survives) on the Capitoline—albeit perhaps at the other end of the hill from the *arx*—at some point in the late Republic, Pina Polo 2006, 88–92; Azoulay 2017 [2014], 141–150; Seemann 2019 for recent literature.

13. Cass. Dio 44.7.4 with Dobesch 1971 [2001]. For Caesar's dismissing his guard, see this chapter nn. 39–41.

14. Multiple assassins, Cic. *Div.* 2.23; cf. Cic. *Phil.* 2.26–30; Capitoline, Cic. *Att.* 14.14.2; speeches, *Att.* 15.11.2; irrational not to kill Antony and Lepidus, *Att.* 14.21.3 and 15.11.2.

15. For emperors depicted as tyrants in Roman history writing, Wickert 1954, 2119–2123 (and in other genres) with 2121 on Domitian; Jerome 1923, 366–380 on Tiberius in Tacitus; Walker 1960 [1952], 149–153, 204–234, on all emperors in Tacitus (although her definition of the tyrant goes beyond the figure familiar from declamation), and see the itemized entries for "tyrant" in the indices of Woodman 2017, 319 and 2018, 343. On Sallust, Livy, and Tacitus, Dunkle 1971, noting especially emphasis on the qualities of *saevitia,* with parallels to declamation (14–15), *crudelitas, avaritia, vis, superbia,* and *libido* (14–15); Scheid 1984 (Caligula, Nero, Vitellius, and Galerius); Soverini 2002 (*saevitia* in Tacitus); Keitel 2007 (Vitellius in Tacitus).

16. Domitian fearful, Suet. *Dom.* 1.2, 3.2, 14.1–4, 15.3, 16.1–2 (mirrored stone, private questioning, 14.4); Pliny, *Pan.* 49.1, with Jones 1996, 117–118; Reeves 2014, 165–166, 298–308. Tyrants in declamation fearful, Sen. *Contr.* 1.7.2, 2.5.2; Calp. Flacc. 13; Lib. *Decl.* 14.9, 37.25; Choricius, XXVI (*Decl.* 7).17, 67, 86 (Foerster and Richtsteig); Syrianus, *in Hermog.* 2.111 (Rabe) with Tabacco 1985, 33–50; a quality the tyrant of declamation shares with those of tragedy, philosophy, and history (34), but which is less marked in declamation, presumably because it conflicts with the

declamatory tyrant depicted as joyful in his cruelty, see chapter 4 n. 67. In linking Domitian to the tyrant of rhetoric I draw heavily upon Reeves 2014. Cf. Tacitus's depiction of Domitian as a stock tyrant, Benferhat 2013; for Dio Chrysostom's, Ventrella 2016. Note that the same sort of analysis of the traditions about Domitian that is undertaken here could just as easily be undertaken about Caligula (and his assassination) on the basis of Joseph. *AJ* book 19.

17. Domitian secluded, Suet. *Dom.* 3.1, 14.4, 21 with Hulls 2014, 180–184; Pliny, *Pan.* 48.5, 49.2, 49.5–6; Cass. Dio 66 (65 Cary).9.5; Aur. Vict. *Caes.* 11.5. For tyrants secluded in declamation, Tabacco 1985, 42–46, adding Lucian, *Cataplus* 11–12. But this is not a major theme in declamation, where (in contrast to the tyrant of philosophy: Pl. *Resp.* 579B; Xen. *Hier.* 3) the tyrant can even have friends, *amici*, Tabacco 1985, 39–41; cf. [Lib.] *Decl.* 43.5; *Prob. Rhet.* 4 (Walz, *RG* 8.402).

18. Domitian's avarice, Suet. *Dom.* 3.2, 10.1, 12.1–2; Suet. *Vesp.* 1.1, Jones 1996, 100. For tyrannical avarice in declamation, *DMin.* 261.9, 329.9; Lucian, *Cataplus* 26; *Tyr.* 5; Sopater, *Diar. Zet.* (Walz, *RG* 8.324 = Weißenberger LXIII pp. 206, 487) with Tabacco 1985, 112, 117–118, 126–131; anticipated in tragedy, Lanza 1977, 53–55.

19. Domitian's cruelty, Suet. *Dom.* 3.2, 8.4, 10.1–2 (devoured by dogs), 10.5, 11; for rending by dogs cf. 15.3, where Domitian has killed in another way a soothsayer who predicts his own death by this means, to prove him wrong; Jones 1996, 84. Cf. for imperial *crudelitas* in Suetonius and the *HA*, Callu 1984, 328. For tyrannical cruelty in declamation, Sen. *Contr.* 1.7.7, 9; 2.5 passim; *DMin.* 322.4, 329.9; Lucian, *Dial. Mort.* 366; *Prob. Rhet.* 67 (Walz, *RG* 8.413), with Tabacco 1985, 89–116. Torture, Suet. *Dom.* 10.5. Torture in declamation, Sen. *Contr.* 1.7.9, 2.5 passim; 5.8, 9.4.14, 16; *DMin.* 269.pr., 4–6, 16; Calp. Flacc. 13; *DM* 16; *RLM* 93; Dio Chrys. 47.24; Lucian, *Cataplus* 26; Lucian, *Tyr.* 5 with Tabacco 1985, for the equipment (88–89), and the techniques (96) (cf. [Phalaris] *Ep.* 147). Declaimers liked torture scenes: Tabacco 1985, 107 refers to "ἔκφρασις delle torture"; cf. van Mal-Maeder 2007, 74–82; Danesi Marioni 2011–2012; Bernstein 2012; 2013, 46–57 (in large part replicating 2012), 133–146; Zinsmaier 2015. Dunkle 1971, 14 happily translates *crudelitas'* near-synonym *saevitia* (Suet. *Dom.* 3.2, 10.1, 10.5, 11.1) as "maniacal sadism," and for its use in association with tyrants in declamation, Tabacco 1985, 88–93; cf. ὠμότης in the Greek, Lib. *Decl.* 14.31; [Lib.] *Decl.* 43.69, 73; Lucian, *Cataplus* 26.

20. Domitian arrogant, Suet. *Dom.* 12.3–13.3; Pliny, *Pan.* 48.4, 49.1; Jones 1996, 105. For tyrannical *superbia* / *hybris* in declamation, Tabacco 1985, 128–129, adding Lucian, *Cataplus* 26; Lucian, *Tyr.* 5, 16; Choricius, XXXV (*Decl.* 9).17, 67 (Foerster and Richtsteig); anticipated in tragedy, Lanza 1977, 59–61.

21. Domitian's sexuality, 1.1, 1.3, 22 with Reeves 2014, 178. For tyrannical *libido* in declamation, Fleskes 1914, 49–53; Dunkle 1971, 16; Winterbottom 1984, 396; Tabacco 1985, 116, 118–125, adding, from the Greek tradition, Dio Chrys. 47.24; Lucian, *Cataplus* 14, 26–27; Lib. *Decl.* 37.22–23; *Decl.* 42 passim; 44.34–36; *Prog.* 8.199 (Foerster) = Gibson p. 183; 8.204 (Foerster) = Gibson p. 189; [Lib.] *Decl.* 43.12, 75; Choricius, XXVI (*Decl.* 7).83–84; XXXV (*Decl.* 9).13–17 (Foerster and Richtsteig); *Prob. Rhet.* 66 (Walz, *RG* 8.413).

22. Domitian hated and feared, Suet. *Dom.* 14.1. Hate and fear of tyrant in declamation, Tabacco 1985, 47–50.

23. If he needed architectural guidance, Seneca's *Thyestes* lines 641–682 could provide it. Unruh 2015 argues that Seneca based his Palace of Atreus on Nero's Golden House, but the similarities to the Palace of Domitian are striking.

24. On the security arrangements, and calling the palace an *arx*, Pliny, *Pan.* 47.4–5, 49.1, with Haensch 2012, 270. Authors also used the term *arx* for Domitian's Alban villa (on which Jones 1992, 27–28, 96–97; 1996, 45): Tac. *Agr.* 45.1 (additionally noting that it was suitable for the keeping of prisoners); Juv. 4.145, with Jones 1992, 27 for the tyrannical implications; cf. Cass. Dio 67.1.2 (*acropolis*).

25. The remains of Domitian's palace have never been properly published, but see MacDonald 1982–1986 [1965], 1.47–74, 187, with the concern for security revealed by the architecture (63 n. 55); water reservoirs (49); *LTUR* 2.193–194; Carandini 2017 [2012] 1.242–247. Recent excavations have muddied the chronological waters somewhat: the palace may have been started by Vespasian, Vonderstein 2007, 26–31, 34–39; Wulf-Rheidt 2015, esp. 6, 12. In addition to archaeology, there are literary sources for Domitian's palace, collected by Jones 1992, 95–96, and esp. Stat. *Silv.* 4.2; Mart. 8.36, studied by Klodt 2001, 45–62. Suetonius mentions only the mirrored portico that may have been part of it, *Dom.* 14.4. For the controversy about security arrangements in the archaeology: Zanker 2002 [2004], 115; Wulf-Rheidt 2012a, 285; 2012b, 99.

26. Domitian in AD 69, Suet. *Dom.* 1.2; Tac. *Hist.* 3.74.1.

27. 49,000 m², Carandini 2017 [2012] 1.243.

28. We know that Fronto taught Marcus Aurelius and Lucius Verus to declaim, and the late fourth-century author of the *HA* takes it for granted that emperors were so educated, Pageau 2015, with 68 n. 3 for Fronto.

29. For the prevalence of thinking about tyranny among the social classes who wrote, see Opelt 1965, 166–168, and *tyrannus* in her index (282). Which is not to say that Domitian could not also be envisaged as the tyrant of philosophy: see Starr 1949 for Epictetus; Philostr. *VA* 7–8 (esp. 7.1–3), with Flinterman 1995, 148–149, 162–170.

30. Chapter 2 n. 2.

31. Witschel 2006 analyses the behavior of "mad emperors," distinguishing several patterns: "god-emperor" (Caligula), "performer-emperor" (Nero, Commodus), "commander-emperor" (Domitian), and "priest-emperor" (Elagabalus).

32. For Domitian's religious activity, Gsell 1894, 75–83; Jones 1992, 99–105; and see this chapter n. 35 for his building. For tyrants as temple robbers in declamation, Fleskes 1914, 63–64; Dunkle 1971, 15; and Tabacco 1985, 126–131 gather and discuss the references; impiety anticipated in tragedy, Lanza 1977, 55–59. Dunkle 1967, 162 n. 23 notes how Cicero picks up this theme (among other topoi about tyrants) in his depiction of Verres.

33. Gsell 1894, 83–87; Grelle 1980; Jones 1992, 106–107; with 1996, 64 for banning castration; Gering 2012, 214–221.

34. Gsell 1894, 165–237; Jones 1992, 126–159; Gering 2012, 245–292; and note also Domitian's eagerness to be depicted in armor in statues and on coins, Wolsfeld 2014, 200–204.

35. Domitian's games, Suet. *Dom.* 4.1–4 and Jones 1992, 102–106; 1996, 35–44. Domitian prefers to eat alone, Braund 1996, 44–45 (and see esp. Juv. 4.37–149; Pliny, *Pan.* 49.6), and is criticized for it, but gives public banquets, Suet. *Dom.* 21; Stat. *Silv.* 1.6.35–50; private banquets, Stat. *Silv.* 4.2; Mart. 9.91 (with Vössing 2004, 312–314, 366, 385–386, 405–406, 466–471, 503–506, 525–527); and Domitian's palace had rooms for banquets with up to 500 guests in total (Zanker 2002 [2004], 113; cf. Mart. 8.39.1–2 and Vössing 2004, 348–352; Mar 2009, 261–262). Acts of ostentatious generosity, Suet. *Dom.* 9.1–3 with Jones 1996, 80–83. Domitian's building projects,

Jones 1992, 79–94; Sablayrolles 1994; Gering 2012, 206–213. He also raised the silver content of the coinage, Jones 1996, 100, which Romans considered a virtuous act, just as lowering it was considered vicious.

36. Happy tyrant, chapter 4 n. 67.

37. Quoted, Cic. *Off.* 3.82 (doubted by Rawson 1994, 439 n. 82); cf. Suet. *Jul.* 30.5.

38. Plut. *Caes.* 64.3 has D. Brutus urge Caesar to go to the Senate on the ides because cancelling the meeting of the Senate would tacitly acknowledge that Rome was in a state of "slavery and tyranny."

39. Spanish bodyguard dismissed, Suet. *Jul.* 86.1; App. *B Civ.* 2.107, 109; Cass. Dio 44.7.4; Nic. Dam. 80, with Jehne 1987, 224–225.

40. New military bodyguard expected when Caesar left on campaign, App. *B Civ.* 2.114. For Caesar's expedition against the Parthians, Pelling 2011, 436–438.

41. For the puzzle of dismissing the bodyguard, Jehne 2009, 128–138; Strauss 2015, 102–104; against advice, Vell. Pat. 2.57.1, with Woodman 1983 ad loc.; for the bodyguard dismissed because of its associations with tyranny, Treu 1948, 208–215; Alföldi 1985, 283–292; Jehne 2009, 136; Pelling 2011, 429 with literature; Jehne 2014, 116; Toher 2017, 325, noticing that δορυφόροι, the word used to describe the bodyguard at Nic. Dam. 80, is the standard term for a tyrant's bodyguard. In Rome Caesar may formally have been given an alternative bodyguard of senators and *equites* (Cass. Dio 44.6.1; Plutarch *Caes.* 57.4 denies it), but if so this new guard existed only τῷ . . . λόγῳ (Cass. Dio 44.7.4) and Caesar was considered not to have an effective guard once the Spaniards departed (Nic. Dam. 80; App. *B Civ.* 2.107, 118; Suet. *Jul.* 86.1; Cass. Dio 44.15.2).

42. Offers throat, Plut. *Caes.* 60.4 with Pelling 2011, 449; *Ant.* 12.4. Cf. the excuses put out after the insult to the Senate, that Caesar was ill (Plut. *Caes.* 60.4; Cass. Dio 44.8.3) or that he was held down (Suet. *Jul.* 78.1) so that he could not rise.

43. Caesar's fatalism: Suet. *Jul.* 86 *neque voluisse se diutius vivere neque curasse* (with Canfora 2007 [1999], 322–323), although it is attributed to his failing health, or his trust in the Senate's oath to protect him, or exhaustion with living perpetually in fear. For not wishing to live in fear, a commonplace for tyrants, cf. Vell. Pat. 2.57.1 (with Woodman 1983 ad loc.); Suet. *Jul.* 87; Plut. *Caes.* 57.4; App. *B Civ.* 2.109; Pelling 2011, 430 (cf. Cic. *Phil.* 2.112).

44. Ignores warnings before the ides: Vell. Pat. 2.57.2; Suet. *Jul.* 75.4; Plut. *Caes.* 62.3, 5; *Brut.* 8.1 (with Moles 2017 [1979] 112–113), cf. 15.3; Plut. *Ant.* 13.1; Cic. *Phil.* 2.34, 74; Cass. Dio 44.15.1. See also Florus 2.13.94; but Nic. Dam. 66 claims he did not know of the conspiracy. Caesar had not always been so indifferent to attempts on his life: Suet. *Jul.* 74.1; Plut. *Caes.* 49.2–3.

45. Ignores portents: Nic. Dam. 83–87; Vell. Pat. 2.57.2; Suet. *Jul.* 81; Plut. *Brut.* 15.1; Plut. *Caes.* 63–64 (with Pelling 2011, 465–476 with literature); App. *B Civ.* 2.115–116, 149, 153; Cass. Dio 44.17–18; Florus 2.13.94.

46. Does not read written warning: Nic. Dam. 66; Vell. Pat. 2.57.2; Suet. *Jul.* 81.4; Florus 2.13.94; App. *B Civ.* 2.116; Cass. Dio 44.18.3; but Plut. *Caes.* 65.2 says that Caesar was prevented from reading it by the crush around him.

47. Wants an unexpected death: Suet. *Jul.* 87; App. *B Civ.* 2.115; Plut. *Caes.* 63.4.

48. Quoted, Suet. *Jul.* 87.

49. I am happy to acknowledge my intellectual debt to Turner (1974) 60–97. Much thought has gone into mythical or historical entities Caesar might have imitated in his last years, Zecchini 2001, 117–135; ver Eecke 2008, 360–397.

## Section III: Rhetoric's Curious Children

1. Similarity of buildings, MacDonald 1982–1986 [1965], 2.111–142.

## Chapter 6: Monumental Nymphaea

1. The section of this chapter on nymphaea is adapted, with addition of recent literature but trimming of much scholarship, from Lendon 2015, which should also be consulted for the author's thanks to colleagues.

Historical summaries of the scholarship on nymphaea, Richard 2012, 1–12; Aristodemou 2012, 25–27; Lamare 2019, 33–43; and Richard 2016; for the wider literature on "water culture" in the Roman world, Rogers 2018a, esp. with "water displays" (46–56). For the ancient terms used to describe large fountains, Settis 1973, 683–740; Letzner 1990, 24–116; Richard 2012, 14–27. Νυμφαῖον or *nymphaeum* was never in antiquity the standard word for such structures, but its modern ubiquity as the term for large, spectacular, ornamented Roman-period fountains makes its use here inevitable.

A definition of a "monumental nymphaeum" would—admitting some exceptions—include elements such as (a) a frontage of at least fifteen meters; (b) a main water receptacle open to the sky; (c) elaborate decoration, usually in the "tabernacle" or "aedicular" (columns and niches) style.

2. For nymphaea in the greater context of cities' other major waterworks, Tuttahs 2007; Richard 2012; Aristodemou 2014. For the modern controversy about spillage into the streets and whether monumental nymphaea could be turned off, Lamare 2019, 192–194, 203; Rogers 2018a, 41 n. 182. See esp. Strabo 14.1.37; Frontin. *Aq.* 111.

3. For the convenient neighborhood fountains of Pompeii, Schmölder-Veit 2009, 115–137.

4. For the placement of nymphaea, Uğurlu 2009, 103–137; on the edges of town, Segal 1997, 162–166; Bru 2011, 48–49; entirely outside the city, as at Side (D-Kl nr. 106 = R nr. 70).

5. Jacobs and Richard 2012.

6. Architectural history questions, Lendon 2015, 123 n. 3 for literature. Functions of nymphaea, practical or symbolic, Richard 2012, 237–258. Symbols of Rome and its power, Lendon 2015, 124 n. 5 for literature. Religious significance, Lendon 2015, 124 n. 6 for literature, adding Lamare 2019, 263–285. Cool refuges, articulating the streetscape, so to be studied in the context of urban design, Lendon 2015, 124 n. 7 for literature, adding Lamare 2019, 220–233.

7. For lists of imperial-period fountains in Asia Minor and their donors (when they can be deduced from inscriptions), Pont 2010, 169–174; Aristodemou 2012, 68–87, with Lendon 2015, 124 n. 9 on the perils of attributing the building of fountains to emperors on the basis of dedicatory inscriptions and the dubious testimony of John Malalas. Arguing that the impetus for building monumental nymphaea in Asia Minor came primarily from Rome, Winter 1996, 177–184; Longfellow 2011, esp. 2, 28, 208–211; that it was local, Richard 2011 with *SEG* LXI 1606; Campagna 2011; Richard 2012, 247–252; Burrell 2012; Richard 2016, 26; and cf. Lamare 2019, 249–261 for North Africa. The evidence and arguments for local motivation are far stronger.

8. Asia Minor: Dorl-Klingenschmid 2001 and Richard 2012; summarily, Pont 2010, 169–176. For Late Antiquity, Jacobs and Richard 2012; Richard 2012, 215–236.

9. The West, Letzner 1990; Rome and its environs, Neuerburg 1965; North Africa, Aupert 1974; Lamare 2019, 295–384.

10. The East: Segal 1997, 151–168; Kamash 2010, 112–117; and Richard's catalogue 2012, 259–280. Greece: Walker 1979; Glaser 1983; Agusta-Boularot 2001; Rogers 2018b; Aristodemou 2018a; of which, so far as I am aware, the only ones to bear comparison in size to the great nymphaea of Asia Minor are the Hadrianic fountain in the Athenian Agora (Glaser 1983, nr. 74 = R nr. 13 and Leigh 2018; c. 19.5 m frontage); the Nymphaeum of Herodes Atticus at Olympia (Glaser 1983, nr. 75 = R nr. 51 and Bol 1984; c. 30 m frontage); the Roman rebuilding of the Arsinoë fountain at Messene (Trabucco della Toretta 2018; 36 m frontage); nymphaeum F25 at Gortyn (R nr. 41; Longfellow 2018; 16 m frontage); and the facing pair at Nicopolis (Walker 1979, 138–148 and Zachos and Leontaris 2018, 39–42; each 12.5 m frontage). I know of no study of nymphaea in the empire's Balkan provinces outside Greece, but nymphaea do appear on the coins of cities in that area: Hadrianopolis (Thrace), and possibly Nicopolis ad Istrum (Moesia), Letzner 1990, 10 and 13.

11. For the aesthetics of monumentality under the Roman Empire, Thomas 2007.

12. On the aqueducts of Asia Minor and their dates, Coulton 1987, esp. 73; Winter 1996, 180–182; Scherrer 2006. For relations between aqueducts and nymphaea, Richard 2012, 52–92; dedicated aqueducts feeding nymphaea (71–74), but noting (57–58) that it was more common for nymphaea to be integrated into existing systems of water distribution, although in many cases those existing systems were ultimately fed by, and required, Roman-period aqueducts.

13. For older fountain forms in Asia Minor, Lendon 2015, 126 n. 15 for literature.

14. See Longfellow 2011, 13–60 for an account of fountains in Republican and early imperial Rome. For the *Meta Sudans*, *LTUR* ad loc.; for provincial copies, Longfellow 2011, 25, 33, 46–49. For the (unconvincing to me) discussion of possible Roman prototypes for the facade nymphaea of Asia Minor, Lendon 2015, 126 n. 16 for literature; *sed contra* Popkin 2016, 157, 218 n. 45.

15. For different building types in Roman Asia Minor and their dates, conveniently, Pont 2010, 25–201. For basilicas in Asia Minor, Stinson 2007; for the coming of Roman-style baths to Asia Minor, Nielsen 1993, 1.101–103.

16. For the monumental gymnasium and bath complex, Yegül 1992, 250–306; Nielsen 1993, 1.103–108, 2.36–39 and a list at 1.105 n. 72; mean size, 1.105. The earliest known complex of this type is the Domitianic so-called Harbor Baths at Ephesus, with a ca. 11,000 $m^2$ footprint (Nielsen 1993, nr. 295).

17. For parallels between the ancient terminology of, and structures of thought in, rhetoric and architecture, E. Thomas 2014, 37–51, 63, 65, 86–87.

18. On the *progymnasmata*, see chapter 1 nn. 6, 51–55; for encomium in the *progymnasmata*, Berardi 2017, 96–110, and Pordomingo 2007 gathering the papyri.

19. Pernot 1993, 1.134–178 gathers the voluminous *testimonia* for encomia of individuals.

20. Baldness: the *Encomium calvitii* of Synesius of Cyrene survives, Lamoureux and Aujoulet 2004, 48–90; parrot, Philostr. *VS* 487.

21. Quint. *Inst.* 3.7.26–27, *laudantur autem urbes similiter atque homines. nam pro parente est conditor, et multum auctoritatis adfert vetustas, ut iis, qui terra dicuntur orti, et virtutes ac vitia circa res gestas eadem quae in singulis: illa propria, quae ex loci positione ac munitione sunt. cives illis ut*

*hominibus liberi sunt decori. est laus et operum: in quibus honor, utilitas, pulchritudo, auctor spectari solet. honor ut in templis, utilitas ut in muris, pulchritudo vel auctor utrubique.* Cities viewed as humans was old in poetry, Kienzle 1936, 9–11.

22. In addition to the brief notice in Quintilian (who provides the *terminus ante quem* for the existence of such rules), accident of survival has left us instructions for praising cities thought to be from the third century AD or after (although there were certainly earlier works upon which the later authors drew): two treatises attributed to Menander Rhetor (I 346–367; II 369–371, 379, 382–388, 391–392, 394, 417, 424, 426–433; text and translation Russell and Wilson 1981; and see Pernot 1981 on the difference between the approaches of the two treatises); [Dion. Hal.] *Rhet.* 257, 275–276 (Usener and Radermacher; English translation in Russell and Wilson [1981] 362–381); [Hermogenes], *Prog.* 18 (Rabe) = Priscian, *Prae.* 24 (*RLM*); Anon. *Excerpta rhetorica* in *RLM* p. 587. For the conventions of encomia upon cities, Pernot 1993, 1.178–216 and Franco 2005, 387–422; for the history of the genre, Classen 1986.

23. Men. Rhet. I 346–351, 353–365.

24. Virtues, old in poetry, Kienzle 1936, 74, 76–79 and e.g., Strabo 5.2.3; Diod. Sic. 5.14.1; *thesis*, old in poetry, Kienzle 1936, 14–28, 39–57, and e.g., Strabo 5.1.11, 5.3.13.

25. Pernot 1993, 1.79–82, 178–188.

26. Men. Rhet. I 365.

27. Men. Rhet. I 363–364.

28. Buildings ought to be praised, e.g., Aristid. *Or.* 17.10–12 (Behr); Philostr. *VS* 532; Choricius II (*Or.* 2).5 (Foerster and Richtsteig). Praise of person's appearance, Pernot 1993, 1.159–161, with 197 on the conflict about praising buildings. Overall, the formula *laudantur urbes similiter atque homines* produced "*une véritable dépréciation des biens extérieurs des cités,*" Pernot 1993, 1.197.

29. Men. Rhet. II 382–383, 386; Pernot 1993, 1.188, 215–216. Causing yet more puzzlement to practitioners, Men. Rhet. I 365; Lib. *Or.* 11.130; [Dion. Hal.] *Rhet.* 276 (Usener and Radermacher), nor was there a natural place in this structure to bring up the honors and titles the city had received from kings and emperors, a subject of great competition in Greek cities under the Roman Empire, see this chapter n. 72.

30. Men. Rhet. I 349.

31. Men. Rhet. I 346–351.

32. Men. Rhet. I 345, 347; II 383–384, 386–387, 392, 427, 433; [Dion. Hal.] *Rhet.* 257 (Usener and Radermacher); Anon. *Excerpta rhetorica* p. 587 line 24 (*RML*); cf. Men. Rhet. I 352, II 423.

33. Men. Rhet. I 349.

34. Dio Chrys. *Or.* 33.2, 17–18, 23–25; 35.13, 18–20; 45.12; Aristid. *Or.* 1 passim; 17.11, 14–15; 18.6, 9; 21.14–15; 26.97 (Behr); there survives also a fragmentary panegyric by Aelius Aristides, which, judging by its title, was wholly devoted to praise of the water of Pergamon (53 [Behr]), with Jones 1991; cf. Philostr. *VS* 491, 525, 557, 613. On praise of rivers, springs, and waterworks in general, Maupai 2003, 33–40, 133–140; Casevitz, Lagacherie, and Saliou 2016, 184, 191.

35. E.g., Aristid. *Or.* 17.14, 21.14 (Behr).

36. Dio Chrys. *Or.* 32.37–38; and cf. the same sneer in John Chrysostom centuries later (*ad populum Antiochenum de statuis* 17 [= *PG* 49, 179]).

37. E.g., Men. Rhet. II 392.

38. Longwinded, Men. Rhet. II 403; myths, II 401–402; cf. in practice Himerius, *Or.* 9.8, 11; and Choricius VI (*Or.* 5).9 (Foerster and Richtsteig) says he will leave the topic of water to a lesser speaker, indicating how hackneyed it had become in *epithalamia*.

39. War and racing, Men. Rhet. II 405–412; rains of autumn, II 408.

40. Men. Rhet. II 433.

41. Men. Rhet. II 440, 444–445, quoting 445.

42. [Dion. Hal.] *Rhet.* 257 (Usener and Radermacher); cf. Men. Rhet. II 423, 427, 429.

43. Pernot 1993, 1.80–81.

44. Hom. *Il.* 4.171, πολυδίψιος; for praise of a city's water in Greek poetry, Kienzle 1936, 54–57. Thucydides, Thuc. 1.46.4, 4.103.5, 7.84.3.

45. Heracleides Criticus, Arenz 2006, fr. I.1, 13, 26, 27 with Heinle 2009, 47, 50; cf. for remarkable water in Hellenistic writings, e.g., Polyb. 9.27; *SEG* XLVIII 1330 lines 15–22 (the so-called "Pride of Halicarnassus"); *Letter of Aristeus* 89–91.

46. Cic. 2*Verr.* 2.2–8.

47. Strabo 8.6.7, 8.6.21, 3.5.7 (for water in Strabo, Pédech 1971, 246); Mela 1.36, 1.55, 1.74.

48. Remarkable, e.g., *HN* 5.110, 5.115, 36.121–125; unremarkable, e.g., 5.74, 5.105, 5.111, 5.118, 5.126, 6.8. For Pliny the Elder as a geographer, Evans 2005; Brodersen 2008. Pausanias on badly and well-watered cities, e.g., 2.3.5, 7.5.10–12, 7.27.11, 10.4.1, 10.33.4–7, 10.35.6. On rivers in the Roman geographical authors, Campbell 2012, 46–82.

49. Solin. 7.21–29, with Brodersen 2016, 302–310 on the author.

50. Calderón Dorda, De Lazzer and Pellizer 2003 for this text and discussion; see Banchich 2010 for an English translation.

51. "In geography we made better progress, for George was able to give a more zoological tinge to the lesson. We would draw giant maps, wrinkled with mountains, and then fill in the various places of interest, together with drawings of the more exciting fauna to be found there. Thus for me the chief products of Ceylon were tapirs and tea; of India tigers and rice; of Australia kangaroos and sheep" (Durrell 1959 [1956], 59–60).

52. Coins: Imhoof-Blumer 1924 [1923], Smyrna (285–287); Alexandria (376); Ephesus (279–280 with Karwiese 2006); also Klementa 1993, 189 n. 498, 198; Dorl-Klingenschmid 2001, 100 n. 501; Maupai 2003, 36–39; and Campbell 2012, 449–450 nn. 268–272 brings the scholarship up to date.

53. For the statues on nymphaea, Kapossy 1969, 63–65; Dorl-Klingenschmid 2001, 86–101; Richard 2011; Aristodemou 2018b; and esp. Aristodemou 2012 with a catalogue. Nymphaea as a class had relatively more "watery" programs of reliefs, with nymphs and tritons and dolphins and the like, than other aedicular or tabernacle buildings—theaters, gates, libraries, and the so-called marble halls of bath and gymnasia complexes: Dorl-Klingenschmid 2001, 80–82, 96–101; Mägele, Richard, and Waelkens 2007, 495 n. 67; Aristodemou 2011a; 2011b; 2012, 100–112, 115–119; 2018b, 202–204, 209; and compare Corinth, Robinson 2013, 373–380. For nymphaea other than those discussed below with prominent watery motifs, e.g., D-Kl nrs. 34, 64, 86, 98, 106.

54. On the Laecanius Bassus fountain (D-Kl nr. 24 = R nr. 34), Jung 2006; Rathmayr 2011, who also treats the statues of the river-gods (135–136, 138). One of the first: priority is contested between the Laecanius Bassus fountain, dating to AD 78–82(?), and the great nymphaeum at

Miletus (D-Kl nr. 64 = R nr. 50; Aristodemou 2008; with Tuttahs 2007, 168 with n. 412 for the date), perhaps dating to the reign of Titus, AD 79–81.

55. On the Ephesus *Domitiansbrunnen* (D-Kl nr. 27 = R nr. 30), Plattner and Schmidt-Colinet 2005, 246–249. "New Marnas," καινοῦ Μάρναντος, *I.Ephesos* 1530 with Scherrer 2006, 48–53.

56. For Nymphaeum F3 at Perge (D-Kl nr. 85 = R nr. 59), Longfellow 2011, 156–161. For other apparent river god statues and fragments, Dorl-Klingenschmid 2001, 100 n. 499; Aristodemou 2012, 102–105; and esp. for those in museum collections that cannot be associated with specific monuments, Kapossy 1969, 23–26.

57. *MAMA* VII 305 with Chastagnol 1981. Jacques 1992 noticed the similarity of the Orcistans' claims to the topoi of panegyric on cities; Kolb 1993, 325–341 argued that the Orcistans were trying to show that they fit an official, legal list of criteria for city status (although that is rendered less likely by the subsequent discovery of an imperial letter actually bearing such a list, Jones 2006); for further literature, Roda 1995, 83–90; Winter 1996, 177 n. 1608. For an English translation and discussion, Van Dam 2007, 368–372.

58. Lib. *Or.* 11 with Saliou 2018, 35 n. 1 for literature on the speech including translations. For English translations and commentary, Downey 1959 and Norman 2000; for fuller treatments, Doukellis 1995, 129–144; Francesio 2004; and Saliou's notes to the text of *Or.* 11 in Casevitz, Lagacherie, and Saliou 2016. Saliou 2006a offers an excellent introduction to the speech, and elsewhere (2006b) discusses the theme of water in it. For other interpretations of the theme of water in the speech, Saliou 2011 and André 2014. For what archaeology has uncovered of the reality—Antioch does seem to have had a remarkable number of baths—Yegül 2000. For water in other speeches of Libanius, Casella 2012, 62–63; Casevitz, Lagacherie, and Saliou 2016, 79.

59. For the Olympias fountain, Casevitz, Lagacherie, and Saliou 2016, 100; Saliou 2018, 49. For the ranking of rivers, Campbell 2012, 67, 71–72, 76, 81, 118–128.

60. R nr. 2; Casevitz, Lagacherie, and Saliou 2016, 159–161.

61. On baths in this speech, Casevitz, Lagacherie, and Saliou 2016, 166–167, 181, 184 with literature.

62. With Saliou 2014, 666 n. 56 and 673 n. 111 for the meaning of φυλή in this passage.

63. A scene described earlier by Aristophanes, *Lys.* lines 327–332 and later by Choricius III (*Or.* 3).46 (Foerster and Richtsteig).

64. A jab particularly at Constantinople, which was then poorly supplied with water, Crow 2012. Cf. Choricius, VI (*Or.* 5).34 (Foerster and Richtsteig) for "A man who, recently chosen *astynomos* by the common vote of the inhabitants, has found out a device both useful and pleasant [the details are not given] to allow the folk to compete with those cities that glory in their water (δέδωκε τοῖς ἐνοικοῦσιν ἐρίζειν πρὸς τὰς ἀγαλλομένας ὕδασι πόλεις)."

65. Cf. Huskinson 2005, 249–250 n. 9. For flowing water metaphors used earlier in descriptions of Rome, Jenkyns 2013, 162–168.

66. ὁ δὲ διαρρεῖ τε ἅπασαν καὶ περιρρεῖ καὶ οὐδὲν ἄμοιρον τῆς ἐπικουρίας ἀφίησιν, with André 2014, 37.

67. Kondoleon 2000, 71–74; Huskinson 2005.

68. Building involving water (usually baths) at Antioch, Malalas, *Chron.* 9.5 (216–217), 9.14 (222), 10.10 (234), 10.18 (243), 10.19 (244), 10.50 (263), 11.9 (276), 11.14 (278), 11.30 (282), 12.2 (283), 12.22 (294), 12.33 (302), 12.38 (307), 13.30 (339), 13.40 (346), 17.17 (422), 17.19 (423); in

other cities, Malalas, *Chron.* 8.1 (192), 10.10 (235), 11.22 (280), 11.25 (281), 12.20 (292), 12.21 (293–294), 13.8 (321), 14.12 (359–360), 14.20 (363), 14.29 (367), 16.10 (399), 16.21 (409), 18.17 (435–436), 18.33 (445), 18.91 (482). For discussion of Malalas's accounts of imperial building, Downey (1938); Saliou (2016). In the same century, in the West, Cassiodorus, *Var.* 8.31, lists baths as part of an implicit definition of a city.

69. For late-antique interest in water cf. (among many) Ausonius, *Ordo urbium nobilium* (with Scafoglio 2014; and of course we have from Ausonius a whole panegyric on a river, his *Mosella*); Rut. Namat. *de Reditu suo*; Libanius, *Or.* 61.7–8, 17–18; Himerius, *Or.* 41.4–7, 10, 14; Greg. Naz. *Or.* 33.6–7; Cassiod. *Var.* 11.14; Choricius III (*Or.* 3).44–49, VI (*Or.* 5).34, VIII (*Or.* 7).13 (Foerster and Richtsteig); Nonnus, *Dionysiaca* book 40; *Life of Thecla* 27 (Dagron 1978, 276–279); Mart. Cap. 6.627–703; Priscian, *Periegesis*; Marek 2000, 377 n. 37 for Greek epigrams and Lamare 2016, 270–273 for Latin, mostly epigraphic. For water, fountains, and baths in late-antique Greek and subsequent Byzantine panegyrics, Fenster 1968, 29, 34, 59, 187; and Bouffartigue 1996, 54–55, noting that *les descripteurs ou laudateurs des villes byzantines omettent rarement de mentionner les bains* (55 n. 71).

70. Puech 2002, esp. 17–23.

71. The Nymphaeum of Herodes Atticus at Olympia (Glaser 1983, nr. 75 = R nr. 51 and Bol 1984) and the Nymphaeum of Herodes Atticus at Alexandria Troas (D-Kl nr. 2 = R nr. 1). Herodes built other waterworks too, Philostr. *VS* 548, 551. For other benefactions by sophists, Janiszewski, Stebnicka, and Szabat 2015; Gros 2016.

72. On competition between Greek cities under the empire, Robert 1977 [1989]; Lendon 1997b, 74–77, 136–137, 170–171; Heller 2006; and Kuhn 2013. For competition especially in building, Maupai 2003, 5–7, 307–327; Pont 2010, 269–296.

73. Diels 1904, 13–14; and see Hor. *Carm.* 3.13.

74. Aristid. *Or.* 26.97 (Behr).

75. Dorl-Klingenschmid 2001, 150–158; Dorl-Klingenschmid 2006, who identifies some competitive fountain building in Hellenistic times as well (383); Longfellow 2011, 188. For the locations of nymphaea in their cities, often near or even outside gates, see this chapter n. 4.

76. On the Nymphaeum of the Tritons (D-Kl nr. 35 = R nr. 43), Campagna 2007; D'Andria 2011, 150–160. For the competition between Hierapolis and Laodicaea, Dorl-Klingschmid 2006. In the matter of the primacy of size among nymphaea, I note for the record that if what are conventionally deemed two separate but adjacent nymphaea at Perge, F2 and F4, are considered to be one (as by Gliwitzky 2010, 35–55 and Martini 2015, 283), and the space between them included, that construction has a longer facade than the Nymphaeum of the Tritons.

77. *CIG* 3909 = Merkelbach and Stauber 1998–2004, 02/12/05.

78. Letzner 1990, 13–19.

79. For this internal competition, sometimes going on for generations, Pont 2010, 387–405; Weiss 2011, 72, 84–114. Ryan 2018, 157–162 stresses instead the cooperation of local notables in such projects: no matter.

80. Lack of new fountains in Greece before the Flavians, Agusta-Boularot 2001; cf. Walker 1979, 290–302, noting early imperial Greece's poverty, and later a skein of restraining classicism. Aristodemou 2017 lists pre-Roman fountains still functioning in Roman-period Greece. Peirene: Robinson 2005; 2011. For Hadrian's fountains and their legacy in Greece, Longfellow 2009.

81. Aphthonius, *Prog.* 40 (Rabe).

82. Robinson 2013, 365 gives a good sense of the lesser ambitions of even a rich city such as Corinth, with the wise observation, "We may wonder if the stature of the city's great old fountains actually discouraged local and regional leaders—the primary benefactors of the city—from trying to compete with new designs."

83. On the cities and rivers of the Three Gauls, Bedon 2008; Britain, Rogers 2013.

84. Baths in the North and West, Nielsen 1993, 1.64–84; 2.11–26. As Laurence, Esmonde Cleary, and Sears 2011 observe, "The vast amounts of water that were consumed by the baths . . . would . . . have been more impressive in the heat of a North African summer than in the midst of a winter on the Rhine where the provision of water could be assumed" (228). Fagan 1999, 166 collects literary passages and inscriptions illustrating how baths contributed to the competitive standing of a city. Exceptions to the comparative modesty of the size of baths in the North and West are Trier's second-century "Barbara" baths (20,640 m$^2$ of interior space; Nielsen 1993, nr. 79), the same city's Constantinian (and perhaps unfinished) "Imperial baths" (15,270 m$^2$ interior space; Nielsen 1993, nr. 81), and the Hadrianic "Large Baths" of Italica in Spain (ca. 16,800 m$^2$ interior space, Gómez Araujo 2010, 72–76).

85. Copying Rome: as the domestic fountains of Gaul did the domestic fountains of Rome and Italy, Dessales 2004. Outside third-century Rome and North Africa (see this chapter nn. 86–87), almost all of the great number of fountains in the West catalogued by Neuerburg 1965 and Letzner 1990 are small.

86. On the Septizodium and the controversies over its size and reconstruction, Popkin 2016, 153–163, 217–218 nn. 40–44 for literature.

87. Amm. Marc. 15.7.3. Lepcis nymphaeum: Jones and Ling 1993; Longfellow 2011, 183–185; Lamare 2019, 343–346; and for evolution of nymphaea in North Africa, Schmölder-Veit 2009, 43–46 and esp. 45; Lamare 2019, 211–220, 233–247, who also discusses earlier fountains in Roman North Africa (211–213). For other major waterworks in Severan North Africa, known only epigraphically, some of which may have been monumental nymphaea, Jouffroy 1986, 241–249; Lamare 2019, 387–403. For the general phenomenon of cities in North Africa striving to rival Severus's improvements to Lepcis, Wilson 2007, 307–313.

88. Yegül 1992, 186–234; Nielsen 1993, 1.84–95, 2.26–32.

89. For the influence of the Septizodium in Asia Minor, Gros 1996, 433; Longfellow 2011, 180–181. On the Fountain at the City Gate at Side (D-Kl nr. 106 = R nr. 70, *ca.* AD 210–240s), see Gliwitzky 2010, 87–122, esp. for the date (109) and for its connection to the Septizodium (94–95); arguing against this connection, Richard 2016, 21–22. On the Miletus nymphaeum (D-Kl nr. 64 = R nr. 50), Aristodemou 2008; Köster 2004, 65–77; Tuttahs 2007, 168–173. Cf. the three-level Nymphaeum of the Tritons at Hierapolis (D-Kl nr. 35 = R nr. 43; AD 222–235?).

## Chapter 7: City Walls, Colonnaded Streets, and the Rhetorical Calculus of Civic Merit

1. *honor ut in templis, utilitas ut in muris, pulchritudo vel auctor utrubique.* See chapter 6 n. 21.

2. Walls impractical: Pinder 2011; Stevens 2016; Müth 2016a; and see Müth, Laufer, and Brasse 2016 (with Müth 2016b) on the state of the debate on the non-defensive—"urbanistic" and "symbolic"—functions of ancient fortifications in general, with a catalogue of ways city walls might be representational as well as defensive: over-large circuits, ornamental gates,

ornamentation in the fabric of the walls themselves, etc. (150–158). Even walls built in Gaul in the late third century AD (when one might think they were indeed sorely needed for defense) display ornamental polychrome facades, Gans 2005; Dey 2010; so there was always a symbolic or representational aspect to building city walls, in addition to a defensive one, even when the security motive for building them is patent and paramount (cf. Hesberg 2005, 71–74; and the security motive is sometimes minimized by scholars even in the case of late third-century walls, Dey 2012, 294–296). Expensive: see Migeotte 2014, 381–388 for the extraordinary financial efforts involved. De Staebler 2007, 195–198 gives an excellent sense of the scale of such building when he calculates that the mid-fourth-century AD wall of Aphrodisias will have required 100,000 cubic meters of stone, and the exterior face alone 65,000 metric tons. The stone of the inner face of the wall would have sufficed to build twenty-six city blocks.

3. Unlike for nymphaea, there are no comprehensive corpora of city walls known to me. Walls are notoriously hard to date—Müth, Sokelicek, Jansen, and Laufer 2016, 2, 5, 10–12 discuss the reasons—and seem less apt to have helpful building inscriptions than other forms of public building. But for lists of walls, see Lehmann-Hartleben 1929, 2102–2105; Rebuffat 1986, 351–354; Gros 1996, 39–54. For the West in general, Esmonde Cleary 2003; Italy and North Africa, Jouffroy 1986; for Italy, Stevens 2017, 315–323; northern Italy, Bonetto 1998; Goffin 2002, 58–64; Gaul, Goudineau 1980, 244–261; North Africa, Daniels 1983, 8–17; Laurence, Esmonde Cleary, and Sears 2011, 158–160; Britain, Esmonde Cleary 2007. On the puzzle of Roman wall building in times of peace, Colin 1987; Esmonde Cleary 2003; Stevens 2017, esp. 11.

4. For the East, Mitchell 1987, 339–342; for Asia Minor, Gros 1996, 52–54; Pont 2010, 189–193: all meager lists because most walls in Asia Minor have been assumed to be Hellenistic, but there is a growing motion to date more Eastern walls (and their repair and bedizening) and city gates to the Roman period, and before the troubles of the third century: Lehmann-Hartleben 1929; Mertens 1969; Maupai 2003, 154–158; Thomas 2007, 109–111; Bekker Nielsen 2008, 51–56; Courtils, Cavalier, and Lemaître 2015, 120–130; Martini 2016; Lohner-Urban and Scherrer 2016. And note also De Staebler 2007, 266–268, who, on the basis of his study of the unquestionably mid-fourth-century AD walls of Aphrodisias, would date many of the walls in Asia Minor traditionally dated to the chaotic third century to the comparatively peaceful middle of the fourth. The more we look, the more we find high Roman imperial walls in the East, especially in the Decapolis: at Gadara (Hoffman 2000) excavation has turned up not only Hellenistic and late-antique walls (as the old scholarship expected) but a Flavian circuit with ornamental gates. Cf. nearby Samaria, Segal 1997, 89; Gerasa, Raja 2012, 140–144; Lichtenberger and Raja 2015, 485 n. 8; Antiochia Hippos, Eisenberg 2016, 618–620; and in Asia Minor, as the result of meticulous study, at Perge and Side (Boatwright 1991, 250–252; Gliwitsky 2010, 63–86, 123–131), suggesting that similarly meticulous study will turn up many more in the Greek East. A careful examination of civic coinage (see, e.g., Price and Trell 1977, 90–91, 243–287) might add significantly to the corpus of Roman-period walls in the East, but without further study we cannot be sure whether a city depicting city walls on its coins is boasting of mere possession of an old wall, or a new or repaired wall.

5. Weiss 2020, 38. Capitolias is yet another city of the Decapolis.

6. Where a builder is clearly known, Rebuffat 2012, 43–63. For the West (but with some Eastern *comparanda*) where imperial involvement, or that of soldiers or officials, is attested in inscriptions, see Horster 2001, 65, 121–156, 170–175, 184–187, 192–196.

7. Size, [Dion. Hal.] *Rhet.* 257, 268, 276, 278, 289 (Usener and Radermacher); Men. Rhet. I 356; II 422; Dio Chrys. *Or.* 31.62, 32.35, 33.17–18, 39.1, 44.9, 47.13, 16; 48.4; Aristid. *Or.* 17.9, 23.24, 26.8–9, 19, 63; 27.13 (Behr); [Aristid.] *Or.* 25.6 (Behr); Lucian, *Patr. Enc.* 1–2; Lib. *Or.* 11.10, 69, 102, 196–211, 228, 270–271; 61.7; *Prog.* 8.353 (Foerster = Gibson pp. 346–347); Himerius, *Or.* 62.5, 39.7, 41.6–7; John Chrysostom, *ad Populum Antiochenum de statuis* 17 (*PG* 49, 178), insisting that a city's virtues were more important than its size, and so revealing the usual assumption; Choricius I (*Or.* 1).43 (Foerster and Richtsteig), with Pernot 1993, 1.192; Casevitz, Lagacherie, and Saliou 2016, 196–197; and for praise of a city's size on inscriptions and coins, Robert 1980, 423–424; cf. Maupai 2003, 64–68, 86–88. Praise of size goes back a long way: in poetry, Kienzle 1936, 91; and see, e.g., Xen. *Anab.* 1.2.6, 7, 20, 23 et passim. For ancient thinking about very large cities in general, Engels 2013 with literature.

8. Old convention, Maupai 2003, 67–68 n. 174; cf. Aristid. *Or.* 1.351. There were lists of cities in rank order by circumference, e.g., Riese 1878, 140; and see Callu 1997, 129–134 and Nicolet 2000. For wall circumferences in Strabo, Pédech 1971, 247. Contrast the various dodges Pliny the Elder (*HN* 3.66–67; cf. Dion. Hal. *Ant. Rom.* 4.13.4–5) must use to give a sense of the size of Rome, which had long outgrown its Servian walls (*moenia* at 3.66 has the sense of "city" or "buildings," on which usage Della Valle 1958): regions, *lares compitales*, number of gates, distance from the forum to the gates, height of buildings. Did the regionary catalogues of Rome and Constantinople serve the same purpose? Other aspects of walls too were noticed in writings: their height, strength, and number of towers, Ruppe 2010, 144–148.

9. [Aristid.] *Or.* 25.7–8 (Behr). Fact of walls bigger than the city, Strabo 6.2.4; Dio Chrys. *Or.* 6.4, 7.38; Auson. *Ordo Nob. Urb.* lines 37–38, 99 (Green); Bonetto 1998, 129–136; Müth, Laufer, and Brasse 2016, 150.

10. Building oversized city walls, Rebuffat 1986, 361; Gros 1996, 47–51; Esmonde Cleary 2003, 73, 75–76, 78 (Trier appears to be a second-century case); Bowden 2011, 110 (Nicopolis in Epirus); Pinder 2011, 71–75 (and Avenches in Flavian times); this was a practice that went back at least to the fourth century BC, Pope 2016, 261–266.

11. Quint. *Inst.* 3.7.26; cf. Men Rhet. I 353–355; Pernot 1993, 1.209–210. For Aphrodisias, see De Staebler 2007, 3, 153, 248–254.

12. Praise of a city's upbringing, Pernot 1993, 1.210–212; esp. Men. Rhet. II 384.

13. City growth praised, Dio Chrys. *Or.* 34.8; [Hermogenes], *Prog.* 18 (Rabe); Men. Rhet. I 355–357; and compared to that of person (cf. Lib. *Or.* 11.69–71, 195), but note that Men. Rhet. I 356–357 praised growth under the category of "origins" rather than "upbringing." The metaphorical description of cities as men (Pernot 1993, 1.193–194 esp. n. 362) could also result in walls being praised as "crowns," [Aristid.] *Or.* 25.7, 9 (Behr); Himerius, *Or.* 62.2; and, of course, statues of the *Tyche* of a city or personifications of the city in art might wear an actual crown representing walls, Thomas 2007, 111–113; Saradi 2006, 135–144.

14. For the connection between harmonious appearance and internal harmony, Ryan 2018; cf. Thomas 2007, 108–110; 2014, 85–86. Internal harmony as an aspect of justice or self-control, Men. Rhet. I 363–364; Lib. *Or.* 11.154, with Casevitz, Lagacherie, and Saliou 2016, 142, tracing the theme back to Plato. Walls could also contribute to the ὕψος, the "sublimity," of the city, which we learn about in [Longinus]'s *On the Sublime*, perhaps a Flavian work: E. Thomas 2014, 51–88. E. Thomas 2014, 75–79 also connects sublimity to the building of nymphaea.

15. Mention of walls as an item of praise in manuals, Quint. *Inst.* 3.7.26–27; Men. Rhet. II 417; cf. in passing II 377, 445; metaphorically, I 349–350; Lib. *Prog.* 8.118 (Foerster = Gibson pp. 102–103). Exclusion of walls where we might expect them, Men. Rhet. I 346–351, 354–365, and even the praise of an acropolis excludes its defensive qualities (352–353); see also II 382–387, with two lists of structures to be praised (the second extensive), but no mention of walls (382 and 386); cf. II 423, 429, 431, 433. Anon. *Excerpta rhetorica* in *RML* p. 587 refers to *moenia*, but meaning "city" or "public buildings," see this chapter n. 8. On the treatment of structures in encomium, Pernot 1993, 1.215–216.

16. Men. Rhet. II 431.

17. Walls as items of praise in speeches, Dio Chrys. *Or.* 31.146, 163; 33.21; [Aristid.] *Or.* 25.7–8, 32, 42, 48–49, 64 (Behr; on which Franco 2008, 218–237, with 226–227 on the walls), both about Rhodes, whose walls were famous (Strabo 14.2.5; Paus. 4.31.5); Himerius, *Or.* 39.6. Aristid. *Or.* 26.79–84, Aristides's encomium on Rome, is a special case, in which he honors the topic of walls, but describes Rome as not fortifying herself, but the fortified boundaries of the empire as metaphorical fortifications of the city, a nice way of dealing with the topic while passing over Rome's beaten up and far-too-small Servian Wall. Walls absent from encomia and encomiastic passages on cities: Dio Chrys. *Or.* 32 (gates in passing at 32.95); Aristid. *Or.* 17–21, all on Smyrna (although gates and walls are mentioned for orientation, 17.14, 19.8, and in order to be adorned with flowers, 20.21; but the walls of Smyrna were notable, Strabo 14.1.37); on Aristides's Smyrnaean orations, Franco 2005, with discussion of Aristides's neglect of the city's walls (404–405); Aristid. *Or.* 23 (with an almost willful avoidance of mentioning walls of Pergamon at 23.20), *Or.* 27 (walls of Cyzicus famous, Flor. *Epit.* 1.40.15; Amm. Marc. 26.8.7; on this speech see Petsalis-Diomidis 2008). Note also Aristid. *Or.* 1 on Athens, with a single passing mention of walls to orient the suburbs (1.20; cf. 1.351) during the physical description of the city (1.9–34), in contrast to the mentions of the walls in the speech's long historical section, 1.252, 1.278, 1.280. On Athens' actual walls in this era, much battered but still prominent, Theocharaki 2020, 206–208. Walls are also absent in the full description of Seleucia given in the *Life of Thecla* 27 (Dagron 1978, 274–279), which appears to rely on rhetorical models; and much the same significant absence is evident in the *Pan. Lat.*, which, however, are not panegyrics on cities (Dey 2010, 35 gathers up the—few—references to city walls to be found); but mention of walls might especially have been expected in *Pan. Lat.* 9/4 about the rebuilding of Autun, which mentions other structures, but not walls, although the rebuilding of walls elsewhere (9/4.18.4) is mentioned, and the walls of Autun (on which Guillaumet and Rebourg 1987 with Amm. Marc. 16.2.1) were famous, Amm. Marc. 15.11.11. Such neglect of walls in panegyric was not always to remain the case: see this chapter n. 49.

18. Walls present in lists of structures, Dio Chrys. *Or.* 31.146, 163; 33.24, 45.12; Aristid. *Or.* 23.68–69 (a passage denouncing pride in such things), 25.3–8; *Pan. Lat.* 6/7.22.4–5. Absent from lists of structures in encomia, Dio Chrys. *Or.* 33.18; 48.9, 12; 50.1; Aristid. *Or.* 17.11 (where buildings are said to compete with each other), 18.6, 19.3, 21.6, 23.20, 26.97 (Rome's subjects compete in building a list of structures, but not walls; but gates do appear), 46.28.

19. E.g., walls are absent from the list of structures built by successive kings at Lib. *Or.* 11.125. Nor do city walls appear at all in Lib. *Or.* 61, the *Monody on Nicomedia*.

20. Downey 1961, 78, 91, 102, 176–178, 259–260, 612–620, 644; Brasse 2010 and Brasse 2016 with up-to-date literature; for Malalas's account, Saliou 2013; 2016, 69–71.

21. On the New City, Saliou 2009, with 240 n. 34 on its walls.

22. As Nock 1954, 80 n. 3 noted, moreover, the term used for walls during that admission of inferiority (270), τοίχους rather than τείχη, should strictly mean building walls, not city fortification walls. If Libanius is to be taken literally, then he has once again avoided mentioning Antioch's city walls; but most commentators seem to accept that city walls are nevertheless meant here, although they decline to adjust the text of Libanius.

23. Heath 2004, 246–247, 278–279, 299–300; Migliario 2007, 33–50; Feddern 2013; Kraus 2016; and for deliberative themes in Latin see Seneca the Elder's *Suasoriae*; Kohl 1915 for Greek.

24. Fr. 112 (L-P), ἄνδρες γάρ πόλεως πύργος ἀρήιοι, with Kienzle 1936, 7–8 for the later poetic tradition.

25. Thuc. 7.77.7; cf. Soph. *OT* lines 56–57; Hdt. 8.61.2; Lycur. *Leoc.* 47; Arist. *Pol.* 1330B-1331A (arguing *contra*); and Smith 1907 and Thomas 2007, 299 n. 90 collect other ancient references.

26. Plut. *Apop. Lac.* 210E-F, with Babbitt 1931, 257 n. d for parallels.

27. Lib. *Prog.* 8.561–564 (Foerster = Gibson pp. 520–523); cf. for this theme Aphthonius, *Prog.* 41–42 (Rabe). For walls as signs of cowardice cf. Aristid. *Or.* 26.79–80; for the related topos that the quality of a city's men is always more important than its built structures, Pernot 1993, 1.197.

28. Grown-up declaimers, Kohl 1915, 18, and esp. Sen. *Suas.* 2.3 and Philostr. *VS* 514, 583–584; cf. Philostr. *VA* 1.38.

29. Summary history of wall building in the imperial West, Laurence, Esmonde Cleary, and Sears 2011, 297–298. Competitive motivations should not apply to wall building in "small towns" in Britannia, Frere 1984, 68–69; *sed contra* Esmonde Cleary 2003, 84.

30. For Britain, Esmonde Cleary 2003, 79–84; 2007, although loyal to a provincial eccentricity most British city walls were of earth rather than stone. Those in danger often erected walls: we see bursts of wall-building after barbarian incursions, e.g., in Dalmatia and Thrace in the 170s (Mihailov 1961; Frere 1984, 69), but towns in dangerous places did not build walls consistently: Boadicea was happy to find Colchester unfortified when she attacked it in AD 60 or 61 (Tac. *Ann.* 14.31.4), and recent research suggests that the Rhine city of Cologne—in the face of the enemy if any Roman city was—was not fortified in stone until the end of the first century AD, and Xanten not until the early second, Gans 2005, 232. Walls were built around towns in second-century AD Mauretania (Akerraz 2012 [2010], 75 n. 1, 78–81), where we know there were troubles (HA *Pius* 5.4; Paus. 8.43.3; *IAM* 2.307.3 lines 12 and 14–16 with Speidel 2017, 262–264, a more serious matter than previously believed); but Rebuffat 1974, 506–514 noted that old walls there might be knocked down and left for a long period before rebuilding and that the new walls might be larger than could easily be defended.

31. Contemporary awareness of the *pax romana*, Brélaz 2008, 155, 163–165. Usefulness of walls against small-scale threats, Thomas 2007, 111.

32. Availability of money, in the west, Rebuffat 1974, 510–512. Repair and upkeep of existing walls, Dio Chrys. *Or.* 31.104.

33. Majority unfortified, Dey 2011, 118–119; cf. Laurence, Esmonde Cleary, and Sears 2011, 151, 158.

34. Dio Chrys. *Or.* 31.104, 125; Aristid. *Or.* 26.70–71, 97.

35. Walls compromised in these various ways, Bonetto 1998, 146–148, 183–184; Stevens 2017, 108–159, 247, with 158 and 254 for the simultaneity of Augustan wall destruction and building. For neglect of walls as customary, see esp. Dio Chrys. *Or.* 31.125. Note also the elimination, or

loss of the military functions of, the ancestral *ephebeiai* in the East, the maintenance of which would have been a more economical means of dealing with local threats than walls: Brélaz 2005, 187–193 (who also denies that the *collegia* of *iuvenes* of Western cities normally had a security function, 183–186), Brélaz 2008, 173–176; and Kennell 2015, 182 collect civic *ephebeiai* that survived and maintained at least exercises at arms into the Roman period (showing that the Romans did not forbid them). For the lapse of military training in eastern cities, cf. Lib. *Or.* 11.157.

36. Growing beyond walls, Laurence, Esmonde Cleary, and Sears 2011, 116, 121; Stevens 2016, 291; Raja 2012, 88. There were of course exceptions, where the circuits were extended to protect new suburbs, Joseph. *BJ* 5.4.2 (Jerusalem under Claudius); Laurence, Esmonde Cleary, and Sears 2011, 59.

37. Gros 1992; Ducrey 1995; and Hansen and Nielsen 2004 for statistics. Cf. Vitr. 2.8.13; and, in the imperial period, an imaginary city would possess walls, Dio Chrys. *Or.* 7.22.

38. Lendon 1997b, 88–89, and see esp. Aristid. *Or.* 1.191, 26.80; cf. Cass. Dio 74 (75 Cary).14.4; Aristid. *Or.* 26.79. For arguments that walls were built in the West out of a generalized desire for prestige, Rebuffat 1974, 506, 510, 513, 522; Gros 1992, 221.

39. Cavallo 1989; Saradi 2006, 119–135; Goodman 2007, 29–31; Thomas 2007, 109, 111–113; Stevens 2017, 72–77.

40. Gates, Thomas 2007, 110–11; Jacobs 2009, 198 with literature; and Lohner-Urban and Scherrer 2016.

41. Seston 1966; Bonetto 1998, 166–169; Stevens 2017, 105–110.

42. Jenkyns 2013, 186–191.

43. Laurence, Esmonde Cleary, and Sears 2011, 148–149; Stevens 2017, 61–72; Jenkyns 2013, 186–191.

44. For the lack of perfect consistency in the functions of early *coloniae* and their possession of walls, Stevens 2017, 7 gathers the literature; 84. On the dangers of assuming too much regularity or system in Roman and Latin colonies of the mid-Republic, Bispham 2006.

45. Connection to colonies, Frere 1984, 65–66; Laurence, Esmonde Cleary, and Sears 2011, 42, 51, 66. Exceptions: colonies without walls, Gros 1992, 219–220. Slow or non-completion of walls of colonies, Esmonde Cleary 2003, 76, 78; Dey 2011, 118; Stevens 2017, 88; or perhaps they were never intended to be finished, Pinder 2011, 68–69; Müth, Laufer, and Brasse 2016, 150.

46. For Augustan wall building, see esp. the essays in Colin 1987; Gros 1996, 39–51; Horster 2001, 164–166.

47. Février 1969, the classic discussion; Bonetto 1998, 171–175 (who is doubtful); Esmonde Cleary 2003, 77–78, accepting the general theory, but offering exceptions (colonies without walls, non-colonies building walls); Daniels 1983; but Horster 2001, 162–167 cautions that we cannot deduce elevation to colonial status merely from the building of a city wall.

48. Competition, Gans 2005, 232.

49. I find myself sympathetic to Dey 2011, 120–123, 139–140 who argues that the Romans were initially rather ashamed of Rome's Aurelian Wall, which is why it appears so rarely in literature before Claudian. But from about AD 400, walls become a prominent aspect of panegyric and related thinking about cities, Fenster 1968, 322, 376 (Fenster's index ad loc. *Mauern*); Saradi 1995 and 2011; Dey 2011, 131 (noting the change), 137–146. Ausonius's *Ordo Nob. Urb.* (ca. AD 390) may mark a turning point, mentioning the walls of five cities out of the seventeen listed,

lines 32, 37, 43, 67, 99, 140–145 (Green); cf. Dey 2011, 122 and Choricius I (*Or.* 1).17 and II (*Or.* 2).16 (Foerster and Richtsteig).

50. Lib. *Or.* 61.7; cf. 46.44. For the colonnades in the encomium on Antioch (*Or.* 11), Francesio 2004, 86–88; Casevitz, Lagacherie, and Saliou 2016, 107, 155–156, 165–166 with parallels elsewhere in Libanius and in other authors; Saliou 2018, 37–38, 48–49. In a useful list of Antiochene monuments mentioned by St. John Chrysostom, Mayer 2012, 91, Antioch's walls (four mentions) receive much the same emphasis as her colonnades (three mentions), implying the artificiality of both Libanius's neglect of the former and his emphasis on the latter.

51. On colonnades in general, Gros 1996, 95–113, with literature, 119; on colonnaded streets, Maupai 2003, 124–132; Thomas 2007, 114–115; Burns 2017. For *corpora* of colonnaded streets: Lehmann-Hartleben 1929, 2106–2110; Williams 1979; Reiter 1992; Bejor 1999; Burns 2017, esp. 325–336, upon whom I have generally relied (and whose collection of older literature is excellent); with Pont 2010, 177–187 for Asia Minor; Segal 1997, 5–53 (with list at 48–49) and Tabaczek 2002, 189–221 for Syria and the Levant; and Jouffroy 1986, 205–208, 241–249 for North Africa.

52. Burns 2017 follows Tabaczek 2002, 210–221 in impeaching most (Tabaczek would impeach all) colonnaded streets said to be earlier than the last years of the first century AD. We suspect that the colonnaded street at Sagalassos, recently dated by its excavators AD 14 to 54 (Burns 2017, 186–188), will duly be consigned to that later period. On Alexandria, Tabaczek 2002, 217–219; Burns 2017, 44–49, with Diod. Sic. 17.52.3; Strabo 17.1.8 (no clear claims to colonnaded streets); Ach. Tat. 5.1 (itself highly rhetorical: Saïd 1994, 230–231)—I think Alexandria's colonnaded streets were probably not early. On the colonnaded streets of Antioch, Lassus 1972; Williams 1979, 68–74; Cabouret 1999; Tabaczek 2002, 211–213; Burns 2017, 121–130, with Joseph. *BJ* 1.21.11; *AJ* 16.5.3 (for Herod the Great); Dio Chrys. *Or.* 47.16; Malalas, *Chron.* 10.8 (232–233); 10.23 (246); 11.24 (280) (claiming Tiberius built them)—probably a real early case of colonnaded streets, I would guess, but an isolated one.

53. Zuiderhoek 2009, 79–80 finds colonnaded structures the second most common whole buildings donated, after religious structures, in Roman Asia Minor, and the third most common building type to receive financial donations for building, after religious structures and and bathgymnasia complexes. We will pass by the question of the origins of colonnaded streets (Greek stoas or Roman porticos? Pre-Greek near-eastern or Egyptian traditions? Religion? Astrology? Shopping needs? Evolving conceptions of the city? MacDonald's "urban armatures"?). For the controversy: Williams 1979, 16–19; Reiter 1992, 59–84; Tabaczek 2002, 226–239; Rababeh, Al Rabady, and Abu-Khafajah 2014; and Burns 2017 esp. 6–10, 311–321.

54. Greece and the northwest provinces: see Burns 2017, 301–310 for dubious cases. Much depends on the definition of a colonnaded street, it being agreed that a proper colonnaded street, built to a single plan, is quite a different thing from a mere street with colonnades on both sides (perhaps a mere series of colonnaded buildings, or with sections perhaps built at various times to different plans, perhaps different in appearance, and perhaps with gaps between the sections; and as such excluded from a list of colonnaded streets *stricto sensu*). Reiter 1992, 420–422 admits Italica in Spain, but Burns 2017, 306 excludes it because its porticos consist of piers rather than columns. Williams 1979, 93–96 admits Athens' Panathenaic Way as it approached the Agora, but Burns 2017, 56–57 is unsure. In Greece only Corinth commands general assent:

Burns 2017, 304–305; cf. Williams 1979, 87–93. But despite these controveries, the general geographical patterns are clear.

55. Saliou 1996, 321–323; Burns 2017, 273–277, 316–318; for the inscriptions and statues on the colonnades at Palmyra, Tabaczek 2002, 110–123; Yon 2017, 500–504; at Gerasa, Tabaczek 2002, 181–183. Major exceptions, where the emperors paid for colonnaded streets, include Antioch (see this chapter n. 52), where emperors continued the efforts allegedly begun by Herod; cities in which certain emperors took a particular interest (Septimius Severus's Lepcis Magna; Philip the Arab's Philippopolis, and presumably Hadrian's Antinoopolis); and the imperial repair of colonnaded streets in cities damaged by earthquakes.

56. Burns 2017, 325–336 and passim.

57. *Via Nova* at Rome, Gorrie 2001, 666–668 with Burns 2017, 301–302 (but the evidence is extremely weak); Lepcis Magna, Burns 2017, 298; and (with literature) the Levant, 282–298 (cf. Bejor 1999, 91–93, arguing for direct imperial benefaction); Tyre, Burns 2017, 293–296. But with the exception of Lepcis, none of these dates is sure. Nor are those for North Africa: while Burns 2017, 325–336 is inclined to date colonnaded streets other than at Lepcis to ca. AD 100, Williams 1979, 131–133 assumed them to be Severan, which would bring the chronology of colonnaded streets even closer to that of nymphaea.

58. Mention of colonnades as objects of praise in manuals, Men. Rhet. II 383, 386, 429, 431, 433; John of Sardis p. 215 line 19 (Rabe).

59. Aphthonius, *Prog.* 38–41 (Rabe); cf. Choricius I (*Or.* 1).17–25 and II (*Or.* 2).30–48 (Foerster and Richtsteig), where confusions of colonnades render *ecphraseis* of churches very hard to follow.

60. Mention in speeches of colonnades as desirable, Dio Chrys. *Or.* 46.9, 47.16, 48.12; in lists of desirable structures, Dio Chrys. *Or.* 33.18, 48.9; Aristid. *Or.* 46.28; *Pan. Lat.* 2(12).21.1; Lib. *Or.* 61.17; Themistius, *Or.* 4.60D (Schenkl and Downey p. 86 line 8); Greg. Naz. *Or.* 33.6; Himerius, *Or.* 39.7, 41.14. And notice that in late-antique art, a depiction of a colonnade can be shorthand for a city, Saradi 2006, 127–128; Popkin 2018. Colonnades of different types: Greek can refer to all colonnaded structures indifferently as "stoas" and to colonnaded streets by a number of other terms in addition: Downey 1937; Williams 1979, 19–29; Reiter 1992, 24–29; Tabaczek 2002, 222–225; Burns 2017, 11. Without context (or excavation) it is often impossible to tell what sort of structure an ancient author means, and so we must accept that we may sometimes confound the various different forms, accepting that most such mentions will have been of the more spectacular streets.

61. Dio Chrys. *Or.* 40 (40.9 columns, roofs, and shops); 45 (45.12 colonnades and fountains); 47 (47.17, 19–20 colonnade); 48 (48.12 colonnade); cf. Pliny *Ep.* 10.81.7 for the colonnade. On Dio's struggle and its context, Bekker Nielsen 2008, esp. 126–127, 130–136; Fuhrmann 2015, 166–170; on the colonnade itself, Burns 2017, 181–183 with literature.

62. Destruction, Dio Chrys. *Or.* 40.8–9, 47.11, 16, 18; in the aftermath of the enterprise Dio was accused of damage to tombs and accounting irregularities, about which we hear from a letter of Pliny the Younger (*Ep.* 10.81), then governor of Bithynia. Increased prestige, Dio Chrys. *Or.* 40.10 (and thus gain benefits from governors, see Lendon 1997b, 204–205); rivalry with other cities, 40.11, 47.16–17 (Antioch).

63. Dio Chrys. *Or.* 47.15; and see also Choricius VIII (*Or.* 7).52; cf. II (*Or.* 2).32 (Foerster and Richtsteig); Tabaczek 2002, 257; and Casevitz, Lagacherie, and Saliou 2016, 167 for parallels,

noting particularly Strabo 13.3.6, who reports the legend that the people of Cyme made their stoas security for a loan, and when the loan was not paid off, they were obliged to walk out in the rain.

64. Lib. *Or.* 11.215–217.

65. Lib. *Or.* 11. 131–193: wisdom, 139, 182, 193; courage, 145, 157–163; justice, 142–143, 146, 154, 188, 190; temperance, 151–154. On a city's virtues, Pernot 1993, 1.212–214. On the theme of education in the speech, Milazzo 1996.

66. Lib. *Or.* 11.196.

67. Lib. *Or.* 11.196–212; for other references to the colonnades, 90. For the columns somehow associated with the palace wall, Casevitz, Lagacherie, and Saliou 2016, 163.

68. Lib. *Or.* 11.213, δοκεῖ μοι τῶν ἐν ταῖς πόλεσι καὶ χαριέστατον εἶναι, προσθείην δ᾽ ἂν ὅτι καὶ χρησιμώτατον, αἱ σύνοδοι καὶ τὸ ἀναμιχθῆναι.

69. Lib. *Or.* 11.214–218 with Leyerle 2018, 261–262 on the connection between colonnades and sociability. On whether this notion of the importance of sociability may be borrowed from philosophy I am not qualified to judge, but those bolder than I may begin their investigations in Magnaldi 1991, 33–46 and Schofield 2012, 176–179.

70. Cabouret 1999, 146 insists that this passage must be taken seriously; cf. Bouffartigue 1996, 54; Francesio 2004, 88; Saliou 2006a, 280; Bührig 2016, 72; and Casevitz, Lagacherie, and Saliou 2016, 167.

71. To the contrary, in Dio Chrys. *Or.* 48 Dio pleads with his townsmen to hide the controversies the building of his colonnade has produced in the city from a visiting Roman governor: his colonnaded street has hardly made the Prusans get along better.

72. See Men. Rhet. I 362 with Pernot 1993, 1.201 for the rhetorical connection of buildings to civic virtues; cf. Dio Chrys. *Or.* 31.146.

73. For this "New Urbanism" I am happy to cite the *National Geographic* (Kunzig 2019, 84–85) in confidence that the views expressed there will be entirely conventional. Ventura da Silva 2011 also finds parallels in modern thinking about urbanism.

74. Rivalry between Side and Perge, Nollé 1993a, 310–316, 1993b, 84–94; for such rivalries over titles see chapter 6 n. 72. On *neokoroi*, Burrell 2004.

75. *SEG* XXXIV 1306 with Roueché 1989 and Weiss 1991, the latter esp. on the sacred (or imperial) *vexillum* (380–381). I have both selected and re-ordered items from this document.

76. Competitive building in Side and Perge, Heinzelmann 2003, 217, accepting his count of structures for the purpose of simplicity (it does not matter for my argument); also Gliwitzky 2010, esp. 193. For Perge's center-of-street canals, see Martini 2015. For Side's smaller side-of-street canals, Reiter 1992, 185–187, 312–314 with literature; and Bricker 2016, 42–53 gives the best account of Side's waterworks, pointing out also the city's re-dedication to water displays in the period from the late third century and after. Pisidian Antioch had a similar channel down a major colonnaded street: Owens and Taşlialan 2009, 314–317; as did Patara, for which see İşkan, Schuler, Aktaş, Reitzenstein, Schmölder-Veit, and Koçek 2016, 92–93, and so may Amastris, if that is the nature of the stinking stream Pliny proposed to cover over (*Ep.* 10.98). Cf. also Pessinus, Devreker and Waelkens 1984, 77–141, where the main street was a river in season.

77. Sestos, Strabo 13.1.22; cf. 5.1.7; snails 13.1.15. For this sort of thinking, Bloomer 1993.

78. Quoted Hdt. 2.35.1; cf. 3.60.

79. Diod. Sic. 1.50.7; cf. 17.52.

80. Men. Rhet. I 359; cf. for how to deal with compulsory topics when the material is weak (showing that they did have to be covered) II 386, 403, 420, 429; [Dion. Hal.] *Ars Rhet.* 265, 275, 278 (Usener and Radermacher); Nicolaus, *Prog.* 50–51 (Felten). Canonical topics could be entirely excluded if weak only when praising the emperor, when "there must be nothing doubtful or controversial, given the supreme glory of the subject," Men. Rhet. II. 368 (cf. II 370–372, 422); and, in practice, this was also—wisely—done when praising governors, Men. Rhet. II 415.

81. Men. Rhet. II 372.

82. Men. Rhet. I 351.

83. Dry, hot, cold, Men. Rhet. I 346–348 (quoted 346); guardian, blooming, I 350 (cf. I 355).

84. Men. Rhet. I 353.

85. [Dion. Hal.] *Ars Rhet.* 257; cf. 275 (Usener and Radermacher).

86. Men. Rhet. I. 353.

87. Men. Rhet. II 386; cf. 383.

88. For the summary comparison, Pernot 1993, 1.308–309, who makes the connection to the *progymnasma* of *synkrisis*.

89. Cities, [Hermogenes], *Prog.* 19 (Rabe) = Priscian, *Prae.* 25 (*RLM*). On the technique of *synkrisis*, Focke 1923 is the classic study; for *comparatio/synkrisis* in the *progymnasmata*, Kneepkens 1994, 293–296; Berardi 2017, 263–273.

90. Wholes by means of parts, Nicolaus, *Prog.* 59–60 (Felten).

91. Begin with obvious similarities and proceed to manufactured, Theon, *Prog.* 113–114 (Spengel); [Hermogenes], *Prog.* 19 (Rabe); Achilles vs. Hector, Aphthonius, *Prog.* 32–33 (Rabe); city vs. country, Lib. *Prog.* 8.353–360 (Foerster = Gibson pp. 346–353).

92. Comparing multiples, Theon, *Prog.* 114–115 (Spengel); Aphthonius, *Prog.* 31 (Rabe).

## Section IV: Lizarding, and Other Adventures in Declamation and the Roman Law

1. Stellion shedding skin, Pliny, *HN* 30.89; for its other fine qualities Garofalo 1992, 61–65 and Garofalo 2008 [2000] [2001], 142–148 gather the ancient references.

2. For *stellionatus* as fraud involving *pignora*, *Dig.* 13.7.16.1 (Marcellus and Paul; on the former, Garofalo 1992, 7–8); *Dig.* 13.7.36.pr. (Ulpian); *Dig.*13.7.1.2 (Ulpian); *Dig.* 47.20.4 (Modestinus); *CJ* 9.34.1 (Alexander Severus); 9.34.2 (Gordian); 9.34.4 (Philip). For discussion of *stellionatus*, Mommsen 1899, 680–681; Volterra 1929 [1999]; Garofalo 1992; Botta 1996, 83–88. The major legal puzzle is distinguishing *stellionatus* from the immensely broad and ill-defined offense of *falsum*, which seems to render a separate offense of *stellionatus* superfluous—Volterra 1929 [1999] 117–120; Mentxaka 1988, 334–335; and Stein 1990, 84—but which distinction the jurists were eager to make because they repeatedly asserted that *stellionatus*, unlike *falsum*, was not *publicum*, *Dig.* 3.2.13.8 (Ulpian), *publicum non est iudicium*; *Dig.* 13.7.36.pr. (Ulpian), *extra ordinem stellionatus nomine plectetur*; *Dig.* 47.11.3 (Ulpian), *stellionatus vel expilatae hereditatis iudicia accusationem quidem habent, sed non sunt publica*; *Dig.* 47.20.1 (Papinian), *actio stellionatus neque publicis iudiciis neque privatis actionibus continetur*; *Dig.* 47.20.2 (Ulpian), *coercitionem extraordinariam*; *Dig.* 47.20.3.pr. (Ulpian), *stellationatus accusatio ad praesidis cognitionem spectat*; cf. *CJ.* 9.34.3 (Gordian). On *cognitio extra ordinem*, Buti 1982; Rüfner 2016; with Garofalo 1992, 24 n. 100 for literature.

3. *Dig.* 47.20.3.1 (Ulpian), *stellionatum autem obici posse his, qui dolo quid fecerunt, sciendum est, scilicet si aliud crimen non sit quod obiciatur . . . ubicumque igitur titulus criminis deficit, illic stellionatus obiciemus. . . . et ut generaliter dixerim, deficiente titulo criminis hoc crimen locum habet, nec est opus species enumerare.* Ulpian refers to (Greek) "written and unwritten" law elsewhere, *Dig.* 1.1.6.1. If Honoré's 2002, 17, 189 dates for the various works of Ulpian be accepted, Ulpian was using both the narrow (fraud with pledges) and the broad (crime without a name) definitions of *stellionatus* at the same time.

4. Thus the passages *igitur titulus criminis deficit, illic stellionatus obiciemus* and *et ut generaliter dixerim, deficiente titulo criminis hoc crimen locum habet, nec est opus species enumerare* (*Dig.* 47.20.3.1 [Ulpian]) were condemned as interpolations even long after interpolation hunting had fallen out of fashion: Levy and Rabel 1935, 524; Volterra 1929 [1999], 109–110, 133, 140; Zilletti 1961, 88–90; Stein 1990, 87–88 (although he had accepted the passages in Stein 1993, 140, written earlier but published later). But Mentxaka 1988, 307–311; Garofalo 1992, 71–72, 126–131; and Garofalo 2008 [2000] [2001], 134–135 n. 39 successfully defend the passages. To that defense might be added that *Dig.* 17.1.29.5 and 40.7.9.1 (both Ulpian) seem to depend on the wider definition of *stellionatus,* as do the Greek translations in the ancient glossaries (Volterra 1929 [1999], 112) and, probably, the references to the (presumably related) crime of *stellatura* in the *HA* (*Pisc. Nig.* 3.8; *Alex.* 15.5). That said, I am indifferent, here and throughout this chapter, to the possibility of pre-Justinianic or Justinianic interpolation in legal texts (Volterra 1929 [1999], 140 argued for Justinianic in this case), because it changes just the date, not the fact, of the changes in the law in which I am interested.

5. Sen. *Contr.* 5.1. For the rhetorical education of jurists, Dingel 1988, 2–5; Mantovani 2014, 597–598; Babusiaux (forthcoming); with Rizzelli 2017, 104–114 for the cultural atmosphere that would encourage juristic borrowing from rhetoric, noting an attested imperial official *a declamationibus Latinis* (105). Wibier 2020, 465–467 argues that law was taught in the rhetorical schools. Another way of illustrating the common culture of jurists and nonjurists is to notice the common use of legal terms in other genres of Latin literature, Peirano 2013, 91 n. 36.

6. *inscripti maleficii sit actio,* Sprenger 1911, 228–230 (discussing the connection to the Greek καινὰ καὶ ἄγραφα ἀδικήματα, and tracing the connection of the declamatory theme to *stellionatus* back to the 1500s); Lanfranchi 1938, 504–507; Bonner 1949, 86–87; Langer 2007, 160–162; Lentano 2014a, 58–62, whose argument I follow here. As a Greek theme: Cyrus, *Diaph. Stas.* 8 (Walz, *RG* 8.392); Latin: Sen. *Contr.* 5.1; *DMin.* 252.*pr.,* and esp. 8; 344.*pr.,* 370.*pr.*

7. Sen. *Contr.* 3.*pr.*17. On this episode, its context and other implications, Berti 2007, 141–142; Schwartz 2015. Cassius Severus's use of it implies the popularity of this theme, as does Quint. *Inst.* 7.4.36. For the details of Cassius Severus's life, Brzoska 1899.

8. *Stellionatus* by *cognitio extra ordinaria,* this chapter n. 2. Berger 1953, 715 emphasizes the freedom a Roman judge would have under *cognitio extra ordinem* to accept the case or not. For offenses that could only be heard under this procedure, *Dig.* 47.11 (Paul and Ulpian), some of them being idiosyncratic to a province, such as damage to the Nile dikes in Egypt (*Dig.* 47.11.10 [Ulpian]).

9. The strict legal authority of juristic *responsa* under the Empire depends on how one views the *ius respondendi,* the power allegedly assigned by Augustus (or Tiberius, or Hadrian) to certain jurists to give authoritative *responsa* (but perhaps only if they agreed). The existence and, if it existed, the details of the *ius respondendi* are, however, imponderable: Tuori 2004 [2007]; Leesen 2010, 22–29, 325–328. For the authority of the *de Officio Proconsulis,* chapter 10 n. 38.

## Chapter 8: Rhetoric and Roman Law

1. By "real Roman jurisprudence" we mean the written, collected Roman law as it is usually understood: the *Digest*, the two *Codices*, the works gathered in *FIRA*, etc. We also allow ourselves to dip into the *LRV* (*Lex Romana Visigothorum*) and the *LRB* (*Lex Romana Burgundionum*). For reasons of space we set aside the large phenomenon of local influence on Roman justice and law in the provinces (Coriat 1997, 411–418 and Peachin 2019, 116 n. 25 gather the writings; see also many of the articles in Czajkowski and Eckhardt 2020) that did not make the journey back into the written, collected Roman law (even to the degree of attracting enough notice to be rejected by a Roman jurist or emperor in a *responsa* or rescript).

2. On the autonomy or isolation of Roman law the classic treatment is Schulz 1936 [1934], 19–39, 124–136; cf. Pugliese 1966; Watson 1995, 64–73, 111–116, 158–171; Lewis 2000 and Palma 1992, 9 n. 17 for literature. Tuori 2007, 71–134 places the debate about the autonomy of the Roman law in its modern historical context, noting that exterior influence on the law was once far more readily accepted.

3. For the style of the classical jurists, Wieacker 2006, 43–44 and Mantovani 2018, 53–78. Nörr 1978 (cf. Wibier 2016), 115 counts only seven mentions of Cicero in the whole *Digest* (and three of them gathered in *Dig.* 1.2.2, a potted history of the Roman law from Pomponius's *Enchiridion*), which is rather astonishing given the emphasis on Cicero in the education jurists will have had (see chapter 1 n. 13).

4. Discussion of the word *color* at *Dig.* 5.2.5 (Marcellus) is traced to 1800–1804 by di Ottavio 2012a (see esp. 107); chapter 10 n. 13 for this passage. Cossa 2012, 335–358 discusses the five other uses of *color* in the *Digest*, with literature. Bretone 2008, 763 notes that jurists strictly avoided the rhetorical terms *controversia* and *ius controversum*.

5. "They glared at each other, mostly, across a great gulf" (Crook 1993, 68). On the separation between jurists and advocates, Leesen 2010, 18–20 with literature, although she herself is against such a strong division (following the polemic of J. W. Tellegen in many works, e.g., 1982, 2–4; Tellegen and Tellegen-Couperus 2000; Tellegen-Couperus and Tellegen 2013, cheerfully admitting in the last that "so far, our work has not changed the commonly held view" [31]). The thoughtful Harries 2006, esp. 27–28, 102, 132, is, after much consideration, inclined to weaken, but not deny, the divide.

6. For convenient histories of the Roman legal profession, Kunkel 1967 [1951]; Schiller 1978, 283–369; for jurists' working habits, Meyer 2004, 251 n. 4, 252 n. 6 gathers the literature; for the education of Roman jurists, Vössing 1997, 387–388 n. 1325; Meyer 2004, 251 n. 3; and Cossa 2012, 310–311 n. 17, 325 n. 44 gather the literature. Riggsby 2015 and Harries 2016 give concise summaries in English.

7. On the "vulgar law," often indeed identified by marks of outside influence, Voss 1982, 2–11; Wieacker 1988, 52 n. 68; 2006, 207–218 with 435–436; and Coriat 1997, 418–419 nn. 440–442 begin to gather the literature; for a summary in English, Liebs 2008. "Noisome weed," Hohmann 1996, 40, also for "the poison of rhetoric" etc.; "bombastic," Schulz 1936 [1934], 82. For Justinianic classicism, Schulz 1936 [1934], 138–139 with literature; Schindler 1966; Wieacker 1988, 49 n. 52; Robinson 2000; Wieacker 2006, 442 with literature.

8. "Dismal reputation," Honoré 1998, 21. On the prose style of late-antique law, Honig 1960, 23–25, 39–61; MacMullen 1990 [1962]; Bauman 1980, 180–189; Voss 1982, 1–81; Eich and Eich

2004; Dillon 2012, 60–89, especially for the date of the change, visible in some genres of imperial constitutions late in the reign of Diocletian and general under Constantine. For modern students' horror at this style, Bauman 1980, 180 n. 147 and Meyer 2004, 251 n. 5 gather expressions of loathing.

9. Peachin 2017, 43–56; Mantovani 2018; if valid, highly useful for analysis of the type undertaken here.

10. Juristic thinking much the same, even if the style has changed, Voss 1982, 80; Crook 1995, 188 and Meyer 2004, 252 with literature. Evans Grubbs 1995, 50 collects opinions upon when the "classical" Roman law ends and the postclassical begins. By the 420s and 430s the office of imperial *quaestor*, responsible in the fourth century for the style of imperial constitutions, was often back in the hands of jurists rather than rhetoricians, Harries 1988, 169–170.

11. In his inaugural lecture at University College London, Jolowicz 1932 elegantly summarized the state of the controversy in his day over the extent and nature of exterior influence on the law, and surprisingly little has changed in actual scholarly practice, even if such influence is now nearly universally admitted in principle. As a test case consider the recent *Oxford Handbook of Roman Law and Society* (Du Plessis, Ando, and Tuori 2016): the editors (5) dismiss the autonomy of Roman law from Roman society as outdated (see also Pölönen 2016 in that volume), but reading the volume itself through is like a passage back in time, and many of the articles later in the book, especially in the sections on "Property" and "Obligation," feel as if they could have been written in 1870 (see Tuori 2007, 174 on this split between approaches), and offer a vision of Roman law entirely innocent of any external influence.

12. Berger 1953, 795–796 offered a bibliography of work to his time.

13. Levy 1951, 5–7, 9–10; 1956, 1–10; practice, Crook 1995, 196; Meyer 2004, 216–249; custom, Humfress 2011 with literature.

14. Collinet 1934; and on precedent ("case law") in general, Harries 2006, 134–148; Metzger 2004.

15. Evans Grubbs 1995, 321–342; on late-antique changes in morality (336–339), with literature, although Evans Grubbs herself demurs. Pressure from inquirers, Connolly 2010, 137–158, 161.

16. Balogh 1951 is the classic study; cf. Scacchetti 1984; Sirks 2002a; with Wieacker 1988, 55–57 for literature.

17. For the controversy, Tuori 2007, 112–120; cf. Leesen 2010, 7–11, 14–15.

18. Mitteis 1891; Taubenschlag 1934 [1959]; 1955, 1 with literature, 51, 54–55; 1959 [1926]; 1959 [1919–1920]; Wieacker 1988, 47–48 nn. 46–47, 50 n. 60 with literature; Evans Grubbs 1995, 2 with literature, 333–335, 339; Amelotti 2001; Meyer 2004, 253 n. 10; Nowak 2010; Humfress 2011, 36, 40–42; Harris 2012; Jakab 2012; Modrzejewski 2014, 337–342; Kantor 2015, 18; and many of the essays in Lamberti, Gröschler, and Milazzo 2015. For a clear statement of the case to the contrary, Watson 1995, 111–116.

19. The controversy about the influence on the Roman law of philosophical ideas or modes of thinking goes back to Voigt 1856–1876; and the vast literature is summarized or listed by Lanfranchi 1938, 6–13; Schiller 1978, 375–376; Wieacker 1988, 618–662; Vander Waerdt 1994; Watson 1995, 158–171; Scarano Ussani 1997; Tuori 2007, 53–58; Leesen 2010, 5–7; Cossa 2012, 306–308 n. 13; Scarano Ussani 2012; Ducos 2014, esp. 303–460; Rizzelli 2014a; Tellegen-Couperus and Tellegen 2016; Giltaij 2016; Mantovani 2018, 79–128. See this chapter n. 31 on the impossibility in many cases of distinguishing philosophical from rhetorical influence.

20. Grammar, Stein 1966, 53–73 is the classic statement; Stein 1972, 14 n. 18 and 29 n. 42 for older literature; Bauman 1980, 133–144; Wieacker 1988, 653–662; Leesen 2010, 11–14.

21. Medicine, Herberger 1981; Scarano Ussani 1989, 12–13, 104–126; 1997, 54, 66–67, 77, 97–99, 129.

22. Antiquarianism, Nörr 1976; Scarano Ussani 2012, 47–71, 87–108; etymology, Babusiaux 2014.

23. Christianity, on which especially Hohenlohe 1937; and the beginnings of the literature can be traced through Hohenlohe 1937; Berger 1953, 796–797; Bauman 1980, 189–218; Wieacker 1988, 51 n. 62; Hunt 1993; and Evans Grubbs 1995, 2–3, 317–318, 340.

24. For general summaries of the law and rhetoric literature, luxuriantly Cossa 2012 and Lentano 2014a, with Calboli's 2016 review to fill in the gaps of the latter; more sparingly, Langer 2007, 17–28; and for concise lists of contributions, Stolfi 2011, 86–88 n. 4 and Cossa 2012, 300–301 n. 3. Major contributions to (or summaries of) the broader controversy at its various stages are Lanfranchi 1938, 2–13, 96 n. 2, 117; Parks 1945, 78–85; Bonner 1949, 45–48; Schiller 1978, 373–375; Wieacker 1988, 51, 54, 627–630, 662 n. 1, 669–675; Hohmann 1996; and Bederman 2001, 84–99.

25. For *stasis* theory especially Stroux 1949 [1926], although the argument was anticipated in the nineteenth century; also La Bua 2006; Babusiaux 2011, 21–61; Rizzelli 2014a, 162 n. 23; and Kacprzak 2016, 207–209 and Babusiaux (forthcoming); with Cossa 2012, 314–315 n. 21, 329 n. 51 for literature. Equity, Cossa 2012, 317–318 n. 25 collects the literature; see Bauman 1980, 112–124, 144–145 in English.

26. Theory of *topica*, esp. Viehweg 1953 [1993]; and see Leesen 2010, esp. 29–32; Babusiaux 2011, 63–174; Tellegen-Couperus and Tellegen 2013, 34–36; Kacprzak 2016, 204–207; with Cossa 2012, 319 n. 27 and Babusiaux (forthcoming) 6–7, 13–16 for literature to date.

27. For definition (which is also a *stasis*), Cossa 2012, 320 n. 29 gathers the literature; and see Nörr 2003 [1972]; Scarano Ussani 2012, 109–115; Querzoli 2013, 117–134; Kacprzak 2016, 205–206 in English. Cf. Wieacker 1988, 628–633, who argues that it was carried from philosophy, by rhetoric, into law.

28. Argument and proof, Cossa 2012, 322–323 n. 37 gathers the literature, and see Puliatti 2011; Querzoli 2013, 138–140; and Kacprzak 2016, 202–204 in English. For the use of *exempla*, see Nörr 2009.

29. *Humanitas*, Honig 1960; Bauman 1980, 174–179 (with literature at 174–175 n. 110, and for the connection to rhetoric esp. 175), 182–218; Palma 1992. The origins of *humanitas* in the law are controversial, and rhetoric is only one possibility: see Kleiter 2010, 139–140 n. 608, 220–221.

30. *Regulae*, Masi Doria 2011; Santorelli 2019.

31. For rhetorical *color*, see this chapter n. 4 and chapter 10 n. 13. A selection of other suggestions for rhetorical influence on the law might begin with the legal understanding of *natura* (Rizzelli 2014a, 158 n. 14 with Citti 2015 for natural law in declamation); rhetoric as a vehicle by which Aristotelian thinking influenced Roman law (Rizzelli 2014a, 183–184 n. 65, 187 n. 72, 239–240 n. 190); rhetoric as a vehicle for Stoic thinking (Rizzelli 2014a, 197; and see Thomas 1978 for abstract thinking in general). See also Nörr 1986a (English summary 1986b), for the influence of rhetoric on juristic thinking about the *lex Aquilia* and indirect causes of death; and about the influence of rhetorical (or philosophical) thinking on categories of legal knowledge (2003). Steinwenter 1947 offered other recollections of rhetorical works in jurists' thinking, if

not the law itself; but he was forcefully countered by Meyer 1951. Leesen 2010, 32 n. 76 collects other scholars who have attempted the same as Steinwenter. In many of these cases (topical thinking, definition, *humanitas*, and *natura* especially), even if such influence be accepted, it is impossible to determine whether it was exerted on legal thinking by rhetoric, philosophy, or philosophy through rhetoric, Nörr 2003 [1972], 713 n. 11; Cossa 2012, 306–308 n. 13.

32. Cf. the implications, if not the conclusions, of Mantovani 2018, 185–188.

33. Tendency towards abstraction: a complaint of Frier 1994, 148 n. 38, whose general judgement of rhetoric and Roman law is that "the fundamental difference in their approaches to legal rules, and to the application of those rules within specific cases, makes the two disciplines not just strange bedfellows, but ultimately irreconcilable" (142). Kacprzak 2016, presumably expected to affirm the relationship by the editors of the *Oxford Handbook of Roman Law and Society*, instead despairs that "to the extent that we want to understand the reasons behind their [Roman jurists'] decisions, as well as the methods by which they reached them, rhetorical theory seems not extremely helpful; as a matter of fact, rather than teaching how to arrive at correct solutions, it provided instructions on how to defend solutions already taken and dependent on personal preferences" (212). Hohmann 1996 estimates the influence of Stroux and his tradition, and *stasis* theory, as greater than I do, but my sense (no more or less subjective than his: neither of us has conducted a census) is that the impact of such thinking on the writings of hard-core students of the Roman law has been slight.

34. Babusiaux 2011; Querzoli 2011a; 2011b; 2013; Bettinazzi 2014.

35. About 160 laws, chapter 10 n. 65. Lentano 2009 [2005], 51–52 nn. 12–16; 2014a, 130; and Lentano 2017b, 168–175 make a general collection of the literature on the laws in declamation, and his bibliographical essay in 2014a, 127–140 is invaluable on declamatory law and its parallels to Roman law.

36. Thomas 1983, 123 counts 173 of the 262 surviving Latin declamations as concerning disputes within families.

37. For the dates of the surviving collections of declamations, chapter 1 n. 4.

38. That Latin declamatory laws we see in the imperial period often appear to be (or pretend to be) laws from the Republic, never displaced by, e.g., Augustan marriage legislation, Calboli Montefusco 1979, 292; expanded by Langer 2007, 83, 106, 119–120 et passim; cf. Lentano 2016, 69.

39. Greek law, see this chapter nn. 18 and 49.

40. For the *giuridicizzazione dell'etica*, Lentano 2009 [2005]; 2011 [2009]; Rizzelli 2012b, 291–293; somewhat anticipated by Beard 1993, 56. A potentially good example is the declamatory law requiring children to support their parents (see chapter 9 nn. 49–50).

41. The classic piece is Lécrivain 1891; see also Bonner 1949, 84–85 for the controversy, which he carried on, arguing for much borrowing from Roman law; but Paoli 1953 [1976] argued for much more Greek, and less Roman, influence, and much mixing.

42. Trying to trace old Roman laws through the laws of declamation, Bornecque 1902, 59–74; Sprenger 1911; Lanfranchi 1938; Bonner 1949, 84–132; Düll 1971; Langer 2007; Wycisk 2008; on this tradition of scholarship, Hömke 2002, 161–164. This is a practice justly complained of by Crook 1993, 70 n. 15, given the gulfs of time often separating the attestations of the Roman and the declamatory law.

43. Winterbottom 1982, 65; Crook 1993; Crook 1995, 163–167.

44. While the gaps in time between surviving Latin declamation (mostly first or early second century AD) and Roman law (mostly early third century AD or after, but often commenting on legal material from the Republic) presented a problem for those trying to trace the latter through the former (see this chapter, n. 42), they present less of a problem for the reverse, because laws used in declamation do not appear to have changed much over time. Scholars trying to trace the influence, as we do, from laws of declamation into the Roman law, are uncommon, but see Tivier 1868, 121–123; Bornecque 1902, 133; Rayment 1952; Evans-Grubbs 1989, 83 n. 118 (the founder of the current tradition of study of this topic); Mantovani 2007 [2006]; Querzoli 2011a; 2011b; and Di Ottavio 2012a.

45. *DMin*. 264 with Bettinazzi 2014, 12–23. The *lex Voconia* concerned the capacity of women to be named as heirs. Cf. Sen. *Contr*. 3.9, where the *lex Cornelia de sicariis et veneficis* is apostrophized within the text of the declamation: "*lex Cornelia, te appello*."

46. For fathers versus sons in Latin declamation, chapter 2 n. 34. My "with a few exceptions" delicately conceals a perfect mare's nest of contradictions in the sources and controversy among scholars: see Mer 1953, 80–82, 95–98; Daube 1953, and Fayer 1994–2005, 1.260–268. But in general a father accusing a son was a *miseriarum ac saevitiae exemplum atrox*, Tac. *Ann*. 4.28.1. Many types of litigation between husbands and wives that appear in Latin declamation were also impossible under the real Roman law, Fayer 1994–2005, 2.363 n. 125; Evans Grubbs 2011, 381: "In general, imperial law did not approve of family members acting against each other in court," with further evidence. As another example, adoption in Latin declamation often violates the Roman law, Bornecque 1902, 68.

47. Livy 1.50.9, *dixisse enim nullam breviorem esse cognitionem quam inter patrem et filium, paucisque transigi verbis posse: ni pareat patri, habiturum infortunium esse*, for which I thank Margaret Imber. On this passage, Lentano 2009 [2005], 45–48, 75–79.

48. Broadly on *patria potestas* in declamation, Brescia 2015a, 63 n. 6 gathers the literature. On the *ius vitae necisque* in declamation, Lanfranchi 1938, 251–254 adding *DMin*. 372.11; Thomas 1984 [2017]; Breij 2006a, 64–71, with 22 cases of fathers killing or wishing to kill sons (64), of which 10 ask a court for a sentence, and who gathers uses of the *lex indemnatorum* (= Breij 2015a, 31–50); cf. Sussman 1994, 168; Langer 2007, 92–93; Lentano 2014a, 48–50, 133; Santorelli 2019. But the picture is mixed, because while applicable laws are spelled out in the preface of a declamation, in the body the unrestricted power of fathers to execute their children without the special authorization to kill a child without trial provided by the *lex indemnatorum* is often stated or implied (e.g., Sen. *Contr*. 2.3.11; *DMin*. 304.3; Calp. Flacc. 53; *DM* 6.14, 17.7, 19.5, 19.12), as are other aspects of *patria potestas*. Note also the rarity in declamation of a father trying a son-in-power himself (Sen. *Contr*. 7.1.pr., 7.1.12; *DMin*. 281.5, 356.1 with Lanfranchi 1938, 211–212, 253; cf. *DMin*. 300.pr.) as the real Roman law allowed: see Düll 1943, 57–70; Kaser 1971 [1955], 62–63; Harris 1986; with Donadio 2012 for full literature and discussion of the controversies about the real-world law, especially whether the father had to convoke a formal court of his relations (the *iudicium domesticum*) to execute a child. Wurm notes that litigants in cases of *abdicatio* appeal to *iudices*, once again indicating that the father was not acting alone by virtue of his *patria potestas* or in a *iudicium domesticum* (1972, 32–34; cf. Lanfranchi 1938, 259 and Krapinger 2007a, 17). On the desuetude of the *ius vitae necisque* in the real world of late Republic and Roman Empire, chapter 10 n. 35.

49. The imagined world of Latin declamation, Berti 2007, 99–110; Breij 2015b, 224–225; Greek, Russell 1983, 22–39; and for the differences between them, Lentano 2014b. On declamation's connection to New Comedy, the novel, and story-telling, Zinsmaier 1993, 1–13 = 2009, 15–29; for law and justice in the Greek novel, Schwartz 2016; for drawing on the New Comedy especially, Bonner 1949, 37–38; Penella 2014, 123 n. 61; Krapinger 2007a, 13 n. 2; Nocchi 2015, 193–199; for plots as well, Fantham 2011 [2004]. For folklore in declamation, Berti 2007, 311–325; Lentano 2012b, 2018a, mediated through Euripides' *Phoenissae*, a popular teaching text (24 n. 50). For pirates, Favreau 2015 and Lentano 2018b, 178–189 with n. 17 for literature; for stepmothers, *novercae*, Casamento 2002, 101–124; van Mal-Maeder 2007, 128–136; Lentano 2012b, 2 n. 4, 5 n. 14; Krapinger and Stramaglia 2015, 14–18; Pingoud and Rolle 2016.

50. Other declamatory laws assumed to be in operation, e.g., Sen. *Contr.* 3.1, 10.4.9; *DMin.* 277.5, 385.*pr.*, 4; Lucian, *Abdicatus* 19.

51. For the *giuridicizzazione dell'etica*, see this chapter n. 40, chapter 9 n. 52.

## Chapter 9: The Attractions of Declamatory Law

1. For all the variants of the law in declamation, Sprenger 1911, 203–204 and Lanfranchi 1938, 462; see also Bornecque 1902, 61; Desanti 1988, 319–323; Langer 2007, 65–66; Wycisk 2008, 269; Casinos Mora 2011, 595–605. The *raptor duarum* scenario is found, *inter alia*, at Sen. *Contr.* 1.5; Calp. Flacc. 51. *mutanda optio raptore convicto*, Sen. *Contr.* 7.8. *maritus virginis raptor, DMin.* 262. For *raptus* in Latin declamation, in addition to the works above, Evans-Grubbs 1989, 68–69, who argues for a difference between the Senecan and pseudo-Quintilianic themes; Packman 1999, 20–21 who observes that in the surviving Latin declamations all cases of *raptus* of females are of unmarried citizen girls by unmarried citizen men, with only one exception (the *Maritus raptor*); Kaster 2001, 317–318, 326–334 with explicit appearances of the *raptarum lex* at 328–329 n. 24; van Mal-Maeder 2007, 24–29; Berti 2007, 85–90; Casinos Mora 2009 for the cases in Calpurnius Flaccus; Querzoli 2011a, 157 nn. 25–27 and 2011b, 84 n. 8 collects thirty-five instances of *raptus* in the surviving Latin declamations (and Grodzynski 1984, 704 n. 11 gathers the instances in Quint. *Inst.*); Brescia 2012, 52–83; 2016, 333–345; in Greek declamation, Heath 1995, 148–149. The *raptor* is listed as a stock character in declamation at Juv. 7.168 and the victim's choice is mentioned at Tac. *Dial.* 35.5, implying how frequently this declamatory law was used. Rape (in our sense) is usually implied in cases of *raptus*, but not always: Querzoli 2011a, 162 and 2011b, 87 collects declamations where this is placed in doubt.

2. Calp. Flacc. 25.

3. For the rhetorical crime of *raptus* and the Roman law, Sprenger 1911, 204–205; Lanfranchi 1938, 462–465; Bonner 1949, 89–91; Langer 2007, 66–70; Wycisk 2008, 269–270.

4. *Raptus* in the Roman law is a complete tangle until the early third century AD because we must deduce pre-Augustan and Augustan law from much later fragments. How *iniuria* (and what sort of *iniuria*, delict or crime? prosecuted by what procedure? did that change?), the *lex de adulteriis*, and *vis* (and whether *vis publica* or *privata*?) went together, succeeded one another (or did not), and indeed whether all three were used, is controversial and probably insoluble. Standard treatments are Goria 1987; Rizzelli 1997, 249–257; Botta 2004, 15–176—especially on the question of *vis* versus the *lex Julia de adulteriis* (24–78) and *iniuria* (72–79), with 2016 for

updated literature; Astolfi 2012, 135–166. Mancini 2011, 153–155 offers a good, up-to-date summary of the state of the question; and see Puliatti 1995, 471–472 n. 1 for a convenient collection of older literature, and Querzoli 2011a, 154–155 n. 11 for recent literature on treating *raptus* as *iniuria*. The best English summary, up through the Augustan legislation, is Moses 1993, 45–59; and Robinson 1995, 71–73 takes the story in English through Justinian. Treated as *iniuria*, *Sent. Paul.* 5.4.1, 5.4.4, 5.4.14; cf. *Dig.* 47.10.1.2, 47.10.9.4, 47.10.15.15–24 (Ulpian) with 47.10.10, 47.10.18.2 (Paul), all from works on the Praetor's Edict, from which Lenel 1907 deduced that the Edict classed *adtempata pudicitia* as *iniuria*; see also *Dig.* 48.5.6.*pr.* (Papinian); 48.6.5.2 (Marcian); *Inst. Just.* 4.4.1; with Balzarini 1983, 193–202 and Hagemann 1998, 61, 71–75, 122–124, 135–137, 194–195, 216, 244–247 on this puzzling matter. As *stuprum* without violence under the *lex Julia de adulteriis*, *Inst. Just.* 4.18.4, *quis sine vi vel virginem vel viduam honeste viventem stupraverit*; with a punishment of *dimidia parte bonorum suorum multatur nec testamentum ei ex maiore parte facere licet* (*Coll.* 5.2.2 = *Sent. Paul.* 2.26.13) later changed to confiscation of half of property for an *honestus*, and, for a *humilis* (*Inst. Just.* 4.18.4), flogging and relegation (Mette-Dittmann 1991, 40, 65). With violence, *lex Iulia de vi publica*, *Dig.* 48.6.3.4 (Marcian), *per vim stupraverit*; *Dig.* 48.6.5.2 (Marcian); 48.5.30(29).9 (Ulpian) *per vim stuprum intulit* (with Mommsen 1899, 664; Rizzelli 1997, 251; cf. *CJ* 9.12.3 [Diocletian and Maximian, AD 293]), which carried a capital penalty, *Dig.* 48.6.10.2 (Ulpian); *Sent. Paul.* 5.26.1. If, as some scholars of the Roman law claim, it was originally *vis privata* (which was not capital) rather than *vis publica* (see Goria 1987, 709–710; Querzoli 2011a, 154–155 n. 11; 2011b, 83 n. 3), that merely pushes the capital penalty back to Marcian (see above, this note), and so does not affect the argument here, unless the capital penalty in Marcian is interpolated (see this chapter n. 7).

5. *Dig.* 48.6.5.2 (Marcian), *cum raptus crimen legis Iuliae de adulteris potestatem excedit*, with Puliatti 1995, 475–477; Botta 2004, 81–95. *Raptus* was still a form of *vis* in AD 293, *CJ* 9.12.3 (Diocletian and Maximian, AD 293).

6. Constantine, *CTh* 9.24.1 (date disputed, but AD 320 or 326 are most likely: see Desanti 1986, 196 n. 1 for the controversy), with Grodzynski 1984; Desanti 1986; Evans-Grubbs 1989; Puliatti 1995, 482–495; Botta 2004, 95–106; Mancini 2011, 156–171; Rizzelli 2012a, 314–316 (with n. 51 for recent literature), 327–333. Puzzle: "It is interesting that this separate legal category, *raptus*, should have arisen in the first place. Forcible rape of any woman was already covered by . . ." (Dixon 2001, 52).

7. *Dig.* 48.6.5.2 (Marcian), cf. *Sent. Paul.* 5.4.4, 5.4.14. Marcian's *ultimum supplicium* is thought interpolated by some, Botta 2004, 83 n. 7, but if so that just pushes the capital penalty to Constantine, which does not affect the argument here. In *CTh* 9.24.1 (Constantine, AD 320 or 326), the exact nature of the penalty (although severe) that applied to free persons has dropped out of the text (or may have been regarded as too obvious to state) although slaves were to be burnt, *CTh* 9.24.1.5 = *CJ* 9.13.1.4 (Justinian, AD 533); but *CTh* 9.8.1 (Constantine, AD 326) makes it clear that it was worse than deportation and confiscation of property, while *CTh* 9.24.2 (Constantius, AD 349), which reduces the penalty imposed by his imperial father to a merely capital one, implies that the penalty under Constantine had been some especially horrid form of execution. On the puzzle of the penalty for *raptores* in *CTh* 9.24.1 see Grodzynski 1984, 706, 711–713; Evans-Grubbs 1989, 66. *Raptus* was still (in principle) capital under Julian (Amm. Marc. 16.5.12) and probably under Jovian, *CTh* 9.25.2 = *CJ* 1.3.5 [Jovian, AD 364]).

8. Quoting *CJ* 9.13.1.2 (Justinian, AD 533; *CJ* 1.3.53 is partially identical), *nec sit facultas raptae virgini vel viduae vel cuilibet mulieri raptorem suum sibi maritum exposcere* (cf. 9.13.1.1g, *nuptae mulieres alii cuilibet praeter raptorem legitime coniungentur*); with Desanti 1987 with 189 n. 2 on the date of the law, which might alternatively be AD 528; Haase 1994; Puliatti 1995, 505–519; Botta 2004, 134–146; Rizzelli 2012a, 332–338. Capital, *CJ* 9.13.1 = 1.3.53 (Justinian, AD 533); cf. *Inst. Just.* 4.18.8; Just. *Nov.* 123.43 (AD 546).

9. Canon law, Goria 1987, 718–719; Evans-Grubbs 1989, 73–76; Karlin-Hayter 1992, 138.

10. Or, of course, *raptae* marrying their *raptores* may have been immemorial custom in the real world (and forgiving the crime a *ius vetus*, at *CTh* 9.24.1.*pr.* with Desanti 1988, 327), and taken into both declamation and law independently (Desanti 1986, 205–207, 212; Evans-Grubbs 1989), which is, *mutatis mutandis*, possible in almost all the cases argued in this chapter.

11. For the "without a dowry" variant, which Bonner considered the root form of the law, Bonner 1949, 89 gathers the references; it therefore also makes sense that *CJ* 9.13.1.1f-1g (Justinian, AD 533) should grant the property of a convicted *raptor* to the victim as a dowry. *Raptor* wealthy, as implied by *CTh* 9.1.1 = *CJ* 3.24.1 (Constantine, AD 317); cf. *CJ* 1.3.53.2 = 9.13.1.1c (Justinian, AD 533). Declamation often suggests that the act of *raptus* was collusive between the man and woman, to coerce parents into consent—"abduction marriage" is the term of art: Kaster 2001, 329 n. 26. And so the law also often suspected, *CTh* 9.24.1 (Constantine, date disputed); *CTh* 9.25.1, 2 (Constantius, AD 354); *CJ* 9.13.1.3b (Justinian, AD 533); and the law also worried that parents were apt to overlook the crime, *CTh* 9.24.1.4 (Constantine, date disputed); *CJ* 9.13.1.2, 3c (Justinian, AD 533). Majorian (*Nov.* 6.4, AD 458), allowing anyone to prosecute the *raptus* of a nun and rewarding the prosecutor with the guilty party's estate, also suggests a failure of victims and family members to act against *raptores*. On the legal and social reality of abduction marriage in the late Empire, and the difficulties faced by those abducted (which apply to victims of simple rape as well), Desanti 1986, 203 n. 36; Evans-Grubbs 1989, 61–67 (the classic discussion) = 1995, 183–193; Arjava 1996, 37–40; Grey 2008.

12. *CTh* 9.24.1 (Constantine, AD 320 or 326) *si quis nihil cum parentibus puellae ante depectus invitam eam rapuerit vel volentem abduxerit, patrocinium ex eius responsione sperans . . . nihil ei secundum ius vetus prosit puellae responsio, sed ipsa puella potius societate criminis obligetur,* with Rizzelli 2012a, 327 n. 83 (drawing on Evans-Grubbs 1989, 82–83), who notes the possible rhetorical inspiration for the situations and language of the Constantinian law.

13. *CTh* 9.24.3 (Valentinian, Valens, and Gratian, AD 374) *sed si quo casu quis vel accusationem differat vel reatum, et opprimi e vestigio atrociter commissa nequiverint, ad persecutionem criminis ex die sceleris admissi quinquennii tribuimus facultatem. quo sine metu interpellationis et complemento accusationis exacto, nulli deinceps copia patebit arguendi, nec de coniugio aut sobole disputandi,* with Goria 1987, 716–717 (noting that if not challenged within the five-year period, the marriage stood); Grodzynski 1984, 714–716; Evans-Grubbs 1989, 66–67; Puliatti 1995, 487; Rizzelli 1997, 256; Botta 2004, 99–100 n. 42. *Contra*, Desanti 1986, and Casinos Mora 2011, for the minority position that the *raptarum lex* was the Roman law from the late first century AD to Constantine, and thus that the declamatory law reflected the Roman law, rather than the other way around. *Raptus* had apparently temporarily ceased to be punished by execution by AD 420: *Const. Sirm.* 10 = *CTh* 9.25.3 (Honorius and Theodosius).

14. Nörr 1969, esp. 16–25.

15. For Justinian's law see this chapter n. 8.

16. Just. *Nov.* 143.*pr.* (AD 563 = Just. *Nov* 150.*pr.*, with slight changes; see Puliatti 1995, 505–506 n. 88 for the date, which might be AD 543: no matter), with Puliatti 1995, 520–522; Botta 2004, 147–151. *Raptus* still capital: *et capitis subiecisse supplicio non tantum raptores, verum comites etiam eorum nec non alios qui eis auxilium tempore invasionis contulisse noscuntur.* The ravished still marrying their ravishers and inheriting from them: *sed mirati sumus, quod conati sunt aliqui dicere raptam mulierum sive volentem sive nolentem, etsi raptoris amplexa sit matrimonium contra nostrae constitutionis tenorem, debere tamen raptoris eam habere substantiam vel quasi legis praemium vel ex testamento forte*; disposition of the late rapist husband's property, Just. *Nov.*143.1. Subsequent to Justinian, the eastern law continued to wobble on the subject of ravishers marrying their victims, it being allowed in the Isaurian *Ecloga*, Karlin-Hayter 1992, 141.

17. *raptor, nisi et suum et raptae patrem intra dies triginta exoraverit, pereat*, Sen. *Contr.* 2.3.*pr.*; *DMin.* 349; Quint. *Inst.* 9.2.90–91 with slightly different wording, with Bornecque 1902, 61; Sprenger 1911, 203; Bonner 1949, 91; Desanti 1988, 326; Wycisk 2008, 275–276.

18. *Dig.* 48.6.5.2 (Marcian), *qui vacantem mulierem rapuit vel nuptam, ultimo supplicio punitur et, si pater iniuriam suam precibus exoratus remiserit, tamen extraneus sine quinquennii praescriptione reum postulare poterit, cum raptus crimen legis Iuliae de adulteriis potestatem excedit.* For *exorare* in both contexts, Bonner 1949, 91; Grodzynski 1984, 721–722; Querzoli 2011a, and 2011b, from whom I take the suggestion of rhetorical influence on Marcian; with Botta 2004, 86–88 nn. 17–18 and Querzoli 2013, 173–174 for recent discussion and literature. Constantine even punished parents who were prepared to forgive a ravisher, *CTh.* 9.24.1.4. But forgiveness by parents did come to extinguish the crime in the barbarian law codes, Arjava 1996, 39.

19. *rapta raptoris mortem aut bona optet, DMin.* 276.*pr.*; cf. 252, 370, with Rayment 1952, 227; Langer 2007, 69–70.

20. *lex Iulia de adulteriis coercendis, Inst. Just.* 4.18.4; *lex Iulia de vi publica, Dig.* 48.6.10.2 (Ulpian) with Santalucia 1998, 88; and also under the *lex Iulia de vi privata*, if, as many scholars think, that, rather than *vis publica*, was in fact the law at issue, *Dig.* 48.7.1.*pr.* (Marcian). Cf. *CTh* 9.8.1 (Constantine, AD 326), *universae eius facultates fisci viribus vindicentur; Const. Sirm.* 10 = *CTh* 9.25.3 (Honorius and Theodosius, AD 420). For Justinian, *CJ* 9.13.1.1f (Justinian, AD 533); Just. *Nov.* 143.*pr.* (AD 563 = Just. *Nov.* 150.*pr.*).

21. On a husband's *ius occidendi* in the pre-*lex Iulia* law, Cantarella 1972, 253–258; Astolfi 2000, 301–343; Fayer 1994–2005, 3.195–211 with literature (197–198 n. 27); on the duty to kill both, Hor. *Sat.* 2.7.61–62; *sed contra* Treggiari 1991, 271–272, but the Republican law does not matter for my argument.

22. For the *ius occidendi* in the *lex Iulia de adulteriis coercendis*, esp. *Dig.* 48.5.21–25, *Coll.* 4.2–12; Rizzelli 1997, 9–66 with a discussion of the limited rights of the betrayed husband (11); Panero Oria 2001, 99–183; Fayer 1994–2005, 3.221–270; with Rizzelli 2014a, 284 n. 271 for recent literature. Treggiari 1991, 282–285 offers a brief account in English. The *lex Iulia* moved the Republican "must kill both" requirement (if indeed it had existed previously) over to fathers, who retained, under extremely limited circumstances, the right to kill daughters and their adulterous lovers. Beginnings to the huge literature on the Augustan marriage legislation are Rizzelli 1997; Santalucia 1998, 201–204; and Querzoli 2013, 210–211 n. 189.

23. Sen. *Contr.* 1.4.*pr.*, *adulterum cum adultera qui deprehenderit, dum utrumque corpus interficiat, sine fraude sit*; 9.1.*pr.*; *DMin.* 244.*pr.*, 277.1, 286.3, 347.*pr.*; Calp. Flacc. 49 (with emphasis

on the requirement to kill both; see Rizzelli 2014a, 293 n. 283); Quint. *Inst.* 7.1.7: *adulterum cum adultera occidere licet*; *DMin.* 284.*pr.* (both must be killed, 284.4); Sulp. Vict. *Inst. Or.* 42 (*RLM* 339; both must be killed); Fortunatus, *Ars Rhet.* 6 (*RLM* 85): *adulteros liceat occidere*; cf. Quint. *Inst.* 5.10.104–105 (both must be killed); *DMin.* 277.5 (both must be killed), 291, 335, 379; with Sprenger 1911, 199–200; Lanfranchi 1938, 439–442; Bonner 1949, 119–121, noting that the husband is the killer in all cases, and that Latin declamation was not interested in fathers killing adulterers (119); Robinson 2002, noting that declamation ignores the restrictions of the *lex Julia* on the husbands' *ius occidendi* (636); cf. Robinson 2003, 64–65; Langer 2007, 70–76; Wycisk 2008, 250–253; Brescia and Lentano 2016, 155–166; Lentano 2014a, 94–100; Lentano 2016, noting that 10 percent of surviving Latin declamation concerns adultery (64), and that declamations on this subject usually assumed a world in which the *lex Iulia de adulteriis coercendis* did not exist (69). On adultery in Latin declamation see also Fantham 2011 [2004], 314–315; Brescia 2012, 31–52; 2015b, 75–81; Brescia and Lentano 2016. In Greek, Penella 2014, 114, noting [Libanius], *Decl.* 40, a case where the father is the killer.

24. The *lex Iulia de adulteriis coercendis* called for those who murdered their wives to be punished capitally under the *lex Cornelia de sicariis* (*Coll.* 4.10.1 with Rizzelli 1997, 12). Pius, Marcus Aurelius, and Commodus: *Coll.* 4.3.6 (Paul); *Dig.* 48.5.39(38).8 (Papinian); cf. *Coll.* 4.12.4 (Paul); *CJ* 9.9.4.1 (Alexander Severus), with Rizzelli 2017, 93–96. Majorian, *LRB* 25 (with Osaba García 1997, 110 n. 109); and note also *LRV PS* 2.27.1 (AD 506; with Osaba García 1997, 107–108) adjusting the classical *Sent. Paul.* 2.26.7 = *Coll.* 4.12.6, which did not allow the husband to kill, to allow him to do so. A husband's killing his wife did not become legal in the East, Just. *Nov.* 117.15. On the evolution of the law after the *lex Iulia*, Cantarella 1972, 258–263; Arjava 1996, 199–201; Osaba García 1997, 62–65, 106–117; Panero Oria 2001, 113–118; Fayer 1994–2005, 3.359–364 with more evidence for the late-antique return of the husband's right to kill his wife.

25. Verbal similarities between the law of declamation and the Roman law of adultery have also been adduced: Lanfranchi 1938, 442–444 (with Venturini 1988, 92–107) sees an *accusatio adulterii ex suspicione* implied in declamation (esp. Sen. *Contr.* 2.7; on this declamation see Berti 2007, 44–77; Lentano 2012a, 12; and Rizzelli 2014a, 246 n. 205 for literature), and finds similar wording in *CTh* 9.7.2 = *CJ* 9.9.29.2 (Constantine, AD 326 with Bettinazzi 2014, 115–118); but Berti 2007, 51 n. 3 considers *ex suspicione* in the declamation a purely rhetorical term of art. For a parallel between *DMin.* 249.*pr.* and *Dig.* 48.5.2.*pr.* (Ulpian) for the term *peragere* for bringing a case of adultery, Rizzelli 1997, 98–99; and for a verbal parallel between Fortunatianus, *Ars Rhet.* 1.15 (*RLM* 93) and Victorinus, *In Lib.* 1.11 (*RLM* 191) with *Dig.* 48.5.2.4 (Ulpian) on *compensatio*, a claim by an adulterer that the husband is guilty of *lenocinium*, and so the adulterer's own fault is reduced (a claim not admitted by Ulpian), Rizzelli 2001, 119, esp. n. 138. For the common use of *dolor* for the emotion felt by the person killing adulterers, *DMin.* 335.7 with *Dig.* 48.5.39.8 (Papinian) and *Coll.* 4.12.4 (Paul); Lentano 2016, 71.

26. See Csillag 1976, 199–205 and Treggiari 1991 for the unpopularity of Augustus's legislation on marriage (77–80) and adultery (294–298).

27. *liceat adulterium in matre et filio vindicare*, Sen. *Contr.* 1.4 (the handless war hero; see Casamento 2004 and Rizzelli 2017, 97–102 on this declamation); cf. Calp. Flacc. 23, 31; Sopater, *Quaest. Div.* (Walz, *RG* 8.261 = Weißenberger XLV, 166 and 443); on this law Bonner 1949, 121–122. For the disowning, *abdicatio*, chapter 10 nn. 49–51.

28. *CJ* 9.9.4.*pr.* (Severus Alexander), *idemque filiis eius qui patri paruerunt praestandum est*; cf. *Coll.* 4.3.2.

29. *Sent. Paul.* 2.26.14 with Mette-Dittman 1991, 39; Fayer 1994–2005, 3.337–341 with literature; and Treggiari 1991, 290 in English.

30. Capital crime, *CTh* 9.40.1 = *CJ* 9.47.16 (Constantine, AD 314); *CJ* 9.9.29.4 (Constantine, AD 326); cf. *CTh* 11.36.4 (Constantius and Constans, AD 339); Arjava 1996, 195–199 and Fayer 1994–2005, 3.337–357 with literature. Evans Grubbs 1995, 216–218 would date the coming of a capital penalty to the reigns of Constantine's sons, but the date has no impact on the argument here. No appeal, *CTh* 11.36.1 (Constantine, AD 314); no amnesty, *CTh* 9.38.1 (Constantine, AD 322); cf. *CTh* 9.38.2–8; *CJ* 1.4.3 (AD 350s–380s); on these provisions, Evans Grubbs 1995, 218; Puliatti 1995, 472–473; Rizzelli 1997, 273 n. 27; and Robinson 2001, wondering why adultery should have been classed as one of the "unpardonable crimes" (124). Note that adultery had, apparently irregularly, sometimes been punished by execution as early as Augustus, and now and again before Constantine, Treggiari 1991, 290, 295–296; Fayer 1994–2005, 3.342–343.

31. Constantine, Christianity, and adultery, Bauman 1980, 212–218 with Arjava 1996, on the controversy (202); also, against Germanic influence (200). Crimes punished more severely under Constantine, Dupont 1955; Liebs 1985, 92–104; MacMullen 1990 [1986], 211–213; and Dillon 2012, passim.

32. Fourteen cases, Pasetti 2015 listed 186–190 (nrs. 25, 36–48), and see, e.g., Sen. *Contr.* 6.6 for the scenario described in all but nr. 25. *Veneficium* and adultery, see this chapter n. 30 under "no appeal" and "no amnesty." The mental link between adultery and poisoning was old: Quint. *Inst.* 5.11.39 offers a fragment from Cato connecting them. For the law of *veneficium* in declamation, Sprenger 1911, 248–249; Lanfranchi 1938, 483–488, who points out in declamation quotations of, clear allusions to, and even an address to (Sen. *Contr.* 3.9) the *lex Cornelia de sicariis et veneficis*; Bonner 1949, 111–112; Hömke 2002, 181–185, 194–198; Langer 2007, 154; Wycisk 2008, 290–297; Longo 2008, 17–26. Adultery can also be connected to murder of other (or unspecified) types, e.g., Hermog. *Stat.* 58 (Rabe).

33. For the Roman law of poisoning, Hömke 2002, 185–194; Rives 2011 [2003]); Pasetti 2011, 14–17 and Querzoli 2011b, 88–91 with literature; and Rizzelli 2014a, 221 n. 143 points out the connection between adultery and poisoning in late-antique law; cf. Querzoli 2011b, 89.

34. *Dig.* 48.8.3.*pr.*-3 (Marcian) with Querzoli 2011b, 88–94. Marcian welcoming to rhetoric: Querzoli 2011a, 153–154 n. 8 and 154 n. 9 notes verbal echoes in other passages.

35. *ingrati sit actio*, with Sprenger 1911, 220–222; Bonner 1949, 87–88; Langer 2007, 185–186; Lentano 2014a, 33–34. Sen. *Ben.* 3.6.1–2; cf. Sen. *Contr.* 3.*pr*.17 and Quint. *Inst.* 7.4.37–38, all tending to imply that this law was overwhelmingly common in Latin declamation, even if only four Latin cases survive to us: Sen. *Contr.* 2.5, 9.1; *DMin.* 333, 368. Sprenger 1911, 220 n. 8 lists Greek examples. On the wider topic of *gratia* and the duty of reciprocity in Latin declamation, Raccanelli 2000, 112–117; Lentano 2009a; Bernstein 2013, 78–113; and Brescia 2016, 325–333.

36. Signorini 2009, 22 n. 12 and Querzoli 2013, 205 n. 181 (= 2009, 207–208 n. 29) with recent literature; *revocatio in servitutem* (Kaser 1971 [1955], 292–293) does not appear in the law until Commodus (*Dig.* 25.3.6.1 [Commodus in Modestinus], with Mommsen 1899, 856), and may only have been generally applied later; others (see Koops 2014, 111–112) believe that *revocatio in servitutem* was not authorized until Constantine.

37. Claudius, Suet. *Claud.* 25.2, *ingratos et de quibus patroni quererentur reuocauit in seruitutem*; cf. *Dig.* 37.14.5 (Ulpius Marcellus). AD 56, Tac. *Ann.* 13.26–27, but the legal situation envisaged is baffling.

38. Nothing inevitable, Querzoli 2009; 2013, 198–232.

39. *DMin.* 259.9, 388.23; and, if rarely, to perform the postmanumission services (*operae*) Roman law required as a manifestation of that gratitude, Sen. *Contr.* 4.8; see Knoch 2018, 155–160.

40. Caligula, Suet. *Calig.* 38.2, *ut ingrata rescidit*; Cass. Dio 59.15.2, emphasizing that this was an extra-legal act. On "ungrateful" wills, Gaudemet 1953.

41. Nero, Suet. *Nero* 32.2, *ut ingratorum in principem testamenta ad fiscum pertinerent.* This may or may not refer to the same practice as Cass. Dio 63 (62 Cary).11.2, Nero requiring the children and freedmen of the executed to leave him half their estates.

42. Pliny, *Pan.* 43.4. For ungrateful testators see also *CJ* 3.28.37.1g (Justinian, AD 531).

43. *CJ* 3.28.28.*pr.* (Constantine, AD 321; cf. *CTh* 2.19.2 for a version of this same law that expands upon of what such gratitude might consist); *CJ* 3.28.30.*pr.* (Justinian, AD 528); 3.28.33.1 (Justinian, AD 529); 3.28.34.1 (Justinian, AD 531); the Diocletianic date is implied by *CJ* 3.29.5 (Diocletian and Maximian, AD 286), on the closely related matter of *inofficiosi donationes*, attempts to get around the laws of testation by giving large gifts before death, which can be challenged, just as wills can, but not by "ungrateful" children (*non ingratis liberis*). For this rule of gratitude, Renier 1942, 255. On the procedure for challenging wills, also potentially the result of rhetorical influence, chapter 10 n. 12.

44. For the tortured wife, Sen. *Contr.* 2.5; cf. for another wife, *DMin.* 368; and Juv. 7.169 refers to the "*malus ingratusque maritus*" as a declamatory theme, suggesting that it was common. Father-in-law versus son-in-law, Sen. *Contr.* 9.1 (although with named characters from Greek history); Rich Man versus Poor Man, *DMin.* 333. For charges of ingratitude in declamation, Querzoli 2009, 213–215; 2013, 217–223.

45. Sen. *Ben.* 3.6.1, *an haec lex, quae in scholis exercetur, etiam in civitate ponenda sit, qua ingrati datur actio*; on which Manning 1986 and Lentano 2009b.

46. Hellegouarc'h 1963, 153–170; Saller 1982, 11–22; Lendon 1997b, 63–69.

47. *CTh* 8.14.1 = *CJ* 8.49.1 (Valens, Valentinian, and Gratian, AD 367), *de Ingratis Liberis*; cf. *Frag. Vat.* 248 (AD 330). Evans-Grubbs 1989, 83 n. 118 asserts the influence of rhetoric on the law here.

48. *CJ* 8.55.10 (Justinian, AD 530); cf. Just. *Nov.* 115.3 (AD 542).

49. *liberi parentes alant aut vinciantur*, Tivier 1868, 122; Bornecque 1902, 63; Sprenger 1911, 238–239, quite properly including the negative formulation of the declamatory law, *liberi parentes in calamitate ne deserant*; Lanfranchi 1938, 274–282; Bonner 1949, 95–96; Langer 2007, 83–86; Wycisk 2008, 148–150; Breij 2015b, 226–236; and for the example, Sen. *Contr.* 1.7. On the declamations hanging from this law, see esp. Beltrami 1997 and the literature gathered by Brescia 2016, 325 n. 12. For those depending on *in calamitate parentes ne deserant*, Zinsmaier 2009, 33–38 = Zinsmaier 1993, 17–21; Santorelli 2012, 135–142 = 2014, 191–197.

50. Duty to support parents, *CJ* 5.25.1–3 (Antoninus Pius, Marcus Aurelius, and Lucius Verus); *Dig.* 25.3.5 (Ulpian, in great detail); *CJ* 8.46.5 (Diocletian and Maximian). On the law, Albertario 1925 [1933]—the classic discussion, but marred by an over-keen nose for

interpolation); Fayer 1994–2005, 1.284–286; Evans Grubbs 2011, 382–383; Sandirocco 2013 with older literature (2 n. 4); Lentano 2009a, 29 n. 40; Saccoccio 2014, 5–22 with exhaustive literature. Note that the Roman law sometimes asserts a duty to support a number of different relations (Halbwachs 2014, 371) not featured in rhetorical law (where it is always parents), and which therefore presumably cannot derive from rhetoric.

51. Emancipated son, *Dig.* 25.3.5.13 (Ulpian); soldier-son, *Dig.* 25.3.5.15 (Ulpian).

52. Santorelli 2012, 140 = 2014, 196; Lentano 2014a, 33–43.

53. *expositum qui agnoverit, solutis alimentis recipiat,* Lanfranchi 1938, 269–271; Bonner 1949, 125–127; Wycisk 2008, 146–148; Bernstein 2009, 344–348. Prefers family who brought him up, Quint. *Inst.* 7.1.14–15. In Roman law, *CJ* 5.4.16 (Diocletian and Maximian); cf. *CJ* 8.51.1 (Alexander Severus); *CTh* 5.10.1 = *CJ* 4.43.2 (Constantine); *Const. Sirm.* 5 (Honorius and Theodosius, AD 419); on the law Lanfranchi 1940; Fayer 1994–2005, 1.196–200. Evans-Grubbs 1989, 83 n. 118 argues for the influence of rhetoric in these laws, as does Casmento 2019, esp. 10, who discusses both the declamatory and Roman laws, and provides recent literature.

54. *Talio, DMin.* 358, *talionis sit actio*; 372; cf. Sen. *Contr.* 10.4.9; *DMin.* 385.4; *DM* 11.5; *talio* for blinding, Calp. Flacc. 9, 43; *DMin.* 297; *DM* 7.4, 11.5; Sen. *Contr.* 3.1; see Sprenger 1911, 226–227; Bonner 1949, 96–97; Langer 2007, 159; Santorelli 2017b, 15 = Santorelli and Stramaglia 2017, 20. Kaster 2001, 329–331 notices a symmetry between the *talio* in declamation and the *raptarum lex*, above. In general, for blinding in Latin declamation, Krapinger and Stramaglia 2015, 29–31.

55. Twelve Tables 1.13 (*RS*), *si membrum rupit, ni cum eo pacit, talio esto*. For *talio* in early Roman law, Scheibelreiter 2012, 23–26 with literature.

56. Aul. Gell. 16.10.8; for the obsolescence of the *lex talionis*, cf. Aul. Gell. 20.1.14–18, discussing *talio* in the Twelve Tables as a thing of the primitive past.

57. Aetna, Strabo 6.2.6, and for more such, Coleman 1990, esp. 46, 60–61.

58. *calumniator idem pateretur quod reus, si convictus esset, DM* 11.*pr.* with Santorelli 2014, 26–32; also *DMin.* 313, 331; cf. Sen. *Contr.* 5.4; with Sprenger 1911, 214–215; Lanfranchi 1938, 560–569; Bonner 1949, 92 for variants and discussion.

59. Pliny, *Pan.* 34.5–35.3; cf. Suet. *Aug.* 32.2; Suet. *Titus* 8.5; Cass. Dio 68.1.2; *HA Alex.* 45.6; *CJ* 4.21.2 (Alexander Severus, AD 223); and cf. for *praevaricatores, Dig.* 47.15.6 (Paul).

60. Constantine, *CTh* 9.10.3 = *CJ* 9.12.7.*pr.* (AD 319) with Centola 1999, 120–121; Dillon 2012, 96 n. 15; cf. *CTh* 9.14.2 = *CJ* 3.27.1 (Valentinian, Theodosius, and Arcadius, AD 391), robbers in fields or on highways may be resisted with force such that *mortem quam minabatur excipiat et id quod intendebat incurrat.* Cf. Just. *Nov.* 117.9.4 (AD 542), where a husband making a false accusation of adultery *subdatur suppliciis, quae esset passa mulier, si huiusmodi fuisset accusatio comprobata. Calumnia*—false accusation—had always been punishable under the Roman law, with *infamia* at the least, and often more severely: Mommsen 1899, 491–498. What interests us here, as it did Mommsen (496), was the evolution of the idea that a false accuser should be punished as guilty of the crime of which he falsely accused another; see esp. Mer 1956, 428–445.

61. *CTh* 9.5.1 = *CJ* 9.8.3 = *FIRA* 1.94 = *CIL* 5.2781 (Constantine, or perhaps Galerius; date disputed; see Dillon 2012, 14) with Centola 1999, 122–123. For other instances of the *talio* in later Roman law, Genzmer 1942.

62. *CTh* 9.1.14 (Gratian, Valentinian, and Theodosius, AD 383); cf. *CTh* 9.1.11 (Valentinian, Valens, and Gratian, with Centola 1999, 139–140 n. 68 for the date); *CTh* 9.2.3 (Gratian,

Valentinian, and Theodosius, AD 380); Symm. *Rel.* 49.1, 3 (AD 384–385). The degree to which, in late antiquity, the penalty attaching to charges brought by *inscriptio* rebounded upon a false accuser, and, if so, for which crimes, is controversial: see Coşkun 2001 with literature. On the *poena talionis* for false accusation in late antiquity, usually traced to Constantine, see also Mer 1953, 212–228; Venturini 1988, 85 n. 57; Harries 1988, 167–168; Santalucia 1998, 283 n. 41; Giomaro 2003, 55–56, 194–195; Santorelli 2014, 30–32.

63. *CTh* 9.1.19.*pr.* = *CJ* 9.2.17.*pr.* = *CJ* 9.46.10 (Honorius and Theodosius, AD 423, with Centola 1999, 149–150), *cum calumniantes ad vindictam poscat similitudo supplicii.* Cf. *CTh* 9.37.4 (Arcadius and Honorius, AD 409), *nec ante a iudice dimitti, quam in reum, probato crimine, vindicetur, aut in accusatorem pari forma sententiae damnatio referatur,* adjusting a prior law, *CJ* 9.42.3 (Valentinian, Valens, and Gratian, AD 369), which does not appear to have had this provision; cf. *LRB* 7.4 (= *FIRA* 2.721); perhaps also *CTh* 9.1.9 = *CJ* 9.46.7 (Valentinian and Valens, AD 366).

64. Foot of deserter, *CJ* 6.1.3 (Constantine; date disputed); hands of peculating officials, *CTh* 1.16.7 (Constantine, AD 331; with Dillon 2012, 139–146); tongue of person who insults the emperor, Amm. Marc. 28.6.20 (it is not perfectly clear from the text whom they had supposedly slandered, but their crime was one of speech: *invidiosa quaedam locutos*); lead, for connivance in *raptus* by a *nutrix*, *CTh* 9.24.1.1 (Constantine; date disputed); cf. *Nov. Maj.* 4.1 (AD 458), amputation of the hands of those who damage public buildings; all with Harries 1999, 136–138, who also offers other and earlier, or apparently earlier, examples. Cf. *HA Alex.* 28.4, 36.2, a work of the imagination from the late fourth century that shows the expectation of mutilation "appropriate" to the crime. For mutilation in late-antique law see Mommsen 1899, 982–983 with more examples, many of which "fit the crime"; MacMullen 1990 [1964], 102; MacMullen 1990 [1986], 212.

65. *CTh* 10.10.2 (Constantine, AD 312), *comprimatur unum maximum humanae vitae malum, delatorum exsecranda pernicies, et inter primos conatus in ipsis faucibus stranguletur, et amputata radicitus invidiae lingua vellatur* (with Centola 1999, 132–133); the interpretation follows immediately in the *CTh*.

66. In early times the amputation of hands may also have been a military punishment, for theft (Frontinus, *Str.* 4.1.16) and desertion (Val. Max. 2.7.11: Fabius Maximus). And cf. in the classical jurists *Dig.* 5.2.8.14 (Ulpian) for an appropriate, if not anatomically appropriate, penalty: he who makes an unsuccessful *querela inofficiosi testamenti* loses what he was to have received under the will that was not overturned; also *Dig.* 48.19.28.12 (Callistratus), an arsonist executed by burning (but that was a normal Roman judicial punishment, if appropriate in this case); *Dig.* 48.19.28.15 (Callistratus) specifies that bandits are to be crucified at the location where they robbed; 48.19.38.*pr.* (Paul): Steal from the mines? Be condemned to the mines. And see *Dig.* 49.19.40 (Paul) for a man named Philoctetes relegated to an island (this may be that rarest of things, a joke in the *Digest*).

67. *excaecati dux sit,* Quint. *DMin.* 297.*pr.* On the duties owed to the blind in Latin declamation, Santorelli and Stramaglia 2017, 15–21 with Cal. Flacc. 9, 43. *qui patrem pulsaverit, manus ei praecidantur,* Sprenger 1911, 240; Bonner 1949, 96–97; Lentano 2009 [2005], 60 n. 40; Santorelli 2014, 32 n. 60. *sacrilegio manus praecidantur,* Sen. *Contr.* 8.2 with Bonner 1949, 106.

68. The ubiquity of mutilated persons in declamation is discussed by Gunderson 2003, 59–60, 75–79; Berti 2007, 325–337; Danesi Marioni 2011–2012.

## Chapter 10: Legal Puzzles, Familiar Laws, and Laws of Rhetoric Rejected by Roman Law

1. Sen. *Contr.* 10.1, *iniuriarum sit actio (pr.)*; cf. Bornecque 1902, 68–69; Sprenger 1911, 225; Lanfranchi 1938, 342–343; Bonner 1949, 115–116. The declaimers (in the person of the Rich Man) clarify the purpose of the Son's wearing mourning dress as *in alienam invidiam facere* (10.1.9); *me quidam propter hoc suspectum habent* (10.1.11); *in convicium . . . sequitur* (10.1.12).

2. Sen. *Contr.* 10.1.9, *omnia iniuriae genera lege conprehensa sunt: pulsare not licet, convicium contra bonos mores non licet . . . nova formula iniuriarum componitur: "quod ille contra bonos mores flevit."*

3. Quoted *Dig.* 47.10.15.25–26 (Ulpian; cf. 28), *ait praetor: "ne quid infamandi causa fiat. si quis adversus ea fecerit, prout quaeque res erit, animaduertam."* *Hoc edictum supervacuum esse Labeo ait, quippe cum ex generali iniuriarum agere possumus.* Labeo won this argument. In the classical law insult of the kind the Rich Man was subjected to was unquestionably *iniuria*, see Daube 1991 [1951], 465–466; Hagemann 1998, 64–71, 75–81, also to be consulted on the evolution of the law of *iniuria* in general. On Labeo and *iniuria*, Bryen 2018.

4. Such is the controversy between Daube 1991 [1951] and Birks 1976.

5. Suet. *Gramm. et Rhet.* 25.5 (Kaster) with Kaster 1995 ad loc., arguing that the historical case must be Augustan or later, despite Suetonius classing it among the *veteres controversiae*; Sprenger 1911, 242 quite properly thought this a real event. In general for slaves and freedmen in Latin declamation, Knoch 2018.

6. *qui voluntate domini in libertate fuerit, liber sit, DMin.* 340.*pr.*-1 with Winterbottom 1984 ad loc.; also *DMin.* 342.*pr.*, 2. On this declamatory law, Sprenger 1911, 260; Lanfranchi 1938, 183–186; Bonner 1949, 19; Sirks 1988; Wycisk 2008, 53–59; Knoch 2018, 149–150.

7. From praetorian *tuitio*, Wlassak 1905, 374–378; Lanfranchi 1938, 183–185; Bonner 1949, 19; Wycisk 2008, 55–56 with literature. From the *lex Junia*, Sirks 1983, 218–221 (still the best piece on Junian Latinity); Sirks 1988, 347 (but shows [354–355] that *DMin.* 342, which uses the declamatory law, contradicts prominent elements of the *lex Junia*; and cf. for other problems [356–358]); and Wycisk 2008, 56 with literature. On the *lex Junia*, for the state of the question, Bettinazzi 2014, 45–64; for older literature on the *lex Junia* and its date, Rodríguez Alvarez 1978, 127–140 for a *catalogue raisonné*, or Sirks 1981, 250–251 n. 9 for a list; for newer literature, Koops 2014.

8. *Dig.* 40.12.28 (Pomponius), *non videtur domini voluntate servus in libertate esse, quem dominus ignorasset suum esse: et est hoc verum: is enim demum voluntate domini in libertate est, qui possessionem libertatis ex voluntate domini consequitur*, with Wlassak 1905, 397–401; cf. *Dig.* 40.12.24.3 (Paul); Ulp. *Tit.* 1.12; *Frag. Dosith.* 4–5, 7 (= *FIRA* 2.618–619); *CJ* 7.4.4 (Alexander Severus, AD 222?) for similar formulations; and cf. Sirks 1983, 235–236 n. 51 for instances where this *voluntas* is implied, adding *CJ* 7.6.1.5 (Justinian, AD 531), 12.33.6.*pr.* (Justinian, AD 529), 12.33.7 (Justinian, AD 531) from Bettinazzi 2014, 147 n. 737.

9. To which we might add that at *CJ* 4.61.1 (Severus and Caracalla) the emperors decided that if a slave were manumitted *iure* before a customs issue arose, he could not be returned to slavery as a result of such an issue, seeming to settle a different aspect of the case presented by the slave boy of Brundisium, which perhaps, by virtue of declamation, lived long in the public mind.

10. Cic. *Inv. Rhet.* 2.149; *Rhet. Her.* 1.23; Livy, *Per.* 68; Mommsen 1899, 921–923, with n. 9 for the black oxen; Cantarella 1991, 264–289 for discussion of the *poena cullei*; Di Ottavio 2012b, 51–52 and Carlà-Uhink 2017, 54 n. 143 for recent collections of literature on this form of execution. Meyer 2004 discusses the special power of wax tablets in Roman legal business.

11. D'Ors 1995, 131–132 collects the literature on Malleolus and his will; Calboli 2018 does the same and summarizes the Italian scholarly controversy in English, pointing to the declamatory form of the reports and to the conflict of laws.

12. *querela inofficiosi testamenti*, Di Ottavio 2012a and 2012b, 1–24 offer invaluable *catalogues raisonnés* of the vast scholarship. Renier 1942 is the classic study.

13. *Dig.* 5.2.5 (Marcellus), *resque illo colore defenditur apud iudicem, ut videatur ille quasi non sanae mentis fuisse, cum testamentum inique ordinaret. Dig.* 5.2.2 (Marcian), *hoc colore inofficioso testamento agitur, quasi non sanae mentis fuerunt, ut testamentum ordinarent. et hoc dicitur non quasi vere furiosus vel demens testatus sit, sed recte quidem fecit testamentum, sed non ex officio pietatis: nam si vere furiosus esset vel demens, nullum est testamentum.* On these passages, and with full literature on the *querela inofficiosi testamenti* and parallels in declamation, Renier 1942, 101–124; Querzoli 2000, 151–179; Di Ottavio 2009 = 2012b, 43–77; 2012a; 2012b, 1–41, 125–134; Querzoli 2013, 147–183; Rizzelli 2014b, 135–154; and Querzoli 2013 for the tendency of Ulpius Marcellus to use terms and concepts borrowed from rhetoric. We have drawn on Di Ottavio's interpretation here. What happened if the *querela* were successful is wonderfully complicated, extending from invalidation of the will (and so the rules of intestacy apply) to adjustment of its terms in favor of the successful litigant: see Buckland 1963, 330–331 in English.

14. For *dementiae sit actio* in declamation, Bornecque 1902, 67–68; Sprenger 1911, 184–186; Bonner 1949, 93–94; Gunderson 2003, 115–149; Langer 2007, 90–92; Di Ottavio 2012b, 79–100; Rizzelli 2014b, 7–79 = 2015. See Longo 2016, 179–187 generally for madness in Latin declamation, and Querzoli 2013, 162–163 n. 43 for literature on madness in Roman law. Quint. *Inst.* 7.4.29–31 (cf. Sulpitius Victor 60 [*RLM* 351]) devotes a special discussion to this law, implying—in addition to the nine cases that survive in Latin declamation—how common the theme was.

15. Suet. *Gramm. et Rhet.* 30.1–2, 6 (Kaster) with Grisé 1982, 142–143 n. 77; Kaster 1995 ad loc.

16. *qui causas <voluntariae> mortis in senatu non reddiderit, insepultus abiciatur, DM* 4.pr. Stramaglia 2013, 84–86 nn. 2–3 gathers the many cases of this law and similar ones known in Latin and Greek declamation; add Penella 2014, 112 for more cases of προσαγγελία in Libanius, whose favorite declamatory law this was. The commonness of this theme is further implied by Quint. *Inst.* 7.4.39, 11.1.56. For discussion of the penalty *insepultus abiciatur*, Zinsmaier 1993, 22–26, 33–39 = 2009, 38–43, 52–58.

17. Suet. *Gramm. et Rhet.* 30.4–5 (Kaster, with Kaster 1995 ad loc.) and Sen. *Contr.* 7.pr.6–7 with Berti 2007, 144–149.

18. On the declamatory law, its variants and origins, Sprenger 1911, 236–238; Lanfranchi 1938, 489–490; Langer 2007, 154–155; Pasetti 2011, 31–34.

19. Roman law on suicide, Vandenbossche 1953 and Wacke 1980 with literature, and especially on the testaments of suicides, van Hooff 1990, 166–173; Langer 2007, 156; Pasetti 2011, 34–36.

20. Suicide anticipatory of condemnation, Grisé 1982, 44–50. On the legal liability of the heirs of the condemned, Brasiello 1971.

21. *Dig.* 48.21.3 (Marcian; citing Antoninus Pius); cf. *Dig.* 28.3.6.7 (Ulpian); *Dig.* 29.5.1.23 (Ulpian); *Dig.* 49.14.45.2 (Paul); and there may be a trace as early as Trajan, *Dig.* 3.2.11.3 (Neratius in Ulpian; Vandenbossche 1953, 488–489). This logic was extended to soldiers who attempted, but failed, to commit suicide, who were normally to be executed but only dismissed from service with *ignominia* if *impatientia doloris aut taedio vitae aut morbo aut furore aut pudore mori maluit, Dig.* 49.16.6.7 (Hadrian in Arrius Menander); cf. *Dig.* 48.19.38.12 (Paul); *Dig.* 48.21.3.6 (Marcian).

22. Hadrian, *Dig.* 48.21.3.5 (Marcian). Calp. Flacc. 38; *DMin.* 337; cf. *DMin.* 335. For killing sons in the real world, Carlà-Uhink 2017, 32–46 for literature.

23. *Dig.* 48.9.8 (Ulpian), and in declamation, *DM* 4; cf. *DMin.* 377. For parricide in the law, see this chapter n. 32; in declamation, n. 34.

24. *Dig.* 48.21.3.6 (Marcian), *et merito, si sine causa sibi manus intulit, puniendus est: qui enim sibi non pepercit, multo minus alii parcet*; Sen. *Contr.* 8.4, *nihil non ausurus fuit qui se potuit occidere. Dig.* 21.1.23.3 (Ulpian), *tamquam non nihil in alium ausurus, qui hoc adversus se ausus est.* The similarity to Seneca naturally caused the Marcian passage to be struck as an interpolation when searching for interpolation was fashionable: Levy and Rabel 1935, 550; Vandenbossche 1953, 503–505, 513–514.

25. *Dig.* 48.21.3.8 (Pius in Marcian) versus *CJ* 6.22.2 (Diocletian and Maximian, AD 290). By AD 364, to end the story, this became moot, because the property even of the condemned went to their children except in the case of *maiestas, CTh* 9.42.6 (Valentinian and Valens, AD 364); cf. *CJ* 9.48.1 (Theodosius and Valentinian, AD 425) and *CJ* 9.49.10 (Theodosius and Valentinian, AD 426), in the second of which half the estate passes to the children.

26. On this declamation, Krapinger 2005; this is much the most famous of the *Major Declamations*, known to other authors in antiquity (9 n. 1) and commented on extensively by scholars; see esp. the articles by Tabacco (collected by Krapinger 2005, 165–166); Crook 1993, 74; and Krapinger 2007b, for literature (189 n. 3) and *Nachleben*.

27. *Coll.* 12.7.10, much discussed: Frier 1982–1983 and 1994 are good introductions in English.

28. Mantovani 2007 [2006], whose view we adopt here: arguments similar (352–369); words in common (369); verbal tics, (374–376 with n. 193, adducing other parallels between Celsus and Quint. *Inst.* and the *DMin.*, on which also Scarano Ussani 1979, 139–155; 1989, 89–90); conclusion (376–377). This all requires, of course, that with Mantovani (336–338) we place *DM* 13 at the end of the first or the beginning of the second century, the very earliest likely era, and hope that it is the genuine work of Quintilian: I am happy to make the ingenious Mantovani responsible for those assumptions.

29. Intellectual children: see Rodríguez González 2015; Rizzelli 2019. So Stagl 2012, comparing *DMin.* 360 esp. to *Dig.* 15.1.52.1 (Paul); *Dig.* 24.3.22.13 (Ulpian); *Dig.* 42.5.17.1 (Ulpian); *CJ* 7.74.1 (Severus and Caracalla, AD 209). For literature on the *favor dotis*, Kleiter 2010, 185–190.

30. Bettinazzi 2012, about *DMin.* 302; but see Avenarius 2015, 59–79 for Greek influence on Roman seating arrangements in the theater. I mention this and the *favor dotis* case with respect, but it is worrying that these arguments each rely on a single surviving declamation.

31. Moot court, Daube 1991 [1951], 486, 497; Evans-Grubbs 1989, 82–83; Mantovani 2007 [2006]; Nörr 2009, 50–51; Bettinazzi 2012, esp. 543–544; Mantovani 2014, 1; Lentano 2016, 75; Casamento 2019, 10.

32. For the Roman law of parricide, Mommsen 1899, 643–646, Nardi 1980—with full discussion of the animals: how many and what kinds? Santalucia 1998, 148–149, 161–162, 262, 292–293; Robinson 1995, 46–47; Carlà-Uhink 2017, 53–61 for literature.

33. Other penalties, *Sent. Paul.* 5.24, *hodie tamen vivi exuruntur vel ad bestias dantur; Dig.* 48.9.9.*pr.* (Modestinus quoting Hadrian); *Dig.* 48.9.1 (Marcian); Constantine, *CTh* 9.15.1 = *CJ* 9.17.1 (AD 318–319), explicitly replacing execution by the sword or burning alive with the *culleus.* See La Bua 2006, 200–201; Robinson 1995, 47.

34. For parricide in declamation, Pasetti 2011, 16–20; Lentano 2015c; Zinsmaier 2009, 208–209 gathers mentions of the *culleus* in Latin declamation; Santorelli and Stramaglia 2017, 87–88 for further literature.

35. *ius vitae necisque* rarely used under high and late Empire, Thomas 1984 [2017] 545–548, "*La vitae necisque potestas n'est pas un fait d'histoire sociale*" (545); Saller 1994, 115–117; Arjava 1998, 153 n. 33; going to court instead, Arjava 1998, 153 n. 37; perhaps compulsory, *Dig.* 48.8.2 (Ulpian), *inauditum filium pater occidere non potest, sed accusare eum apud praefectum praesidemque provinciae debet*, with Nótári 2013, 37–38, naturally denounced as interpolated when such things were fashionable; but cf. *CJ* 8.46.3 (Alexander Severus, AD 227). *CTh* 4.8.6.*pr.* = *CJ* 8.46.10 (Constantine, AD 323) seems to refer to the *ius vitae necisque* as a purely historical phenomenon in Constantine's day. And *CTh* 9.13.1 = *CJ* 9.15.1 (Valentinian and Valens, AD 365) assumes that a father's power does not extend to execution, and bids the father in such cases to let a judge deal with the peccant child, *quod si atrocitas facti ius domesticae emendationis excedit, placet enormis delicti reos dedi iudicum notioni.* For the law see Fayer 1994–2005, 1.170–178; Carlà-Uhink 2017, 46–47.

36. For the *ius vitae necisque* in Latin declamation, see chapter 8 n. 48.

37. Legal ignorance of Roman officials, Brunt 1975 [1990], 132–136; Peachin 1996, 14–65; for the makeup of the governor's *consilia*, panels of advisors, Weaver 2002, and Kantor 2017, 60–73, who mentions (72) the rare legal experts, all, we guess, experts on local rather than Roman law. For the imperfect legal knowledge of Tacitus and Cassius Dio, both high officials, Rogers 1933; for Aulus Gellius, who served as a *iudex* at Rome, see Holford-Strevens 2003 [1988], 294–301; Querzoli 2008. For a less pessimistic account of the legal knowledge available to a governor from his staff, Lehne-Gstreinthaler 2016, 90–95. For governors acting *extra ordinem*, see section iv n. 2. Starace 2007, 509 usefully connects the influence of rhetoric on the law to governors acting *extra ordinem*, and the latitude they enjoyed thereby.

38. Ulpian's works at Ephesus, *I.Ephesos* II 217 with Kantor 2009, 249–256; alas, the inscription may date anywhere from the Severans to Constantine. For fragments of Roman juristic texts found in Egyptian papyri, Taubenschlag 1955, 37–40.

39. Jurists around the emperor, Peachin 2016. Did the emperor pay attention? Sometimes: Peachin 2001. For the use of juristic opinions in actual cases, Katzoff 1982 collects the small number of cases known from the Egyptian papyri, implying that the use of *responsa* in court was rare. For the press of imperial work, book 10 of Pliny's letters gives a good sense, along with Millar 1977.

40. The penetration of the use and knowledge of Roman law in the Roman provinces, especially in advance of widespread Roman citizenship (and the near universality of such citizenship after AD 212) is controversial. The traditional view, that Roman law was only available to Roman citizens and rarely used in the provinces, has recently been challenged by scholars who argue that Roman governors accepted and encouraged its use by non-Romans as well, whether or not they formally employed the *fictio civitatis* (Gaius, *Inst.* 4.37), whereby a non-Roman-citizen could be treated as a Roman citizen for legal purposes: Ando 2011a, 1–36; Kantor 2009, esp. 265;

Kantor 2015, 15–18; Dolganov 2020; *sed contra* for much more limited penetration by Roman law, Maehler 2005 who gathers the older literature arguing the same (136–137); Yiftach-Firanko 2009, 553–557, Fournier 2010, 543–547; and Trajan in Pliny, *Ep.* 10.113, *quod semper tutissimum est, sequendam cuiusque civitatis legem puto.* I think that the case for the widespread early use of Roman law in the provinces has not yet been fully made, but am indifferent to the result: even at Rome knowledge of the Roman law was always a minority accomplishment, and the argument is between those who think that in the provinces it was merely rare and those who think it was vanishingly rare (the classic text on the legal ignorance of litigants is *C. Tanta* 17). In either case education in rhetoric, which nearly every upper-class Greek or Latin speaker possessed, will have been much more common.

41. Quint. *Inst.* 7.4.10–11, 27–31; cf. Sen. *Contr.* 2.3.13 for the *actio dementiae* of declamation's being parallel to asking for a *curator*.

42. For the rhetorical *actio dementiae*, see this chapter n. 14. For the nonuse of the more severe aspects of *patria potestas*, see this chapter n. 35.

43. On the *curator furiosi*, *CJ* 5.70.7 (Justinian, AD 530) offers a summary of earlier jurisprudence, and see Diliberto 1984—especially on the limits of the power of the *curator*; Fayer 1994–2005, 1.559–582 with literature for the legal tradition on this subject, which goes back to the Twelve Tables. Son allowed to be *curator*, *Dig.* 26.5.12.1 (Antoninus Pius, Marcus Aurelius, and Lucius Verus in Ulpian), forbidden earlier *quasi indecorum sit patrem a filio regi.* Allowing a son to be *curator* perhaps under rhetorical influence, Rizzelli 2019, 103–104.

44. On the rhetorical *actio malae tractationis*, Bornecque 1902, 67; Sprenger 1911, 192–194; Bonner 1949, 94–95; Stramaglia 1999, 94–95, 105–107; Hömke 2002, 164–181; Breij 2006b, 89–98 = Breij 2015a, 60–70; 2015b, 236–243. The law was derived, it is generally agreed, from the Athenian γραφὴ κακώσεως.

45. Sen. *Contr.* 3.7, 4.6, 5.3; Calp. Flacc. 51; *DM* 8, 18, 19; with Bonner 1949, 94 for the conflict with *patria potestas*; Langer 2007, 160; Breij 2006b, 96 = 2015a, 68. The declamatory law also had a wider remit: "the withholding of the finery that suits a *matrona*; the refusal to supply servants or to allow one's wife to go out in public; physical abuse; infidelity; the withholding of sexual favours" (Breij 2006b, 95–96 = 2015a, 67–68).

46. Langer 2007, 158–160.

47. Quint. *Inst.* 7.4.11. Solazzi 1899—the book mentioned in the text; Söllner 1969; Treggiari 1991, 350–361; Hömke 2002, 166–167, gathering the legal literature at n. 393; Fayer 1994–2005, 2.698–714, 734–738; 3.79–81.

48. The *lex Iulia et Papia* (on which Astolfi 1996) may come up once in Quint. *Inst.*, albeit not by name, Tellegen-Couperus 2003.

49. Lucian, *Abdicatus* 8 gives a clear account of the legal process envisaged; cf. Wurm 1972, 25–39. Translating *abdicatio* with the English "repudiate" conveys the force of the act and the wrath usually involved, avoiding a periphrasis such as "expel from the household and disinherit," but is not be confused with the Roman law term *repudium*, which was a stage in divorce (Kaser 1971 [1955], 81), and also used when an heirship (718) or a legacy (753) was refused.

50. For the Greek legal tradition, Sciortino 2003, 335 n. 6; Modrzejewski 2014, 334–336. Papyri: *P.Cair.Masp.* III 67353 = *Sel. Pap.* I 87 (AD 569; trans. Hunt and Edgar, adjusted) and *P.Cair. Masp.* I 67097 = *Jur. Pap.* 13 = *FIRA* 3.33–37 (560s or 570s; trans. Urbanik, adjusted) with

Migliorini 2001, 279–286, 320–328; Urbanik 2008. Guast 2018, 192 n. 17 lists instances of ἀποκήρυξις in the Greek declamatory material.

51. *CJ* 8.46.6 (Diocletian and Maximian, AD 287): *abdicatio, quae Graeco more ad alienandos liberos usurpabatur et apokeryxis dicebatur, Romanis legibus non comprobatur*, with Wurm 1972, 80–82. On *abdicatio* (the relationship between the Roman and Greek laws, and the existence of *abdicatio* outside the world of literature before Diocletian and Maximian banned it, are vexed), Lanfranchi 1938, 254–267; Düll 1943, 71–116—unreliable in parts; Bonner 1949, 101–103; Levick 1972; Wurm 1972; Migliorini 2001, 279–333; Sirks 2002b, 712–713; Sciortino 2003; Krapinger 2007a, 13–19; with Lentano 2009 [2005], 61–64, esp. n. 44; 2014a, 43–50, 63–64, 79–83; Masi Doria 2012; and Rizzelli 2012b, 272–273 nn. 5–7 for full literature.

52. *Relegatio*, Mommsen 1899, 968; Düll 1943, 66–67, 72, 96, 99–103 (making the connection to *abdicatio*); Wurm 1972, 48–64. *Exheredatio*, Kaser 1971 [1955], 703–713 (noting some highly technical limitations on this—see also Buckland 1963, 321–332—the most important of which, the danger of the *querela inofficiosi testamenti*, is discussed above); Wurm 1972, 61, 69–77. In some instances, *DMin.* 374.*pr.*; Cal. Flacc. 14.*pr.*; Quint. *Inst.* 3.6.96, 98; and Julius Victor, *Ars Rhet.* 4.9 (*RLM* 394), the inability of the *abdicatus* to inherit is specified (*abdicatus de bonis paternis nihil habeat*), which might imply that *abdicatio* did not always include disinheritance, were there not more examples where disinheritance is assumed, Lanfranchi 1938, 260, and esp. Quint. *Inst.* 7.4.11. Apparently superfluous laws (often to guide the declaimer, or to set up a clear conflict with another law) are hardly unknown in declamation, e.g., Quint. *Inst.* 3.6.96, *testamenta legibus facta rata sint: intestatorum parentium liberi heredes sint* and *in adoptionem dare liceat*, all from the same passage in Quintilian as *abdicatus ne quid de bonis patris capiat*, with Fantham 2011 [2004], 310.

53. Quint. *Inst.* 7.4.11, *nam quae in scholis abdicatorum, haec in foro exheredatorum a parentibus et bona apud centumviros repetentium ratio est.*

54. Langer 2007, 138 counts thirty-nine cases of *abdicatio* in the Latin declamatory corpus; cf. Lanfranchi 1938, 254 n. 3; Wurm 1972, 25–26. Quint. *Inst.* 7.4.27–28, by devoting a special discussion to *abdicatio*, reinforces how common it was in declamation; cf. Sulpitius Victor, *Inst. Or.* 59 (*RLM* 350); Cyrus, *Diaph. Stas.* 13 (Walz, *RG* 8.394–395). For discussion of Latin declamations involving *abdicatio*, Thomas 1983, 126–132; Fantham 2011 [2004]; Brescia and Lentano 2009, 76–84; Greek declamations involving ἀποκήρυξις, Russell 1983, 31–32; Johansson 2015 on Libanius and Choricius; see also Lucian, *Abdicatus*; Sopater, *Quaest. Div.* (Walz, *RG* 8.16 = Weißenberger III, pp. 16, 281; Walz, *RG* 8.78 = Weißenberger XIII, pp. 54, 322; Walz, *RG* 8.175 = Weißenberger XXVII, pp. 112, 386; Walz, *RG* 8.227 = Weißenberger XXXVIII, pp. 145, 421; Walz, *RG* 8.244 = Weißenberger XLII, pp. 155, 431; Walz, *RG* 8.270 = Weißenberger XLVI, pp. 171, 449; Walz, *RG* 8.336 = Weißenberger LXVIII, pp. 214, 495); Cyrus, *Diaph. Stas.* 13 (Walz, *RG* 8.394–395); *Prob. Rhet.* 6, 23, 39 (Walz, *RG* 8.403, 406, 408–409).

55. Sen. *Contr.* 1.6.

56. Sen. *Contr.* 2.2, with Ovid at 2.2.8–12; see Mastrorosa 2002 on this declamation.

57. Lib. *Decl.* 27 and 34 with Johansson 2015, 273–277.

58. On Hermogenes, Levick 1972, 688, pointing out that he could also be Aurelius Hermogenes, governor of Asia in AD 286–305. Hermogenes could, of course, have been asking about the application of a living custom of ἀποκήρυξις in the Greek East (Humfress 2011, 41–42), of

which we have papyrus evidence (Wurm 1972, 47–48; and see this chapter n. 50), but what is significant is that the emperors chose to reply about a law of declamation, *abdicatio*.

59. Pliny, *HN* 7.150; Suet. *Aug.* 65.1 (*ferox*; cf. Tac. *Ann.* 1.3.4); *Tib.* 15.2. On this episode Levick 1972, esp. 675 n. 5, and 677 n. 17, 683 n. 44 for other uses of the term *abdicatio* outside declamation and authors writing about declamation; also Düll 1943, 96–101; Wurm 1972, 24.

60. See this chapter n. 51.

61. The *luxuriosus*, Sirks 2002b; for the *cura prodigi* in the law, Fayer 1994–2005, 1.582–587; Wycisk 2008, 45–48 notes the difference between how a *luxuriosus* child was treated in declamation and in the law.

62. *ultimum patriae potestatis fulmen*, *DM* 9.10; cf. 9.2 and *DMin.* 376.3, where the exercise of *maiestas patria* threatens *abdicatio* rather than death; see Lentano 2009 [2005], 63 n. 45; Santorelli 2019, 76.

63. As they resisted too, at least in part, far more insistent pressures, such as Christianity, even in areas, such as marriage and divorce, where Christianity had very strong opinions: see, e.g., Wolff 1950.

64. Ando 2011a, 1–36, and see this chapter n. 40.

65. Counting from Winterbottom 1984, 597–602, who lists the laws in the *DMin.*, and adding those from the *DM*, Sen. *Contr.*, and Calp. Flacc., but excluding, for purposes of possible inclusion in the Roman law, (a) all those that clearly reflect the existing Roman law; (b) all those involving tyrannicide, the rewards of the *vir fortis*, and military service otherwise, including treachery in war, most of which are highly fanciful; (c) laws implicit in the scenario of the declamation, but that are not explicitly stated to be laws governing the declamation (some declamations do not state laws in their prefaces, see e.g., Sen. *Contr.* 1.6.*pr.*, 2.1.*pr.*; *DMin.* 260.*pr.*).

# Conclusion

1. Philostr. *VS* 559–561 and *SEG* XXIX 127 = Oliver nr. 184 (EM 13366); with Ameling 1983, 1.143–150, 2.182–211; Tobin 1997, 35–47; and esp. Kennell 1997.

2. Philostr. *VS* 559 with Tobin 1997, 285–294 and Kennell 1997, 351–356 for consideration of what a charge of tyranny might have meant. The breakdown of Herodes's relations with the Athenians can unexpectedly be traced by the increasingly elaborate protection curses—no fewer than twenty-five survive—he ordered inscribed on the bases of the statues of the dead favorites with which he littered his estates (Tobin 1997, 113–160; Philostr. *VS* 559): evidently passing Athenians had taken to mutilating them.

3. Philostr. *VS* 547; Suet. *Vesp.* 13; with Graindor 1930, 12–17 and Tobin 1997, 15–16. Incompetently confiscated, at least in part, because his son (Herodes's father) "happened" to discover a gigantic treasure under the floorboards of one of his houses, and so the family fortunes were restored, Philostr. *VS* 548.

4. Use in invective, Kennell 1997, 353; and see chapter 2 nn. 5–6; chapter 4 n. 55. "Tyrants" in papyri, Bryen 2013, 97–98, 159–160.

5. Rarity in reality, see the slim pickings of Plaß 1859, 2.189–190; Berve 1967, 1.412–416, 435–440, and Kennell 1997, 353–355. Jones 2017 found no contemporary references in Strabo.

6. For Eurycles of Sparta, Bowersock 1961; cf. for perhaps similar cases Pliny, *Ep.* 6.31.3; Boatwright 1991; Ventoux 2017.

7. For the degree to which Hellenistic cities had already evolved into *de facto* or *de jure* oligarchies before the Romans came, or under Roman pressure during the Republic, see van der Vliet 2012, Wiemer 2013, and the essays in Börm and Luraghi 2018 for the state of the question (I thank Nicholas Lindberg for this literature). For the Roman Empire see esp. Quaß 1993; Fernoux 2011; the essays in van Nijf and Alston 2011; and Brélaz 2016 for the state of the question. The matter, alas, often devolves into a fruitless debate about the meaning of the word "democracy."

8. Martin 2013.

9. See esp. Paschidis 2008 for Hellenistic times, and for Roman note esp. the offices of *curator civitatis* or *rei publicae* and *defensor civitatis*, *CTh* 1.29–30; Jones 1964, 145, 279–280, 479–480, 726–731, with Burton 1979 for the *curator*, and Frakes 2001, 2018 and Schmidt-Hofner 2014 for the *defensor*.

10. For declamation's assumption that the events occur in a generic *res publica*, Casamento 2018, 64–67.

11. Habinek 2005, 75–77. "Indeed, we might say that in both the Greek-speaking and Roman-speaking world, rhetoric kept the dream of the city-state alive in the context of empire" (76).

12. Three of the seven surviving deliberative speeches in Seneca the Elder that constitute our body of Latin *suasoriae* address monarchs: Alexander (*Suas.* 1 and *Suas.* 4), and Agamennon (*Suas.* 3): in two others the speakers address larger groups, the three-hundred Spartans (*Suas.* 2) and the Athenian Assembly (*Suas.* 5). The Greek material, of which we know much more, concentrating as it does on Classical Athens, has more addresses to assemblies, Kohl 1915, nrs. 29, 30, 36, 38, et passim, than to monarchs, nrs. 28, 33, 35, 37, 206A, 337–342, 344, 346–347, chiefly Xerxes and Alexander.

13. Truisms, but the habit of Roman thinking of their society in terms of law, which especially English-speaking scholars have tended to forget, is usefully reiterated in the recent scholarship by Ando 2011a, 2011b, and 2015; and for the Greeks under Roman rule, by Bryen 2012.

14. For violence in the papyri, Bryen 2013; more broadly in the Roman world, MacMullen 1974 and Fagan 2011.

15. *P.Yale* I 61 with Kelly 2011, 112 n. 152, 269–270; Fournier 2010, 574–579.

16. Esp. Kelly 2011, 75–122; Bryen 2013, 41–44, 126–164.

17. Sen. *Contr.* 3.pr.13, *scholam quasi ludum esse, forum arenam*.

18. Chapter 2 nn. 18–23.

19. Lentano 2019 identifies this world as a Roman utopia.

20. The classic description of the common fictional society created by Greek rhetorical training is in Russell 1983, 21–39, and his term "Sophistopolis" has been adopted by many subsequent scholars. Russell does not, however, discuss the possible influence of Sophistopolis on the real Roman world.

21. On the concept of the "the imaginary," descending from Jacques Lacan, through Cornelius Castoriadis, Benedict Anderson, Bronislaw Baczko, and Charles Taylor, see Strauss 2006 or Rundell 2017, with Bieger, Saldívar, and Voelz 2013 for examples of the use of the concept by historians, and with an intellectual history of the theory as used by historians (x-xviii). It is less new to classicists: Loraux 1986 [1981] introduced it to the field.

22. Petr. *Sat.* 1.1, *et ideo ego adulescentulos existimo in scholis stultissimos fieri, quia nihil ex his, quae in usu habemus, aut audiunt aut vident*. Cf. Tac. *Dial.* 35.5, *materiae abhorrenti a veritate*; see chapter 1 n. 62 for a collection of similar criticisms.

23. Quoted Bloomer (2015b) 347–348; cf. the lapidary formulation of Cribiore (2001) 244: "Life imitated school."

24. See Reardon 1971, 235–405 and Anderson 1990, 108–110 for the survival of independent intellectual traditions among the Greeks under the Empire.

25. For Tacitus, Woodman 1988, 160–196; Frontinus, Peachin 2004, 151–154.

26. Quoted Parks 1945, 108.

# ABBREVIATIONS OF SOME
# MODERN WORKS

ABBREVIATIONS OF ANCIENT WORKS (sometimes expanded in the notes so as to be understood more readily) are taken in the first instance from the *Oxford Classical Dictionary*, 4th ed. (2012), and failing that the *Oxford Latin Dictionary* (1982), Lewis and Short's *Latin Dictionary* (1879), and LSJ (1940). Where it seems helpful, the editor of an edition used may be given in the notes.

D-KL    C. Dorl-Klingenschmid, *Prunkbrunnen in kleinasiatischen Städten: Funktion im Kontext*, 168–260. Munich, 2001.

FGrH    F. Jacoby. *Die Fragmente der griechischen Historiker*. Berlin and Leiden, 1923–1958.

FIRA    S. Riccobono, J. Baviera, C. Ferrini, J. Furlani, and V. Arangio-Ruiz, eds. *Fontes iuris romani anteiustiniani*. 3 vols. Florence, 1st ed. 1909; Florence, 2nd ed. 1940–1943.

Gibson    C. A. Gibson. *Libanius'* Progymnasmata. *Model Exercises in Greek Prose Composition and Rhetoric*. Atlanta, 2008.

LSJ    H. G. Liddell, R. Scott, and H. Stuart Jones. *A Greek-English Lexicon*. 9th ed. Oxford, 1940.

LTUR    E. M. Steinby, ed. *Lexicon topographicum urbis Romae*. 6 vols. Rome, 1993–2000.

MRR    T. R. S. Broughton. *Magistrates of the Roman Republic*. 3 vols. New York and Atlanta, 1951–1986.

Oliver   J. H. Oliver. *Greek Constitutions of Early Roman Emperors from Inscriptions and Papyri.* Philadelphia, 1989.

PG   *Patrologiae cursus completus. Series graeca.* Edited by J.-P. Migne. 167 vols. Paris, 1857–1866.

R   J. Richard. *Water for the City, Fountains for the People: Monumental Fountains in the Roman East. An Archaeological Study of Water Management,* 259–280. Turnhout, 2012.

RE   A. Pauly, G. Wissowa, and W. Kroll, eds. *Realencyclopädie der classischen Altertumswissenschaft.* Stuttgart, 1894–1980.

RLM   K. Halm. *Rhetores Latini Minores.* Leipzig, 1863.

RRC   M. H. Crawford. *Roman Republican Coinage.* 2 vols. Cambridge, 1974.

RS   M. H. Crawford, ed. *Roman Statutes.* 2 vols. London, 1996.

Walz, RG   C. Walz. *Rhetores Graeci.* 9 vols. Stuttgart and Tübingen, 1832–1836.

Weißenberger   M. Weißenberger. *Sopatri Quaestionum Divisio. Sopatros. Streitfälle: Gliederung und Ausarbeitung kontroverser Reden.* Würzburg, 2010.

# WORKS CITED

Adams, J. N. 1982. *The Latin Sexual Vocabulary*. Baltimore.

Adams, J. N. 2003. *Bilingualism and the Latin Language*. Cambridge.

Adams, J. N. 2007. *The Regional Diversification of Latin 200 BC–AD 600*. Cambridge.

Agusta-Boularot, S. 2001. "Fontaines et fontaines monumentales en Grèce de la conquête romain à l'époque flavienne: permanence ou renouveau architectural?" In *Constructions publiques et programmes édilitaires en Grèce entre le II^e siècle av. J.-C. et le I^er siècle ap. J.-C.*, edited by J.-Y. Marc and J.-C. Moretti, 167–236. Paris.

Ahl, F. 1984. "The Art of Safe Criticism in Greece and Rome." *American Journal of Philology* 105: 174–208.

Akerraz, A. 2012 [2010]. "Les fortifications de la Maurétane Tingitane." In *Enceintes urbaines, sites fortifiés, forteresses d'Afrique du Nord*, edited by J. Leclant and F. Déroche, 75–96 (Paris, 2012). Reprinted from *Comptes rendus des séances de l'Académie des Inscriptions et Belles-Lettres* 154 (2010) 539–561.

Albertario, E. 1925 [1933]. *Sul diritto agli alimenti (Note di diritto romano)*, Pubblicazione della Università Cattolica del Sacro Cuore (scienze giudice) 7.2 (Milan, 1925). Reprinted in E. Albertario, *Studi di diritto romano*, vol. 1, 250–279 (Milan, 1933).

Alföldi, A. 1952. *A Conflict of Ideas in the Late Roman Empire*. Translated by H. Mattingly. Oxford.

Alföldi, A. 1955. "Gewaltherrscher und Theaterkönig." In *Late Classical and Early Mediaeval Studies in Honor of Albert Mathias Friend, Jr.*, edited by K. Weitzmann, 15–55. Princeton.

Alföldi, A. 1985. Clementia Caesaris. In A. Alföldi, *Caesar in 44 v. Chr.*, edited by H. Wolff, E. Alföldi-Rosenbaum, and G. Stumpf, vol. 1, 173–386. Bonn.

Amande, C. 1993–1994. "Tradizione e attualità nella figura del tiranno nelle orazioni di Libanio." *Rendiconti della Accademia di Archeologia, Lettere e Belle Arti. Napoli: Società Nazionale di Scienze, Lettere ed Arti* n.s. 64: 535–567.

Amato, E. and J. Schamp eds. 2005. *ΗΘΟΠΟΙΙΑ. Le représentation de caractères entre fiction scolaire et réalité vivante à l'époque impériale et tardive*. Salerno.

Ameling, W. 1983. *Herodes Atticus*. 2 vols. Hildesheim.

Amelotti, M. 2001. "Leggi greche in diritto romano." *Minima epigraphica et papyrologica* 4 (2001) 11–24. Also appeared in *Symposion 1997. Vorträge zur griechischen und hellenistischen Rechtsgeschichte / Communicazioni sul diritto greco ed ellenistico*, edited by E. Cantarella and G. Thür, 225–234 (Böhlau, 2001).

Anderson, G. 1989. "The *Pepaideumenos* in Action: Sophists and their Outlook in the Early Empire." *Aufstieg und Niedergang der römischen Welt* II.33.1: 79–208.

Anderson, G. 1990. "The Second Sophistic: Some Problems of Perspective." In *Antonine Literature*, edited by D. A. Russell, 91–110. Oxford.

Anderson, G. 1993. *The Second Sophistic. A Cultural Phenomenon in the Roman Empire*. London.

Anderson, G. 1995. "*Ut ornatius et uberius dici posset*: Morals into Epigram in the Elder Seneca." In *Ethics and Rhetoric. Classical Essays for Donald Russell on his Seventy-Fifth Birthday*, edited by D. C. Innes, H. Hine, and C. Pelling, 75–91. Oxford.

Ando, C. 2011a. *Law, Language, and Empire in the Roman Tradition*. Philadelphia.

Ando, C. 2011b. "Law and the Landscape of Empire." In *Figures d'empire, fragments de mémoire: Pouvoirs et identités dans le monde romain impérial, II$^e$ s. av. n. è.-VI$^e$ s. de n. è*, edited by S. Benoist, A. Daguet-Gagey, and C. Hoët-van Cauwenberghe, 25–47. Villeneuve d'Ascq.

Ando, C. 2015. *Roman Social Imaginaries. Language and Thought in Contexts of Empire*. Toronto.

André, L.-N. 2014. "L'image de la fluidité dans la construction du paysage urbain d'Antioche chez Libanios: proposition pour une poétique de 'l'effet retour.'" In *ΕΝ ΚΑΛΟΙΣ ΚΟΙΝΟΠΡΑΓΙΑ. Hommages à la mémoire de Pierre-Louis Malosse et Jean Bouffartigue*, edited by E. Amato, 29–51. Nantes.

Arena, V. 2012. Libertas *and the Practice of Politics in the Late Roman Republic*. Cambridge.

Arenz, A. 2006. *Herakleides Kritikos. Über die Städte in Hellas. Eine Periegese Griechenlands am Vorabend des Chremonideischen Krieges*. Munich.

Aristodemou, G. [A.] 2008. "Miletus (Antiquity), Nymphaeum of Flavius." In *Encyclopedia of the Hellenic World, Asia Minor* (22.1.2013), http://www.ehw.gr/l.aspx?id=8190.

Aristodemou, G. [A.] 2011a. "Theatre Façades and Façade Nymphaea. The Link Between." *Bulletin de correspondance hellénique* 135: 163–197.

Aristodemou, G. A. 2011b. "Sculptured Decoration of Monumental Nymphaea at [*sic*] the Eastern Provinces of the Roman Empire." In *Roma y las provincias: modelo y difusión*, edited by T. Nogales and I. Rodà, vol. 1, 149–160. Rome.

Aristodemou, G. A. 2012. *Ο γλυπτός διάκοσμος νυμφαίων και κρηνών, στο ανατολικό τμήμα της ρωμαϊκής αυτοκρατορίας*. Thessalonica.

Aristodemou, G. A. 2014. "Monumental Fountain Structures: The Role of Nymphaea within the Urban Context of the Cities of the Graeco-Roman East." In *IWA Regional Symposium on Water, Wastewater and Environment: Traditions and Culture*, edited by I. K. Kalavrouziotis and A. N. Angelaki, 523–535. Patras. https://www.academia.edu/4718172/G_Aristodemou _Monumental_Fountain_Structures_The_Role_of_Nymphaea_within_the_Urban _Context_of_the_Cities_of_the_Graeco_Roman_East_pp_523_535.

Aristodemou, G. A. 2017. "Fountain Culture in the Greek Provinces before Hadrian. Introducing the Concept of Luxury." In *Wasserwesen zur Zeit des Frontinus. Bauwerke—Technik—Kultur*, edited by G. Wiplinger and W. Letzner, 315–329. Louvain.

Aristodemou, G. A. 2018a. "Fountain Sculptures and Personal Propaganda in Roman Greece." In *Γλυπτική και κοινωνία στη ρωμαϊκή Ελλάδα: Καλλιτεχνικά προϊόντα, κοινωνικές προβολές*, edited by P. Karanastasi, T. Stephanidou-Tiveriou, and D. Damaskos, 351–366. Thessalonica.

Aristodemou, G. A. 2018b. "Fountain Figures from the Greek Provinces: Monumentality in Fountain Sculptures of Roman Greece as Revealed through their Sculptural Display

Programs and their Patrons." In *Great Waterworks in Roman Greece. Aqueducts and Monumental Fountain Structures. Function in Context*, edited by G. A. Aristodemou and T. P. Tassios, 193–217. Oxford.

Arjava, A. 1996. *Women and Law in Late Antiquity*. Oxford.

Arjava, A. 1998. "Paternal Power in Late Antiquity." *Journal of Roman Studies* 88: 147–165.

Arruzza, C. 2019. *A Wolf in the City. Tyranny and the Tyrant in Plato's* Republic. New York.

Ash, R. 2018. *Tacitus,* Annals *Book XV.* Cambridge.

Asheri, D. 1971. "La declamazione 261 di Quintiliano." In *Studi in onore di Edoardo Volterra I*, 309–321. Milan.

Astolfi, R. 1996. *La Lex Julia et Papia*, 4th ed. Padua.

Astolfi, R. 2000. *Il matrimonio nel diritto romano preclassico*. Padua.

Astolfi, R. 2012. *Studi sul matrimonio nel diritto romano postclassico e giustinianeo*. Naples.

Atherton, C. 1996. "What Every Grammarian Knows?" *Classical Quarterly* 46: 239–260.

Atherton, C. 1998. "Children, Animals, Slaves, and Grammar." In *Pedagogy and Power. Rhetorics of Classical Learning*, edited by Y. L. Too, 214–244. Cambridge.

Aupert, P. 1974. *Le nymphée de Tipasa et les nymphées et "septizonia" nord-africaines*. Rome.

Avenarius, M. 2015. "Vom théatron zur Bühne totalitärer Gesellschaftsstrukturen. Die Rezeption griechischer Elemente in die Theaterordnung des Prinzipats, deren Instrumentalisierung zur politischen Einvernahme der Gesellschaft und die staatsbezogene Ausgeltung des Ehe- und Familienrechts." In *Il diritto romano e le culture straniere. Influenze e dipendenze interculturali nell'antichità*, edited by F. Lamberti, P. Gröschler, and F. Milazzo, 59–121. Lecce.

Azoulay, V. 2017 [2014]. *The Tyrant-Slayers of Ancient Athens. A Tale of Two Statues*. (New York, 2017). Translated by J. Lloyd from *Les tyrannicides d'Athènes* (Paris, 2014).

Babbitt, F. C. 1931. *Plutarch's* Moralia III, *172A-263C*. Cambridge MA.

Babusiaux, U. 2011. *Papinians* Quaestiones. *Zur rhetorischen Methode eines spätklassischen Juristen*. Munich.

Babusiaux, U. 2014. "Funktionen der Etymologie in der juristischen Literatur." In Meditationes in iure et historia. *Essays in Honour of Laurens Winkel*, edited by R. van den Bergh, G. van Niekerk, P. Pichonnaz, P. J. Thomas, D. G. Kleyn, F. Lucrezi, and J. Mutton, vol. 1, 39–60. Pretoria.

Babusiaux, U. (forthcoming) "Römische Rechtsrhetorik." In *Historisches Wörterbuch der Rhetorik*, edited by K. von Schlieffen. Tübingen.

Balbo, A. 2011. "Riflessi dell'oratoria reale nei discorsi sulla morte di Cesare: il caso di Bruto." *I Quaderni del Ramo d'Oro* 4: 152–167.

Balbo, A. 2013. "Marcus Junius Brutus the Orator: Between Philosophy and Rhetoric." In *Community and Communication: Oratory and Politics in Republican Rome*, edited by C. Steel and H. van der Blom, 315–328. Oxford.

Balbo, A. 2016. "Ri-leggere un retore: riflessioni lessicali su Calpurnio Flacco." In *Fabrique de la déclamation antique (controverses et suasoires)*, edited by R. Poignault and C. Schneider, 49–65. Lyon.

Balogh, E. 1951. "Adaptation of Law to Economic Conditions According to Roman Law." *Atti del congresso internazionale di diritto romano e di storia del diritto II*, 263–355. Milan.

Balzarini, M. 1983. *De iniuria extra ordinem statui*. Padua.

Banchich, T. M., trans. 2010. *Pseudo-Plutarch. About Rivers and Mountains and Things Found in Them*. Buffalo NY.

Bannard, P. 2015. "Military Training." In *A Companion to Ancient Education*, edited by W. M. Bloomer, 483–495. Chichester.

Bannert, H. 2015. "[Education in] Medicine." In *A Companion to Ancient Education*, edited by W. M. Bloomer, 413–429. Chichester.

Barnes, J. 1989 [1997]. "Antiochus of Ascalon." In Philosophia Togata. *Essays on Philosophy and Roman Society*, edited by J. Barnes and M. Griffin, 51–96 (Oxford, 1989). Reprinted as Philosophia Togata I. *Essays on Philosophy and Roman Society*, 51–96 (Oxford, 1997).

Barrow, R. 2015. "The Persistence of Ancient Education." In *A Companion to Ancient Education*, edited by W. M. Bloomer, 281–291. Chichester.

Bauman, R. A. 1980. "The '*Leges iudiciorum publicorum*' and their Interpretation in the Republic, Principate and Later Empire." *Aufstieg und Niedergang der römischen Welt* II.13: 103–233.

Beard, M. 1993. "Looking (Harder) for Roman Myth: Dumézil, Declamation and the Problems of Definition." In *Mythos in mythenloser Gesellschaft: Das Paradigma Roms*, edited by F. Graf, 44–64. Stuttgart.

Becht, E. 1911. *Regeste über die Zeit von Cäsars Ermordung bis zum Umschwung in der Politik des Antonius (15 März bis 1 Juni anno 43 v. Chr.)*. Freiburg.

Bederman, D. J. 2001. *Classical Canons: Rhetoric, Classicism, and Treaty Interpretation*. Aldershot.

Bedon, R. 2008. "Les villes des Trois Gaules et leur recherche d'une proximité de l'eau: gestion des atouts et des difficultés créés par le presence de rivières et de marécages." In *Vers une gestion intégrée de l'eau dans l'empire romain*, edited by E. Hermon, 99–106. Rome.

Bejor, G. 1999. *Vie colonnate. Paesaggi urbani del mondo antico*. Rome.

Bekker Nielsen, T. 2008. *Urban Life and Local Politics in Roman Bithynia: The Small World of Dion Chrysostomos*. Aarhus.

Beltrami, L. 1997. "I doveri alimentari erga parentes." In *Pietas e allattamento filiale. La vicenda, l'exemplum, l'iconografia*, edited by R. Raffaelli, R. M. Danese, and S. Lanciotti, 73–101. Urbino.

Benferhat, Y. 2013. "Tacite et le tyran en filigrane dans les *Histoires*." In *Le tyran et sa postérité dans la littérature latine de l'Antiquité à la Renaissance*, edited by H. Casanova-Robin and C. Lévy, 187–202. Paris.

Bengtson, H. 1970. *Zur Geschichte des Brutus*. Munich.

Berardi, F. 2017. *La retorica degli esercizi preparatori: glossario ragionato dei progymnásmata*. Hildesheim.

Berger, A. 1953. *Encyclopedic Dictionary of Roman Law*. Philadelphia.

Bernstein, N. W. 2009. "Adoptees and Exposed Children in Roman Declamation: Commodification, Luxury, and the Threat of Violence." *Classical Philology* 104: 331–353.

Bernstein, N. W. 2012. "'Torture Her until She Lies': Torture, Testimony, and Social Status in Roman Rhetorical Education." *Greece and Rome* 59: 165–177.

Bernstein, N. W. 2013. *Ethics, Identity, and Community in Later Roman Declamation*. New York.

Berry, D. H. and M. Heath. 1997. "Oratory and Declamation." In *Handbook of Classical Rhetoric in the Hellenistic Period, 330 B.C.–A.D. 400*, edited by S. E. Porter, 393–420. Leiden.

Berti, E. 2007. Scholasticorum Studia. *Seneca il Vecchio e la cultura retorica e letteraria della prima età imperiale*. Pisa.

Berve, H. 1967. *Die Tyrannis bei den Griechen*. 2 vols. Munich.

Bettinazzi, M. 2012. "La *lex Roscia* e la declamazione 302 ascritta a Quintiliano. Sull'uso delle declamazioni come documento dell'esperienza giuridica romana." In Leges Publicae. *La legge nell'esperienza giuridica romana*, edited by J.-L. Ferrary, 515–544. Pavia.

Bettinazzi, M. 2014. *La legge nelle declamazioni quintilianee. Una nuova prospettiva per lo studio della* lex Voconia, *della lex* Iunia Norbana *e della* lex Iulia de adulteriis. Saarbrücken.

Bieger, L., R. Saldívar, and J. Voelz eds. 2013. *The Imaginary and Its Worlds. American Studies after the Transnational Turn*. Hanover NH.

Billows, R. A. 2009. *Julius Caesar: The Colossus of Rome*. Abingdon.

Birks, P. 1976. "*Infamandi causa facta* in Disguise?" *Acta Juridica* 83: 83–104.

Bispham, E. 2006. "*Coloniam Deducere*: How Roman was Roman Colonization during the Middle Republic?" In *Greek and Roman Colonization*, edited by G. Bradley and J.-P. Wilson, 73–160. Swansea.

Bloomer, W. M. 1993. "The Superlative *Nomoi* of Herodotus's Histories." *Classical Antiquity* 12: 30–50.

Bloomer, W. M. 1997a. "A Preface to the History of Declamation: Whose Speech? Whose History?" In *The Roman Cultural Revolution*, edited by T. Habinek and A. Schiesaro, 199–215 (Cambridge, 1997). Also printed in W. M. Bloomer, *Latinity and Literary Society at Rome*, 110–153 (Philadelphia, 1997).

Bloomer, W. M. 1997b. "Schooling in *Persona*: Imagination and Subordination in Roman Education." *Classical Antiquity* 16: 57–78.

Bloomer, W. M. 2007. "Roman Declamation: The Elder Seneca and Quintilian." In *A Companion to Roman Rhetoric*, edited by W. Dominik and J. Hall, 297–306. Malden MA.

Bloomer, W. M. 2011a. *The School of Rome. Latin Studies and the Origins of Liberal Education*. Berkeley and Los Angeles.

Bloomer, W. M. 2011b. "Quintilian on the Child as a Learning Subject." *Classical World* 105: 109–137.

Bloomer, W. M. ed. 2015a. *A Companion to Ancient Education*. Chichester.

Bloomer, W. M. 2015b. "Quintilian on Education." In *A Companion to Ancient Education*, edited by W. M. Bloomer, 347–357. Chichester.

Bloomer, W. M. 2017. "*Latinitas*." In *The Oxford Handbook of the Second Sophistic*, edited by D. S. Richter and W. A. Johnson, 67–79. New York.

Boatwright, M. T. 1991. "Plancia Magna of Perge. Women's Roles and Status in Roman Asia Minor." In *Women's History and Ancient History*, edited by S. B. Pomeroy, 249–272. Chapel Hill.

Börm, H. and N. Luraghi eds. 2018. *The Polis in the Hellenistic World*. Stuttgart.

Boesche, R. 1996. *Theories of Tyranny from Plato to Arendt*. University Park PA.

Boissier, G. 1875. *L'opposition sous les Césars*. Paris.

Bol, R. 1984. *Das Statuenprogramm des Herodes-Atticus-Nymphäums*. Berlin.

Bonetto, J. 1998. *Mura e città nella transpadana romana*. Portogruaro.

Bonner, S. F. 1949. *Roman Declamation in the Late Republic and Early Empire*. Liverpool.

Bonner, S. F. 1977. *Education in Ancient Rome*. Berkeley and Los Angeles.

Bons, J. A. E. 2007. "Gorgias the Sophist and Early Rhetoric." In *A Companion to Greek Rhetoric*, edited by I. Worthington, 37–46. Malden MA.

Booth, A. D. 1978. "The Appearance of the *Schola Grammatici*." *Hermes* 106: 117–125.

Booth, A. D. 1979a. "The Schooling of Slaves in First-Century Rome." *Transactions of the American Philological Association* 109: 11–19.

Booth, A. D. 1979b. "Elementary and Secondary Education in the Roman Empire." *Florilegium* 1: 1–14.

Bornecque, H. 1902. *Les déclamations et les déclamateurs d'après Sénèque le Père*. Lille.

Botermann, H. 1968. *Die Soldaten und die römische Politik in der Zeit von Caesars Tod bis zur Begründung des zweiten Triumvirats*. Munich.

Botta, F. 1996. *Legittimazione, interesse ed incapacità all'accusa nei publica iudicia*. Cagliari.

Botta, F. 2004. Per vim inferre. *Studi su* stuprum *violento e* raptus *nel diritto romano e bizantino*. Cagliari.

Botta, F. 2016. "*Stuprum per vim illatum*. Violenza e crimini sessuali nelle fonti giuridiche dall'età classica a Giustiniano." In F. Lucrezi, F. Botta, and G. Rizzelli, *Violenza sessuale e società antiche: profili storico-giuridici*, 3rd ed., 87–157. Lecce.

Boudon-Millot, V. 2008. "Un étudiant sans école, un maître sans disciples: l'exemple paradoxal de Galien de Pergame." In *L'enseignement supérieur dans les mondes antiques et médiévaux*, edited by H. Hugonnard-Roche, 265–282. Paris.

Bouffartigue, J. 1996. "La tradition de l'éloge de la cité dans le monde grec." In *La fin de la cité antique et le début de la cité médiévale de la fin du III⁰ siècle à l'avènement de Charlemagne*, edited by C. Lepelley, 43–58. Bari.

Bouyssou, G.-S. 2013. "Le tyran ou le banquet impossible." In *Le banquet du monarque dans le monde antique*, edited by C. Grandjean, C. Hugoniot, and B. Lion, 71–86. Rennes.

Bowden, W. 2011. "'Alien Settlers Consisting of Romans': Identity and Built Environment in the Julio-Claudian Foundations of Epirus in the Century after Actium." In *Roman Colonies in the First Century of their Foundation*, edited by R. J. Sweetman, 101–116. Oxford.

Bowersock, G. W. 1961. "Eurycles of Sparta." *Journal of Roman Studies* 51: 112–118.

Bowersock, G. W. 1969. *Greek Sophists in the Roman Empire*. Oxford.

Bowie, E. [L.] 1970 [1974]. "The Greeks and their Past in the Second Sophistic." *Past and Present* 46 (1970) 3–41. Reprinted in *Studies in Ancient Society*, edited by M. I. Finley, 166–209 (London, 1974).

Bowie, E. L. 1982. "The Importance of Sophists." *Yale Classical Studies* 27: 29–59.

Bowie, E. [L.] 2004. "The Geography of the Second Sophistic: Cultural Variations." In *Paideia: The World of the Second Sophistic*, edited by B. E. Borg, 65–75. Berlin.

Bowie, E. L. 2009. "'*Quid Roma Athenis?*' How Far did Imperial Greek Sophists or Philosophers Debate the Legitimacy of Roman Power?" In *Ordine e sovversione nel mondo greco e romano*, edited by G. Urso, 223–240. Pisa.

Brasiello, U. 1971. "Sulla persecuzione degli eredi del colpevole nel campo criminale." In *Studi in onore di Edoardo Volterra*, vol. 4, 325–345. Milan.

Brasse, C. 2010. "Von der Stadtmauer zur Stadtgeschichte. Das Befestigungssystem von Antiochia am Orontes." In *Neue Forschungen zu antiken Stadtbefestigungen im östlichen*

*Mittelmeerraum und im Vorderen Orient*, edited by J. Lorentzen, F. Pirson, P. Schneider, and U. Wulf-Rheidt, 261–282. Istanbul.

Brasse, C. 2016. "Antiochia am Orontes." In *Ancient Fortifications. A Compendium of Theory and Practice*, edited by S. Müth, P. I. Schneider, M. Schnelle, and P. D. De Staebler, 261–266. Oxford.

Braund, S. M. 1996. "The Solitary Feast: A Contradiction in Terms?" *Bulletin of the Institute of Classical Studies* 41: 37–52.

Breij, B. 2006a. "*Vitae Necisque Potestas* in Roman Declamation." *Advances in the History of Rhetoric* 9: 55–79.

Breij, B. 2006b. "Pseudo-Quintilian's *Major Declamations* 18 and 19: Two *Controversiae Figuratae*." *Rhetorica* 24: 79–105.

Breij, B. 2009. "Pseudo-Quintilian's *Major Declamations*: Beyond School and Literature." *Rhetorica* 27: 354–369.

Breij, B. 2011. "Dilemmas of *Pietas* in Roman Declamation." In *Sacred Words: Orality, Literacy, and Religion*, edited by A. P. M. H. Lardinois, J. H. Blok, and M. G. M. van der Poel, 329–348. Leiden.

Breij, B. 2015a. *[Quintilian] The Son Suspected of Incest with His Mother (Major Declamations 18–19)*. Cassino.

Breij, B. 2015b. "The Law in the *Major Declamations* Ascribed to Quintilian." In *Law and Ethics in Greek and Roman Declamation*, edited by E. Amato, F. Citti, and B. Huelsenbeck, 219–248. Berlin.

Breij, B. 2016. "Rich and Poor, Father and Son in *Major Declamation 7*." In *Fabrique de la déclamation antique (controverses et suasoires)*, edited by R. Poignault and C. Schneider, 275–290. Lyon.

Breitenstein, N. 2009. *Petronius, Satyrica 1–15. Text, Übersetzung, Kommentar*. Berlin.

Brélaz, C. 2005. *La sécurité publique en Asie Mineure sous le Principat (I^er-III^ème s. ap. J.-C.)*. Basel.

Brélaz, C. 2008. "L'adieu aux armes: la défense de la cité grecque dans l'empire romain pacifié." In *Sécurité collective et ordre public dans les sociétés anciennes*, edited by C. Brélaz and P. Ducrey, 155–196. Geneva.

Brélaz, C. 2016. "Democracy and Civic Participation in Greek Cities under Roman Imperial Rule: Political Practice and Culture in the Post-Classical Period." *CHS Research Bulletin* 4, no. 2. https://research-bulletin.chs.harvard.edu/2016/11/01/democracy-civic-participation/.

Brescia, G. 2004. *Il miles alla sbarra. [Quintiliano] Declamazioni maggiori, III*. Bari.

Brescia, G. 2012. *La donna violata. Casi di stuprum e raptus nella declamazione latina*. Lecce.

Brescia, G. 2015a. "Declamazione e mito." In *La declamazione latina. Prospettive a confronto sulla retorica di scuola a Roma antica*, edited by M. Lentano, 59–88. Naples.

Brescia, G. 2015b. "Ambiguous Silence: *Stuprum* and *Pudicitia* in Latin Declamation." In *Law and Ethics in Greek and Roman Declamation*, edited by E. Amato, F. Citti, and B. Huelsenbeck, 75–93. Berlin.

Brescia, G. 2016. "*Rapta raptoris aut mortem optet aut nuptias*. Rischi ed equivoci della seduzione nella declamazione latina." In *Fabrique de la déclamation antique (controverses et suasoires)*, edited by R. Poignault and C. Schneider, 323–352. Lyon.

Brescia, G. and M. Lentano. 2009. *Le ragioni del sangue. Storie di incesto e fratricidio nella declamazione latina*. Naples.

Brescia, G. and M. Lentano. 2016. "La norma nascosta. Storie di adulterio nella declamazione latina." In *Giuristi nati. Anthropologia e diritto romano*, edited by A. McClintock, 135–184. Bologna.

Bretone, M. 2008. Ius Controversum *nella giurisprudenza classica. Atti della Accademia Nazionale dei Lincei, Memorie* ser. 9, vol. 23, fasc. 3: 755–880. Rome.

Bricker, B. L. 2016. *Virtue from Necessity in the Urban Waterworks of Roman Asia Minor.* Unpublished PhD dissertation, University of California at Santa Barbara. https://www.alexandria.ucsb.edu/lib/ark:/48907/f3cf9q4k.

Brightbill, J. D. 2015. *Roman Declamation: Between Creativity and Constraints*. Unpublished PhD dissertation, University of Chicago. https://knowledge.uchicago.edu/record/492?ln=en.

Brink, C. O. 1989. "Quintilian's *de Causis corruptae eloquentiae* and Tacitus' *Dialogus de Oratoribus*." *Classical Quarterly* 39: 472–503.

Brodersen, K. 2008 "Einführung. Die Geographie des Plinius." In *Gaius Plinius Secundus. Naturkunde, Bd. 2: Geographie*, edited by R. König, 225–236. Darmstadt.

Brodersen, K. 2016. "The Geographies of Pliny and his 'Ape' Solinus." In *Brill's Companion to Ancient Geography*, edited by S. Bianchetti, M. R. Cataudella, and H.-J. Gehrke, 298–310. Leiden.

Brown, P. 1992. *Power and Persuasion in Late Antiquity: Towards a Christian Empire*. Madison WI.

Bru, H. 2011. *Le pouvoir impérial dans les provinces syriennes. Représentations et célébrations d'Auguste à Constantin (31 av. J.-C.—337 ap. J.-C.)*. Leiden.

Brunt, P. A. 1975 [2013]. "Stoicism and the Principate." *Papers of the British School at Rome* 43 (1975) 7–35. Reprinted in P. A. Brunt, *Studies in Stoicism*, edited by M. Griffin and A. Samuels, 275–304 (Oxford, 2013).

Brunt, P. A. 1975 [1990]. "The Administrators of Roman Egypt." *Journal of Roman Studies* 65 (1975) 124–147. Reprinted in P. A. Brunt, *Roman Imperial Themes*, 215–254 (Oxford, 1990).

Bryen, A. Z. 2012. "Judging Empire. Courts and Culture in Rome's Eastern Provinces." *Law and History Review* 30: 771–811.

Bryen, A. Z. 2013. *Violence in Roman Egypt. A Study in Legal Interpretation*. Philadelphia.

Bryen, A. [Z.] 2018. "Labeo's *iniuria*: Violence and Politics in the Age of Augustus." *Chiron* 48: 17–52.

Brzoska, J. 1899. "Cassius nr. 89." *RE* III.2 cols. 1744–1747.

Buckland, W. W. 1963. *A Textbook of Roman Law from Augustus to Justinian*, 3rd ed. Cambridge.

Bührig, C. 2016. "The Stage of Palmyra: Colonnaded Streets, Spaces for Communication and Activities in the Eastern Roman Empire." In *Palmyrena: City, Hinterland and Caravan Trade Between Orient and Occident*, edited by J. C. Meyer, E. H. Seland, and N. Anfinset, 59–75. Oxford.

Burckhardt, J. 1949 [1853]. *The Age of Constantine the Great* (Berkeley and Los Angeles, 1949). Translated by M. Hadas from *Die Zeit Constantin's des Großen* (2nd ed., Leipzig, 1880 [1st ed., Leipzig, 1853]).

Burns, R. 2017. *Origins of the Colonnaded Streets in the Cities of the Roman East*. Oxford.

Burrell, B. 2004. Neokoroi: *Greek Cities and Roman Emperors*. Leiden.

Burrell, B. 2012. Review of B. Longfellow, *Roman Imperialism and Civic Patronage: Form, Meaning, and Ideology in Monumental Fountain Complexes* (New York, 2011). *American Journal of Archaeology* 116.2. http://www.ajaonline.org/online-review-book/1107.

Burton, G. 1979. "The *Curator Rei Publicae*: Towards a Reappraisal." *Chiron* 9: 465–487.

Buti, I. 1982. "La '*cognitio extra ordinem*': da Augusto a Diocleziano." *Aufstieg und Niedergang der römischen Welt* II.14: 29–59.

Cabouret, B. 1999. "Sous les portiques d'Antioche." *Syria* 76: 127–150.

Cairns, F. 1972. *Generic Composition in Greek and Roman Poetry*. Edinburgh.

Calboli, G. 2010. "Quintilien et les déclamateurs." In *Quintilien ancien et moderne*, edited by P. Galand, F. Hallyn, C. Lévy, and W. Verbaal, 11–28. Turnhout.

Calboli, G. 2016. "*Rhetorica et ius*. Le declamazioni e l'attività giudiziaria a Roma." Review of M. Lentano, *Retorica e diritto. Per una lettura giuridica della declamazione latina* (Lecce, 2014). *Maia* 68: 807–818.

Calboli, G. 2018. "Rhetorical Performance and Law: The First Example of How a Real or Invented Law Suited a Rhetorical Rule." In *Papers on Rhetoric XIV*, edited by L. Calboli Montefusco and M. Silvana Celentano, 19–42. Perugia.

Calboli Montefusco, L. 1979. Consulti Fortunatiani Ars Rhetorica. Bologna.

Calderón Dorda, E., A. De Lazzer, and E. Pellizer. 2003. *Plutarcho Fiumi e Monti*. Naples.

Callu, J.-P. 1984. "Le jardin des supplices au Bas-Empire." In *Du châtiment dans la cité. Supplices corporels et peine de mort dans le monde antique*, 313–359. Rome.

Callu, J.-P. 1997. "Antioche la grande. La cohérence des chiffres." *Mélanges de l'École française de Rome* 109: 127–169.

Campagna, L. 2007. "Le recenti indagni al Ninfeo dei Tritoni (Regio II): nuovi dati per lo studio del monumento." In *Hierapolis di Frigia I. Le attività delle campagne di scavo e restauro 2000–2003*, edited by F. D'Andria and M. P. Caggia, 311–332. Istanbul.

Campagna, L. 2011. "Le fontane nelle città dell'impero romano: 'a monument indelibly associated with the emperor'?" Review of B. Longfellow, *Roman Imperialism and Civic Patronage: Form, Meaning, and Ideology in Monumental Fountain Complexes* (New York, 2011). *Journal of Roman Archaeology* 24: 648–656.

Campbell, B. 2012. *Rivers and the Power of Ancient Rome*. Chapel Hill.

Canfora, L. 2007 [1999]. *Julius Caesar. The Life and Times of the People's Dictator* (Berkeley and Los Angeles, 2007). Translated by M. Hill and K. Windle from *Giulio Cesare: Il dittatore democratico* (Rome, 1999).

Cantarella, E. 1972. "Adulterio, omicidio legittimo et causa d'onore in diritto romano." In *Studi in onore di Gaetano Scherillo*, edited by A. Biscardi and C. Castello, 243–274. Milan.

Cantarella, E. 1991. *I supplizi capitali in Grecia e a Roma*. Milan.

Capriglione, J. C. 2007. "La scuola dell'architecto, τεχνίτης ma non troppo." In *Escuela y literatura en Grecia Antigua*, edited by J. A. Fernández Delgado, F. Pordomingo, and A. Stramaglia, 251–272. Cassino.

Carandini, A. ed. 2017 [2012]. *The Atlas of Ancient Rome*. 2 vols. (Princeton, 2017). Translated by A. C. Halavais from *Atlante di Roma Antica* (Milan, 2012).

Carlà-Uhink, F. 2017. "Murder among Relatives. Intrafamilial Violence in Ancient Rome and its Regulation." *Journal of Ancient History* 5: 26–65.

Casamento, A. 2002. Finitimus oratori poeta. *Declamazioni retoriche e tragedie senecane*. Palermo.

Casamento, A. 2004. "Le mani dell'eroe. In nota a Sen. *Contr.* 1, 4." *Pan* 22: 243–253.

Casamento, A. 2018. "Lo spazio della città nelle declamazioni in lingua latina." In *Papers on Rhetoric XIV*, edited by L. Calboli Montefusco and M. Silvana Celentano, 59–74. Perugia.

Casamento, A. 2019. "*Patres non tantum natura*. L'*expositio* di minori nelle declamazioni in lingua latina: il caso di Ps. Quint. *Dec. Min.* 278." *Camenae* 23: 1–12.

Casella, M. 2012. "Les discours de Libanios (discours 33–64) et la topographie d'Antioche." In *Les sources de l'histoire du paysage urbain d'Antioche sur l'Oronte*, 57–67. Saint-Denis.

Casevitz, M., O. Lagacherie, and C. Saliou. 2016. *Libanios discours tome III. Discours XI Antiochicos*. Paris.

Casinos Mora, F. J. 2009. "Sobre la verosimilitud de la llamada *Lex Raptarum* en las Declamationes de Calpurnio Flaco." In *Perfiles de Grecia y Roma. Actas del XII Congreso Español de Estudios Clásicos*, edited by J. F. González Castro, J. Siles Ruiz, J. de la Villa Polo, G. Hinojo Andrés, M. A. Almela Lumbreras, and P. Cañizares Ferriz, vol. 1, 981–988. Madrid.

Casinos Mora, F. J. 2011. "*Lex raptarum* y matrimonio expiatorio." In *Estudios jurídicos en homenaje al Profesor Alejandro Guzmán Brito*, edited by P.-I. Carvajal and M. Miglietta, vol. 1, 595–623. Alessandria.

Cavallo, G. 1989. "Il segno della mura. L'iconografia della città nel libro antico." In *Storia di Roma IV. Caratteri e morfologie*, edited by E. Gabba and A. Schiavone, 267–300. Turin.

Centola, D. A. 1999. *Il crimen calumniae. Contributo allo studio del processo criminale romano*. Naples.

Champlin, E. 2013. "The Odyssey of Tiberius Caesar." *Classica et Mediaevalia* 64: 199–246.

Chankowski, A. S. 2010. *L'éphébie hellénistique. Étude d'une institution civique dans les cités grecques des îles de la Mer Égée et de l'Asie Mineure*. Paris.

Chastagnol, A. 1981. "L'inscription constantinienne de Orcistus." *Mélanges de l'École française de Rome* 93: 381–416.

Chiron, P. 2007. "The Rhetoric to Alexander." In *A Companion to Greek Rhetoric*, edited by I. Worthington, 90–106. Malden MA.

Chiron, P. 2017. "Les *progymnasmata* de l'Antiquité gréco-latine." *Lustrum* 59: 7–130.

Christ, K. 1994. *Caesar. Annäherungen an einen Diktator*. Munich.

Christensen, J. P. 2015. "Trojan Politics and the Assemblies of *Iliad* 7." *Greek, Roman, and Byzantine Studies* 55: 25–51.

Citti, F. 2015. "*Quaedam iura non lege, sed natura*: Nature and Natural Law in Roman Declamation." In *Law and Ethics in Greek and Roman Declamation*, edited by E. Amato, F. Citti, and B. Huelsenbeck, 95–131. Berlin.

Clark, D. L. 1949. "Some Values of Roman *Declamatio*. The *Controversia* as a School Exercise in Rhetoric." *Quarterly Journal of Speech* 35: 280–283.

Clarke, M. L. 1951. "The Thesis in the Roman Rhetorical Schools of the Republic." *Classical Quarterly* ns. 1: 159–166.

Clarke, M. L. 1968. "Cicero at School." *Greece and Rome* 15: 18–22.

Clarke, M. L. 1971. *Higher Education in the Ancient World*. London.

Clarke, M. L. 1981. *The Noblest Roman. Marcus Brutus and his Reputation*. Ithaca NY.

Clarke, M. L. 1996 [1953]. *Rhetoric at Rome. A Historical Survey* (3rd ed., London, 1996 [1st ed., London, 1953]).

Classen, C. J. 1986. *Die Stadt im Spiegel der* Descriptiones *und* Laudes urbium *in der antiken und mittelalterlichen Literatur bis zum Ende des zwölften Jahrhunderts.* Hildesheim.

Cogitore, I. 2013. "Des tyrans 'de papier' dans les *Controverses* transmises par Sénèque le Père?" In *Le tyran et sa postérité dans le littérature latine de l'Antiquité à la Renaissance*, edited by H. Casanova-Robin and C. Lévy, 161–185. Paris.

Cole, T. 1991. *The Origins of Rhetoric in Ancient Greece.* Baltimore.

Coleman, K. M. 1990. "Fatal Charades: Roman Executions Staged as Mythological Enactments." *Journal of Roman Studies* 80: 44–73.

Colin, M.-G. ed. 1987. *Les enceintes Augustéennes dans l'Occident romain (France, Italie, Espagne, Afrique du Nord).* Nimes.

Collinet, P. 1934. "Le rôle des juges dans le formation du droit romain classique." In *Recueil d'études sur les sources du droit en l'honneur de François Gény*, edited by E. Lambert, vol. 1, 23–31. Paris.

Connolly, J. 1998. "Mastering Corruption. Constructions of Identity in Roman Oratory." In *Women and Slaves in Greco-Roman Culture: Differential Equations*, edited by S. R. Joshel and S. Murnaghan, 130–151. London.

Connolly, J. 2001a. "Problems of the Past in Imperial Greek Education." In *Education in Greek and Roman Antiquity*, edited by Y. L. Too, 339–372. Leiden.

Connolly, J. 2001b. "Reclaiming the Theatrical in the Second Sophistic." *Helios* 28: 75–96.

Connolly, J. 2007a. "The New World Order: Greek Rhetoric in Rome." In *A Companion to Greek Rhetoric*, edited by I. Worthington, 139–165. Malden MA.

Connolly, J. 2007b. "Virile Tongues: Rhetoric and Masculinity." In *A Companion to Roman Rhetoric*, edited by W. Dominik and J. Hall, 83–97. Malden MA.

Connolly, J. 2016. "Imaginative Fiction Beyond Social and Moral Norms." In *Reading Roman Declamation. The Declamations Ascribed to Quintilian*, edited by M. T. Dinter, C. Guérin, and M. Martinho, 191–208. Berlin.

Connolly, S. 2010. *Lives Behind the Laws. The World of the Codex Hermogenianus.* Bloomington IN.

Corbeill, A. 2001. "Education in the Roman Republic: Creating Traditions." In *Education in Greek and Roman Antiquity*, edited by Y. L. Too, 261–287. Leiden.

Corbeill, A. 2007. "Rhetorical Education and Social Reproduction in the Republic and Early Empire." In *A Companion to Roman Rhetoric*, edited by W. Dominik and J. Hall, 69–82. Malden MA.

Corbeill, A. 2016. "A Student Speaks for Social Equality in the Roman Classroom (Quintilian, *Declamationes Minores* 260)." In *Reading Roman Declamation. The Declamations Ascribed to Quintilian*, edited by M. T. Dinter, C. Guérin, and M. Martinho, 11–23. Berlin.

Coriat, J.-P. 1997. *Le prince législateur. La technique législative des Sévères et les méthodes de création du droit impérial à la fin du principat.* Rome.

Corrigan, K. 2015. *Brutus. Caesar's Assassin.* Barnsley.

Coşkun, A. 2001. "*Civiliter vel criminaliter agere de falso*—zu Inhalt und Bedeutung einer prozessrechtlichen Reform Gratians (*CTh* 9,19,4 A. 376 / 9,20,1 A. 378)." *Tijdschrift voor Rechtsgeschiedenis / Revue d'Histoire du Droit / The Legal History Review* 69: 21–41.

Cossa, G. 2012. "I giuristi e la retorica." In *Dogmengeschichte und historische Individualität der römischen Juristen / Storia dei dogmi e individualità storica dei giuristi romani*, edited by C. Baldus, M. Miglietta, G. Santucci, and E. Stolfi, 299–363. Trent.

Coulton, J. J. 1987. "Roman Aqueducts in Asia Minor." In *Roman Architecture in the Greek World*, edited by S. Macready and F. H. Thompson, 72–84. London.

Courtils, J. des, L. Cavalier, and S. Lemaître. 2015. "Le rempart de Xanthos. Recherches 1993–2010." In *Turm und Tor. Siedlungsstrukturen in Lykien und benachbarten Kulturlandschaften*, edited by B. Beck-Brandt, S. Ladstätter, and B. Yener-Marksteiner, 103–178. Vienna.

Cracco Ruggini, L. 2003. "Iatrosofistica pagana, 'filosophia' christiana e medicina (IV-VI secolo)." In Consuetudinis Amor: *Fragments d'histoire romaine (II^e-VI^e siècles) offerts à Jean-Pierre Callu*, edited by F. Chausson and E. Wolff, 189–216. Rome.

Cribiore, R. 1996. *Writing, Teachers, and Students in Greco-Roman Egypt*. Atlanta.

Cribiore, R. 2001. *Gymnastics of the Mind. Greek Education in Hellenistic and Roman Egypt*. Princeton.

Cribiore, R. 2007. *The School of Libanius in Late Antique Antioch*. Princeton.

Cribiore, R. 2009. "The Value of a Good Education: Libanius and Public Authority." In *A Companion to Late Antiquity*, edited by P. Rousseau, 233–245. Chichester.

Cristofoli, R. 2002. *Dopo Cesare. La scena politica romana all'indomani del cesaricidio*. Naples.

Crook, J. A. 1993. "Once Again the *Controversiae* and the Roman Law." In Multarum Artium Scientia: *A "Chose" for R. Godfrey Tanner Contributed by his Allies upon Rumours of his Retirement*, edited by K. Lee, C. Mackie, and H. Tarrant, 68–76. Auckland.

Crook, J. A. 1995. *Legal Advocacy in the Roman World*. Ithaca NY.

Crow, J. 2012. "Water and Late Antique Constantinople: 'It Would be Abominable for the Inhabitants of this Beautiful City to be Compelled to Purchase Water.'" In *Two Romes. Rome and Constantinople in Late Antiquity*, edited by L. Grig and G. Kelly, 116–135. New York.

Csillag, P. 1976. *The Augustan Laws on Family Relations*. Budapest.

Czajkowski, K., and B. Eckhardt eds. 2020. *Law in the Roman Provinces*. Oxford.

D'Andria, F. 2011. "Gods and Amazons in the Nymphaea of Hierapolis." In *Roman Sculpture in Asia Minor*, edited by F. D'Andria and I. Romeo, 150–172. Portsmouth RI.

Dagron, G. 1978. *Vie et miracles de Sainte Thècle*. Brussels.

Dahlheim, W. 1996 [2005]. "Die Iden des März 44 v. Chr." In *Das Attentat in der Geschichte*, edited by A. Demandt, 39–59. (Cologne, 1996). Reprinted in W. Dahlheim, *Julius Caesar. Die Ehre des Kriegers und die Not des Staates*, 218–257 (Paderborn, 2005).

Daly, L. W. 1950. "Roman Study Abroad." *American Journal of Philology* 71: 40–58.

Danesi Marioni, G. 2011–2012. "Lo spettacolo della crudeltà. Mutilazioni e torture in due *Controversiae* (10, 4 e 5) di Seneca Retore (e nel cinema di oggi)." *Quaderni di Anazetesis* 9: 17–45.

Daniels, C. 1983. "Town Defences in Roman North Africa: A Tentative Historical Survey." In *Roman Urban Defences in the West*, edited by J. Maloney and B. Hobley, 5–19. London.

Daube, D. 1953. "Actions between *Paterfamilias* and *Filiusfamilias* with *Peculium Castrense*." In *Studi in Memoria di Emilio Albertario*, edited by V. Arangio-Ruiz and G. Lavaggi, vol. 1, 433–474. Milan.

Daube, D. 1991 [1951]. "*Ne quid infamandi causa fiat*. The Roman Law of Defamation." In D. Daube, *Collected Studies in Roman Law*, edited by D. Cohen and D. Simon, vol. 1, 465–500

(Frankfurt, 1991). Reprinted from *Atti del congresso internazionale di diritto romano e di storia del diritto: Verona 27-28-29-IX-1948*, edited by G. Moschetti, vol. 3, 413–450 (Milan, 1951).

David, J.-M. 1992. *Le patronat judiciaire au dernier siècle de la république romaine.* Rome.

De Hoz, M. P. 2007. "Testimonios epigráficos sobre la educación griega de época imperial." In *Escuela y literatura en Grecia Antigua*, edited by J. A. Fernández Delgado, F. Pordomingo, and A. Stramaglia, 307–332. Cassino.

De Salvo, L. 2001. "Libanio e i tiranni (a proposito di Lib. *or.* 57, 51 ss)." *Mediterraneo Antico* 4: 631–645.

De Staebler, P. D. 2007. *The City Wall of Aphrodisias and Civic Identity in Late Antique Asia Minor.* Unpublished PhD dissertation, Institute of Fine Arts, New York University.

Del Corso, L. 2007. "Le pratiche scholastiche nelle testimonianze epigrafiche di età ellenistica." In *Escuela y literatura en Grecia Antigua*, edited by J. A. Fernández Delgado, F. Pordomingo, and A. Stramaglia, 141–190. Cassino.

Della Valle, G. 1958. "Moenia." *Rendiconti della Accademia di Archeologia Lettere e Belle Arti di Napoli* 33: 167–176.

Delorme, J. 1960. Gymnasion. *Étude sur les monuments consacrés à l'éducation en Grèce.* Paris.

Desanti, L. 1986. "Costantino, il ratto e il matrimonio riparatore." *Studia et Documenta Historiae et Iuris* 52: 195–217.

Desanti, L. 1987. "Giustiniano e il ratto." *Annali dell'Università di Ferrara; n.s.; sezione 5: scienze giuridiche* 1: 187–201.

Desanti, L. 1988. "Osservazioni sul matrimonio riparatore nelle fonti retoriche e nelle fonti giuridice." *Atti del III seminario romanistico gardesano*, 319–330. Milan.

Desbordes, F. 1993. "Le texte caché: problèmes figurés dans la déclamation latine." *Revue des études latines* 71: 73–86.

Dessales, H. 2004. "Les fontaines privées de la Gaule romaine. Le adoption de modèles venus de Rome?" *Dossiers d'archéologie* 295: 20–29.

Dettenhofer, M. H. 1992. Perdita Iuventus. *Zwischen den Generationen von Caesar und Augustus.* Munich.

Devreker, J. and M. Waelkens. 1984. *Les fouilles de la Rijksuniversiteit te Gent a Pessinonte, 1967–1973, I.* Bruges.

Dey, H. [W.] 2010. "Art, Ceremony, and City Walls: The Aesthetics of Imperial Resurgence in the Late Roman West." *Journal of Late Antiquity* 3: 3–37.

Dey, H. W. 2011. *The Aurelian Wall and the Refashioning of Imperial Rome, AD 271–855.* Cambridge.

Dey, H. [W.] 2012. "*Spolia*, Milestones and City Walls: The Politics of Imperial Legitimacy in Gaul." In *Patrons and Viewers in Late Antiquity*, edited by S. Birk and B. Poulsen, 291–310. Aarhus.

Di Ottavio, D. 2009. "Sui precedenti retorici della '*querela inofficiosi testamenti*' nel I sec. a.C." *Index* 37: 293–317.

Di Ottavio, D. 2012a. "Una bibliografia ragionata in tema di *querela inofficiosi testamenti*: schede di lettura." In *Scritti di storia del diritto e bibliografia giuridica offerti a Giuliano Bonfanti*, edited by U. Petronio and O. Diliberto, 81–220. Macerata.

Di Ottavio, D. 2012b. *Richerche in tema di "querela inofficiosi testamenti" I. Le origini.* Naples.

Dickey, E. 2012–2015. *The* Colloquia *of the* Hermeneumata Pseudodositheana. 2 vols. Cambridge.

Diels, H. 1904. Laterculi Alexandrini *aus einem Papyrus ptolemäischer Zeit. Abhandlungen der königlich Preussischen Akademie der Wissenschaften. Phil.-Hist. Klasse* 2: 1–16.

Diliberto, O. 1984. *Studi sulle origini della "cura furiosi."* Naples.

Dillon, J. N. 2012. *The Justice of Constantine: Law, Communication, and Control.* Ann Arbor.

Dingel, J. 1988. Scholastica Materia: *Untersuchungen zu den* Declamationes minores *und der* Institutio oratoria *Quintilians.* Berlin.

Dixon, S. 2001. "Rape in Roman Law and Myth." In S. Dixon, *Reading Roman Women. Sources, Genres and Real Life,* 45–55. London.

Dobesch, G. 1971 [2001]. "Nahm Caesar die ihm verliehene Leibwache von Senatoren und Rittern an? Zum Text von Dio XLIV 7,4." *Jahreshefte des Österreichischen Archäologischen Institutes in Wien, Beiheft* 49.2 (1971) 61–64. Reprinted in G. Dobesch, *Ausgewählte Schriften,* edited by H. Heftner and K. Tomaschitz, vol. 1, 427–432 (Cologne, 2001).

Dobesch, G. 1978 [2001]. "Nikolaos von Damaskus und die Selbstbiographie des Augustus." *Grazer Beiträge. Zeitschrift für die klassische Altertumswissenschaft* 7 (1978) 91–174. Reprinted in G. Dobesch, *Ausgewählte Schriften,* edited by H. Heftner and K. Tomaschitz, vol. 1, 205–273 (Cologne, 2001).

Dodds, E. R. 1959. *Plato* Gorgias. Oxford.

Dolganov, A. 2020. "*Nutricula causidicorum.* Legal Practitioners in Roman North Africa." In *Law in the Roman Provinces,* edited by K. Czajkowski and B. Eckhardt, 358–416. Oxford.

Dominik, W. and J. Hall eds. 2007. *A Companion to Roman Rhetoric.* Malden MA.

Donadio, N. 2012. "*Iudicium domesticum,* riprovazione sociale e persecuzione pubblica di atti commessi da sottoposti alla *patria potestas.*" *Index* 40: 175–195.

Donié, P. 1996. *Untersuchungen zum Caesarbild in der römischen Kaiserzeit.* Hamburg.

Dorl-Klingenschmid, C. 2001. *Prunkbrunnen in kleinasiatischen Städten: Funktion im Kontext.* Munich.

Dorl-Klingenschmid, C. 2006. "Brunnenbauten als Medium des interkommunalen Wettbewerbs." In Cura Aquarum *in Ephesus,* edited by G. Wiplinger, vol. 2, 381–386. Louvain.

D'Ors, X. 1995. "Una recapitulacion sobre XII Tablas V.7a: '*si furiosus escit.*'" *Revista de Estudios Histórico-Juridicos (Sección Derecho Romano)* 17: 131–145.

Doukellis, P. N. 1995. *Libanios et la terre: discours et idéologie politique.* Beirut.

Downey, G. 1937. "The Architectural Significance of the Use of the Words *Stoa* and *Basilike* in Classical Literature." *American Journal of Archaeology* 41: 194–211.

Downey, G. 1938. "Imperial Building Records in Malalas." *Byzantinische Zeitschrift* 38: 1–15, 299–311.

Downey, G. 1959. "Libanius' *Oration in Praise of Antioch* (*Oration* XI)." *Proceedings of the American Philosophical Society* 103: 652–686.

Downey, G. 1961. *A History of Antioch in Syria from Seleucus to the Arab Conquest.* Princeton.

Drecoll, C. 2004. "Sophisten und Archonten: *Paideia* als gesellschaftliches Argument bei Libanios," In Paideia: *The World of the Second Sophistic,* edited by B. E. Borg, 403–417. Berlin.

Drossart, P. 1970. "Le psychodrame des Ides de Mars." *Bulletin de l'Association Guillaume Budé,* 4th ser. nr. 3: 375–389.

Drumann, W. and P. Groebe 1906 [1837]. *Geschichte Roms in seinem Übergange von der republikanischen zur monarchischen Verfassung oder Pompeius, Caesar, Cicero und ihre Zeitgenossen nach Geschlechtern und mit genealogischen Tabellen*, vol. 3 (2nd ed., Leipzig, 1906 [1st ed. Königsberg, 1837]).

Du Plessis, P. J., C. Ando, and K. Tuori eds. 2016. *The Oxford Handbook of Roman Law and Society*. Oxford.

Ducos, M. 2008. "L'enseignement du droit dans le monde romain." In *L'enseignement supérieur dans les mondes antiques et médiévaux*, edited by H. Hugonnard-Roche, 13–28. Paris.

Ducos, M. 2014. *Les Romains et la loi. Recherches sur les rapports de la philosophie grecque et de la tradition romaine à la fin de la République*. Paris.

Ducrey, P. 1995. "La muraille est-elle un élément constitutif d'une cité?" In *Sources for the Ancient Greek City-State*, edited by M. H. Hansen, 245–256. Copenhagen.

Düll, R. 1943. "*Iudicium domesticum, abdicatio* und *apoceryxis*." *Zeitschrift der Savigny-Stiftung für Rechtsgeschichte, Romanistische Abteilung* 63: 54–116.

Düll, R. 1971. "Bruchstücke verschollener römischer Gesetze und Rechtssätze." In *Studi in onore di Edoardo Volterra*, vol. 1, 113–139. Milan.

Dugan, J. 2005. *Making a New Man. Ciceronian Self-Fashioning in the Rhetorical Works*. Oxford.

Dugan, J. 2007. "Modern Critical Approaches to Roman Rhetoric." In *A Companion to Roman Rhetoric*, edited by W. Dominik and J. Hall, 9–22. Malden MA.

Dunkle, J. R. 1967. "The Greek Tyrant and Roman Political Invective of the Late Republic." *Transactions of the American Philological Association* 98: 151–171.

Dunkle, J. R. 1971. "The Rhetorical Tyrant in Roman Historiography: Sallust, Livy, and Tacitus." *Classical World* 65: 12–20.

Dupont, C. 1955. *Le droit criminel dans les constitutions de Constantin: les peines*. Lille.

Durrell, G. 1959 [1956]. *My Family and Other Animals* (Harmondsworth, 1959 [London, 1956]).

Eck, W. 2000. "Latein als Sprache politischer Kommunikation in Städten der östlichen Provinzen." *Chiron* 30: 641–660.

Eck, W. 2009. "The Presence, Role and Significance of Latin in the Epigraphy and Culture of the Roman Near East." In *From Hellenism to Islam. Cultural and Linguistic Change in the Roman Near East*, edited by H. M. Cotton, R. G. Hoyland, J. J. Price, and D. J. Wasserman, 15–42. Cambridge.

Edmondson, J. 2008. "Public Dress and Social Control in Late Republican and Early Imperial Rome." In *Roman Dress and the Fabrics of Roman Culture*, edited by J. Edmondson and A. Keith, 21–46. Toronto.

Eich, P. and A. Eich 2004. "Thesen zur Genese des Verlautbarungsstils des spätantiken kaiserlichen Zentrale." *Tyche* 19: 75–104.

Eisenberg, M. 2016. "Graeco-Roman *Poliorketics* and the Development of Military Architecture in Antiochia Hippos of the Decapolis as a Test Case." In *Focus on Fortifications. New Research on Fortifications in the Ancient Mediterranean and the Near East*, edited by R. Frederiksen, S. Müth, P. I. Schneider, and M. Schnelle, 609–622. Oxford.

Engels, D. 2013. "'L'étendue de la cité est une objet que l'homme politique ne doit pas négliger'. Les critiques de la mégapole dans l'Antiquité méditerranéenne." *Latomus* 72: 1055–1085.

Epstein, D. F. 1987. "Caesar's Personal Enemies on the Ides of March." *Latomus* 46: 566–570.

Esmonde Cleary, S. 2003. "Civil Defences in the West under the High Empire." In *The Archaeology of Roman Towns. Studies in Honour of John S. Wacher*, edited by P. Wilson, 73–85. Oxford.

Esmonde Cleary, S. 2007. "Fortificación urbana en la *Britannia* Romana: ¿Defensa militar o monumento cívico?" In *Murallas de ciudades romanas en el occidente del Imperio: Lucus Augusti como paradigma*, edited by A. Rodríguez Colmenero and I. Rodá de Llanza, 155–165. Lugo. Original English version, "Urban Fortifications in Roman Britain: Military Defence or Civic Monument?" https://www.academia.edu/31676236/Urban_Fortification_in_Roman_Britain_military_defence_or_civic_monument.

Étienne, R. 1973. *Les Ides de Mars. L'assassinat de César ou de la dictature?* Paris.

Evans, R. 2005. "Geography without People: Mapping in Pliny *Historia Naturalis* Books 3–6." *Ramus* 34: 47–74.

Evans-Grubbs, J. 1989. "Abduction Marriage in Antiquity: A Law of Constantine (*CTh* IX.24.1) and its Social Context." *Journal of Roman Studies* 79: 59–83.

Evans Grubbs, J. 1995. *Law and Family in Late Antiquity: The Emperor Constantine's Marriage Legislation*. Oxford.

Evans Grubbs, J. 2011. "Promoting *Pietas* through Roman Law." In *A Companion to Families in the Greek and Roman Worlds*, edited by B. Rawson, 377–392. Chichester.

Fagan, G. G. 1999. *Bathing in Public in the Roman World*. Ann Arbor.

Fagan, G. G. 2011. "Violence in Roman Social Relations." In *The Oxford Handbook of Social Relations in the Roman World*, edited by M. Peachin, 467–495. New York.

Fairweather, J. 1981. *Seneca the Elder*. Cambridge.

Fantham, E. 2002 [2011]. "Quintilian on the Uses and Methods of Declamation." In *Hispania terris omnibus felicior. Premesse ed esiti di un processo di integrazione*, edited by G. Urso, 271–280 (Pisa, 2002). Reprinted in E. Fantham, *Roman Readings. Roman Response to Greek Literature from Plautus to Statius and Quintilian*, 320–330 (Berlin, 2011).

Fantham, E. 2009. "Rhetoric and Ovid's Poetry." In *A Companion to Ovid*, edited by P. E. Knox, 26–44. Chichester.

Fantham, E. 2011 [2004]. "Disowning and Dysfunction in the Declamatory Family." In E. Fantham, *Roman Readings: Roman Response to Greek Literature from Plautus to Statius and Quintilian*, edited by E. Fantham, 302–319 (Berlin, 2011). Reprinted from *Materiali e discussioni per l'analisi dei testi classici* 53 (2004) 65–82.

Favreau, A.-M. 2015. "Les pirates entre roman et déclamation." In *Présence de la déclamation antique (controverses et suasoires)*, edited by R. Poignault and C. Schneider, 257–284. Clermont-Ferrand.

Fayer, C. 1994–2005. *La familia romana. Aspetti giuridici antiquari*. 3 vols. Rome.

Feddern, S. 2013. *Die Suasorien des älteren Seneca*. Berlin.

Felber, D. 1961. "Caesars Streben nach der Königswürde." In *Einzeluntersuchungen zur altitalischen Geschichte*, edited by F. Altheim and D. Felber, 211–284. Frankfurt.

Fenster, E. 1968. Laudes Constantinopolitanae. Munich.

Fernández Delgado, J. A. 2007. "Influencia literaria de los *progymnasmata*." In *Escuela y literatura en Grecia Antigua*, edited by J. A. Fernández Delgado, F. Pordomingo, and A. Stramaglia, 273–306. Cassino.

Fernández López, J. 2005. "Mujeres en sofistópolis: estereotipos femeninos en la declamación romana." In *Las hijas de Pandora: historia, tradición y simbología*, edited by I. M. Calero Secall and V. Alfaro Bech, 241–254. Málaga.

Fernoux, H.-L. 2011. *Le demos et la cité. Communautés et assemblées populaires en Asie Mineure à l'époque impériale.* Rennes.

Festugière, A. J. 1959. *Antioche païenne et chrétienne. Libanius, Chrysostome et les moines de Syrie.* Paris.

Février, P. A. 1969. "Enceinte et colonie (de Nîmes à Vérone, Toulouse et Tipasa)." *Rivista di studi liguri* 35: 277–286.

Fiori, R. 2011. Bonus vir. *Politica filosofia retorica e diritto nel de officiis di Cicerone.* Naples.

Fish, J. 2011. "Not all Politicians are Sisyphus: What Roman Epicureans were Taught about Politics." In *Epicurus and the Epicurean Tradition*, edited by J. Fish and K. R. Sanders, 72–104. Cambridge.

Flamerie de Lachapelle, G. 2011. Clementia. *Recherches sur la notion de clémence à Rome, du début du 1er siècle a.C. à la mort d'Auguste.* Paris.

Fleskes, W. 1914. *Vermischte Beiträge zum literarischen Porträt des Tyrannen im Anschluss an die Deklamationen.* Bonn.

Fleury, P. 2006. *Lectures de Fronton. Un rhéteur latin à l'époque de la Seconde Sophistique.* Paris.

Flinterman, J.-J. 1995. *Power,* Paideia *and Pythagoreanism. Greek Identity, Conceptions of the Relationship between Philosophers and Monarchs and Political Ideas in Philostratus'* Life of Apollonius. Amsterdam.

Flinterman, J.-J. 2004. "Sophists and Emperors: A Reconnaissance of Sophistic Attitudes." In Paideia: *The World of the Second Sophistic*, edited by B. E. Borg, 359–376. Berlin.

Focke, F. 1923. "*Synkrisis.*" *Hermes* 58: 327–368.

Fortenbaugh, W. W. 1996. "On the Composition of Aristotle's Rhetoric." In *ΛHNAIKA. Festschrift für Carl Werner Müller*, edited by C. Mueller-Goldingen and K. Sier, 165–188. Stuttgart.

Fournier, J. 2010. *Entre tutelle romaine et autonomie civique. L'administration judiciaire dans les provinces hellénophones de l'empire romain (129 av. J.-C.—235 apr. J.-C.).* Paris.

Frakes, R. M. 2001. Contra potentium iniurias: *The* Defensor Civitatis *and Late Roman Justice.* Munich.

Frakes, R. M. 2018. "The *Defensor Civitatis* and the Late Roman City." *Antiquité tardive* 26: 127–147.

Francesio, M. 2004. *L'idea di città in Libanio.* Stuttgart.

Franchet d'Espèrey, S. 2016. "La *controversia figurata* chez Quintilien (*Inst.* 9.2.65–99). Quelle figure pour quel plaisir?" In *Reading Roman Declamation. The Declamations Ascribed to Quintilian*, edited by M. T. Dinter, C. Guérin, and M. Martinho, 51–90. Berlin.

Franco, C. 2005. *Elio Aristide e Smirne.* Rome.

Franco, C. 2008. "Aelius Aristides and Rhodes: Concord and Consolation." In *Aelius Aristides between Greece, Rome, and the Gods*, edited by W. H. Harris and B. Holmes, 217–249. Leiden.

Frazel, T. D. 2009. *The Rhetoric of Cicero's* In Verrem. Göttingen.

Frere, S. S. 1984. "British Urban Defences in Earthwork." *Britannia* 15: 63–74.

Friedel, H. 1937. *Der Tyrannenmord in Gesetzgebung und Volksmeinung der Griechen.* Stuttgart.

Friend, C. 1999. "Pirates, Seducers, Wronged Heirs, Poison Cups, Cruel Husbands, and other Calamities: The Roman School Declamations and Critical Pedagogy." *Rhetoric Review* 17.2: 300–320.

Frier, B. W. 1982–1983. "Bees and Lawyers." *Classical Journal* 78: 105–114.

Frier, B. W. 1994. "Why did the Jurists Change Roman Law? Bees and Lawyers Revisited." *Index* 22: 135–149.

Fron, C. 2017. "Der ewige Wettkampf. Zur Konkurrenz unter kaiserzeitlichen Sophisten." In *Sophisten in Hellenismus und Kaiserzeit. Orte, Methoden und Personen der Bildungsvermittlung,* edited by B. Wyss, R. Hirsch-Luipold, and S.-J. Hirschi, 159–176. Tübingen.

Fuhrmann, C. J. 2015. "Dio Chrysostom as a Local Politician: A Critical Reappraisal." In *Aspects of Ancient Institutions and Geography. Studies in Honor of Richard J. A. Talbert,* edited by L. L. Brice and D. Slootjes, 161–176. Leiden.

Gaebel, R. E. 1969–1970. "The Greek Word-Lists to Vergil and Cicero." *Bulletin of the John Rylands Library* 52: 284–325.

Gaines, R. N. 2007. "Roman Rhetorical Handbooks." In *A Companion to Roman Rhetoric,* edited by W. Dominik and J. Hall, 163–180. Malden MA.

Galand, P., F. Hallyn, C. Lévy, and W. Verbaal. 2010. *Quintilien. Ancien et moderne.* Turnhout.

Gans, U.-W. 2005. "Zur Datierung der römischen Stadtmauer von Köln und zu den farbigen Steinornamenten in Gallien und Germanien." *Jahrbuch des Römisch-Germanischen Zentralmuseums Mainz* 52: 211–236.

Garofalo, L. 1992. *La persecuzione dello stellionato in diritto romano.* Padua.

Garofalo, L. 2008 [2000] [2001]. "*Stellionatus*: Storia di una parola." In L. Garofalo, *Piccoli scritti di diritto penale romano,* 125–153 (Milan, 2008). Reprinted from *Archivio giuridico* 220 (2000) 415–452 and "Scientia Iuris" *e linguaggio nel sistema giuridico romano,* edited by F. Sini and R. Ortu, 195–229 (Milan, 2001).

Gaudemet, J. 1953. "'*Testamenta ingrata et pietas Augusti.*' Contribution à l'étude du sentiment impérial." In *Studi in onore di Vincenzo Arangio-Ruiz nel XLV anno del suo insegnamento,* vol. 3, 115–137. Naples.

Gelzer, M. 1918. "M. Junius Brutus, der Caesarmörder" = "Junius nr. 53," *RE* X.1 cols. 973–1020.

Gelzer, M. 1968 (1960). *Caesar, Politician and Statesman* (Cambridge MA, 1968). Translated by P. Needham from *Caesar, Politiker und Staatsman* (6th ed., Wiesbaden, 1960).

Genzmer, E. 1942. "Talion in klassischen und nachklassischen Recht? Erwägungen über Ursprung und Grundgedanken des Edikts *Quod quisque juris in alterum statuerit, ut ipse eodem jure utatur.*" *Zeitschrift der Savigny-Stiftung für Rechtsgeschichte, Romanistische Abteilung* 62: 122–142.

Gering, J. 2012. *Domitian, dominus et deus? Herrschafts- und Machtstrukturen im römischen Reich zur Zeit des letzten Flaviers.* Rahden.

Gesche, H. 1976. *Caesar.* Erträge der Forschung 51. Darmstadt.

Gibson, C. A. 2008. *Libanius's Progymnasmata: Model Exercises in Greek Prose Composition and Rhetoric.* Atlanta.

Gibson, C. A. 2013. "Doctors in Ancient Greek and Roman Rhetorical Education." *Journal of the History of Medicine* 68: 529–550.

Gibson, C. A. 2014. "Better Living through Prose Composition? Moral and Compositional Pedagogy in Ancient Greek and Roman *progymnasmata.*" *Rhetorica* 32: 1–30.

Gildenhard, I. 2006. "Reckoning with Tyranny: Greek Thoughts on Caesar in Cicero's *Letters to Atticus* in Early 49." In *Ancient Tyranny,* edited by S. Lewis, 197–209. Edinburgh.

Gildenhard, I. 2011. *Creative Eloquence. The Construction of Reality in Cicero's Speeches*. Oxford.

Giltaij, J. 2016. "Greek Philosophy and Classical Roman Law, a Brief Overview." In *The Oxford Handbook of Law and Society*, edited by P. J. Du Plessis, C. Ando, and K. Tuori, 188–199. Oxford.

Giomaro, A. M. 2003. *Per lo studio della* calumnia. *Aspetti di "deontologia" processuale in Roma antica*. Turin.

Giorgini, G. 2009. "Plato and the Ailing Soul of the Tyrant." In *Le philosophe, le roi, le tyran*, edited by S. Gastaldi and J.-F. Pradeau, 111–127. Sankt Augustin.

Glaser, F. 1983. *Antike Brunnenbauten (KPHNAI) in Griechenland*. Vienna.

Gleason, M. W. 1995. *Making Men. Sophists and Self-Presentation in Ancient Rome*. Princeton.

Gleason, M. W. 2009. "Shock and Awe: The Performance Dimension of Galen's Anatomy Demonstrations." In *Galen and the World of Knowledge*, edited by C. Gill, T. Whitmarsh, and J. Wilkins, 85–114. Cambridge.

Gliwitzky, C. 2010. *Späte Blüte in Side und Perge. Die pamphylische Bauornamentik des 3. Jahrhunderts n. Chr.* Bern.

Goffin, B. 2002. *Euergetismus in Oberitalien*. Bonn.

Goldhill, S. 2009. "Rhetoric and the Second Sophistic." In *The Cambridge Companion to Ancient Rhetoric*, edited by E. Gunderson, 228–241. Cambridge.

Gómez Araujo, L. 2010. "El agua y las termas en la ciudad romana: el caso de Itálica (Santiponce, Sevilla)." In *Actas del II Coloquio Internacional Irrigación, Energía y Abastecimento de Agua: La cultura del agua en el Arco Mediterráneo*, edited by J. Sobrino Simal and L. Cervera Pozo, 65–86. Alcalá de Guadaira.

Goodman, P. J. 2007. *The Roman City and its Periphery*. London.

Goria, F. 1987. "Ratto (dir. rom.)." In *Enciclopedia del diritto*, edited by F. Calasso, 38: 707–724. Milan.

Gorrie, C. 2001. "The Septizodium of Septimius Severus Revisited: The Monument in its Historical and Urban Context." *Latomus* 60: 653–670.

Gotter, U. 1996. *Der Diktator ist tot! Politik in Rom zwischen den Iden des März und der Begründung des Zweiten Triumvirats*. Stuttgart.

Goudineau, C. 1980. "Les villes de la paix romaine." In *Histoire de la France urbaine*, edited by G. Duby, vol. 1, 232–390. Paris.

Graindor, P. 1930. *Un milliardaire antique. Hérode Atticus et sa famille*. Cairo.

Grelle, F. 1980. "La 'correctio morum' nella legislazione flavia." *Aufstieg und Niedergang der römischen Welt* II.13: 340–365.

Greschat, K. 2018. "'Early Impressions are Hard to Eradicate from the Mind.' The Lasting Influence of Domestic Education in Western Late Antiquity." In *Teachers in Late Antique Christianity*, edited by P. Gemeinhardt, O. Lorgeoux, and M. Munkholt Christensen, 165–183. Tübingen.

Grey, C. 2008. "Two Young Lovers: An Abduction Marriage and its Consequences in Fifth-Century Gaul." *Classical Quarterly* 58: 286–302.

Griffin, J. 1985 [1976]. "Augustan Poetry and the Life of Luxury." In J. Griffin, *Latin Poets and Roman Life*, 1–31. (London, 1985). Reprinted from *Journal of Roman Studies* 66 (1976) 87–105.

Griffin, J. 1985 [1981]. "Genre and Real Life in Latin Poetry." In J. Griffin, *Latin Poets and Roman Life*, 48–64 (London, 1985). Reprinted from *Journal of Roman Studies* 71 (1981) 39–49.

Griffin, M. 1976. *Seneca. A Philosopher in Politics*. Oxford.

Griffin, M. 1989 [1997]. "Philosophy, Politics, and Politicians at Rome." In Philosophia Togata. *Essays on Philosophy and Roman Society*, edited by M. Griffin and J. Barnes, 1–37 (Oxford, 1989). Reprinted as Philosophia Togata I. *Essays on Philosophy and Roman Society*, 1–37 (Oxford, 1997).

Grimaldi, W. M. A. 1996. "How Do We Get From Corax-Tisias to Plato-Aristotle in Greek Rhetorical Theory?" In *Theory, Text, Context. Issues in Greek Rhetoric and Oratory*, edited by C. L. Johnstone, 19–43. Albany NY.

Grisé, Y. 1982. *Le suicide dans la Rome antique*. Montreal.

Grodzynski, D. 1984. "Ravies et Coupables. Un essai d'interprétation de la loi IX, 24, 1 du Code Théodosien." *Mélanges de l'École française de Rome* 96: 697–726.

Gros, P. 1992. "*Moenia*: aspects défensifs et aspects représentatifs des fortifications." In Fortificationes antiquae, edited by S. Van de Maele and J. M. Fossey, 211–225. Amsterdam.

Gros, P. 1996. *L'architecture romaine de début du III$^e$ siècle av. J.-C. à la fin du Haut-Empire I. Les monuments publics*. Paris.

Gros, P. 2016. "L'évergétisme édilitaire au temps de la seconde sophistique: le cas d'Éphèse." *Revue archéologique* 62: 329–360.

Gselle, S. 1894. *Essai sur le règne de l'empereur Domitien*. Paris.

Guast, W. 2018. "Lucian and Declamation." *Classical Philology* 113: 189–205.

Guast, W. 2019. "Greek Declamation Beyond Philostratus' Second Sophistic." *Journal of Hellenic Studies* 139: 172–186.

Guillaumet, J.-P. and A. Rebourg. 1987. "L'enceinte d'Autun." In *Les enceintes Augustéennes dans l'Occident romain (France, Italie, Espagne, Afrique du Nord)*, edited by M.-G. Colin, 41–49. Nîmes.

Gunderson, E. 1998. "Discovering the Body in Roman Oratory." In *Parchments of Gender: Deciphering the Bodies of Antiquity*, edited by M. Wyke, 169–189. Oxford.

Gunderson, E. 2000. *Staging Masculinity. The Rhetoric of Performance in the Roman World*. Ann Arbor.

Gunderson, E. 2003. *Declamation, Paternity, and Roman Identity*. Cambridge.

Gunderson, E. 2016. "Declamatory Play." In *Fabrique de la déclamation antique (controverses et suasoires)*, edited by R. Poignault and C. Schneider, 179–195. Lyon.

Haase, R. 1994. "Justinian I. und der Frauenraub (*raptus*)." *Zeitschrift der Savigny-Stiftung für Rechtsgeschichte, Romanistische Abteilung* 111: 458–470.

Habinek, T. 2005. *Ancient Rhetoric and Oratory*. Malden MA.

Hadot, I. 2005 [1984]. *Arts libéraux et philosophie dans la pensée antique* (2nd ed., Paris, 2005 with addenda pp. 309–494 [1st ed., Paris, 1984]).

Haehling, R. von 2000. "*Rex* und *Tyrannus*. Begriffe und Herrscherbilder der römischen Antike." In Basileus *und* Tyrann. Herrscherbilder und Bilder von Herrschaft in der Englischen Renaissance, edited by U. Baumann, 13–33. Frankfurt.

Haensch, R. 2012. "*Arx imperii*? Der Palast auf dem Palatin als das politisch-administrative Zentrum in der Reichshauptstadt Rom nach dem Zeugnis der schriftlichen Quellen." In

*Politische Räume in vormodernen Gesellschaften. Gestaltung—Wahrnehmung—Funktion*, edited by O. Dally, F. Fless, R. Haensch, F. Pirson, and S. Sievers, 267–276. Rahden.

Hagel, S. and T. Lynch. 2015. "Musical Education in Greece and Rome." In *A Companion to Ancient Education*, edited by W. M. Bloomer, 401–412. Chichester.

Hagemann, M. 1998. Iniuria. *Von den XII-Tafeln bis zur Justinianischen Kodifikation*. Cologne.

Håkanson, L. 1986. "Die quintilianischen Deklamationen in der neueren Forschung." *Aufstieg und Niedergang der römischen Welt* II.32.4: 2272–2306.

Håkanson, L. 2014. "Der Satzrhythmus der 19 Größeren Deklamationen und des Calpurnius Flaccus." In L. Håkanson, *Unveröffentlichte Schriften I*, edited by B. Santorelli, 47–130. Berlin.

Halbwachs, V. 2014. "*Haec disceptatio in factum constitit*: Bemerkungen zur *Pietas* im römischen Unterhaltsrecht." In Meditationes in iure et historia. *Essays in Honour of Laurens Winkel*, edited by R. van den Bergh, G. van Niekerk, P. Pichonnaz, P. J. Thomas, D. G. Kleyn, F. Lucrezi, and J. Mutton, vol. 1, 371–382. Pretoria.

Hall, J. 2014. *Cicero's Use of Judicial Theater*. Ann Arbor.

Hansen, M. H. and T. H. Nielsen. 2004. "City Walls as Evidence for *Polis* Identity." In *An Inventory of Archaic and Classical Poleis*, edited by M. H. Hansen and T. H. Nielsen, 135–137. Oxford.

Harries, J. 1988. "The Imperial Quaestor from Constantine to Theodosius II." *Journal of Roman Studies* 78: 148–172.

Harries, J. 1999. *Law and Empire in Late Antiquity*. Cambridge.

Harries, J. 2006. *Cicero and the Jurists. From Citzens' Law to the Lawful State*. London.

Harries, J. 2016. "Legal Education and Training of Lawyers." In *The Oxford Handbook of Roman Law and Society*, edited by P. J. Du Plessis, C. Ando, and K. Tuori, 151–175. Oxford.

Harris, E. M. 2012. "*Hypotheca* in Roman Law and ὑποθήκη in Greek Law." In *Transferts culturels et droits dans le monde grec et hellénistique*, edited by B. Legras, 433–441. Paris.

Harris, W. V. 1986. "The Roman Father's Power of Life and Death." In *Studies in Roman Law in Memory of A. Arthur Schiller*, edited by R. S. Bagnall and W. V. Harris, 81–95. Leiden.

Harris, W. V. 1989. *Ancient Literacy*. Cambridge MA.

Hawley, R. 1995. "Female Characterization in Greek Declamation." In *Ethics and Rhetoric. Classical Essays for Donald Russell on his Seventy-Fifth Birthday*, edited by D. C. Innes, H. Hine, and C. Pelling, 255–267. Oxford.

Hayne, L. 1971. "Lepidus' Role after the Ides of March." *Acta Classica* 14: 109–117.

Heath, M. 1994. "The Substructure of *Stasis*-Theory from Hermagoras to Hermogenes." *Classical Quarterly* 44: 114–129.

Heath, M. 1995. *Hermogenes. On Issues*. Oxford.

Heath, M. 2002. "Rhetoric in Mid-Antiquity." In *Classics in Progress. Essays on Ancient Greece and Rome*, edited by T. P. Wiseman, 419–439. Oxford.

Heath, M. 2002–2003. "Theon and the History of the *Progymnasmata*." *Greek, Roman, and Byzantine Studies* 43: 129–160.

Heath, M. 2004. *Menander: A Rhetor in Context*. Oxford.

Hedrick, C. W. 2011. "Literature and Communication." In *The Oxford Handbook of Social Relations in the Roman World*, edited by M. Peachin, 167–190. New York.

Heinle, M. 2009. "Stadtbilder im Hellenismus—Wahrnehmung urbaner Strukturen in hellenistischer Zeit." In *Stadtbilder im Hellenismus*, edited by A. Matthaei and M. Zimmermann, 41–69. Berlin.

Heintzeler, G. 1927. *Das Bild des Tyrannen bei Platon. Ein Beitrag zur Geschichte der griechischen Staatsethik.* Stuttgart.

Heinzelmann, M. 2003. "Städtekonkurrenz und kommunaler Bürgersinn. Die Säulenstraße von Perge als Beispiel monumentaler Stadtgestaltung durch kollektiven Euergetismus." *Archäologischer Anzeiger* [no vol.]: 197–220.

Hellegouarc'h, J. 1963. *Le vocabulaire Latin des relations de partis politiques sous la République.* Paris.

Heller, A. 2006. *"Les bêtises des Grecs." Conflits et rivalités entre cités d'Asie et de Bithynie à l'époque romaine (129 a.C.-235 p.C.).* Bordeaux.

Herberger, M. 1981. *Dogmatik. Zur Geschichte von Begriff und Methode in Medizin und Jurisprudenz.* Frankfurt.

Hesberg, H. von 2005. *Römische Baukunst.* Munich.

Heusch, C. 2005. "Die Ethopoiie in der griechischen und lateinischen Antike: Von der rhetorischen *Progymnasma*-Theorie zur literarischen Form." In *ΗΘΟΠΟΙΙΑ. La représentation de caractères entre fiction scolaire et réalité vivante à l'époque impériale et tardive*, edited by E. Amato and J. Schamp, 11–33. Salerno.

Heuss, A. 1971. "Aristoteles als Theoretiker des Totalitarismus." *Antike und Abendland* 17: 1–44.

Higham, T. F. 1958. "Ovid and Rhetoric." In *Ovidiana. Recherches sur Ovide*, edited by N. I. Herescu, 32–48. Paris.

Hillard, T. 2013. "Graffiti's Engagement. The Political Graffiti of the Late Roman Republic." In *Written Space in the Latin West, 200 BC to AD 300*, edited by G. Sears, P. Keegan, and R. Laurence, 105–122. London.

Hömke, N. 2002. *Gesetzt den Fall, ein Geist erscheint. Komposition und Motivik der ps-quintilianischen* Declamationes maiores *X, XIV, und XV.* Heidelberg.

Hömke, N. 2007. "'Not to Win, but to Please': Roman Declamation Beyond Education." In *Papers on Rhetoric VIII. Declamation*, edited by L. Calboli Montefusco, 103–127. Rome.

Hoffman, A. 2000. "Die Stadtmauern der hellenistisch-römischen Dekapolisstadt Gadara. Zusammenfassender Bericht über die seit 1991 durchgeführten Ausgrabungen und Untersuchungen." *Archäologischer Anzeiger* [no vol.]: 176–233.

Hohenlohe, C. 1937. *Einfluß des Christentums auf das* Corpus iuris civilis. Vienna.

Hohmann, H. 1996. "Classical Rhetoric and Roman Law: Reflections on a Debate." *Rhetorik* 15: 15–41.

Holford-Strevens, L. 2003 [1988]. *Aulus Gellius. An Antonine Scholar and his Achievement.* (2nd ed., Oxford 2003 [1st ed., London, 1988]).

Honig, R. M. 1960. Humanitas *und Rhetorik in spätrömischen Kaisergesetzen.* Göttingen.

Honoré, T. 2002. *Ulpian. Pioneer of Human Rights.* 2nd ed. Oxford.

Honoré, T. 1998. *Law in the Crisis of the Empire, 379–455 AD. The Theodosian Dynasty and its Quaestors.* Oxford.

Horsfall, N. 1974. "The Ides of March: Some New Problems." *Greece and Rome* 21: 191–199.

Horsfall, N. 1979. *"Doctus Sermones Utriusque Linguae." Echos du monde classique / Classical News and Views* 23: 79–95.

Horster, M. 2001. *Bauinschriften römischer Kaiser. Untersuchungen zu Inschriftenpraxis und Bautätigkeit in Städten des westlichen Imperium Romanum in der Zeit des Prinzipats.* Stuttgart.

Hulls, J.-M. 2014. "The Mirror in the Text: Privacy, Performance, and the Power of Suetonius' Domitian." In *Suetonius the Biographer. Studies in Roman Lives,* edited by T. Power and R. K. Gibson, 178–196. Oxford.

Humfress, C. 2011. "Law and Custom under Rome." In *Law, Custom, and Justice in Late Antiquity and the Early Middle Ages,* edited by A. Rio, 23–47. London.

Hunt, D. 1993. "Christianizing the Roman Empire: The Evidence of the *Code.*" In *The Theodosian Code,* edited by J. Harries and I. Wood, 143–158. Ithaca NY.

Huskinson, J. 2005. "Rivers of Roman Antioch." In *Personification in the Greek World: From Antiquity to Byzantium,* edited by E. Stafford and J. Herrin, 247–264. Aldershot.

Imber, M. 2001. "Practised Speech. Oral and Written Conventions in Roman Declamation." In *Speaking Volumes. Orality and Literacy in the Greek and Roman World,* edited by J. Watson, 199–216. Leiden.

Imber, M. 2008. "Life Without Father. Declamation and the Construction of Paternity in the Roman Empire." In *Role Models in the Roman World: Identity and Assimilation,* edited by S. Bell and I. L. Hansen, 161–169. Ann Arbor.

Imhoof-Blumer, F. 1924 [1923]. *Fluss- und Meergötter auf griechischen und römischen Münzen* (Geneva, 1924). Reprinted from the *Revue Suisse de Numismatique* 23 (1923) 173–421.

Inglebert, H. 2004. "Éducation et culture chez les Chrétiens de l'Antiquité Tardive." In *Que reste-t-il de l'éducation classique? Relire 'le Marrou': Histoire de l'éducation dans l'Antiquité,* edited by J.-M. Pailler and P. Payen, 333–341. Toulouse.

Innes, D. C. 1985. "Theophrastus and the Theory of Style." In *Theophrastus of Eresus: On his Life and Work,* edited by W. W. Fortenbaugh, P. M. Huby, and A. A. Long, 251–267. New Brunswick NJ.

Isaac, B. 1993. *The Limits of Empire: The Roman Army in the East.* Oxford.

İşkan, H., C. Schuler, Ş. Aktaş, D. Reitzenstein, A. Schmölder-Veit, and M. Koçak eds. 2016. *Patara. Lykiens Tor zur römischen Welt.* Darmstadt.

Jacobs, I. 2009. "Gates in Late Antiquity in the Eastern Mediterranean." *BABESCH* 84: 197–213.

Jacobs, I. and J. Richard. 2012. "'We Surpass the Beautiful Waters of Other Cities by the Abundance of Ours': Reconciling Function and Decoration in Late Antique Fountains." *Journal of Late Antiquity* 5: 3–71.

Jacques, F. 1992. "Les moulins d'Orcistus. Rhétorique et géographie au IVᵉ s." In *Institutions, société et vie politique dans l'empire romain au IVᵉ siécle ap. J.-C.,* edited by M. Christol, S. Demougin, Y. Duval, C. Lepelley, and L. Pietri, 431–446. Rome.

Jakab, É. 2012. "Geld und Sport. Rezeption griechischer Topoi in der römischen Jurisprudenz." *Revue Internationale des droits de l'Antiquité* 59: 93–125.

Janiszewski, P., K. Stebnicka, and E. Szabat. 2015. *Prosopography of Greek Rhetors and Sophists of the Roman Empire.* Oxford.

Jedrkiewicz, S. 2002. "Il tirannicidio nella cultura classica. *Hybris* tirannica e tirannicidio: realtà e rappresentazione." In *Antichità e rivoluzioni da Roma a Costantinopoli a Mosca,* edited by P. Catalano and G. Lobrano, 3–26. Rome.

Jehne, M. 1987. *Der Staat des Dictators Caesar*. Cologne.

Jehne, M. 1998. "Die Ermordung des Dictators Caesar und das Ende der römischen Republik." In *Große Verschwörungen. Staatsstreich und Tyrannensturz von der Antike bis zur Gegenwart*, edited by U. Schultz, 33–47, 256–261. Munich.

Jehne, M. 2005. "History's Alternative Caesars. Julius Caesar and Current Historiography." In *Julius Caesar: New Critical Essays*, edited by H. Zander, 59–70. New York.

Jehne, M. 2009. *Der große Trend, der kleine Sachzwang und das handelnde Individuum. Caesars Entscheidungen*. Munich.

Jehne, M. 2014. *Caesar*, 5th ed. Munich.

Jenkyns, R. 2013. *God, Space, and City in the Roman Imagination*. Oxford.

Jerome, T. S. 1923. *Aspects of the Study of Roman History*. New York.

Johansson, M. 2015. "Nature over Law: Themes of Disowning in Libanius' Declamations." In *Law and Ethics in Greek and Roman Declamation*, edited by E. Amato, F. Citti, and B. Huelsenbeck, 269–286. Berlin.

Johansson, T., and P. Lalander. 2012. "Doing Resistance—Youth and Changing Theories of Resistance." *Journal of Youth Studies* 15: 1078–1088.

Johnstone, M. A. 2015. "Tyrannized Souls: Plato's Depiction of the 'Tyrannical Man.'" *British Journal for the History of Philosophy* 23: 423–437.

Jolowicz, H. F. 1932. "Academic Elements in Roman Law." *The Law Quarterly Review* 48: 171–190.

Jones, A. H. M. 1964. *The Later Roman Empire, 284–602*. 2 vols. Oxford.

Jones, B. and R. Ling. 1993. "6. The Great Nymphaeum." In *The Severan Buildings of Lepcis Magna: An Architectural Survey*, edited by J. B. Ward-Perkins, 79–87. London.

Jones, B. W. 1992. *The Emperor Domitian*. London.

Jones, B. W. 1996. *Suetonius* Domitian. London.

Jones, C. P. 1991. "Aelius Aristides, 'On the Water in Pergamon.'" *Archäologischer Anzeiger* [no vol.]: 111–117.

Jones, C. P. 2004. "Multiple Identities in the Age of the Second Sophistic." In *Paideia: The World of the Second Sophistic*, edited by B. E. Borg, 13–21. Berlin.

Jones, C. P. 2006. "A Letter of Hadrian to Naryka (Eastern Locris)." *Journal of Roman Archaeology* 19: 151–162.

Jones, C. P. 2017. "Strabo and the 'Petty Dynasts.'" In *Auguste et l'Asie Mineure*, edited by L. Cavalier, M.-C. Ferriès, and F. Delrieux, 349–356. Bordeaux.

Jones Hall, L. 2004. *Roman Berytus. Beirut in Late Antiquity*. Abingdon.

Jordović, I. 2011. "Aristotle on Extreme Tyranny and Extreme Democracy." *Historia* 60: 36–64.

Jordović, I. 2019. *Taming Politics. Plato and the Democratic Roots of Tyrannical Man*. Stuttgart.

Jouffroy, H. 1986. *La construction publique en Italie et dans l'Afrique romaine*. Strasbourg.

Jung, K. 2006. "Das *Hydrekdocheion* des Gaius Laecanius Bassus in Ephesos." In Cura Aquarum in Ephesus, edited by G. Wiplinger, vol. 1, 79–86. Louvain.

Kacprzak, A. 2016 "Rhetoric and Roman Law." In *The Oxford Handbook of Law and Society*, edited by P. J. Du Plessis, C. Ando, and K. Tuori, 200–213. Oxford.

Kah, D. and P. Scholz, eds. 2004. *Das hellenistiche Gymnasion*. Berlin.

Kamash, Z. 2010. *Archaeologies of Water in the Roman Near East, 63 BC–AD 636*. Piscataway NJ.

Kamp, A. 1985. "Die aristotelische Theorie der Tyrannis." *Philosophisches Jahrbuch* 92: 17–34.

Kantor, G. 2009. "Knowledge of Law in Roman Asia Minor." In *Selbstdarstellung und Kommunikation. Die Veröffentlichung staatlicher Urkunden auf Stein und Bronze in der römischen Welt*, edited by R. Haensch, 249–265. Munich.

Kantor, G. 2015. "Greek Law under the Romans." In *The Oxford Handbook of Ancient Greek Law*, edited by E. M. Harris and M. Canevaro. https://www.oxfordhandbooks.com/view/10.1093/oxfordhb/9780199599257.001.0001/oxfordhb-9780199599257-e-25.

Kantor, G. 2017. "*Qui in consilio estis*: The Governor and his Advisors in the Early Empire." *Istoricheskij Vestnik* 19: 50–86.

Kapossy, B. 1969. *Brunnenfiguren der hellenistischen und römischen Zeit*. Zurich.

Karlin-Hayter, P. 1992. "Further Notes on Byzantine Marriage: *Raptus*—ἁρπαγή or μνηστείαι?" *Dumbarton Oaks Papers* 46: 133–154.

Karwiese, S. 2006. "*Polis Potamōn*—Stadt der Flüsse. Die Gewässer auf den ephesischen Münzen." In Cura Aquarum *in Ephesus*, edited by G. Wiplinger, vol. 1, 17–22. Louvain.

Kaser, M. 1971 [1955]. *Das römische Privatrecht*, vol. 1 (2nd ed., Munich, 1971 [1st ed., Munich, 1955]).

Kaster, R. A. 1983. "Notes on 'Primary' and 'Secondary' Schools in Late Antiquity." *Transactions of the American Philological Association* 113: 323–346.

Kaster, R. A. 1988. *Guardians of Language: The Grammarian and Society in Late Antiquity*. Berkeley and Los Angeles.

Kaster, R. A. 1995. *C. Suetonius Tranquillus*. De Grammaticis et Rhetoribus. Oxford.

Kaster, R. A. 1998. "Becoming 'CICERO.'" In *Style and Tradition. Studies in Honor of Wendell Clausen*, edited by P. Knox and C. Foss, 248–263. Stuttgart.

Kaster, R. A. 2001. "Controlling Reason: Declamation in Rhetorical Education at Rome." In *Education in Greek and Roman Antiquity*, edited by Y. L. Too, 317–337. Leiden.

Katzoff, R. 1982. "'*Responsa Prudentium*' in Roman Egypt." In *Studi in onore di Arnaldo Biscardi*, edited by F. Pastori, vol. 2, 523–535. Milan.

Keeline, T. J. 2018. *The Reception of Cicero in the Early Roman Empire*. Cambridge.

Keitel, E. 2007. "Feast Your Eyes on This: Vitellius as a Stock Tyrant (Tac. *Hist.* 3.36–39)." In *A Companion to Greek and Roman Historiography*, edited by J. Marincola, vol. 2, 441–446. Malden MA.

Kelly, B. 2011. *Petitions, Litigation, and Social Control in Roman Egypt*. Oxford.

Kennedy, G. [A.] 1972. *The Art of Rhetoric in the Roman World, 300 B.C.—A.D. 300*. Princeton.

Kennedy, G. [A.] 1983. *Greek Rhetoric under Christian Emperors*. Princeton.

Kennedy, G. A. 2003. Progymnasmata. *Greek Textbooks of Prose Composition and Rhetoric*. Atlanta.

Kennell, N. M. 1997. "Herodes Atticus and the Rhetoric of Tyranny." *Classical Philology* 92: 346–362.

Kennell, N. M. 2015. "The *Ephebeia* in the Hellenistic Period." In *A Companion to Ancient Education*, edited by W. M. Bloomer, 172–183. Chichester.

Keyt, D. 1999. *Aristotle* Politics: *Books V and VI*. Oxford.

Kienzle, E. 1936. *Der Lobpreis von Städten und Ländern in der älteren griechische Dichtung*. Basel.

Kim, L. 2017. "Atticism and Asianism." In *The Oxford Handbook of the Second Sophistic*, edited by D. S. Richter and W. A. Johnson, 41–66. New York.

Kleiter, T. 2010. *Entscheidungskorrekturen mit unbestimmter Wertung durch die klassische römische Jurisprudenz.* Munich.

Klementa, S. 1993. *Gelagerte Flußgötter des Späthellenismus und der römischen Kaiserzeit.* Cologne.

Klodt, C. 2001. *Bescheidene Größe. Die Herrschergestalt, der Kaiserpalast und die Stadt Rom: Literarische Reflexionen monarchicher Selbstdarstellung.* Göttingen.

Kneepkens, C. H. 1994. "*Comparatio.*" In *Historisches Wörterbuch der Rhetorik,* edited by G. Ueding, vol. 2, 293–299. Tübingen.

Knoch, S. 2018. *Sklaven und Freigelassene in der lateinischen Deklamation.* Hildesheim.

König, J. 2011. "Competitiveness and Anti-Competitiveness in Philostratus' *Lives of the Sophists.*" In *Competition in the Ancient World,* edited by N. Fisher and H. Van Wees, 279–300. Swansea.

Köster, R. 2004. *Die Bauornamentik von Milet 1. Die Bauornamentik der frühen und mittleren Kaiserzeit.* Berlin.

Kohl, R. 1915. De scholasticarum declamationum argumentis ex historia petitis. Paderborn.

Kolb, F. 1993. "Bemerkungen zur urbanen Ausstattung von Städten im Westen und im Osten des römischen Reiches anhand von Tacitus, *Agricola* 21 und der Konstantinischen Inschrift von Orkistos." *Klio* 75: 321–341.

Kolb, F. 2015. "Alföldi, Caesar and the German Tradition of Research on Caesar." In *Andreas Alföldi in the Twenty-First Century,* edited by J. H. Richardson and F. Santangelo, 153–165. Stuttgart.

Kondoleon, C. 2000. "Mosaics of Antioch." In *Antioch: The Lost Ancient City,* edited by C. Kondoleon, 63–77. Princeton.

Koops, E. 2014. "Masters and Freedmen: Junian Latins and the Struggle for Citizenship." In *Integration in Rome and in the Roman World,* edited by G. de Kleijn and S. Benoist, 105–126. Leiden.

Korenjak, M. 2000. *Publikum und Redner. Ihre Interaktion in der sophistischen Rhetorik der Kaiserzeit.* Munich.

Kraft, K. 1969. *Der goldene Kranz Caesars und der Kampf um die Entlarvung des "Tyrannen."* Darmstadt.

Krapinger, G. 2005. *[Quintilian] Die Bienen des armen Mannes (Größere Deklamationen, 13).* Cassino.

Krapinger, G. 2007a. *[Quintilian] Der Gladiator (Größere Deklamationen, 9).* Cassino.

Krapinger, G. 2007b. "Die Bienen des armen Mannes in Antike und Mittelalter." In *Theatron. Rhetorische Kultur in Spätantike und Mittelalter/Rhetorical Culture in Late Antiquity and the Middle Ages,* edited by M. Grünbart, 189–201. Berlin.

Krapinger, G. and A. Stramaglia. 2015. *[Quintilian] Der Blinde auf der Türschwelle (Größere Deklamationen, 2).* Cassino.

Kraus, M. 2005. "*Progymnasmata, Gymnasmata.*" In *Historisches Wörterbuch der Rhetorik,* edited by G. Ueding, vol. 7, 159–191. Tübingen.

Kraus, M. 2013. "Rhetoric or Law? The Role of Law in Late Ancient Greek Rhetorical Exercises." In *The Purpose of Rhetoric in Late Antiquity: From Performance to Exegesis,* edited by A. J. Quiroga Puertas, 123–137. Tübingen.

Kraus, M. 2016. "Rhetorik und Macht: Theorie und Praxis der deliberativen Rede in der Dritten Sophistik—Libanios und Aphthonios." In *La rhétorique du pouvoir. Une exploration de l'art oratoire délibératif grec*, edited by P. Derron, 299–331. Geneva.

Kremmydas, C. 2013. "Hellenistic Oratory and the Evidence of Rhetorical Exercises." In *Hellenistic Oratory: Continuity and Change*, edited by C. Kremmydas and K. Tempest, 139–163. Oxford.

Kremmydas, C. and K. Tempest. 2013. "Introduction: Exploring Hellenistic Oratory." In *Hellenistic Oratory: Continuity and Change*, edited by C. Kremmydas and K. Tempest, 1–17. Oxford.

Kuhn, C. T. 2013. "Der Rangstreit der Städte im römischen Kleinasien: Anmerkungen zu Kontext und Datierung von *I.Laodikeia* 10." *Zeitschrift für Papyrologie und Epigraphik* 186: 195–204.

Kühnert, F. 1961. *Allgemeinbildung und Fachbildung in der Antike*. Berlin.

Kunkel, W. 1967 [1951]. *Herkunft und soziale Stellung der römischen Juristen* (2nd ed., Graz, 1967 [1st ed., Weimar, 1951]).

Kunzig, R. 2019. "Rethinking Cities." *National Geographic* 235.4 (April): 73–97.

La Bua, G. 2006. "Diritto e retorica: Cicerone *Iure Peritus* in Seneca Retore e Quintiliano." In *Atti del XII Colloquium Tullianum*. Rome. = *Ciceroniana*, n.s. 12: 181–203.

La Bua, G. 2019. *Cicero and Roman Education. The Reception of the Speeches and Ancient Scholarship*. Cambridge.

Laes, C. 2015. "Masters and Apprentices." In *A Companion to Ancient Education*, edited by W. M. Bloomer, 474–482. Chichester.

Laes, C. and J. Strubbe. 2014 [2008]. *Youth in the Roman Empire. The Young and Restless Years?* (Cambridge, 2014). Translated from *Jeugd in het Romeinse Rijk: Jonge jaren, wilde haren?* (Louvain, 2008).

Lamare, N. 2016. "Architecture et motif littéraire de la fontaine, Orient-Occident." In *Parure monumentale et paysage dans le poésie épigraphique de l'Afrique romaine*, edited by C. Hamdoune, 263–273. Bordeaux.

Lamare, N. 2019. *Les fontaines monumentales en Afrique romaine*. Rome.

Lamberti, F., P. Gröschler, and F. Milazzo eds. 2015. *Il diritto romano e le culture straniere. Influenze e dipendenze interculturali nell'antichità*. Lecce.

Lamoureux, J. and N. Aujoulet. 2004. *Synésios de Cyrène, Tome 4: Opuscules 1*. Paris.

Lanciotti, S. 1977–1978. "Silla e la tipologie del tiranno nella letteratura latina repubblicana (I)" and "(II)." *Quaderni di Storia* 6 (1977) 129–153 and 8 (1978) 191–225.

Lanfranchi, F. 1938. *Il diritto nei retori Romani. Contributo alla storia dello sviluppo del diritto romano*. Milan.

Lanfranchi, F. 1940. "'*Ius exponendi*' e obbligo alimentare nel diritto romano-classico." *Studia et Documenta Historiae et Iuris* 6: 5–69.

Langer, V. I. 2007. Declamatio Romanorum. *Dokument juristischer Argumentationstechnik, Fenster in Gesellschaft ihrer Zeit und Quelle des Rechts?* Frankfurt.

Langlands, R. 2006. *Sexual Morality in Ancient Rome*. Cambridge.

Lanza, D. 1977. *Il tiranno e il suo pubblico*. Turin.

Lassus, J. 1972. *Antioch-on-the-Orontes V. Les portiques d'Antioche*. Princeton.

Laurence, R., S. Esmonde Cleary, and G. Sears. 2011. *The City in the Roman West, c. 250 BC–c. AD 250.* Cambridge.

Lausberg, H. 1998 [1973]. *Handbook of Literary Rhetoric,* edited by D. E. Orton and R. D. Anderson (Leiden, 1998). Translated by M. T. Bliss, A. Jansen, and D. E. Orton from *Handbuch der literarischen Rhetorik* (2nd ed., Munich, 1973).

Lécrivain, C. 1891. "Le droit grec et le droit romain dans les *Controverses* de Sénèque le Père et dans les *Déclamations* de Quintilien et de Calpurnius Flaccus." *Nouvelle revue historique de droit français et étranger* 15: 680–691.

Leesen, T. G. 2010. *Gaius Meets Cicero: Law and Rhetoric in the School Controversies.* Leiden.

Lefèvre, E. 2008. *Philosophie unter der Tyrannis. Ciceros* Tusculanae Disputationes. Heidelberg.

Lehmann-Hartleben, E. 1929. "Städtebau Italiens und des römischen Reiches," *RE* IIIA.2 cols. 2016–2124.

Lehne-Gstreinthaler, C. 2016. "'Jurists in the Shadows': The Everyday Business of the Jurists of Cicero's Time." In *Cicero's Law. Rethinking Roman Law of the Late Republic,* edited by P. J. Du Plessis, 88–99. Edinburgh.

Lehnert, G. 1920. "Bericht über die Literatur zu den lateinischen Deklamationen bis 1914." *Jahresbericht über die Fortschritte der klassischen Altertumswissenschaft* 183: 204–267.

Leigh, S. 2018. "The Monumental Fountain in the Athenian Agora: Reconstruction and Interpretation." In *Great Waterworks in Roman Greece. Aqueducts and Monumental Fountain Structures. Function in Context,* edited by G. A. Aristodemou and T. P. Tassios, 218–234. Oxford.

Lendon, J. E. 1997a. "Spartan Honor." In *Polis and Polemos. Essays on Politics, War, and History in Ancient Greece in Honor of Donald Kagan,* edited by C. D. Hamilton and P. Krentz, 105–126. Claremont CA.

Lendon, J. E. 1997b. *Empire of Honour: The Art of Government in the Roman World.* Oxford.

Lendon, J. E. 2002. "Primitivism and Ancient Foreign Relations." *The Classical Journal* 97: 375–384.

Lendon, J. E. 2005. *Soldiers and Ghosts. A History of Battle in Classical Antiquity.* New Haven.

Lendon, J. E. 2006. "The Legitimacy of the Roman Emperor: Against Weberian Legitimacy and Imperial 'Strategies of Legitimation.'" In *Herrschaftsstrukturen und Herrschaftspraxis. Konzepte, Prinzipien und Strategien der Administration im römischen Kaiserreich,* edited by A. Kolb, 53–63. Berlin.

Lendon, J. E. 2009. "Historians without History: Against Roman Historiography." In *Cambridge Companion to the Roman Historians,* edited by A. Feldherr, 41–61. Cambridge.

Lendon, J. E. 2015. "Rhetoric and Nymphaea in the Roman Empire." *Chiron* 45: 123–149.

Lenel, O. 1907. *Das* Edictum Perpetuum. Leipzig.

Lentano, M. 1998. *L'eroe va a scuola. La figura del* vir fortis *nella declamazione latina.* Naples.

Lentano, M. 1999. "La declamazione latina. Rassegna di studi e stato delle questioni (1980–1998)." *Bollettino di Studi Latini* 29: 571–621.

Lentano, M. 2009 [2005]. "Padri alla sbarra." In M. Lentano, *Signa Culturae. Saggi di antropologia e letteratura latina,* 44–79 (Bologna, 2009). Reprinted from M. Lentano, "'Un nome più grande di qualsiasi legge.' Declamazione latina e *patria potestas.*" *Bollettino di Studi Latini* 35 (2005) 558–589.

Lentano, M. 2009a. "Il beneficio impossibile." In M. Lentano, *Signa Culturae. Saggi di antropologia e letteratura latina*, 15–43. Bologna.

Lentano, M. 2009b. "La gratitudine e la memoria. Una lettura del *de Beneficiis*." *Bollettino di Studi Latini* 39: 1–28.

Lentano, M. 2011 [2009]. "Die Stadt der Gerichte. Das Öffentliche und das Private in der römischen Deklamation." In *Römische Werte und römische Literatur im frühen Prinzipat*, edited by A. Haltenhoff, A. Heil, and F.-H. Mutschler, 209–232 (Berlin, 2011). Translated by C. O. Mayer, with changes, from "La città dei giudici." In M. Lentano, *Signa Culturae. Saggi di antropologia e letteratura latina*, 189–210 (Bologna, 2009).

Lentano, M. 2012a. "Non è un paese per donne. Notizie sulla condizione femminile a Sofistopoli." In G. Brescia, *La donna violata: casi di* stuprum *et* raptus *nella declamazione latina*, 5–27. Lecce.

Lentano, M. 2012b. "Il vascello del parricida. Un tema declamatorio tra mito e retorica (Seneca, *Controversiae*, 7, 1)." *Bollettino di Studi Latini* 42: 1–14.

Lentano, M. 2013–2014. "L'etopea prefetta. I declamatori e il prestito delle voce." *I Quaderni del Ramo d'Oro on-line* 6: 66–77. http://www.qro.unisi.it/frontend/node/166.

Lentano, M. 2014a. *Retorica e diritto. Per una lettura giuridica della declamazione latina*. Lecce.

Lentano, M. 2014b. "Musica per orecchie romane. Nota a ps.-Quint. *decl. mai.* 4, 7." *Bollettino di Studi Latini* 44: 166–177.

Lentano, M., ed. 2015a. *La declamazione latina. Prospettive a confronto sulla retorica di scuola a Roma antica*. Naples.

Lentano, M. 2015b. "Declamazione e antropologia." In *La declamazione latina. Prospettive a confronto sulla retorica di scuola a Roma antica*, edited by M. Lentano, 149–173. Naples.

Lentano, M. 2015c. "*Parricidii sit actio*: Killing the Father in Roman Declamation." In *Law and Ethics in Greek and Roman Declamation*, edited by E. Amato, F. Citti, and B. Huelsenbeck, 133–153. Berlin.

Lentano, M. 2016. "*Auribus vestris non novum crimen*. Il tema dell'adulterio nelle *Declamationes minores*." In *Le Declamazioni minori dello Pseudo-Quintiliano*, edited by A. Casamento, D. van Mal-Maeder, and L. Pasetti, 63–80. Berlin.

Lentano, M. 2017a. *La declamazione a Roma. Breve profilo di un genere minore*. Palermo.

Lentano, M. 2017b. "Le declamazioni pseudo-quintilianee (1986–2014)." *Lustrum* 59: 131–191.

Lentano, M. 2018a. "'Onde si immolino tre vergini o più.' Un motivo mitologico nella declamazione latina." *Maia* 70: 10–27.

Lentano, M. 2018b. "Cose dell'altro mondo. La figura del pirata nella cultura latina." In *Latrocinium maris. Fenomenologia e repressione della pirateria nell'esperienza romana e oltre*, edited by I. G. Mastrorosa, 173–192. Rome.

Lentano, M. 2019. "A scuolo di utopia. La città dei sofisti e l'impero della legge." In *Il volto umano del diritto*, edited by F. Casucci, 65–73. Naples.

Leonard, I. A. 1949. *Books of the Brave. Being an Account of Books and of Men in the Spanish Conquest and Settlement of the Sixteenth-Century New World*. Cambridge MA.

Letzner, W. 1990. *Römische Brunnen und Nymphaea in der westlichen Reichshälfte*. Münster.

Levick, B. M. 1972. "Abdication and Agrippa Postumus." *Historia* 21: 674–697.

Lévy, C. 2012. "Other Followers of Antiochus." In *The Philosophy of Antiochus*, edited by D. Sedley, 290–306. Cambridge.

Levy, E. 1951. *West Roman Vulgar Law: The Law of Property.* Philadelphia.

Levy, E. 1956. *Weströmisches Vulgarrecht. Das Obligationenrecht.* Weimar.

Levy, E. and E. Rabel. 1935. Index Interpolationum quae in Iustiniani Digestis inesse dicuntur, vol. 3. Weimar.

Lewis, A. D. E. 2000. "The Autonomy of Roman Law." In *The Moral World of the Law,* edited by P. Coss, 37–47. Cambridge.

Lewis, S. 2009. *Greek Tyranny.* Exeter.

Leyerle, B. 1994. "John Chrysostom on Almsgiving and the Use of Money." *Harvard Theological Review* 87: 29–47.

Leyerle, B. 2018. "Imagining Antioch, or The Fictional Space of Alleys and Markets." In *Antioch II. The Many Faces of Antioch: Intellectual Exchange and Religious Diversity, CE 350–450,* edited by S.-P. Bergjan and S. Elm, 255–278. Tübingen.

Lichtenberger, A. and R. Raja. 2015. "New Archaeological Research in the Northwest Quarter of Jerash and its Implications for the Urban Development of Roman Gerasa." *American Journal of Archaeology* 119: 483–500.

Liebeschuetz, J. H. W. G. 1972. *Antioch. City and Imperial Administration in the Later Roman Empire.* Oxford.

Liebs, D. 1985. "Unverhohlene Brutalität in den Gesetzen der ersten christlichen Kaiser." In *Römisches Recht in der europäischen Tradition. Symposion aus Anlaß des 75. Geburtstags von Franz Wieacker,* edited by O. Behrends, M. Diesselhorst, and W. E. Voss, 89–116. Ebelsbach.

Liebs, D. 2008. "Roman Vulgar Law in Late Antiquity." In *Aspects of Law in Late Antiquity Dedicated to A. M. Honoré on the Occasion of the Sixtieth Year of His Teaching in Oxford,* edited by B. Sirks, 35–53. Oxford.

Lintott, A. 1968. *Violence in Republican Rome.* Oxford.

Lintott, A. 1970. "The Tradition of Violence in the Annals of the Early Roman Republic." *Historia* 19: 12–29.

Lintott, A. 2009. "The Assassination." In *A Companion to Julius Caesar,* edited by M. Griffin, 72–82. Chichester.

Lohner-Urban, U. and P. Scherrer. 2016. "Hellenistische Prunktore—Ein wissenschaftlicher Irrtum? Vorläufige Grabungsergebnisse vom Osttor von Side aus der Kampagne 2012." In *Focus on Fortifications. New Research on Fortifications in the Ancient Mediterranean and the Near East,* edited by R. Frederiksen, S. Müth, P. I. Schneider, and M. Schnelle, 232–243. Oxford.

Longfellow, B. 2009. "The Legacy of Hadrian: Roman Monumental Civic Fountains in Greece." In *The Nature and Function of Water, Baths, Bathing, and Hygiene from Antiquity through the Renaissance,* edited by C. Kosso and A. Scott, 211–232. Leiden.

Longfellow, B. 2011. *Roman Imperialism and Civic Patronage: Form, Meaning, and Ideology in Monumental Fountain Complexes.* New York.

Longfellow, B. 2018. "Reflecting the Past: The Nymphaeum near the so-called Praetorium at Gortyn." In *Great Waterworks in Roman Greece. Aqueducts and Monumental Fountain Structures. Function in Context,* edited by G. A. Aristodemou and T. P. Tassios, 246–258. Oxford.

Longo, G. 2008. *[Quintiliano] La pozione dell'odio (Declamazioni maggiori, 14–15).* Cassino.

Longo, G. 2016. "La medicina nelle *Declamazioni maggiori* pseudo-quintilianee." In *Reading Roman Declamation. The Declamations Ascribed to Quintilian*, edited by M. T. Dinter, C. Guérin, and M. Martinho, 167–187. Berlin.

Loraux, N. 1986 [1981]. *The Invention of Athens. The Funeral Oration in the Classical City.* (Cambridge MA, 1986). Translated by A. Sheridan from *L'invention d'Athènes: histoire de l'oraison funèbre dans la "cité classique"* (Paris, 1981).

Luciani, S. 2009. "Cypsélos, Pisistrate, Phalaris, Denys et les autres: la figure du tyran dans l'oeuvre philosophique de Cicéron." In *Pouvoirs des hommes, pouvoir des mots, des Gracques à Trajan. Hommages au Professeur Paul Marius Martin*, edited by O. Devillers and J. Meyers, 153–165. Louvain.

MacDonald, W. L. 1982–1986 [1965]. *The Architecture of the Roman Empire: An Introductory Study.* 2 vols. (2nd ed., New Haven, 1982–1986 [1st ed. New Haven, 1965]).

MacMullen, R. 1966. *Enemies of the Roman Order.* Cambridge MA.

MacMullen, R. 1974. *Roman Social Relations, 50 BC—AD 284.* New Haven.

MacMullen, R. 1976. *Roman Government's Response to Crisis, AD 235–337.* New Haven.

MacMullen, R. 1988. *Corruption and the Decline of Rome.* New Haven.

MacMullen, R. 1990 [1962]. "Roman Bureaucratese." In R. MacMullen, *Changes in the Roman Empire: Essays in the Ordinary*, 67–77 (Princeton, 1990). Reprinted from *Traditio* 18 (1962) 364–378.

MacMullen, R. 1990 [1964]. "Some Pictures in Ammianus Marcellinus." In R. MacMullen, *Changes in the Roman Empire: Essays in the Ordinary*, 78–106 (Princeton, 1990). Reprinted from *Art Bulletin* 46 (1964) 435–455.

MacMullen, R. 1990 [1986]. "Judicial Savagery in the Roman Empire." In R. MacMullen, *Changes in the Roman Empire: Essays in the Ordinary*, 204–217 (Princeton, 1990). Reprinted from *Chiron* 16 (1986) 147–166.

Maehler, H. 2005. "Greek, Egyptian, and Roman Law." *Journal of Juristic Papyri* 35: 121–140.

Mägele, S., J. Richard, and M. Waelkens. 2007. "A Late-Hadrianic Nymphaeum at Sagalassos (Pisidia, Turkey): A Preliminary Report." *Istanbuler Mitteilungen* 57: 469–504.

Magnaldi, G. 1991. *L'οἰκείωσις peripatetica in Ario Didimo e nel 'de Finibus' di Cicerone.* Florence.

Malitz, J. 2003. *Nikolaos von Damaskus. Leben des Kaisers Augustus.* Darmstadt.

Malosse, P.-L. 2006. "Sophistiques et tyrannies." In *Approches de la Troisième Sophistique. Hommages à Jacques Schamp*, edited by E. Amato, 157–178. Brussels.

Mancini, G. 2011. "*Pro tam magna sui confidentia*." In *I diritti degli altri in Grecia e a Roma*, edited by A. Maffi and L. Gagliardi, 152–190. Sankt Augustin.

Manning, C. 1986. "'*Actio Ingrati*' (Seneca, *de Benef.* 3, 6–17): A Contribution to Contemporary Debate?" *Studia et Documenta Historiae et Iuris* 52: 61–72.

Mantovani, D. 2007 [2006]. "I giuristi, il retore e le api. *Ius controversum* e natura nella *Declamatio maior XIII*." In *Testi e problemi del giusnaturalismo romano*, edited by D. Mantovani and A. Schiavone, 323–385 (Pavia, 2007). Reprinted from *Seminarios complutenses de derecho romano* 19 (2006) 205–283.

Mantovani, D. 2014. "Declamare le Dodici Tavole: una parafrasi di *XII Tab.* V, 3 nella *Declamatio Minor 264*." In Meditationes in iure et historia. *Essays in Honour of Laurens Winkel*, edited by

R. van den Bergh, G. van Niekerk, P. Pichonnaz, P. J. Thomas, D. G. Kleyn, F. Lucrezi, and J. Mutton, vol. 2, 597–605. Pretoria.

Mantovani, D. 2018. *Les juristes écrivains de la Rome antique. Les oeuvres des juristes comme littérature*. Paris.

Mar, R. 2009. "La *Domus Flavia*, utilizzo e funzioni del palazzo di Domiziano." In Divus Vespasianus. *Il bimillenario dei Flavi*, edited by F. Coarelli, 250–263. Rome.

Marek, C. 2000. "Der Dank der Stadt an einem *comes* in Amisos unter Theodosius II." *Chiron* 30: 367–387.

Marrou, H.-I. 1938. *Saint Augustin et la fin de la culture antique*. Paris.

Marrou, H.-I. 1949. *Saint Augustin et la fin de la culture antique*. Retractatio. Paris.

Marrou, H.-I. 1956. *A History of Education in Antiquity* (New York, 1956). Translated by G. Lamb from *Histoire de l'éducation dans l'Antiquité* (3rd ed. Paris, 1955).

Marrou, H.-I. 1971 [1948]. *Histoire de l'éducation dans l'Antiquité* (7th ed. Paris, 1971 [1st ed., Paris, 1948]: only the page numbers change between editions).

Martin, J. 1974. *Antike Rhetorik. Technik und Methode*. Munich.

Martin, K. 2013. Demos, Boule, Gerousia. *Personifikationen städtischer Institutionen auf kaiserzeitlichen Münzen aus Kleinasien*. 2 vols. Bonn.

Martin, P. M. 1982–1994. *L'idée de royauté à Rome*. 2 vols. Clermont-Ferrand.

Martin, P. M. 1988. *Tuer César!* Brussels.

Martini, W. 2015. "Nymphäum und Tor. Zur Wasserkultur in Perge in Pamphylien." In *Turm und Tor. Siedlungsstrukturen in Lykien und benachbarten Kulturlandschaften*, edited by B. Beck-Brandt, S. Ladstätter, and B. Yener-Marksteiner, 279–289. Vienna.

Martini, W. 2016. "Form, Funktion und Bedeutung der Stadtmauern von Perge in Pamphylien." In *Focus on Fortifications. New Research on Fortifications in the Ancient Mediterranean and the Near East*, edited by R. Frederiksen, S. Müth, P. I. Schneider, and M. Schnelle, 220–231. Oxford.

Masi Doria, C. 2011. "Principii e regole. Valori e razionalità come forme del discorso giuridico." In *Tra retorica e diritto. Linguaggi e forme argomentative nella tradizione giuridica*, edited by A. Lovato, 19–41. Bari.

Masi Doria, C. 2012. "'*Libertorum bona ad patronos pertineant*': su Calp. Flacc. *decl. exc.* 14." *Index* 40: 313–325.

Mastrorosa, I. [G.] 2002. "Rhetoric between Conjugal Love and *patria potestas*: Seneca the Elder, *Contr.* 2.2." In *Papers on Rhetoric IV*, edited by L. Calboli Montefusco, 165–190. Rome.

Mastrorosa, I. G. 2013. "Aspirations tyranniques et *adfectio regni* dans la Rome archaïque et dans la première époque républicaine. Cicéron et Tite-Live." In *Le tyran et sa postérité dans le littérature latine de l'Antiquité à la Renaissance*, edited by H. Casanova-Robin and C. Lévy, 123–139. Paris.

Matijević, K. 2006. *Marcus Antonius. Consul—Proconsul—Staatsfeind. Die Politik der Jahre 44 und 43 v. Chr.* Rahden.

Mattern, S. [P.] 1999. *Rome and the Enemy. Imperial Strategy in the Principate*. Berkeley and Los Angeles.

Mattern, S. P. 2013. *The Prince of Medicine: Galen in the Roman Empire*. New York.

Maupai, I. 2003. *Die Macht der Schönheit. Untersuchungen zu einem Aspekt des Selbstverständnisses und der Selbstdarstellung griechischer Städte in der römischen Kaiserzeit*. Bonn.

Maurice, L. 2013. *The Teacher in Ancient Rome: The* Magister *and his World.* Plymouth.

May, J. 1996. "Cicero and the Beasts." *Syllecta Classica* 7: 143–153.

Mayer, R. 2001. *Tacitus.* Dialogus de Oratoribus. Cambridge.

Mayer, W. 2012. "The Topography of Antioch Described in the Writings of John Chrysostom." In *Les sources de l'histoire du paysage urbain d'Antioche sur l'Oronte*, 81–100. Saint-Denis.

Mayor, J. E. B. 1878. *Thirteen Satires of Juvenal.* 2nd ed. 2 vols. London.

McCall, J. B. 2002. *The Cavalry of the Roman Republic.* London.

McNamee, K. 1998. "Another Chapter in the History of *Scholia.*" *Classical Quarterly* 48: 269–288.

Meier, M. 2012. "(K)ein Tyrannenmord: Der Tod des Iulius Caesar 44 v. Chr." In *Politische Morde in der Geschichte. Von der Antike bis zur Gegenwart*, edited by G. Schild and A. Schindling, 11–36. Paderborn.

Meier, M. 2014. *Caesar und das Problem der Monarchie in Rom.* Heidelberg.

Mentxaka, R. 1988. "*Stellionatus.*" *Bullettino dell'Istituto di diritto romano* 91: 277–335.

Mer, L. 1953. *L'accusation dans la procédure pénale du Bas-Empire Romain.* Unpublished dissertation, Rennes.

Merkelbach, R. and J. Stauber. 1998–2004. *Steinepigramme aus dem griechischen Osten.* 5 vols. Stuttgart, Leipzig, and Munich.

Mertens, J. 1969. "Sondages dans la grande colonnade et sur l'enceinte." In *Apamée de Syrie. Bilan des recherches archéologiques 1965–1968*, edited by J. Balty, 61–73. Brussels.

Mette-Dittmann, A. 1991. *Die Ehegesetze des Augustus.* Stuttgart.

Metzger, E. 2004. "Roman Judges, Case Law, and Principles of Procedure." *Law and History Review* 22: 243–275.

Meulder, M. 2008. "Un monstre platonicien: le tyran." *Revue de philosophie ancienne* 26: 79–100.

Meyer, E. 1922. *Caesars Monarchie und das Principat des Pompeius.* 3rd ed. Stuttgart.

Meyer, E. 1951. "Die Quaestionen der Rhetorik und die Anfänge juristischer Methodenlehre." *Zeitschrift der Savigny-Stiftung für Rechtsgeschichte, Romanistische Abteilung* 68: 30–73.

Meyer, E. A. 2004. *Legitimacy and Law in the Roman World:* Tabulae *in Roman Belief and Practice.* Cambridge.

Michelfeit, J. 1964. "Der König und sein Gegenbild in Ciceros 'Staat.'" *Philologus* 108: 262–287.

Migeotte, L. 2014. *Les finances des cités grecques aux périodes classique et hellénistique.* Paris.

Migliario, E. 1989. "Luoghi retorici e realtà sociale nell'opera di Seneca il Vecchio." *Athenaeum* 67: 525–549.

Migliario, E. 2007. *Retorica e storia. Una lettura delle* Suasoriae *di Seneca Padre.* Bari.

Migliorini, M. 2001. *L'adozione tra prassi documentale e legislazione imperiale nel diritto del tardo Impero Romano.* Milan.

Mihailov, G. 1961. "La fortification de la Thrace par Antonin le Pieux et Marc Aurèle." *Studi Urbinati* 35: 42–56.

Milazzo, A. M. 1996. "L'elogio della retorica nell'*Antiochicus* di Libanio." *Cassiodorus* 2: 73–97.

Millar, F. 1969. "P. Herennius Dexippus: The Greek World and the Third Century Invasions." *Journal of Roman Studies* 59: 12–29.

Millar, F. 1977. *The Emperor in the Roman World.* London.

Mitchell, S. 1987. "Imperial Building in the Eastern Roman Provinces." *Harvard Studies in Classical Philology* 91: 333–365.

Mitteis, L. 1891. *Reichsrecht und Volksrecht in den östlichen Provinzen des römischen Kaiserreichs.* Leipzig.

Modrzejewski, J. M. 2014. *Loi et coutume dans l'Égypte grecque et romaine.* Warsaw.

Moles, J. [L.] 1987. "The Attacks on L. Cornelius Cinna, Praetor in 44 BC." *Rheinisches Museum für Philologie* 130: 124–128.

Moles, J. [L.] 1997. "Plutarch, Brutus and Brutus' Greek and Latin Letters." In *Plutarch and his Intellectual World. Essays on Plutarch,* edited by J. Mossman, 141–168. London.

Moles, J. L. 2017 [1979]. *A Commentary on Plutarch's Brutus.* Edited by C. Pelling (*Histos* Supplement 7, Newcastle, 2017): a postumous publication, with updated bibliography, of the author's 1979 Oxford DPhil thesis. https://research.ncl.ac.uk/histos/documents/SV07.MolesBrutus.pdf.

Momigliano, A. 1941. "II. Epicureans in Revolt." In A. Momigliano, review of Benjamin Farrington, *Science and Politics in the Ancient World. Journal of Roman Studies* 31: 149–157 at 151–157.

Mommsen, Th. 1887–1888. *Römisches Staatsrecht.* 3rd ed. 3 vols. Leipzig.

Mommsen, Th. 1899. *Römisches Strafrecht.* Leipzig.

Morgan, T. 1998. *Literate Education in the Hellenistic and Roman Worlds.* Cambridge.

Morgan, T. 2007. "Rhetoric and Education." In *A Companion to Greek Rhetoric,* edited by I. Worthington, 303–319. Malden MA.

Morstein-Marx, R. 2004. *Mass Oratory and Political Power in the Late Roman Republic.* Cambridge.

Morstein-Marx, R. 2012. "Political Graffiti in the Late Roman Republic: 'Hidden Transcripts' and 'Common Knowledge.'" In *Politische Kommunikation und öffentliche Meinung in der antiken Welt,* edited by C. Kuhn, 191–217. Stuttgart.

Moses, D. C. 1993. "Livy's Lucretia and the Validity of Coerced Consent in Roman Law." In *Consent and Coercion to Sex and Marriage in Ancient and Medieval Societies,* edited by A. E. Laiou, 39–81. Washington.

Müth, S. 2016a. "Urbanistic Functions and Aspects." In *Ancient Fortifications. A Compendium of Theory and Practice,* edited by S. Müth, P. I. Schneider, M. Schnelle, and P. D. De Staebler, 159–172. Oxford.

Müth, S. 2016b. "Functions and Semantics of Fortifications: An Introduction." In *Focus on Fortifications. New Research on Fortifications in the Ancient Mediterranean and the Near East,* edited by R. Frederiksen, S. Müth, P. I. Schneider, and M. Schnelle, 183–192. Oxford.

Müth, S., A. Sokolicek, B. Jansen, and E. Laufer. 2016. "Methods of Interpretation." In *Ancient Fortifications. A Compendium of Theory and Practice,* edited by S. Müth, P. I. Schneider, M. Schnelle, and P. D. De Staebler, 1–23. Oxford.

Müth, S., E. Laufer, and C. Brasse. 2016. "Symbolische Funktionen." In *Ancient Fortifications. A Compendium of Theory and Practice,* edited by S. Müth, P. I. Schneider, M. Schnelle, and P. D. De Staebler, 126–158. Oxford.

Najock, D. 2007. "Unechtes und Zweifelhaftes unter den Deklamationen des Libanios—die statistische Evidenz." In *Theatron. Rhetorische Kultur in Spätantike und Mittelalter/Rhetorical Culture in Late Antiquity and the Middle Ages,* edited by M. Grünbart, 305–355. Berlin.

Nardi, E. 1980. *L'otre dei parricidi e le bestie incluse.* Milan.

Neri, V. 1997. "L'usurpatore come tiranno nel lessico politico della tarda antichità." In *Usurpationen in der Spätantike,* edited by F. Paschoud and J. Szidat, 71–86. Stuttgart.

Neuerburg, N. 1965. *L'architettura delle fontane e dei ninfei nell'Italia antica.* Naples.

Nicolet, C. 2000. "Fragments pour une géographie urbaine comparée: à propos d'Alexandrie." In *Mégapoles méditerranéennes. Géographie urbaine rétrospective,* edited by C. Nicolet, R. Ilbert, and J.-Ch. Depaule, 245–252. Paris.

Nielsen, I. 1993. *Thermae et Balnea. The Architecture and Cultural History of Roman Public Baths.* 2nd ed. 2 vols. Aarhus.

Nilsson, M. P. 1955. *Die Hellenistische Schule.* Munich.

Nippel, W. 2017. "Zur Monarchie in der politischen Theorie des 5. und 4. Jahrhunderts v. Chr." In *Monarchische Herrschaft im Altertum,* edited by S. Rebenich, 245–261. Berlin.

Nocchi, F. R. 2015. "Declamazione e Teatro." In *La declamazione latina. Prospettive a confronto sulla retorica di scuola a Roma antica,* edited by M. Lentano, 175–209. Naples.

Nocchi, F. R. 2019. "*Ambigua signa* e signa animi: le lacrime del tiranno." *Camenae* 23: 1–18.

Nock, A. D. 1954. "The Praises of Antioch." *Journal of Egyptian Archaeology* 40: 76–82.

Nollé, J. 1993a. "Die feindlichen Schwestern—Betrachtungen zur Rivalität der pamphylischen Städte." In *Die epigraphische und altertumskundliche Erforschung Kleinasiens: Hundert Jahre Kleinasiatische Kommission der Österreichischen Akademie der Wissenschaften,* edited by G. Dobesch and G. Rehrenböck, 297–317. Vienna.

Nollé, J. 1993b. *Side im Altertum. Geschichte und Zeugnisse I.* Bonn.

Norman, A. F. 2000. *Antioch as a Centre of Hellenic Culture as Observed by Libanius.* Liverpool.

Nörr, D. 1969. *Die Entstehung der* longi temporis praescriptio. *Studien zum Einfluß der Zeit im Recht und zur Rechtspolitik in der Kaiserzeit.* Cologne.

Nörr, D. 1976. "Der Jurist im Kreis der Intellektuellen: Mitspieler oder Aussenseiter? (Gellius, *Noctes Atticae* 16. 10)." In *Festschrift für Max Kaser zum 70. Geburtstag,* edited by D. Medicus and H. H. Seiler, 57–90. Munich.

Nörr, D. 1978. "Cicero-Zitate bei den klassischen Juristen." *Ciceroniana* n.s. 3: 111–150.

Nörr, D. 1986a. Causa Mortis. *Auf den Spuren einer Redewendung.* Munich.

Nörr, D. 1986b. "*Causam Mortis Praebere.*" In *The Legal Mind: Essays for Tony Honoré,* edited by N. MacCormick and P. Birks, 203–217. Oxford.

Nörr, D. 2003 [1972]. *Divisio und partitio. Bemerkungen zur römischen Rechtsquellenlehre und zur antiken Wissenschaftstheorie.* In D. Nörr, Historiae Iuris Antiqui. *Gesammelte Schriften,* edited by T. J. Chiusi, W. Kaiser, and H.-D. Spengler, vol. 2, 705–774 (2nd ed., Goldbach, 2003 [1st ed., Berlin, 1972]).

Nörr, D. 2009. "*Exempla nihil per se valent.* Bemerkungen zu Paul. 15 *quaest.* D. 46, 3, 98, 8; 72 *ad ed.* D. 45, 1, 83, 5)." *Zeitschrift der Savigny-Stiftung für Rechtsgeschichte, Romanistische Abteilung* 126: 1–54.

North, H. 1952. "The Use of Poetry in the Training of the Ancient Orator." *Traditio* 8: 1–33.

Nótári, T. 2013. "Remarks on Two Aspects of *patria potestas* in Roman Law." *Fiat Iustitia* 2: 29–49.

Nowak, M. 2010. "*Titius heres esto.* The Role of the [*sic*] Legal Practice in the [*sic*] Law-Creation in Late Antiquity." *Journal of Juristic Papyri* 41: 161–184.

Ogilvie, R. M. 1965. *A Commentary on Livy Books 1–5.* Oxford.

Opelt, I. 1965. *Die lateinischen Schimpfwörter und verwandte sprachliche Erscheinungen.* Heidelberg.

Orions, G. H. 1941. "Walter Scott, Mark Twain, and the Civil War." *South Atlantic Quarterly* 40: 342–359.

Ortmann, U. 1988. *Cicero, Brutus und Octavian—Republikaner und Caesarianer. Ihr gegenseitiges Verhältnis im Krisenjahr 44/43 v. Chr.* Bonn.

Osaba García, E. 1997. *El adulterio uxorio en la* Lex Visigothorum. Madrid.

Owens, E. J. and M. Taşlialan. 2009. "'Beautiful and Useful': The Water Supply of Pisidian Antioch and the Development of the Roman Colony." In *The Nature and Function of Water, Baths, Bathing, and Hygiene from Antiquity through the Renaissance,* edited by C. Kosso and A. Scott, 301–317. Leiden.

Packman, Z. M. 1999. "Rape and Consequences in the Latin Declamations." *Scholia* 8: 17–36.

Pagán, V. E. 2004. *Conspiracy Narratives in Roman History.* Austin.

Pagán, V. E. 2007–2008. "Teaching Torture in Seneca *Controversiae* 2.5." *Classical Journal* 103: 165–182.

Pageau, V. 2015. "L'empereur déclamateur dans l'*Histoire Auguste.*" In *Présence de la déclamation antique (controverses et suasoires),* edited by R. Poignault and C. Schneider, 57–73. Clermont-Ferrand.

Palma, A. 1992. Humanior Interpretatio. "*Humanitas*" *nell'interpretazione e nella normazione da Adriano ai Severi.* Turin.

Panero Oria, P. 2001. Ius occidendi et ius accusandi *en la* lex Iulia de adulteriis coercendis. Valencia.

Paoli, U. E. 1953 [1976]. "Droit attique et droit romain dans les rhéteurs Latins." *Revue historique de droit français et étranger* 31 (1953) 175–199. Reprinted in U. E. Paoli, *Altri studi di diritto greco e romano* (Milan, 1976) 79–101.

Parker, E. R. 1946. "The Education of Heirs in the Julio-Claudian Family." *American Journal of Philology* 67: 29–50.

Parks, E. P. 1945. *The Roman Rhetorical Schools as a Preparation for the Courts under the Early Empire.* Baltimore.

Parry, R. D. 2007. "The Unhappy Tyrant and the Craft of Inner Rule." In *The Cambridge Companion to Plato's Republic,* edited by G. R. F. Ferrari, 386–414. Cambridge.

Paschidis, P. 2008. *Between City and King. Prosopographical Studies on the Intermediaries between the Cities of the Greek Mainland and the Aegean and the Royal Courts in the Hellenistic Period (322–190 BC).* Athens.

Pasetti, L. 2008. "Filosofia e retorica di scuola nelle '*Declamazioni Maggiori*' pseudoquintilianee." In *Retorica ed educazione delle élites nell'antica Roma,* edited by F. Gasti and E. Romano, 113–147. Pavia.

Pasetti, L. 2011. *[Quintiliano] Il veleno versato (Declamazioni maggiori, 17).* Cassino.

Pasetti, L. 2015. "Cases of Poisoning in Greek and Roman Declamation." In *Law and Ethics in Greek and Roman Declamation,* edited by E. Amato, F. Citti, and B. Huelsenbeck, 155–199. Berlin.

Pasetti, L. 2016. "Lingua e stile dell''io' nella declamazione latina." In *Fabrique de la déclamation antique (controverses et suasoires),* edited by R. Poignault and C. Schneider, 135–159. Lyon.

Patillon, M. 1988. *La theorie du discours chez Hermogene le rheteur.* Paris.

Patillon, M. 2002a. *Pseudo-Aelius Aristide Arts rhétoriques, Tome I.* Paris.

Patillon, M. 2002b. *Apsinès Art rhétorique. Problèmes à faux-semblant.* Paris.

Patillon, M. 2007. "Les modèles littéraires dans l'apprentissage de la rhétorique." In *Escuela y literatura en Grecia Antigua,* edited by J. A. Fernández Delgado, F. Pordomingo, and A. Stramaglia, 511–521. Cassino.

Patillon, M. 2009. Corpus Rhetoricum, *Tome II. Hermogène. Les états de cause.* Paris.

Patillon, M. 2012. Corpus Rhetoricum, *Tome IV. Prolégomènes au de Ideis. Hermogéne, Les caté-gories stylistiques du discours* (de Ideis); *Synopses des exposés sur les* Ideai. Paris.

Patillon, M. and G. Bolognesi. 1997. *Aelius Théon.* Progymnasmata. Paris.

Peachin, M. 1996. Iudex vice Caesaris. *Deputy Emperors and the Administration of Justice during the Principate.* Stuttgart.

Peachin, M. 2001. "Jurists and the Law in the Early Roman Empire." In *Administration, Prosopography and Appointment Policies in the Roman Empire,* edited by L. de Blois, 109–120. Amsterdam.

Peachin, M. 2004. *Frontinus and the* curae *of the* curator aquarum. Stuttgart.

Peachin, M. 2016. "Lawyers in Administration." In *The Oxford Handbook of Law and Society,* edited by P. J. Du Plessis, C. Ando, and K. Tuori, 164–175. Oxford.

Peachin, M. 2017. "In Search of a Roman Rule of Law." *Legal Roots* 6: 19–64.

Peachin, M. 2019. "Rome's Emperor of Law. Review of Kaius Tuori, *The Emperor of Law. The Emergence of Imperial Jurisdiction* (Oxford, 2016)." *Iura* 67: 81–117.

Pédech, P. 1971. "La géographie urbaine chez Strabon." *Ancient Society* 2: 234–253.

Peirano, I. 2013. "*Non subripiendi causa sed palam mutuandi:* Intertextuality and Literary Deviancy between Law, Rhetoric, and Literature in Roman Imperial Culture." *American Journal of Philology* 134: 83–100, 133–148.

Pelling, C. 2011. *Plutarch* Caesar. Oxford.

Penella, R. J. 2011. "Menelaus, Odysseus, and the Limits of Eloquence in Libanius, *Declamations* 3 and 4." In *Libanios, le premier humaniste. Études en hommage à Bernard Schouler,* edited by O. Lagacherie and P.-L. Malosse, 93–105. Alessandria.

Penella, R. J. 2014. "Libanius' *Declamations.*" In *Libanius: A Critical Introduction,* edited by L. van Hoof, 107–127. Cambridge.

Penella, R. J. 2015. "The *Progymnasmata* and Progymnasmic Theory in Imperial Greek Education." In *A Companion to Ancient Education,* edited by W. M. Bloomer, 160–171. Chichester.

Pérez Galicia, G. 2011. "Las cartas de Libanio como claves de la nueva retórica de la *paideia.*" In *Libanios, le premier humaniste. Études en hommage à Bernard Schouler,* edited by O. Lagacherie and P.-L. Malosse, 79–91. Alessandria.

Pernot, L. 1981. "Topique de topographie: l'espace dans la rhétorique épidictique grecque à l'époque impériale." In *Arts et légendes d'espaces: figures du voyage et rhétoriques du monde,* edited by C. Jacob and F. Lestringant, 99–109. Paris.

Pernot, L. 1993. *La rhétorique de l'éloge dans le monde gréco-romain.* 2 vols. Paris.

Pernot, L. 2000 [2005]. *La rhétorique dans l'Antiquité* (Paris, 2000). Translated by W. E. Higgins as *Rhetoric in Antiquity* (Washington DC, 2005).

Pernot, L. 2008. "Aspects méconnus de l'enseignement de la rhétorique dans le monde gréco-romaine à l'époque impériale." In *L'enseignement supérieur dans les mondes antiques et médiévaux,* edited by H. Hugonnard-Roche, 283–306. Paris.

Pernot, L. 2015. *Epideictic Rhetoric. Questioning the Stakes of Ancient Praise.* Austin.

Petit, C. 2018. *Galien de Pergame ou le rhétorique de la Providence.* Leiden.

Petit, P. 1957. *Les étudiants de Libanius.* Paris.

Petsalis-Diomidis, A. 2008. "The Body in the Landscape: Aristides' *Corpus* in Light of the *Sacred Tales.*" In *Aelius Aristides between Greece, Rome, and the Gods,* edited by W. V. Harris and B. Holmes, 131–150. Leiden.

Pina Polo, F. 1996. Contra arma verbis. *Der Redner vor dem Volk in der späten römischen Republik.* Translated by E. Liess. Stuttgart.

Pina Polo, F. 2006. "The Tyrant Must Die: Preventive Tyrannicide in Roman Political Thought." In *Repúblicas y ciudadanos: Modelos de participación cívica en el mundo antiguo,* edited by F. Marco Simón, F. Pina Polo, J. Remesal Rodríguez, 71–101 (Barcelona, 2006). Published in Spanish as "El Tirano debe morir: el tiranicidio preventivo en el pensamiento político romano." *Actas y Comunicaciones del Instituto de Historia Antigua y Medieval* 2 (2006) 1–24.

Pina Polo, F. 2017. "The 'Tyranny' of the Gracchi and the *Concordia* of the Optimates: An Ideological Construct." In *Costruire la memoria. Uso e abuso della storia fra tarda repubblica e primo principato,* edited by R. Cristofoli, A. Galimberti, and F. Rohr Vio, 5–33. Rome.

Pinder, I. 2011. "Constructing and Deconstructing Roman City Walls: The Role of Urban Enceintes as Physical and Symbolic Borders." In *Places in Between. The Archaeology of Social, Cultural and Geographical Borders and Borderlands,* edited by D. Mullin, 67–79. Oxford.

Pingoud, J. and A. Rolle. 2016. "*Noverca et mater crudelis.* La perversion féminine dans les *Grandes Déclamations* à travers l'intertextualité." In *Reading Roman Declamation. The Declamations Ascribed to Quintilian,* edited by M. T. Dinter, C. Guérin, and M. Martinho, 147–166. Berlin.

Plaß, H. G. 1859. *Die Tyrannis in ihren beiden Perioden bei den alten Griechen.* 2 vols. Leipzig.

Plattner, G. A. and A. Schmidt-Colinet. 2005. "Beobachtungen zu drei kaiserzeitlichen Bauten in Ephesos." In *Synergia. Festschrift für Friedrich Krinzinger,* edited by B. Brandt, V. Gassner, and S. Ladstätter, vol. 1, 243–255. Vienna.

Pölönen, J. 2016. "Framing 'Law and Society' in the Roman World." In *The Oxford Handbook of Law and Society,* edited by P. J. Du Plessis, C. Ando, and K. Tuori, 8–20. Oxford.

Poignault, R., and C. Schneider, eds. 2015. *Présence de la déclamation antique (controverses et suasoires).* Clermont-Ferrand.

Pollitt, J. J. 2015. "Education in the Visual Arts." In *A Companion to Ancient Education,* edited by W. M. Bloomer, 375–386. Chichester.

Pont, A.-V. 2010. *Orner la cité. Enjeux culturels et politiques du paysage urbain dans l'Asie gréco-romain.* Bordeaux.

Pope, S. 2016. "Protection and Trade: Girding the City." In *A Companion to Greek Architecture,* edited by M. M. Miles, 254–272. Chichester.

Popkin, M. L. 2016. *The Architecture of the Roman Triumph. Monuments, Memory, and Identity.* Cambridge.

Popkin, M. L. 2018. "Urban Images in Glass from the Late Roman Empire: The Souvenir Flasks of Puteoli and Baiae." *American Journal of Archaeology* 122: 427–461.

Pordomingo, F. 2007. "Ejercicios preliminares de la composición retórica y literaria en papiro: el encomio." In *Escuela y literatura en Grecia Antigua,* edited by J. A. Fernández Delgado, F. Pordomingo, and A. Stramaglia, 405–453. Cassino.

Portmann, W. 1988. *Geschichte in der spätantiken Panegyrik.* Frankfurt.

Porter, S. E. ed. 1997. *Handbook of Classical Rhetoric in the Hellenistic Period, 330 B.C.–A.D. 400.* Leiden.

Price, M. J. and B. L. Trell. 1977. *Coins and their Cities. Architecture on the Ancient Coins of Greece, Rome, and Palestine.* London.

Pritchard, D. M. 2015. "[Education in] Athens." In *A Companion to Ancient Education*, edited by W. M. Bloomer, 112–122. Chichester.

Puech, B. 2002. *Orateurs et sophistes grecs dans les inscriptions d'époque impériale*. Paris.

Pugliese, G. 1966. "L'autonomia del diritto rispetto agli altri fenomeni e valori sociali nella giurisprudenza romana." In *La storia del diritto nel quadro delle scienze storiche*, 161–192. Florence.

Puliatti, S. 1995. "La dicotomia *vir-mulier* e la disciplina del ratto nelle fonti legislative tardo-imperiali." *Studia et Documenta Historiae et Iuris* 61: 471–529.

Puliatti, S. 2011. "Alla ricerca della verità. La discrezionalità del giudice tra retorica e diritto." In *Tra retorica e diritto. Linguaggi e forme argomentative nella tradizione giuridica*, edited by A. Lovato, 43–84. Bari.

Quaß, F. 1993. *Die Honoratiorenschicht in den Städten des griechischen Ostens. Untersuchungen zur politischen und sozialen Entwicklung in hellenistischer und römischer Zeit*. Stuttgart.

Querzoli, S. 2000. *I testamenta e gli officia pietatis. Tribunale centumvirale, potere imperiale e giuristi tra Augusto e i Severi*. Naples.

Querzoli, S. 2008. "Il sapere giuridico nella cultura del *civiliter eruditus* secondo Gellio." In *Cultura letteraria e diritto nei primi due secoli del Principato*, edited by S. Querzoli and G. Calboli, 31–54. Rovigo.

Querzoli, S. 2009. "Il *beneficium* della *manumissio* del pensiero di Ulpio Marcello." *Ostraka* 18: 203–220.

Querzoli, S. 2011a. "La *puella rapta*: paradigmi retorici e apprendimento del diritto nelle Instituzioni di Elio Marciano." *Annali Online Lettere-Ferrara* 1–2: 153–169. http://annali.unife.it/lettere/article/view/242.

Querzoli, S. 2011b. "About *Raptus* and *Veneficium* in Marcian's Institutions." *Ostraka* 20: 83–94.

Querzoli, S. 2013. *Scienza giuridica e cultura retorica in Ulpio Marcello*. Naples.

Rababeh, S., R. Al Rabady, and S. Abu-Khafajah. 2014. "Colonnaded Streets within the Roman Cityscape: A 'Spatial' Perspective." *Journal of Architecture and Urbanism* 38: 293–305.

Rabe, H. 1931. Prolegomenon Sylloge. Leipzig.

Raccanelli, R. 2000. "Parenti e amici a confronto. Per un sistema degli affetti nelle declamazioni latine (Ps.Quint. *decl.mai.* 9 e 16; *decl.min.* 321)." *Bollettino di Studi Latini* 20: 106–133.

Raja, R. 2012. *Urban Development and Regional Identity in the Eastern Roman Provinces, 50 BC-AD 250. Aphrodisias, Ephesos, Athens, Gerasa*. Copenhagen.

Ramsey, J. 2008. "At What Hour did the Murderers of Julius Caesar Gather on the Ides of March 44 B.C.?" In *In Pursuit of Wissenschaft: Festschrift für William M. Calder III zum 75. Geburtstag*, edited by S. Heilen, R. Kirstein, R. S. Smith, S. M. Trzaskoma, R. L. Van der Wal, and M. Vorwerk, 351–363. Hildesheim.

Raschle, C. R. 2011. "Thémistios et la Seconde Sophistique: le thème du tyran." In *Perceptions of the Second Sophistic and its Times—Regards sur la Seconde Sophistique et son époque*, edited by T. S. Schmidt and P. Fleury, 216–234. Toronto.

Rathmayr, E. 2011. "Die Skulpturenausstattung der C. Laecanius Bassus Nymphaeum in Ephesos." In *Roman Sculpture in Asia Minor*, edited by F. D'Andria and I. Romeo, 130–149. Portsmouth RI.

Rawson, B. 2003. *Children and Childhood in Roman Italy*. Oxford.

Rawson, E. 1975 [1991]. "Caesar's Heritage: Hellenistic Kings and their Roman Equals." *Journal of Roman Studies* 65 (1975) 148–159. Reprinted in E. Rawson, *Roman Culture and Society,* 169–188 (Oxford, 1991).

Rawson, E. 1985. *Intellectual Life in the Late Roman Republic.* Baltimore.

Rawson, E. 1986 [1991]. "Cassius and Brutus: The Memory of the Liberators." In *Past Perspectives: Studies in Greek and Roman Historical Writing,* edited by I. S. Moxon, J. D. Smart, and A. J. Woodman, 101–119 (Cambridge, 1986). Reprinted in E. Rawson, *Roman Culture and Society,* 488–507 (Oxford, 1991).

Rawson, E. 1994. "Caesar: Civil War and Dictatorship." In *The Cambridge Ancient History.* 2nd ed. *Volume IX, The Last Age of the Roman Republic,* edited by J. A. Crook, A. Lintott, and E. Rawson, 424–467. Cambridge.

Rayment, C. S. 1952. "Three Notes on the [*sic*] Roman Declamation." *Classical Weekly* 45: 225–228.

Reardon, B. P. 1971. *Courants littéraires grecs des IIᵉ et IIIᵉ siècles après J.-C.* Paris.

Rebuffat, R. 1974. "Enceintes urbaines et insécurité en Maurétanie Tingitane." *Mélanges de l'École française de Rome* 86: 501–522.

Rebuffat, R. 1986. "Les fortifications urbaines du monde romain." In *La fortification dans l'histoire du monde grec,* edited by P. Leriche and H. Tréziny, 345–361. Paris.

Rebuffat, R. 2012. "Qui va payer l'enceinte urbaine?" In *Enceintes urbaines, sites fortifiés, forteresses d'Afrique du Nord,* edited by J. Leclant and F. Déroche, 25–74. Paris.

Reeves, H. S. 2014. *The Stock Tyrant and the Roman Emperors. The Influence of the Traditional Portrait of Tyranny on Suetonius' Caesares.* Unpublished PhD Dissertation, University of Virginia.

Reinhardt, T. and M. Winterbottom. 2006. *Quintilian,* Institutio Oratoria. Book 2. Oxford.

Reiter, W. M. N. 1992. *Die Säulenstraßen Kleinasiens.* Unpublished *Magisterarbeit,* Geisteswissenschaftliche Fakultät, Universität Wien, 1992.

Renier, E. 1942. *Étude sur l'histoire de la* querela inofficiosi *en droit romain.* Liége.

Rice Holmes, T. 1923. *The Roman Republic and the Founder of the Empire.* 3 vols. Oxford.

Richard, J. 2011. "In the Élites' Toolkit. Decoding the Initiative and Reference System Behind the Investment in the Architecture and Decoration of Roman Nymphaea." *Facta* 5: 65–100.

Richard, J. 2012. *Water for the City, Fountains for the People. Monumental Fountains in the Roman East: An Archaeological Study of Water Management.* Turnhout.

Richard, J. 2016. "Where Do We Go Now? The Archaeology of Monumental Fountains in the Roman and Early Byzantine East." In *Fountains and Water Culture in Byzantium,* edited by B. Shilling and P. Stephenson, 15–35. Cambridge.

Richlin, A. 1997. "Gender and Rhetoric: Producing Manhood in the Schools." In *Roman Eloquence: Rhetoric in Society and Literature,* edited by W. J. Dominik, 90–110. London.

Richlin, A. 2011. "Old Boys: Teacher-Student Bonding in Roman Oratory." *Classical World* 105: 91–107.

Richter, D. S. and W. A. Johnson, eds. 2017. *The Oxford Handbook of the Second Sophistic.* New York.

Riese, A. 1878. Geographi latini minores. Heilbronn.

Riggsby, A. M. 2015. "Roman Legal Education." In *A Companion to Ancient Education,* edited by M. W. Bloomer, 444–451. Chichester.

Rives, J. B. 2011 [2003]. "Magic in Roman Law. The Reconstruction of a Crime." In *The Religious History of the Roman Empire*, edited by J. A. North and S. R. F. Price, 71–108 (Oxford, 2011). Reprinted from *Classical Antiquity* 22 (2003) 313–339.

Rizzelli, G. 1997. Lex Iulia de adulteriis. *Studi sulla disciplina di* adulterium, lenocinium, stuprum. Lecce.

Rizzelli, G. 2001. "Agostino, Ulpiano e Antonino." In Iuris Vincula. *Studi in onore di Mario Talamanca,* vol. 7, 71–120. Naples.

Rizzelli, G. 2012a. "La violenta sessuale su donne nell'esperienza di Roma antica. Note per una storia degli stereotypi." In *El cisne II. Violencia, proceso y discurso sobre género*, edited by E. Höbenreich, V. Kühne, and F. Lamberti, 295–377. Lecce.

Rizzelli, G. 2012b. "Sen. *contr.* 2.4 e la legislazione matrimoniale augustea. Qualche considerazione." *Index* 40: 271–312.

Rizzelli, G. 2014a. "*Adulterium*, immagini, etica, diritto." In Ubi tu Gaius. *Modelli familiari, pratiche sociali, e diritti delle persone nell'età del principato*, edited by F. Milazzo, 145–322. Milan.

Rizzelli, G. 2014b. *Modelli di "follia" nella cultura dei giuristi romani*. Lecce.

Rizzelli, G. 2015. "Declamazione e diritto." In *La declamazione latina. Prospettive a confronto sulla retorica di scuola a Roma antica*, edited by M. Lentano, 211–270. Naples.

Rizzelli, G. 2017. *Padri romani. Discorsi, modelli, norme*. Lecce.

Rizzelli, G. 2019. "Fra giurisprudenza e retorica scolastica. Note sul *ius* a Sofistopoli." Iura *and Legal Systems* 6: 102–114.

Robert, L. 1977 [1989]. "La titulature de Nicée et de Nicomédie: La gloire et la haine." *Harvard Studies in Classical Philology* 81 (1977) 1–39. Reprinted in L. Robert, *Opera Minora Selecta 6* (Amsterdam, 1989) 211–249.

Robert, L. 1980. *À travers l'Asie Mineure. Poètes, prosateurs, monnaies grecques, voyageurs et géographie*. Athens.

Robinson, B. A. 2005. "Fountains and the Formation of Cultural Identity at Roman Corinth." In *Urban Religion in Roman Corinth: Interdisciplinary Approaches*, edited by D. N. Schowalter and S. J. Friesen, 111–140. Cambridge MA.

Robinson, B. A. 2011. *Histories of Peirene: A Corinthian Fountain in Three Millennia*. Princeton.

Robinson, B. A. 2013. "Playing in the Sun: Hydraulic Architecture and Water Displays in Imperial Corinth." *Hesperia* 82: 341–384.

Robinson, O. F. 1995. *The Criminal Law of Ancient Rome*. Baltimore.

Robinson, O. F. 2000. "Roman Criminal Law: Rhetoric and Reality. Some Forms of Rhetoric in the Theodosian Code." In *Au-delà des frontières. Mélanges de droit romain offerts à Witold Wołodkiewicz*, edited by M. Zabłocka, J. Krzynówek, J. Urbanik, and Z. Służewska, vol. 2, 765–785. Warsaw.

Robinson, O. F. 2001. "Unpardonable Crimes: Fourth Century Attitudes." In *Critical Studies in Ancient Law, Comparative Law and Legal History*, edited by W. Cairns and O. F. Robinson, 117–126. Oxford.

Robinson, O. F. 2002. "Quintilian and Adultery." In Iurisprudentia universalis. *Festschrift für Theo Mayer-Maly zum 70. Geburtstag*, edited by M. J. Schermaier, J. M. Rainer, and L. C. Winkel, 631–638. Cologne.

Robinson, O. [F.] 2003. "Quintilian (book III) and his Use of Roman Law." In *Quintilian and the Law*, edited by O. Tellegen-Couperus, 59–66. Louvain.

Rochette, B. 1997. *Le latin dans le monde grec. Recherches sur la diffusion de la langue et des lettres latines dans les provinces hellénophones de l'Empire romain*. Brussels.

Roda, S. 1995. "La polis ellenistica e la *civitas romana:* gli spazi della civiltà." In Graecia capta. *De la conquista de Grecia a la helenización de Roma*, edited by E. Falque and F. Gascó, 83–103. Huelva.

Rodríguez Alvarez, L. 1978. *Las leyes limitadoras de las manumisiones en epoca augustea*. Oviedo.

Rodríguez González, A. M. 2015. "Las declamaciones quintilianeas y la experiencia jurídica romana." *Seminarios Complutenses de Derecho Romano* 28: 941–957.

Rogers, J. 2009. *Kung Fu Monkey* blog http://kfmonkey.blogspot.com/2009/03/ephemera-2009-7.html.

Rogers, A. 2013. *Water and Roman Urbanism: Towns, Waterscapes, Land Transformation and Experience in Roman Britain*. Leiden.

Rogers, D. K. 2018a. "Water Culture in Roman Society." *Ancient History* 1: 1–118.

Rogers, D. K. 2018b. "Shifting Tides: Approaches to the Public Water-Displays of Roman Greece." In *Great Waterworks in Roman Greece. Aqueducts and Monumental Fountain Structures. Function in Context*, edited by G. A. Aristodemou and T. P. Tassios, 173–192. Oxford.

Rogers, R. S. 1933. "Ignorance of the Law in Tacitus and Dio: Two Instances from the History of Tiberius." *Transactions of the American Philological Association* 64: 18–27.

Roisman, H. M. 2007. "Right Rhetoric in Homer." In *A Companion to Greek Rhetoric*, edited by I. Worthington, 429–446. Malden MA.

Romano, E. 1990. *La capanna e il tempio. Vitruvio o dell'architettura*. 2nd ed. Palermo.

Roskam, G. 2007. *Live Unnoticed (λάθε βιώσας). On the Vicissitudes of an Epicurean Doctrine*. Leiden.

Rossi, R. F. 1953. "Bruto, Cicerone et la congiura contro Cesare." *La parola del passato* 8: 26–47.

Roueché, C. 1989. "*Floreat Perge.*" In *Images of Authority: Papers Presented to Joyce Reynolds on the Occasion of her 70th birthday*, edited by C. Roueché and M. M. Mackenzie, 206–228. Cambridge.

Rüfner, T. 2016. "Imperial *Cognitio* Process." In *The Oxford Handbook of Law and Society*, edited by P. J. Du Plessis, C. Ando, and K. Tuori, 257–269. Oxford.

Rundell, J. 2017. *Imaginaries of Modernity: Politics, Cultures, Tensions*. Abingdon.

Ruppe, U. 2010. "Die Stadtmauer von Priene—Zweckbau, Identifikationsobjekt oder Machtsymbol?" In *Neue Forschungen zu antiken Stadtbefestigungen im östlichen Mittelmeerraum und im Vorderen Orient*, edited by J. Lorentzen, F. Pirson, P. Schneider, and U. Wulf-Rheidt, 141–163. Istanbul.

Russell, D. A. 1983. *Greek Declamation*. Cambridge.

Russell, D. A. and N. G. Wilson. 1981. *Menander Rhetor*. Oxford.

Rutherford, I. 1998. *Canons of Style in the Antonine Age: Idea-Theory in its Literary Context*. Oxford.

Ryan, G. 2018. "Building Order: Unified Cityscapes and Elite Collaboration in Roman Asia Minor." *Classical Antiquity* 37: 151–185.

Sablayrolles, R. 1994. "Domitien, l'Auguste ridicule." *Pallas* 40: 113–144.

Saccoccio, A. 2014. "Dall'obbligo alla prestazione degli alimenti alla *obligatio ex lege.*" *Roma e America. Diritto romano comune* 35: 3–40.

Sahlins, M. 1996. *Waiting for Foucault*. 2nd ed. Cambridge.

Saïd, S. 1994. "The City in the Greek Novel." In *The Search for the Ancient Novel*, edited by J. Tatum, 216–236. Baltimore.

Saliou, C. 1996. "Du portique à la rue à portiques. Les rues à colonnades de Palmyre dans le cadre de l'urbanisme romain impérial: originalité et conformisme." *Annales archéologiques arabes syriennes* 42: 319–330.

Saliou, C. 2006a. "Antioche décrite par Libanios. La rhétorique de l'espace urbain et ses enjeux au milieu du quatrième siècle." In *Approches de la Troisième Sophistique. Hommages à Jacques Schamp*, edited by E. Amato, 273–285. Brussels.

Saliou, C. 2006b. "Rhétorique et réalités: l'eau dans l'*Éloge d'Antioche* (Libanios, *Or.* XI)." *Chronos. Revue d'Histoire de l'Université de Balamand* 13: 7–27.

Saliou, C. 2009. "Le palais impériale d'Antioche et son contexte à l'époque de Julien. Réflexions sur l'apport des sources littéraires à l'histoire d'un espace urbain." *Antiquité Tardive* 17: 235–250.

Saliou, C. 2011. "Jouir sans entraves? La notion de τρυφή dans l'*Éloge d'Antioche* de Libanios." In *Libanios, le premier humaniste. Études en hommage à Bernard Schouler*, edited by O. Lagacherie and P.-L. Malosse, 153–165. Alessandria.

Saliou, C. 2013. "La forme mouvante d'une ville: Antioch au fil de l'Oronte." In *Architectures urbains, formes et temps: Mélanges offerts à Pierre Pinon*, edited by M. Lambert-Bresson and A. Térade, 284–290. Paris.

Saliou, C. 2014. "Bains et histoire urbaine. L'exemple d'Antioche sur l'Oronte dans l'Antiquité." In *25 siècles de bain collectif en Orient. Proche-Orient, Égypte et péninsule Arabique*, edited by M. F. Boussac, S. Denoix, T. Fornet, and B. Redon, 657–685. Cairo.

Saliou, C. 2016. "Malalas' Antioch." In *Die Weltchronik des Johannes Malalas*, edited by M. Meier, C. Radtki, and F. Schulz, 59–76. Stuttgart.

Saliou, C. 2018. "Libanius' *Antiochicus*, Mirror of a City? Antioch in 356, Praise and Reality." In *Antioch II. The Many Faces of Antioch: Intellectual Exchange and Religious Diversity, CE 350–450*, edited by S.-P. Bergjan and S. Elm, 35–52. Tübingen.

Saller, R. P. 1982. *Personal Patronage under the Early Empire*. Cambridge.

Saller, R. P. 1994. *Patriarchy, Property and Death in the Roman Family*. Cambridge.

Sandirocco, L. 2013. "*Non solum alimenta praestari debent.*" *Rivista di diritto romano* 13 https://www.ledonline.it/rivistadirittoromano/allegati/dirittoromano13Sandirocco-Alimenta.pdf.

Santalucia, B. 1998. *Diritto e processo penale nell'antica Roma*. 2nd ed. Milan.

Santorelli, B. 2012. "Il tiranno e il *corpus vicarium* nella *XVI Declamazione maggiore* pseudoquintilianea." *Materiali e discussioni per l'analisi dei testi classici* 69: 119–144.

Santorelli, B. 2014. *[Quintiliano] Il ricco accusatto di tradimento (Declamazioni maggiori, 11). Gli amici garanti (Declamazioni maggiori, 16)*. Cassino.

Santorelli, B. 2017a. "Metrical and Accentual Clausulae as Evidence for the Date and Origin of Calpurnius Flaccus." In *Reading Roman Declamation. Calpurnius Flaccus*, edited by M. T. Dinter, C. Guérin, and M. Martinho, 129–140. Berlin.

Santorelli, B. 2017b. "Cecità e insegamento retorico antico." *Lexis* 35: 10–27.

Santorelli, B. 2019. "*Poteram quidem fortiter dicere: 'Pater iussi'*. L'autorità paterna a scuola, tra retorica e diritto." In L. Capogrossi Colognesi, F. Cenerini, F. Lamberti, M. Lentano, G. Rizzelli, and B. Santorelli, *Anatomie della paternità. Padri e famiglia nella cultura romana*, edited by A. Atorino, R. D'Alessio, and L. Parenti, 73–88. Lecce.

Santorelli, B. and A. Stramaglia. 2015. "La declamazione perduta." In *La declamazione latina. Prospettive a confronto sulla retorica di scuola a Roma antica*, edited by M. Lentano, 271–304. Naples.

Santorelli, B. and A. Stramaglia. 2017. *[Quintiliano] Il muro con le impronte di una mano (Declamazioni Maggiori, 1)*. Cassino.

Saradi, H. [G.] 1995. "The *Kallos* of the Byzantine City: The Development of a Rhetorical *Topos* and Historical Reality." *Gesta* 34: 37–56.

Saradi, H. G. 2006. *The Byzantine City in the Sixth Century. Literary Images and Historical Reality*. Athens.

Saradi, H. [G.] 2011. "The Monuments in the Late Byzantine *Ekphraseis* of Cities." *Byzantinoslavika—Revue Internationale des Études Byzantines* 69 supp. 3: 179–192.

Scacchetti, M. G. 1984. "Note sulle differenze di metodo fra Sabiniani e Proculiani." In *Studi in onore di Arnaldo Biscardi*, edited by F. Pastori, vol. 5, 369–404. Milan.

Scafoglio, G. 2014. "Città e acque nell'*Ordo Urbium Nobilium* di Ausonio." In *ΕΝ ΚΑΛΟΙΣ ΚΟΙΝΟΠΡΑΓΙΑ. Hommages à la mémoire de Pierre-Louis Malosse et Jean Bouffartigue*, edited by E. Amato, 405–419. Nantes.

Scarano Ussani, V. 1979. *Valori e storia nella cultura giuridica fra Nerva e Adriano. Studi su Nerazio e Celso*. Naples.

Scarano Ussani, V. 1989. *Empiria e dogmi. La scuola proculiana fra Nerva e Adriano*. Turin.

Scarano Ussani, V. 1997. *L'Ars dei Giuristi. Considerazione sullo statuto epistemologico della giurisprudenza romana*. Turin.

Scarano Ussani, V. 2012. *Disciplina iuris e altri saperi. Studi sulla cultura di alcuni giuristi romani fra tarda repubblica e secondo secolo d. C.* Naples.

Schamberger, M. 1917. De declamationum Romanorum argumentis observationes selectae. Halle.

Scheibelreiter, P. 2012. "*Pharmakos, aries* und *talio*. Rechtsvergleichende Überlegungen zum frühen römischen und griechischen Strafrecht." In *Strafe und Strafrecht in den antiken Welten*, edited by R. Rollinger, M. Lang, and H. Barta, 23–47. Wiesbaden.

Scheid, J. 1984. "La mort du tyran. Chronique de quelques morts programmées." In *Du châtiment dans la cité. Supplices corporels et peine de mort dans la monde antique*, 177–190. Rome.

Scherrer, P. 2006. "Die Fernwasserversorgung von Ephesos in der römischen Kaiserzeit: Synopse der epigraphischen Quellen." In Cura Aquarum *in Ephesus*, edited by G. Wiplinger, vol. 1, 45–58. Louvain.

Schiesaro, A. 2002. "Ovid and the Professional Discourses of Scholarship, Religion, Rhetoric." In *The Cambridge Companion to Ovid*, edited by P. Hardie, 62–75. Cambridge.

Schiller, A. A. 1978. *Roman Law: Mechanisms of Development*. The Hague.

Schindler, K.-H. 1966. *Justinians Haltung zur Klassik. Versuch einer Darstellung an Hand seiner Kontroversen entscheidenden Konstitutionen*. Cologne.

Schmidt, W. A. 1847. *Geschichte der Denk- und Glaubensfreiheit im ersten Jahrhundert der Kaiserherrschaft und des Christenthums*. Berlin.

Schmidt-Hofner, S. 2014. "Der *Defensor Civitatis* und die Entstehung des Notabelnregiments in den spätrömischen Städten." In *Chlodwigs Welt. Organization von Herrschaft um 500*, edited by M. Meier and S. Patzold, 487–522. Stuttgart.

Schmitthenner, W. C. G. 1958. *The Armies of the Triumviral Period: A Study of the Origins of the Roman Imperial Legions*. Unpublished Oxford DPhil thesis.

Schmitthenner, W. [C. G.] 1962. "Das Attentat auf Caesar am 15 März 44 v. Chr." *Geschichte in Wissenschaft und Unterricht* 11: 685–695.

Schmitz, T. [A.] 1997. *Bildung und Macht. Zur sozialen und politischen Funktion der zweiten Sophistik in der griechischen Welt der Kaiserzeit*. Munich.

Schmitz, T. A. 1999. "Performing History in the Second Sophistic." In *Geschichtsschreibung und politischer Wandel im 3. Jh. n. Chr. Kolloquium zu Ehren Karl-Ernst Petzold*, edited by M. Zimmermann, 71–92. Stuttgart.

Schmitz, T. A. 2017. "Professionals of *Paideia*? The Sophists as Performers." In *The Oxford Handbook of the Second Sophistic*, edited by D. S. Richter and W. A. Johnson, 169–180. New York.

Schmitz, W. 2006. "Die Macht über die Sprache: Kommunikation, Politik und soziale Ordnung in Sparta." In *Das frühe Sparta*, edited by A. Luther, M. Meier, and L. Thommen, 89–111. Stuttgart.

Schmölder-Veit, A. 2009. *Brunnen in den Städten des westlichen römischen Reiches*. Wiesbaden.

Schneider, C. 2000. "Quelques réflexions sur la date de publication de 'Grandes Déclamations' pseudo-quintiliennes." *Latomus* 59: 614–632.

Schneider, C. 2016. "L'oeil à l'oeuvre dans le *Tombeau ensorcelé* du pseudo-Quintilien (*Decl.* 10)." In *Reading Roman Declamation. The Declamations Ascribed to Quintilian*, edited by M. T. Dinter, C. Guérin, and M. Martinho, 109–125. Berlin.

Schofield, M. 1986. "*Euboulia* in the *Iliad*." *Classical Quarterly* 36: 6–31.

Schofield, M. 2012. "Antiochus on Social Virtue." In *The Philosophy of Antiochus*, edited by D. Sedley, 173–187. Cambridge.

Schofield, M. 2015. "Seneca on Monarchy and the Political Life: *De Clementia, De Tranquillitate Animi, De Otio*." In *The Cambridge Companion to Seneca*, edited by S. Bartsch and A. Schiesaro, 68–81. Cambridge.

Schulz, F. 1936 [1934]. *Principles of Roman Law* (Oxford, 1936). Translated by M. Wolff from *Prinzipien des römischen Rechts* (Munich, 1934).

Schwartz, P. 2015. "Forensic Intrusion into the Schools of Rhetoric: A Reading of Cassius Severus' Attack on Cestius Pius." In *Law and Ethics in Greek and Roman Declamation*, edited by E. Amato, F. Citti, and B. Huelsenbeck, 63–74. Berlin.

Schwartz, P. 2016. "Tyrans et tyrannicides dans les *Petites déclamations*." In *Reading Roman Declamation. The Declamations Ascribed to Quintilian*, edited by M. T. Dinter, C. Guérin, and M. Martinho, 267–278. Berlin.

Schwartz, S. 2016. *From Bedroom to Courtroom. Law and Justice in the Greek Novel*. Groningen.

Schwartz Frydman, P. 2016. "Cestio Pío, lector de Cicerón y de Virgilio." In *Fabrique de la déclamation antique (controverses et suasoires)*, edited by R. Poignault and C. Schneider, 245–255. Lyon.

Sciortino, S. 2003. "C. 8.46.6: Brevi osservazioni in tema di *abdicatio* ed *apokhruxis*." *Annali del Seminario Giuridico della Università di Palermo* 48: 333–378.

Sedley, D. 1997. "The Ethics of Brutus and Cassius." *Journal of Roman Studies* 87: 41–53.

Sedley, D. 2010. "Philosophy." In *The Oxford Handbook of Roman Studies*, edited by A. Barchiesi and W. Scheidel, 701–712. Oxford.

Sedley, D., ed. 2012. *The Philosophy of Antiochus.* Cambridge.

Seeck, O. 1902. *Kaiser Augustus.* Bielefeld.

Seel, O. 1939. "Caesar und seine Gegner." *Erlanger Universitäts-Reden* 24. Erlangen.

Seelye, J. D. 2001. "Ivan Who?: A Second Look at the Other Book that is Supposed to Have Started the Civil War." In *Finding Colonial Americas. Essays Honoring J. A. Leo Lemay,* edited by C. Mulford and D. S. Shields, 415–433. Cranbury NJ.

Seemann, L. 2019. "Die Tyrannenmörder auf dem Kapitol." *Historia* 68: 95–114.

Segal, A. 1997. *From Function to Monument. Urban Landscapes of Roman Palestine, Syria, and Provincia Arabia.* Oxford.

Seston, W. 1966. "Les murs, les portes et les tours des enceintes urbaines et le problème des *res sanctae* en droit romain." In *Mélanges d'archéologie et d'histoire offerts à André Piganiol,* edited by R. Chevallier, vol. 3, 1489–1498. Paris.

Settis, S. 1973. "'Esedra' e 'ninfeo' nella terminologia architettonica del mondo romano. Dall'età repubblicana alla tarda antichità." *Aufstieg und Niedergang der römischen Welt* I.4: 661–745.

Shackleton Bailey, D. R. 1980. *Cicero* Epistulae ad Quintum fratrem et M. Brutum. Cambridge.

Sidoli, N. 2015. "Mathematics Education." In *A Companion to Ancient Education,* edited by W. M. Bloomer, 387–400. Chichester.

Sigismund, S. 2008. *Der politische Mord in der späten römischen Republik.* Hamburg.

Sigmund, C. 2014. *"Königtum" in der politischen Kultur des spätrepublikanischen Rom.* Berlin.

Signorini, R. 2009. Adsignare Libertum. *La disponibilità del patronatus tra normazione senatoria ed interpretatio giurisprudenziale.* Milan.

Sinclair, P. 1993. "The *Sententia* in *Rhetorica ad Herennium*: A Study in the Sociology of Rhetoric." *American Journal of Philology* 114: 561–580.

Sinclair, P. 1995. "Political Declensions in Latin Grammar and Oratory 55 BCE–CE 39." In *Roman Literature and Ideology.* Ramus *Essays for J. P. Sullivan,* edited by A. J. Boyle, 92–109. Bendigo, Australia.

Sirago, V. 1956. "Tyrannus. Teoria e prassi antitirannica in Cicerone e suoi contemporanei." *Rendiconti dell'Accademia di Archeologia Lettere e Belle Arti di Napoli* n.s. 31: 179–225.

Sirks, A. J. B. 1981. "Informal Manumission and the Lex *Junia." Revue internationale des droits de l'antiquité* 3rd ser. 28: 247–276.

Sirks, A. J. B. 1983. "The *lex Junia* and the Effects of Informal Manumission and Iteration." *Revue internationale des droits de l'antiquité* 3rd ser. 30: 211–292.

Sirks, [A. J.] B. 1988. "Juridical Rationality in Rhetorics [*sic*]: The Roman Law in the Minor Declamations Ascribed to Quintilian, nos. 340 and 342." In *Atti del III Seminario Romanistico Gardesano. Promosso dall'Istituto Milanese di diritto Romano et storia dei diritti Antichi,* 332–359. Milan.

Sirks, [A. J.] B. 2002a. "Sailing in the Off-Season with Reduced Financial Risk." In Speculum Iuris. *Roman Law as a Reflection of Social and Economic Life in Antiquity,* edited by J.-J. Aubert and [A. J.] B. Sirks, 134–150. Ann Arbor.

Sirks, [A. J.] B. 2002b. "Der Playboy im römischen Recht." In Iurisprudentia Universalis. *Festschrift für Theo Mayer-Maly zum 70. Geburtstag,* edited by M. J. Schermaier, J. M. Rainer, and L. C. Winkel, 709–718. Cologne.

Smith, C. 2006. "*Adfectio Regni* in the Roman Republic." In *Ancient Tyranny,* edited by S. Lewis, 49–64. Edinburgh.

Smith, C. F. 1907. "What Constitutes a State?" *Classical Journal* 2: 299–302.

Solazzi, S. 1899. *La restituzione della dote nel diritto romano*. Città di Castello.

Söllner, A. 1969. *Zur Vorgeschichte und Funktion der* Actio Rei Uxoriae. Cologne.

Soverini, P. 2002. "*Saevitia* tirannica e regime imperiale in Seneca e in Tacito." In *TEPΨΙΣ. In ricordo di M. L. Coletti*, edited by M. S. Celentano, 173–195. Alessandria.

Speidel, M. A. 2017. "Antoninus Pius, das Militär und der Krieg. Epigraphische Korrekturen zur literarischen Überlieferung." In *Jenseits des Narrativs. Antoninus Pius in den nicht-literarischen Quellen*, edited by C. Michels and P. F. Mittag, 255–268. Stuttgart.

Sprenger, J. 1911. Questiones in rhetorum romanorum declamationes iuridicae. Halle.

Stagl, J. F. 2012. "La *'lis de dotibus socrus et nurus'* e il potere del *'favor dotis'* (Quint. *Decl.* 360)." *Index* 40: 326–341.

Starace, P. 2007. "Venuleio, il parricidio, i servi, la natura." In *Testi e problemi del giusnaturalismo romano*, edited by D. Mantovani and A. Schiavone, 497–518. Pavia.

Starr, C. G. 1949. "Epictetus and the Tyrant." *Classical Philology* 44: 20–29.

Stein, P. 1966. Regulae Iuris. *From Juristic Rules to Legal Maxims*. Edinburgh.

Stein, P. 1972. "The Two Schools of Jurists in the Early Roman Principate." *Cambridge Law Journal* 31: 8–31.

Stein, P. 1990. "The Origins of *Stellionatus*." *Iura* 41: 79–89.

Stein, P. 1993. "The Crime of Fraud in the Uncodified Civil Law." *Current Legal Problems* 46: 135–147.

Steinwenter, A. 1947. "Rhetorik und römischer Zivilprozeß." *Zeitschrift der Savigny-Stiftung für Rechtsgeschichte, Romanistische Abteilung* 65: 69–120.

Stenger, J. 2009. *Hellenische Identität in der Spätantike. Pagane Autoren und ihr Unbehagen an der eigenen Zeit*. Berlin.

Stevens, S. 2016. "*Candentia Moenia*. The Symbolism of Roman City Walls." In *Focus on Fortifications. New Research on Fortifications in the Ancient Mediterranean and the Near East*, edited by R. Frederiksen, S. Müth, P. I. Schneider, and M. Schnelle, 288–299. Oxford.

Stevens, S. 2017. *City Boundaries and Urban Development in Roman Italy*. Louvain.

Stevenson, T. 2015. *Julius Caesar and the Transformation of the Roman Republic*. Abingdon.

Stewens, W. 1963. *Marcus Brutus als Politiker*. Zurich.

Stinson, P. 2007. "Imitation and Adaptation in Architectural Design: Two Roman Basilicas at Ephesus and Aphrodisias." In *Neue Zeiten—Neue Sitten. Zu Rezeption und Integration römischen und italischen Kulturguts in Kleinasien*, edited by M. Meyer, 91–100. Vienna.

Stolfi, E. 2011. "'*Argumentum auctoritatis*,' citazioni e forme di approvazione nella scrittura dei giuristi romani." In *Tra retorica e diritto. Linguaggi e forme argomentative nella tradizione giuridica*, edited by A. Lovato, 85–135. Bari.

Storch, R. H. 1995. "Relative Deprivation and the Ides of March: Motive for Murder." *Ancient History Bulletin* 9: 45–52.

Stramaglia, A. 1999. *[Quintiliano] I gemelli malati: un caso di vivisezione (Declamazioni maggiori, 8)*. Cassino.

Stramaglia, A. 2010. "Come si insegnava a declamare? Riflessioni sulle *'routines'* scholastiche nell'insegamento retorico antico." In *Libri di scuola e pratiche didattiche. Dall'Antichità al Rinascimento*, edited by L. Del Corso and O. Pecere, 111–151. Cassino.

Stramaglia, A. 2013. *[Quintiliano] L'astrologo (Declamazioni maggiori, 4)*. Cassino.

Stramaglia, A. 2015. "Temi 'sommersi' e trasmissione dei testi nella declamazione antica (con un regesto di papiri declamatori)." In *Nel segno del testo. Edizioni, materiali e studi per Oronzo Pecere*, edited by L. del Corso, F. De Vivo, and A. Stramaglia, 147–178. Florence.

Strasburger, H. 1968 [1953]. *Caesar im Urteil seiner Zeitgenossen* (Darmstadt, 1968). Reprinted from *Historische Zeitschrift* 175 (1953) 225–264.

Strasburger, H. 1990. *Ciceros philosophisches Spätwerk als Aufruf gegen die Herrschaft Caesars.* Hildesheim.

Strauss, B. 2015. *The Death of Caesar.* New York.

Strauss, C. 2006. "The Imaginary." *Anthropological Theory* 6: 322–344.

Strobel, C. 2009. "The Lexica of the Second Sophistic: Safeguarding Atticism." In *Standard Languages and Language Standards: Greek, Past and Present*, edited by A. Georgakopoulou and M. Silk, 93–107. Farnham.

Stroh, W. 2003. "*Declamatio*." In *Studium declamatorium. Untersuchungen zu Schulübungen und Prunkreden von der Antike bis zur Neuzeit*, edited by J. Dingel, B.-J. Schröder, and J.-P. Schröder, 5–34. Munich.

Stroup, S. C. 2007. "Greek Rhetoric Meets Rome: Expansion, Resistance, and Acculturation." In *A Companion to Roman Rhetoric*, edited by W. Dominik and J. Hall, 23–37. Malden MA.

Stroux, J. 1949 [1926]. "*Summum ius summa iniuria. Ein Kapitel aus der Geschichte der Interpretatio Iuris*." In J. Stroux, *Römische Rechtswissenschaft und Rhetorik*, 7–66 (Potsdam, 1949). Reprinted from *Festschrift Paul Speiser-Sarasin zum 80. Geburtstag am 16. Oktober 1926*, 115–156 (Leipzig, 1926) (*non vidi*).

Sumi, G. S. 2005. *Ceremony and Power. Performing Politics in Rome Between Republic and Empire.* Ann Arbor.

Suolahti, J. 1955. *The Junior Officers of the Roman Army in the Republican Period.* Helsinki.

Sussman, L. A. 1984. "The Elder Seneca and Declamation Since 1900: A Bibliography." *Aufstieg und Niedergang der römischen Welt* II.32.1: 557–577.

Sussman, L. A. 1994. *The Declamations of Calpurnius Flaccus.* Leiden.

Sussman, L. A. 1995. "Sons and Fathers in the *Major Declamations* Ascribed to Quintilian." *Rhetorica* 13: 179–192.

Swain, S. 1996. *Hellenism and Empire. Language, Classicism, and Power in the Greek World, AD 50–250.* Oxford.

Swist, J. J. 2017. "Sophistry and Sorcery in Libanius' *Declamations*." *Greek, Roman, and Byzantine Studies* 57: 431–453.

Syme, R. 1939. *The Roman Revolution.* Oxford.

Syme, R. 1980 [1984]. "No Son for Caesar?" *Historia* 29 (1980) 422–437. Reprinted in R. Syme, *Roman Papers*, edited by A. R. Birley, vol. 3, 1236–1250 (Oxford, 1984).

Tabacco, R. 1978. "Povertà e ricchezza. L'unità tematica della declamazione XIII dello Pseudo-Quintiliano." *Materiali e contributi per la storia della narrativa greco-latina* 2: 37–70.

Tabacco, R. 1979. "*Apes pauperis* [ps.-Quint. XIII]. Articolazione tematica ed equilibri strutturali." *Atti dell'Accademia Pontaniana* 28: 81–104.

Tabacco, R. 1980. "Le declamazioni maggiori pseudoquintilianee (Rassegna critica degli studi dal 1915 al 1979)." *Bollettino di Studi Latini* 10: 82–112.

Tabacco, R. 1985. "Il tiranno nelle declamazioni di scuola in lingua latina." *Memorie della Accademia delle Scienze di Torino II. Classe di Scienze Morali, Storiche, Filologiche* ser. 5, v. 9 (1–2): 1–141.

Tabaczek, M. 2002. *Zwischen Stoa und Suq: Die Säulenstraßen im Vorderen Orient in römischer Zeit unter besonderer Berücksichtigung von Palmyra.* Unpublished PhD Dissertation, Cologne. https://kups.ub.uni-koeln.de/1380.

Tarver, T. 1997. "Varro and the Antiquarianism of Philosophy." In Philosophia Togata *II. Plato and Aristotle at Rome*, edited by J. Barnes and M. Griffin, 130–164. Oxford.

Tatum, W. J. 2008. *Always I am Caesar.* Malden MA.

Taubenschlag, R. 1934 [1959]. "Der Einfluss der Provinzialrechte auf das römische Privatrecht." *Atti del Congresso Internazionale di Diritto Romano*, vol. 1, 281–315 (Pavia, 1934). Reprinted in R. Taubenschlag, Opera Minora, vol. 1, 421–460 (Warsaw, 1959).

Taubenschlag, R. 1955. *The Law of Greco-Roman Egypt in the Light of the Papyri, 332 B.C.–640 AD.* 2nd ed. Warsaw.

Taubenschlag, R. 1959 [1919–1920]. "Le droit local dans les *Digesta* et *responsa* de Cervidius Scaevola." In R. Taubenschlag, *Opera Minora*, vol. 1, 505–517 (Warsaw, 1959). Reprinted from *Bulletin de l'Académie Polonaise des Sciences et des Lettres, Classe de philologie, Classe d'histoire et de philosophie* [no vol.] (1919–1920): 45–55.

Taubenschlag, R. 1959 [1926]. "Le droit local dans les constitutions prédioclétiennes." In R. Taubenschlag, *Opera Minora*, vol. 1, 519–533 (Warsaw, 1959). Reprinted from *Mélanges de droit romain dédiés à Georges Cornil*, edited by F. de Zulueta and J. Van Kan, vol. 2, 497–512 (Paris, 1926).

Teegarden, D. A. 2014. *Death to Tyrants! Ancient Greek Democracy and the Struggle against Tyranny.* Princeton.

Teitler, H. C. 1985. Notarii *and* Exceptores. Amsterdam.

Tellegen, J. W. 1982. *The Roman Law of Succession in the Letters of Pliny the Younger*, vol. 1. Zutphen.

Tellegen, J. W. and O. Tellegen-Couperus. 2000. "Law and Rhetoric in the *Causa Curiana*." *Orbis Iuris Romani* 6: 171–202.

Tellegen-Couperus, O. 2003. "A Clarifying *Sententia* Clarified: On *Institutio Oratoria* VIII.5.19." In *Quintilian and the Law. The Art of Persuasion in Law and Politics*, edited by O. Tellegen-Couperus, 213–221. Louvain.

Tellegen-Couperus, O., and J. W. Tellegen. 2013. "*Artes Urbanae*: Roman Law and Rhetoric." In *New Frontiers. Law and Society in the Roman World*, edited by P. J. Du Plessis, 31–50. Edinburgh.

Tellegen-Couperus, O., and J. W. Tellegen. 2016. "Reading a Dead Man's Mind: Hellenistic Philosophy, Rhetoric and Roman Law." In *Cicero's Law. Rethinking Roman Law of the Late Republic*, edited by P. J. Du Plessis, 26–49. Edinburgh.

Tempest, K. 2017. *Brutus. The Noble Conspirator.* New Haven.

Theocharaki, A. M. 2020. *The Ancient Circuit Walls of Athens.* Berlin.

Thomas, E. 2007. *Monumentality and the Roman Empire: Architecture in the Antonine Age.* Oxford.

Thomas, E. 2014. "On the Sublime in Architecture." In *Art and Rhetoric in Roman Culture*, edited by J. Elsner and M. Meyer, 37–88. Cambridge.

Thomas, H. 2014. *World Without End. Spain, Philip II, and the First Global Empire*. New York.

Thomas, Y. 1978. "Le droit entre les mots et les choses. Rhétorique et jurisprudence à Rome." *Archives de philosophie de droit* 23: 93–114.

Thomas, Y. 1983. "Paura dei padri e violenza dei figli: immagini retoriche e norme di diritto." In *La paura dei padri nella società antica e medievale*, edited by E. Pellizer and N. Zorzetti, 113–140. Rome.

Thomas, Y. 1984 [2017]. *"Vitae necisque potestas.* Le père, la cité, la mort." In *Du châtiment dans la cité. Supplices corporels et peine de mort dans le monde antique*, 499–548 (Rome, 1984). Reprinted with additions as "Le puissance de vie et de mort." In Y. Thomas, *La mort du père. Sur le crime de parricide à Rome*, edited by P. Napoli, 165–200, 271–288 (Paris, 2017).

Tivier, H. 1868. De arte declamandi et de romanis declamatoribus. Paris.

Tobin, J. 1997. *Herodes Attikos and the City of Athens. Patronage and Conflict under the Antonines.* Amsterdam.

Toher, M. 2005. "Tillius and Horace." *Classical Quarterly* 55: 183–189.

Toher, M. 2006. "The Earliest Depiction of Caesar and the Later Tradition." In *Julius Caesar in Western Culture*, edited by M. Wyke, 29–44. Malden MA.

Toher, M. 2017. *Nicolaus of Damascus. The Life of Augustus and the Autobiography.* Cambridge.

Tomassi, G. 2014. "Continuità e innovazione nel *Tirannicida* di Coricio di Gaza (*op.* XXVI [*decl.* 7] F./R.)." In *Discorso pubblico e declamazione scolastica a Gaza nella tarda antichità. Coricio di Gaza e la sua opera*, edited by E. Amato, L. Thévenet, and G. Ventrella, 204–229. Bari.

Tomassi, G. 2015. "Tyrants and Tyrannicides: Between Literary Creation and Contemporary Reality in Greek Declamation." In *Law and Ethics in Greek and Roman Declamation*, edited by E. Amato, F. Citti, and B. Huelsenbeck, 249–267. Berlin.

Tomassi, G. 2017. "La pratica declamatoria nella scuola di Gaza: il caso del *Tirannicida* di Coricio." In *L'École de Gaza: espace littéraire de identité culturelle dans l'Antiquité tardive*, edited by E. Amato, A. Corcella, and D. Lauritzen, 339–366. Louvain.

Trabucco della Torretta, M. 2018. "New Water from Old Spouts: The Case of the Arsinoe Fountain of Messene." In *Great Waterworks in Roman Greece. Aqueducts and Monumental Fountain Structures. Function in Context*, edited by G. A. Aristodemou and T. P. Tassios, 235–245. Oxford.

Trampedach, K. 2006. "Die Tyrannis als Wunsch- und Schreckbild." In *Gewalt und Ästhetik. Zur Gewalt und ihrer Darstellung in der griechischen Klassik*, edited by B. Seidensticker and M. Vöhler, 3–27. Berlin.

Treggiari, S. 1991. *Roman Marriage. Iusti Coniuges from the Time of Cicero to the Time of Ulpian.* Oxford.

Treggiari, S. 2015. "The Education of the Ciceros." In *A Companion to Ancient Education*, edited by W. M. Bloomer, 240–251. Chichester.

Treu, M. 1948. "Zur *clementia* Caesars." *Museum Helveticum* 5: 197–217.

Tuori, K. 2004 [2007]. "The *ius respondendi* and the Freedom of Roman Jurisprudence." *Revue internationale des droits de l'antiquité* 51 (2004) 295–337. Reprinted in K. Tuori, *Ancient Roman Lawyers and Modern Legal Ideals*, 73–111 (Frankfurt, 2007).

Tuori, K. 2007. *Ancient Roman Lawyers and Modern Legal Ideals*. Frankfurt.

Turchetti, M. 2001. *Tyrannie et tyrannicide de l'Antiquité à nos jours.* Paris.

Turner, V. 1974. *Dramas, Fields, and Metaphors. Symbolic Action in Human Society.* Ithaca NY.

Turner, V. and E. Turner. 1978. *Image and Pilgrimage in Christian Culture. Anthropological Perspectives*. New York.

Tuttahs, G. 2007. *Milet und das Wasser—Ein Leben in Wohlstand und Not in Antike, Mittelalter und Gegenwart*. Siegburg.

Twain, M. 1982 [1883]. *Mississippi Writings: The Adventures of Tom Sawyer; Life on the Mississippi; Adventures of Huckleberry Finn; Pudd'nhead Wilson* (New York, 1982 [Boston, 1883]).

Uğurlu, N. B. 2009. *The Roman Nymphaea in the Cities of Asia Minor: Function in Context*. Saarbrücken.

Unruh, D. B. 2015. "The Predatory Palace: Seneca's *Thyestes* and the Architecture of Tyranny." In *Urban Dreams and Realities in Antiquity*, edited by A. M. Kemezis, 246–272. Leiden.

Urbanik, J. 2008. "Dioskoros and the Law (on Succession): *Lex Falcidia* Revisited." In *Les archives de Dioscore d'Aphrodité cent ans après leur découverte. Histoire et culture dans l'Égypte byzantine*, edited by J.-L. Fournet, 117–142. Paris.

Ureña Bracero, J. 2007. "Algunas consideraciones sobre la autoría de los *progymnasmata* atribuidos a Libanio." In *Escuela y literatura en Grecia Antigua*, edited by J. A. Fernández Delgado, F. Pordomingo, and A. Stramaglia, 645–690. Cassino.

Ürögdi, G. 1980. "Caesar, Marcus Antonius und die im Tempel der Ops aufbewahrten öffentlichen Gelder." In *Les 'dévaluations' à Rome: époque républicaine et impériale*, edited by G. Vallet, vol. 2, 49–57. Rome.

Valachova, C. 2018. "The Garden and the Forum. Epicurean Adherence and Political Affiliation in the Late Republic." In *Institutions and Ideology in Republican Rome*, edited by H. van der Blom, C. Gray, and C. Steel, 147–164. Cambridge.

Van Dam, R. 2007. *The Roman Revolution of Constantine*. New York.

van den Berg, C. S. 2014. *The World of Tacitus' Dialogus de Oratoribus. Aesthetics and Empire in Ancient Rome*. Cambridge.

van der Poel, M. 2007. "Material for a History of the Latin Declamation in the Renaissance." In *Papers on Rhetoric VIII: Declamation*, edited by L. Calboli Montefusco, 267–291. Rome.

van der Vliet, E. C. L. 2012. "The Durability and Decline of Democracy in Hellenistic *Poleis*." *Mnemosyne* 65: 771–786.

Van Hoof, L. 2010. "Greek Rhetoric and the Later Roman Empire. The Bubble of the 'Third Sophistic.'" *Antiquité Tardive* 18: 211–224.

van Hooff, A. J. L. 1990. *From* Autothanasia *to Suicide. Self-Killing in Classical Antiquity*. London.

van Mal-Maeder, D. 2003 [2007]. "L'autre voix. Représentations de femmes dans les déclamations latines." In *Gender Studies in Altertumswissenschaften: Rollenkonstrukte in der antiken Texten*, edited by T. Fuhrer and S. Zinsli, 93–105 (Trier, 2003). Reprinted in D. van Mal-Maeder, *La fiction de déclamations*, 97–107 (Leiden, 2007).

van Mal-Maeder, D. 2007. *La fiction des déclamations*. Leiden.

van Nijf, O. [M.] 2001. "Local Heroes: Athletics, Festivals, and Elite Self-Fashioning in the Roman East." In *Being Greek under Rome. Cultural Identity, the Second Sophistic and the Development of Empire*, edited by S. Goldhill, 306–334. Cambridge.

van Nijf, O. M. and R. Alston, eds. 2011. *Political Culture in the Greek City after the Classical Age*. Louvain.

Vandenbossche, A. 1953. "Recherches sur le suicide en droit romain." In *ΠΑΓΚΑΡΠΕΙΑ. Mélanges Henri Grégoire*, edited by J. Moreau, vol. 4, 471–516. Brussels.

Vander Waerdt, P. A. 1994. "Philosophical Influence on Roman Jurisprudence? The Case of Stoicism and Natural Law." *Aufstieg und Niedergang der römischen Welt* II.36.7: 4851–4900.

Vanderspoel, J. 2007. "Hellenistic Rhetoric in Theory and Practice." In *A Companion to Greek Rhetoric*, edited by I. Worthington, 124–138. Malden MA.

Ventoux, O. 2017. "Le premier des citoyens à Pergame sous les Haut-Empire: C. Antius Aulus Iulius Quadratus." In *The Politics of Honour in the Greek Cities of the Roman Empire*, edited by A. Heller and O. M. van Nijf, 339–369. Leiden.

Ventrella, G. 2016. "Da esercizio retorico a realtà vivente. La declamazione contro i tiranni nella polemica anti-Domizianea di Dione di Prusa (*Or.* 6)." In *Fabrique de la déclamation antique (controverses et suasoires)*, edited by R. Poignault and C. Schneider, 393–410. Lyon.

Ventura da Silva, G. 2011. "Qualche riflessione sull'idea di città nell'*Oratio* XI di Libanio." In *Libanios, le premier humaniste. Études en hommage à Bernard Schouler*, edited by O. Lagacherie and P.-L. Malosse, 133–140. Alessandria.

Venturini, C. 1988. "'*Accusatio Adulterii*' e politica costantiniana (per un riesame di *CTh* 9, 7, 2)." *Studia et Documenta Historiae et Iuris* 54: 66–109.

Ver Eecke, M. 2008. *La République et le roi. Le mythe de Romulus à la fin de la République romaine.* Paris.

Viehweg, T. 1953 [1993]. *Topik und Jurisprudenz. Ein Beitrag zur rechtswissenschaftlichen Grundlagenforschung* (Munich, 1953). Translated by W. C. Durham, Jr. as *Topics and Law. A Contribution to Basic Research in Law* (Frankfurt, 1993).

Vinthagen, S. and A. Johansson 2013. "'Everyday Resistance': Exploration of a Concept and its Theories." *Resistance Studies* 1: 1–46.

Vix, J.-L. 2010. *L'enseignement de la rhétorique au II$^e$ siècle ap. J.-C. à travers les discours 30–34 d'Aelius Aristide.* Turnhout.

Voigt, M. 1856–1876. *Das ius naturale, aequum et bonum, und ius gentium der Römer.* 4 vols. Leipzig.

Volterra, E. 1929 [1999]. "*Stellionatus*." *Studi Sassaresi* 7 (1929) 107–143. Reprinted in E. Volterra, *Diritto criminale e diritti dell'antico oriente mediterraneo* (= *Scritti guiridici* 7), 21–57 (Naples, 1999).

Vonderstein, M. ed. 2007. *Die Kaiserpaläste auf dem Palatin in Rom. Neue deutsche Forschungen / I palazzi imperiali sul Palatino a Roma. Le nuove ricerche tedesche.* Berlin.

Voss, W. E. 1982. *Recht und Rhetorik in den Kaisergesetzen der Spätantike. Eine Untersuchung zum nachklassischen Kauf- und Übereignungsrecht.* Frankfurt.

Vössing, K. 1995. "*Non scholae sed vitae*—der Streit um die Deklamationen und ihre Funktion als Kommunikationstraining." In *Kommunikation durch Zeichen und Wort*, edited by G. Binder and K. Ehlich, 91–136. Trier.

Vössing, K. 1997. *Schule und Bildung im Nordafrika der Römischen Kaiserzeit.* Brussels.

Vössing, K. 2004. *Mensa Regia. Das Bankett beim hellenistischen König und beim römischen Kaiser.* Munich.

Vössing, K. 2010. "Der Kaiser und die Deklamationen." In *Neronia VIII. Bibliothèques, livres et culture écrite dans l'empire romain de César à Hadrian*, edited by Y. Perrin, 301–314. Brussels.

Wacke, A. 1980. "Der Selbstmord im römischen Recht und in der Rechtsentwicklung." *Zeitschrift der Savigny-Stiftung für Rechtsgeschichte, Romanistische Abteilung* 97: 26–77.

Walker, B. 1960. *The Annals of Tacitus: A Study in the Writing of History.* 2nd ed. Manchester.

Walker, S. E. C. 1979. *The Architectural Development of Roman Nymphaea in Greece.* Unpublished PhD dissertation, University of London.

Walter, G. 1938. *Brutus et la fin de la République.* Paris.

Walters, J. 1997. "Soldiers and Whores in a Pseudo-Quintilian Declamation." In *Gender and Ethnicity in Ancient Italy,* edited by T. Cornell and K. Lomas, 109–114. London.

Wassmann, H. 1996. *Ciceros Widerstand gegen Caesars Tyrannis. Untersuchungen zur politischen Bedeutung der philosophischen Spätschriften.* Bonn.

Watson, A. 1995. *The Spirit of Roman Law.* Athens GA.

Weaver, P. 2002. "*Consilium Praesidis*: Advising Govenors." In *Thinking like a Lawyer: Essays on Legal History and General History for John Crook on his Eightieth Birthday,* edited by P. McKechnie, 43–62. Leiden.

Webb, R. 2001. "The *Progymnasmata* as Practice." In *Education in Greek and Roman Antiquity,* edited by Y. L. Too, 289–316. Leiden.

Webb, R. 2009. Ekphrasis, *Imagination and Persuasion in Ancient Rhetorical Theory and Practice.* Farnham.

Weiss, C. F. 2011. *Living Fluidly: Uses and Meanings of Water in Asia Minor (Second Century BCE—Second Century CE).* Unpublished PhD dissertation, Brown University.

Weiss, D. 2020. "The Founder's Tomb. Frescoes Discovered in a Jordanian Village Narrate the Early Days of a Once-Cosmopolitan City on the Eastern Edge of the Roman Empire." *Archaeology* 73.2 (March/April): 38–41.

Weiss, P. 1991. "*Auxe Perge*: Beobachtungen zu einem bemerkenswerten städtischen Dokument des späten 3. Jahrhunderts n. Chr." *Chiron* 21: 353–393.

Welch, K. 2015. "Programme and Narrative in *Civil Wars* 2.118–4.138." In *Appian's Roman History. Empire and Civil War,* edited by K. Welch, 277–304. Swansea.

Westlake, H. D. 1994. "Dion and Timoleon." In *The Cambridge Ancient History.* 2nd ed. *Volume VI, The Fourth Century B.C.,* edited by D. M. Lewis, J. Boardman, S. Hornblower, and M. Ostwald, 693–722. Cambridge.

Wheeler, E. L. 1993. "Methodological Limits and the Mirage of Roman Strategy Part I" and "Part II." *Journal of Military History* 57: 7–41 and 215–240.

Whitmarsh, T. 2001. *Greek Literature and the Roman Empire: The Politics of Imitation.* Oxford.

Whitmarsh, T. 2005. *The Second Sophistic.* Oxford.

Wibier, M. 2016. "Cicero's Reception in the Juristic Tradition of the Early Empire." In *Cicero's Law. Rethinking Roman Law in the Late Republic,* edited by P. J. Du Plessis, 100–122. Edinburgh.

Wibier, M. 2020. "Legal Education and Legal Culture in Gaul during the Principate." In *Law in the Roman Provinces,* edited by K. Czajkowski and B. Eckhardt, 462–485. Oxford.

Wickert, L. 1954. "*Princeps (civitatis),*" *RE* XXII.2 cols. 1998–2296.

Wieacker, F. 1988. *Römische Rechtsgeschichte,* vol. 1. Munich.

Wieacker, F. 2006. *Römische Rechtsgeschichte,* vol. 2, edited by J. G. Wolf. Munich.

Wiemer, H.-U. 2003. "Vergangenheit und Gegenwart im *Antiochikos* des Libanios." *Klio* 85: 442–468.

Wiemer, H.-U. 2013. "Hellenistic Cities: The End of Greek Democracy?" In *A Companion to Ancient Greek Government,* edited by H. Beck, 54–69. Chichester.

Wilde, O. 1921 [1889]. "The Decay of Lying," *Intentions.* 14th ed. 1–54 (London, 1921). Reprinted from *The Nineteenth Century. A Monthly Review* 25 (January-June, 1889): 35–56.

Williams, C. J. 1979. *The Development of Monumental Street Architecture with Special Emphasis on Roman Asia Minor*. Unpublished PhD diss. University of London, Institute of Archaeology.

Williams, G. 1978. *Change and Decline. Roman Literature in the Early Empire*. Berkeley and Los Angeles.

Williams, G. 1980. *Figures of Thought in Roman Poetry*. New Haven.

Wilson, A. 2007. "Urban Development in the Severan Empire." In *Severan Culture*, edited by S. Swain, S. Harrison, and J. Elsner, 290–326. Cambridge.

Winter, E. 1996. *Staatliche Baupolitik und Baufürsorge in den römischen Provinzen des kaiserzeitlichen Kleinasien*. Bonn.

Winterbottom, M. 1982 [2019]. "Cicero and the Silver Age." In *Éloquence et rhétorique chez Cicéron*, edited by W. Ludwig, 237–266 (Geneva, 1982). Reprinted in M. Winterbottom, *Papers on Quintilian and Ancient Declamation*, edited by A. Stramaglia, F. Romana Nocchi, and G. Russo, 66–86 (Oxford, 2019).

Winterbottom, M. 1982. "Schoolroom and Courtroom." In *Rhetoric Revalued. Papers from the International Society for the History of Rhetoric*, edited by B. Vickers, 59–70. Binghamton NY.

Winterbottom, M. 1984. *The Minor Declamations Ascribed to Quintilian*. Berlin.

Winterbottom, M. 1998 [2019]. "Quintilian the Moralist." In *Quintiliano: historia y actualidad de la retórica*, edited by E. del Río Sanz, J. A. Caballero López, and T. Albaladejo Mayordomo, 317–334 (Calahorra, 1998). Reprinted in M. Winterbottom, *Papers on Quintilian and Ancient Declamation*, edited by A. Stramaglia, F. Romana Nocchi, and G. Russo, 176–190 (Oxford, 2019).

Wirszubski, Ch. 1950. *Libertas as a Political Idea at Rome during the Late Republic and Early Principate*. Cambridge.

Wiseman, T. P. 2009. *Remembering the Roman People: Essays on Late-Republican Politics and Literature*. Oxford.

Witschel, C. 2006. "Verrückte Kaiser? Zur Selbststilisierung und Außenwahrnehmung nonkonformer Herrscherfiguren in der römischen Kaiserzeit." In *Einblicke in die Antike: Orte—Praktiken—Strukturen*, edited by C. Ronning, 87–129. Munich.

Wlassak, M. 1905. "Die prätorischen Freilassungen." *Zeitschrift der Savigny-Stiftung für Rechtsgeschichte, Romanistische Abteilung* 26: 367–431.

Woerther, F. 2012. *Hermagoras: fragments et témoignages*. Paris.

Wolff, C. 2015. *L'éducation dans le monde romain*. Paris.

Wolff, H. J. 1950. "Doctrinal Trends in Postclassical Roman Marriage Law." *Zeitschrift der Savigny-Stiftung für Rechtsgeschichte, Romanistische Abteilung* 67: 261–319.

Wolsfeld, A. 2014. "Der Kaiser im Panzer. Die bildische Darstellung Neros und Domitians im Vergleich." In *Nero und Domitian. Mediale Diskurse der Herrscherrepräsentation im Vergleich*, edited by S. Bönisch-Meyer, L. Cordes, V. Schulz, A. Wolsfeld, and M. Ziegert, 181–216. Tübingen.

Woodman, A. J. 1983. *Velleius Paterculus. The Caesarian and Augustan Narrative (2.41–93)*. Cambridge.

Woodman, A. J. 1988. *Rhetoric in Classical Historiography*. London.

Woodman, A. J. 2017. *The Annals of Tacitus Books 5 and 6*. Cambridge.

Woodman, A. J. 2018. *The Annals of Tacitus Book 4*. Cambridge.

Worthington, I., ed. 2007. *A Companion to Greek Rhetoric*. Malden MA.

Wülfing, P. 2003. "Classical and Modern Gesticulation Accompanying Speech: An Early Theory of Body Language by Quintilian." In *Quintilian and the Law*, edited by O. Tellegen-Couperus, 265–275. Louvain.

Wulf-Rheidt, U. 2012a. "Der Palast auf dem Palatin—Zentrum im Zentrum. Geplanter Herrschersitz oder Produkt eines langen Entwicklungsprozesses?" In *Politische Räume in vormodernen Gesellschaften. Gestaltung—Wahrnehmung—Funktion*, edited by O. Dally, F. Fless, R. Haensch, F. Pirson, and S. Sievers, 277–289. Rahden.

Wulf-Rheidt, U. 2012b. "Nutzungsbereiche des flavischen Palastes auf dem Palatin in Rom." In *Orte der Herrschaft. Charakteristika von antiken Machtzentren*, edited by F. Arnold, A. Busch, R. Haensch, and U. Wulf-Rheidt, 97–112. Rahden.

Wulf-Rheidt, U. 2015. "The Palace of the Roman Emperors on the Palatine in Rome." In *The Emperor's House. Palaces from Augustus to the Age of Absolutism*, edited by M. Featherstone, J.-M. Spieser, G. Tanman, and U. Wulf-Rheidt, 3–18. Berlin.

Wurm, M. 1972. Apokeryxis, Abdicatio *und* Exheredatio. Munich.

Wyatt-Brown, B. 2001. *The Shaping of Southern Culture. Honor, Grace, and War, 1760s-1890s.* Chapel Hill.

Wycisk, T. 2008. Quidquid in foro fieri potest—*Studien zum römischen Recht bei Quintilian.* Berlin.

Wylie, G. 1998. "The Ides of March and the Immovable Icon." In *Studies in Latin Literature and Roman History IX*, edited by C. Deroux, 167–185. Brussels.

Xenophontos, S. 2015. "[Education in] Plutarch." In *A Companion to Ancient Education*, edited by W. M. Bloomer, 335–346. Chichester.

Yegül, F. 1992. *Baths and Bathing in Classical Antiquity.* Cambridge MA.

Yegül, F. 2000. "Baths and Bathing in Roman Antioch." In *Antioch: The Lost Ancient City*, edited by C. Kondoleon, 146–151. Princeton.

Yiftach-Firanko, U. 2009. "Law in Graeco-Roman Egypt: Hellenization, Fusion, Romanization." In *The Oxford Handbook of Papyrology*, edited by R. Bagnall, 541–560. Oxford.

Yon, J.-B. 2017. "Le reflet des honneurs." In *The Politics of Honour in the Greek Cities of the Roman Empire*, edited by A. Heller and O. M. van Nijf, 496–526. Leiden.

Zachos, K. L. and L. Leontaris. 2018. "The Aqueduct of Actian Nicopolis." In *Great Waterworks in Roman Greece. Aqueducts and Monumental Fountain Structures. Function in Context*, edited by G. A. Aristodemou and T. P. Tassios, 26–49. Oxford.

Zadorojnyi, A. V. 2019. "Competition and Competitiveness in Pollux's *Onomasticon*." In *Eris vs. Aemulatio. Valuing Competition in Classical Antiquity*, edited by C. Damon and C. Pieper, 324–342. Leiden.

Zanker, P. 1993. "The Hellenistic Grave Stelai from Smyrna: Identity and Self-Image in the Polis." In *Images and Ideologies: Self-Definition in the Hellenistic World*, edited by A. Bulloch, E. S. Gruen, A. A. Long, and A. Stewart, 212–231. Berkeley and Los Angeles.

Zanker, P. 2002 [2004]. "Domitian's Palace on the Palatine and the Imperial Image." In *Representations of Empire: Rome and the Mediterranean World*, edited by A. K. Bowman, H. M. Cotton, M. Goodman, and S. Price, 105–130 (Oxford, 2002). Reprinted in German as "Domitians Palast auf dem Palatin als Monument kaiserlicher Selbstdarstellung." In *Die Kaiserpaläste auf dem Palatin in Rom*, edited by A. Hoffmann and U. Wulf, 86–99 (Mainz, 2004).

Zecchini, G. 2001. *Cesare e il* mos maiorum. Stuttgart.

Ziebarth, E. 1914. *Aus dem griechischen Schulwesen. Eudamos von Milet und Verwandtes.* 2nd. ed. Leipzig.

Zilletti, U. 1961. "Annotazioni sul *crimen stellionatus." Archivio giuridico* 161: 72–107.

Zinsmaier, T. 1993. *Der von Bord geworfene Leichnam. Die sechste der neunzehn größeren pseudoquintilianischen Deklamationen.* Frankfurt.

Zinsmaier, T. 2009. *[Quintilian] Die Hände der blinden Mutter (Größere Deklamationen, 6).* Cassino.

Zinsmaier, T. 2015. "Truth by Force? Torture as Evidence in Ancient Rhetoric and Roman Law." In *Law and Ethics in Greek and Roman Declamation,* edited by E. Amato, F. Citti, and B. Huelsenbeck, 201–218. Berlin.

Zuiderhoek, A. 2009. *The Politics of Munificence in the Roman Empire.* Cambridge.

# INDEX

*abdicatio*, 141, 143–147; and Greek term *apokēruxis*, 143; legality of, 144–145; as metaphorical term, 145; as a term in declamation only, 143–144. *See also* law, declamatory; law, Roman

*About Rivers and Mountains and Things Found in Them* [Ps.-Plutarch], 78

Academy, Old (Platonic), 40

*accusatio ingrati liberti*, 125–126, 128. *See also* freedman; law, Roman, and children, ungrateful

accuser, false. *See delator*; *talio*

Achaean League, 49

Achilles, xii, 18, 103–104, 153

acropolis. *See* Capitoline; citadel

*actio dementiae*, 135, 141–142. *See also* law, declamatory, on madness; law, Roman, on madness; madness

*actio malae tractationis*, 141, 143–147. *See also* law, declamatory, and wife; law, Roman, and wife

*actio rei uxoriae*, 142. *See also* dowry

actor, punishment of, 123

Adrianople, battle of, 23

adultery, laws about. *See* law, Roman

advice, speeches of. *See* declamation, deliberative; *suasoriae*

Aelius Aristides, 74, 84, 90–91

*Aeneid*, 3

Agamemnon, 10–11

Agesilaus, 93

Agrippa Postumus, 145

Albucius Silus, C., 136

Alcaeus, 93

Alexamenus, 49

Alexander the Great, xii, 80

Alexandria (Egypt): colonnaded streets at, 97; medical school at, 4; remarkable structures of, 103; Serapeum in, 99

Alföldi, Andreas, 23–24

*Amadis de Gaulia*, xii

Amazons, xi-xii

Ammianus Marcellinus, 86

amphitheater, games in, 60

*andreia*, 73, 100. *See also* city, praise of, topics for; declamation, demonstrative, of cities

Antigoneia, 81

Antioch: city walls of, 82, 91–92, 97; colonnaded streets of, 97, 99–101; history of, 91–92; mythical history of, 80; New City, district of, 92; nymphaeum at, 81; physical description of, 81–82; praise of, 80–83, 104; *thesis* of, 80–81; water supply of, 80–83

Antoninus Pius (Roman emperor), 123, 137–138

Antony, Mark (Marcus Antonius), 29, 31–36, 37–38, 40–41, 48, 54–56; as consul, 31, 38–39

Aphrodisias, 90–91

Aphthonius, 99

*apokēruxis*. *See abdicatio*

Apollo *Sminthiakos*, 75

Appian, 51, 54

apprenticeship, 4–5, 8–9

aqueduct, 69, 83. *See also* nymphaea, monumental

Argos, 76–77

Aristophanes, 7–8

Aristotle, 28; *Politics* of, 41; *Rhetoric* of, 6

arithmetic. *See* mathematics

armed forces. *See* Caesar, veterans of; military training; soldiers

*artes liberales. See* general education

*arx. See* Capitoline; citadel

Ascra, 104

Asia Minor, competitive benefactions in, 153

Asianism (style of oratory), 10

assassins of Caesar. *See* conspirators against Caesar

astronomy, 7

Athanasius of Alexandria, 10

Athens: buildings at, 156; Hadrianic fountain at, 190n10; Herodes Atticus, accused of being tyrant at, 149; Odeon at, 148; place for further education, 4, 9; plague at, 149; ruling class in, 6; sophists at, 5–6, 148–149; water supply of, 77

athletics, 7–8, 154, 162n39

*Atlas Shrugged*, xii

Atticism: as Greek vocabulary choice, 12, 18; as style of Latin oratory, 10

Atticus, friend of Cicero, 45

augury, 29, 63

Augustus (Roman emperor), 36, 39, 124, 145

Aulus Gellius, 129

Aurelian Wall (Rome), 200n49

basilica, 70

baths: in Antioch, 91; in Asia Minor, 86; complex, development of, 70, 85–86; in North Africa, 86; public and private, 79, 81–83

bees, 138, 146–147. *See also* law, declamatory, on bees; law, Roman, on bees

benefactor. *See* nymphaea, monumental

Beirut, 12

Bibulus (son of Porcia), 53

bilingualism, 4, 12, 45, 149

biology, 7

Bloomer, W. Martin, 19–20, 167n29

bodyguard: Caesar's Spanish, 55, 62–63; of a tyrant, 55

Boeotia, 77–78

book-rolls. *See* scrolls

*boulē. See* city council

Bourdieu, Pierre, 20

Britain, walls in, 94

Brundisium, 133–134

brutalism (architectural style), 67

Brutus, Decimus Junius (conspirator against Caesar), 29–31, 35, 41–42, 183n71; age of, 44–45. *See also* conspirators against Caesar

Brutus, Lucius Junius, 42–43

Brutus, Marcus Junius (conspirator against Caesar), 9, 30–33, 49–50, 52, 54; age of, 44–45; family tradition of, 42–43; as legal and constitutional rigorist, 38–39, 175n14; as orator, 44; philosophy of, 31, 37, 39–41, 44, 48; rhetorical education of, 44–50 (*see also* tyrannicide; tyrant); speech of after assassination of Caesar, 31, 33, 37, 49–50, 51, 56 (*see also* conspirators against Caesar); and wife Porcia, 52–53

Bucolianus (conspirator against Caesar), 171n7

Butler, Judith, 20

Caesar, Gaius Julius: assassination of, xiii-xiv, 29–36, 55, 154; assassins of (*see* conspirators against Caesar); bodyguard of (*see* bodyguard); campaign against Parthians, 62; clemency of, 53; funeral of, 36, 54; inaction of before assassination, 62–63; influence of rhetorical education on, 62–63; last words of, 171n9; modern writings on assassination of, 169n1; mother of, 17; official will of, 36; supporters of, 29–31, 34, 37, 40–41, 48; veterans of, 33–34, 38; viewed as king, 42; viewed as tyrant, 32–33, 45–46, 62–63

*calculator*, 4, 160n12

California, xi-xii

Caligula (Roman emperor), 14–15, 60, 126

Callipus of Athens, 40

Calpurnius Flaccus, 158n4

A NOTE ON THE TYPE

This book has been composed in Arno, an Old-style serif typeface in the
classic Venetian tradition, designed by Robert Slimbach at Adobe.